# *THE ELLIOTT WAVE WRITINGS OF A.J. FROST AND RICHARD RUSSELL*

***Edited by Robert R. Prechter***

Published by
New Classics Library

The Elliott Wave Writings of A.J. Frost and Richard Russell

Second Edition 2017
Second Printing 2018



Printed in the United States of America

ISBN: 978-1-61604-028-4
Library of Congress Catalog Card Number: 2017937420

Publisher: New Classics Library
Gainesville, Georgia USA

Elliott Wave International
www.elliottwave.com
Address for comments: customercare@elliottwave.com

## ***ACKNOWLEDGMENTS***

Thanks go to five people who were instrumental in putting this book together. Peter Kendall spent months sifting through and collating all the material. Sally Webb formatted the book, Karen Latvala proofread it, Leigh Tipton handled the charts, and Pam Kimmons designed the book jacket. Everyone on the project did a marvelous job, which is why this labor of love made it to print.

# *CONTENTS*

# *EDITOR'S NOTE*

A.J. Frost was A. Hamilton Bolton's successor as the dean of the Wave Principle. Everything he ever had published on the subject is in this book. In his 1967 and 1970 Elliott Wave supplements to *The Bank Credit Analyst*, Frost not only forecasted the ending level for the 1966-1974 bear market in the Dow to the point but entertains us with two spirited Q&A's. Also included is the 1968 supplement by Russell L. Hall, which was co-written with Frost. We've spiced up the volume with letters between Dr. Max Resnick and Charles J. Collins, which fill the space of the never-issued 1969 BCA supplement. Both men interpreted the 1966-1968 rise as a "B" wave, a conclusion that history confirmed immediately and dramatically. Clearly, had Collins been asked to pen a 1969 BCA forecast, he would have called the 1968 top and further enhanced the publication's amazing track record. These reprints, together with those in our companion volume, *The Complete Elliott Wave Writings of A. Hamilton Bolton*, complete the presentation of the BCA's entire Elliott Wave output.

Another treat we have included is a long-lost article by Collins from the April 17, 1970 issue of *Barron's*. We've added some more spice with a number of newspaper articles covering Frost's opinions when he wasn't being published. The interview from the April 6, 1974 *Financial Post* of Toronto, penned by later *Barron's* writer, author and *Forbes* senior editor Peter Brimelow, details Frost's expectations for the ultimate bear market low.

The path to that low was blazed brilliantly by the incomparable Richard Russell of *Dow Theory Letters*, who conferred often with Frost. Every word Russell wrote about the Wave Principle is here, including one of the greatest market calls of all time: his recognition of the end of the bear market at the December 1974 low.

Ending our tome is a delightful section revealing some of A.J.'s more general thoughts on the Wave Principle and markets. It's the fun part. You can read it first or for dessert.

We now have a nearly uninterrupted six-decade record of real-time Elliott Wave analysis. *R.N. Elliott's Market Letters* covers real time analysis from 1938 to 1946. *The Complete Elliott Wave Writings of A. Hamilton Bolton* covers 1953 to 1966. This volume, *The Elliott Wave Writings of A.J. Frost and Richard Russell,* covers 1967 to 1980, ending shortly after the advent of *The Elliott Wave Theorist* in 1979. Prechter's analysis began in 1976 for Merrill Lynch and is detailed to 1983 in *Elliott Wave Principle* (chapters 4, 5, 8 and the Appendix) and updated in *At the Crest of the Tidal Wave.* With the publication of this book, the library is now complete.

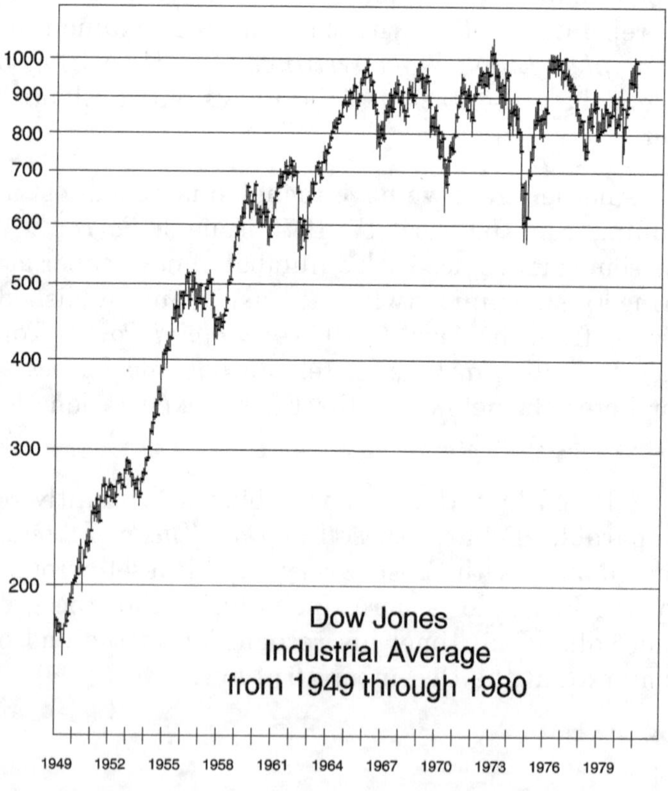

# *AUTHORS' BIOGRAPHIES*

## *A BIOGRAPHICAL MEMOIR OF A.J. FROST*

### *BY*

### *ROBERT R. PRECHTER*

A.J. Frost's favorite phrase is "Live love, love life, and don't let the bastards get you down." As you will see in this biography, he had quite a breadth of life experience. My dear friend is nearly a Fibonacci 89 years old as this is written, a fitting time to publish a book celebrating his achievements.

For the record, most of Frost's friends call him "Jack." Upon belatedly noticing that I was the only one calling him "A.J.", the name on his *Bank Credit Analyst* publications, I asked him one day if he wanted me to switch. He thought for a moment and replied, "No, A.J. is fine. In fact, I rather like it." So that nickname is used liberally in this memoir.

#### EARLY LIFE

A.J. Frost's great-great grandfather traveled from England to Ottawa in the early 1800s. England needed cut Canadian white pine for ships, as Napoleon had put an embargo on timber going to England from elsewhere. The French controlled the river, so the English built a canal and commandeered the timber out. The type of adventurers such a project attracted made Ottawa wilder than Dodge City, qualifying the raucous town as "the roughest, toughest, nastiest place in British North America."

Alfred John ("Jack") Frost was born in Claresholm, Alberta, on January 31, 1908. His father, who had been valedictorian of his class, became mayor of the town and President of the McLeod Liberal Association. Frost's father was a good speaker, and approaching the 1911 election, he had the nomination for the House of Commons "in his pocket." Before the election, he suddenly took ill and died of tuberculosis at age 31. He left behind a debt from gambling on the wheat exchange (perhaps creating an inherited family impetus to find out what makes markets tick). At three years of age, the fatherless young Jack, with sister and mother, moved in with his grandparents in "a fairly large house" where his mother was raised. The house was in Hanover, Ontario, which is near Owen Sound, a town that was "settled by my great grandfather and grandmother" on his father's side.

Frost's father's brother, Harold R. Frost, K.C., a Toronto lawyer, owned a cruiser and had a cottage at Pointe au Baril on Georgian Bay, where his family had lived for a few generations. When he was 14 to 16 years of age, Frost joined his uncle's family, including his cousin Irving, for three summers of camping and cruising around the 30,000 islands. One summer they were joined by his uncle's friend, Dr. William T. Gunn, who was head of the Congregational Church in Canada and widely celebrated for being the catalyst that united the Methodist and Presbyterian churches. He told Jack, "What's important in life is not what you believe, but what you are." The man's introspection and depth powerfully influenced Jack, who decided then to become a churchman.

In 1926, Frost became a registered student of Theology at Queen's University, Kingston, Ontario, with the intention of following a career with the United Church of Canada. His mother had taught school for fifty years and saved enough to finance the higher education of both him and his sister Florence. His sister entered higher education at 16 and graduated at 19. Frost's mother, he says, "once told me my brain was filled with cobwebs." Apparently this comment only compared him to his exceptional sister, as all his professional life, he was to be rewarded for his mental acuity in business, government, academia, finance and authorship.

As his mother made only $1000 a year, Frost sold pots, pans and Fuller brushes to help pay his way through university. In the summer after his first year, he arranged to get $15 a week and expenses from the Church in exchange for providing some services in a "mission field" in a remote area of northern Ontario. In this capacity, he preached his first funeral service at 19 years of age. In 1983 and 1984, Frost set down some of his memories of that time:

> Both summers, I went west with friends, who were ministers' sons. They were given "charges" next to mine and both had a small church and a manse and were given a car. I had none of these luxuries, only two old plugs.
>
> My first assignment as a student missionary was in Pine Grove near Minnitaki at the age of nineteen. My salary was $15 per week plus board, lodging and transportation. It was a great summer, spent with sturdy people of pioneer stock. Many farms were only small clearings in the bush. Clover and hay were the principal crops. It cost $20 to clear an acre of land, and most farmers found it difficult to make a living.
>
> The family where I was billeted were kind, generous and very poor. I made my home with Mr. and Mrs. C.A. Crigger, who had two lovely daughters and a young son by the name of Ivan. I had brought a bicycle with me, but distances between charges were too long and the muddy roads too rough, so I sold my bike to Ivan for $12 and bought a horse for $50 with church funds. Horseback riding was my only means of communication between the various school houses in the district, which also served as churches on Sunday. One Sunday, when I was urging my horse to a fast trot, the old plug smelled a bear and reared up. I toppled into a mud puddle. Fortunately the

horse did not run away, so I recovered in time to conduct the church service.

One of my first experiences came shortly after my arrival in May 1927. An elderly resident died, and his daughter asked me to conduct a funeral service. The service was held in the deceased's home. It was a regional sort of funeral, and afterwards a dear old lady approached me and said, "Mr. Frost, this was the happiest funeral I ever attended." I was a bit startled and replied, "Madam, I did not know the deceased, so I decided to preach to the living and not to the dead." It was a facetious remark, and from the peculiar look on her face, I decided that in the future I would try to be more diplomatic. Unfortunately, this was not the first time my tongue caused me some psychological pain. For instance, in Dryden, I preached on July 12th or thereabouts to the Orange Order, expounding from the pulpit, "Thanks to your immortal Prince, William of Orange, our souls are no longer fettered to any King or any Pope." What a bold statement to make, but not quite as awful as the one I made on a sunny Sunday in late July when many good farmers were doing their best to harvest their hay crop. I said, "I would rather let my hay rot in the field than my soul rot in hell." These remarks were completely out of place and helped convince me that I really was not cut out for the high calling of the Christian ministry. I now apologize to any of the old-timers who happened to remember them. I was young, brash and full of beans.

Another incident also sticks in my mind. I visited a family deep in the forest. The head of the family, an old farmer, asked me to read and pray, so we all knelt down in a circle. When I was well into my prayer, an enormous old sow wandered through an open back door, into the centre of our circle. The sow started to grunt, so I terminated my prayer with a rather quick "Amen." The old farmer got up and started kicking the sow.

I shall never forget Mrs. Crigger. She took good care of me, but I did get tired of pickled moose meat several times a week. I also remember Sam Parks, a kindly gentleman who took pity on me and built me a pulpit. Also I remember the local school teacher - a dried-up old maid of 21 years - who winked at me during one of my sermons and caused me to lose my place. Besides preaching, I helped the Reverend Rivers of Dryden to run an unsuccessful boy's camp for two weeks. All told, however, it wasn't too bad a summer.

The next summer, I was posted to a mission twenty miles from the nearest store, in the badlands of Alberta. I took up residence in an old granary that had no light and was overrun with mice and gophers. It had no outhouse, either, and was two miles from a fresh water pump. Again, I was supplied with an old plug of a horse and an army saddle, the same as in the previous year. This summer almost broke my health. However, there were redeeming features. A farmhand walked eight miles every Sunday to attend divine service. On the last Sunday I was there, a farmer placed what would be today roughly one thousand dollars in cash on the collection plate.

For the summer, I had diligently prepared twenty sermons, which were the result of a great deal of reading and hard work. Unfortunately, they were stolen by an honor graduate in moral philosophy, who later became ordained in the United Church. Further, a friend of mine for whom I had great regard was kicked out of Theology after two years because he got married and his young son arrived eight months after the marriage. This upset me terribly, because he would have made a top-flight clergyman.

I was so miserable that summer that when I returned to the university, I didn't go to church for a year. After careful consideration, I decided that I would change my course in life. Dr. Kent, who was Principal of the Theological College, was most indignant, especially when I told him I had decided to switch to Commerce. He exploded, "What has bookkeeping got to do with the Kingdom of God?" I regret now that I did not answer him.

## PROFESSIONAL LIFE

So Frost abandoned the preaching profession and studied to take up accountancy. While a student, he audited the books of a large life insurance company in order to help pay expenses. Through the years of the Great Depression, Frost kept focused on several ambitious goals and achieved them all. In 1932, he received his Bachelor of Commerce degree and on May 24 married his first wife, Olive Thompson, nicknamed Timmie. In 1934, Frost got his Chartered Accountant (C.A.) designation. While working days, he attended night classes at Osgoode Hall (now part of York University), at that time the only law school in Ontario. In 1937, he received his Barrister At Law degree and was admitted to the Ontario Institute of Chartered Accountants and the Ontario Bar.

Frost's marriage was stable and happy, and Timmie was unfailingly supportive. According to their daughter, Joan, "Timmie thought the sun rose and set on Jack. She was a terrific sport and shared Jack's sense of fun. During their over fourty years of marriage, Timmie never left his side."

As a specialist in legal accountancy, Frost launched his new profession by going to work for the government's Board of Review, with the responsibility of investigating old estates that had been accused of avoiding succession (inheritance) taxes. He found himself so frequently annoyed with the Board's position that upon occasion, he quietly gave parts of the government's case to the defendants to help them out.

In his modest yet influential position with the government, Frost met a number of well-to-do businessmen and began receiving offers of employment. In 1939, he accepted a position with the Toronto General Trust Corporation (now Canada Trust). Soon after joining the firm, he traveled to Banker's Trust in New York to form a plan for improving his firm's internal audits. With the president's blessing, he hired the sharpest people he could find to form a controller's department. After a few years, new management came in and regarded him as too strong an influence on the trust company's president. In 1952, they sent him to Ottawa to become a branch manager, where he remained until 1959. In that capacity, Frost successfully recommended the takeover of another trust company, which expanded the Ottawa branch considerably.

In 1959, Frost was elected a Fellow in the Institute of Chartered Accountants for "distinguished service to the accountancy profession." Though having traveled a long way down the path to become president of the trust company, Frost began to find himself frustrated with the lawyer-dominated headquarters in Toronto and the efforts of the young WWII-brigadier son-in-law of the firm's president to oust him so that *he* could become president. In the midst of these complications, Alec Reid, president of the Mutual Funds Management Corporation in Vancouver, offered Frost a 50% pay increase to become the general manager of MFM. In 1959, Frost resigned from the trust company and accepted the new position. Thus, the young brigadier succeeded in his goal, but as it turned out, he died two years later.

A few months later, Alec Reid persuaded the money management firm of Bolton-Tremblay, as well as the National Life Insurance Corporation, to buy into his company. In 1960, MFM moved its headquarters to Montreal, into the same offices used by Bolton-Tremblay. Frost was named Vice President of the firm and became a partner of Hamilton Bolton. Among Bolton's partners Maurice Tremblay, Donald Storey and A.J. Frost, Frost was the only one who took an interest in the Wave Principle, so Bolton started him on keeping an hourly chart. (For more on Bolton, see

Frost's memoir in *The Complete Elliott Wave Writings of A. Hamilton Bolton.*) Frost recalls making a number of $1 bets on the market with his new friend "Hammy" and being quite amused the times he won. His biggest market triumph of the time occurred at the October 1962 "Cuban Crisis" low in the stock market. Here is A.J.'s recollection of the event:

> Bolton seldom missed important turning points, but he did miss the Cuban crisis low in October 1962, mainly because he was in Greece at the time. In his absence, I was keeping an hourly chart of the DJIA. He happened to phone me from Athens, and I had the good fortune to note that, from the June 1962 low, the Dow Industrials had moved up in a three wave sequence and then down in a five wave sequence. With only a cursory knowledge of the Wave Principle, then, I caught the Cuban crisis low to within two hours. The Cuban crisis low was so obvious that Bolton expressed regret at leaving the country, as he was sure he would have caught it. He would, no doubt, have given it some publicity. That experience confirmed my faith in Elliott, and I continued to keep an hourly chart for the next twenty years.

While with Bolton-Tremblay, Frost obtained his Chartered Financial Analyst (C.F.A.) designation at Bolton's urging, who in 1959-1960 had served a term as president of the National Federation of Financial Analysts Societies (now the Financial Analysts Federation). Although happily entrenched in his new position, during this time Frost received five offers from trust companies to get back into the banking business. He firmly told them all "no" until a professional friend took him to dinner one evening. Over several hours, the friend convinced Frost to return to the business by offering everything he wanted. As a result, Frost accepted a position as general manager and Ottawa branch manager of Guaranty Trust Company of Canada. Later that same night, Queens University, on whose advisory board Frost had been serving, called and offered him an assistant professorship on a full professor's salary. "You're a few hours too late!" said Frost.

Frost left Bolton-Tremblay in 1963, and he and Timmie moved to Manotick near Ottawa, buying a home on a golf course on the Rideau River. Although he enjoyed playing golf, he regretted his professional decision. For one thing, "Guaranty Trust was a disaster; they had no ethics, particularly in the matter of estate fees." Fortunately, along with all his other affiliations, Frost was also president of the Association of Canadian Better Business Bureaus at the time, and after only a few months, he left Guaranty Trust to become executive director of the BBB.

As a member of the exclusive Rideau Club, a gentlemen's dining and social organization, Frost began to form close relationships with members of the Canadian prime minister's cabinet. Those relationships led him in an entirely new direction.

In 1966, Frost got a call from the Minister of Public Works, who requested that he join the National Capital Commission, which had the responsibility of spending $30-40 million annually to develop Ottawa's public works and manage the appearance of Canada's capital, as well as 1,800 square miles of greenbelts, parkways and parks straddling the Ottawa River. In January 1968, Frost was appointed to the full-time post of NCC Chairman. As chairman, Frost worked closely with 72 municipalities, eight counties, the provinces of Ontario and Quebec and the federal government, which put him on a first-name basis with Prime Minister Mike Pearson, "Mike" to close friends. Frost worked for the NCC for several years and oversaw numerous city projects.

After two years as Chairman, Frost was ousted from the position with the advent of the new political regime. A year later, he was appointed a judge with the Tax Appeal Board (later the Tax Review Board and now the Federal Tax Court of Canada). For the next eight years, he heard nearly 500 cases and traveled to every major city. Somewhat of a maverick, Frost displeased the federal powers by deciding 47% of his cases in favor of the taxpayer and against the Crown. He once adjudicated the principle that a status Indian living on a reserve, regardless of his place of employment, was not required to pay income tax. Frost's decision was reversed on appeal to Federal Court, then upheld seven years later by the Supreme Court of Canada, which overruled the Federal Court. On one occasion, the Tax Department seized a company's assets long enough to send it into receivership and force the owner into bankruptcy, only to discover that the company had been innocent. According to one observer, Frost gave the tax department "its worst scolding in history."

During this time, Ham Bolton remained Frost's best friend and also the man that he most admired. They corresponded often about the market. It was quite a blow when Bolton died in early 1967 at the young age of 53. To this day, Frost remains bitter, blaming those closest to Hammy for killing him with drink, neglect and stress. "One of them," says Frost, "was a volatile person who would fly into a rage from time to time." Another applied constant psychological pressure to Hammy. This former failed businessman, says Frost, "was a horse's ass. He had no patience for 'Elliott' and hated Hammy for investigating it. He bugged Hammy *continuously* about it. The man once offered me his girlfriend for the weekend, which I declined. He later sent her to Sweden to get an abortion at the firm's expense. He hasn't the moral principles of a groundhog. Bolton got cancer of the liver from drinking too much with the likes of him. Hammy was a shy person and just too polite to tell him off."

After Bolton's death, Donald Storey wanted to continue publishing the annual Elliott Wave Supplements for business reasons: they were popular. Storey contacted Frost and commissioned him to write the 1967 supplement. A year later, Frost co-wrote the 1968 supplement with Russell Hall, who was a broker in Ottawa. They split the fee, but left off Frost's name because he was working for the government and didn't want his name on a commercial publication. There was no Elliott Wave supplement in 1969. The last supplement was written by Frost in 1970. After that, the BCA was out of the "Elliott" business.

In 1971, Jack was introduced to Frances Reilly by a long time friend of the Reilly family from Ottawa. Frances was a former school teacher and nurse whose late husband had been a prominent Victoria, B.C. physician. After Frost's wife Timmie died of liver cancer in May 1973, Jack renewed his acquaintance with Frances, a delightful, energetic woman eighteen years his junior, and was soon calling her his "sweetie-pie." On December 7, 1973, they were married. Frances kept her home in Victoria but traveled the country with him as he served on the Tax Review Board. They also maintained Frost's Manotick home for a few more years to have a place to stay in the summers (which was vacation time for tax judges) and when his tax cases took him to Ottawa.

## FROST AND PRECHTER

I wrote my first letter to A.J. in November 1976, when I was 27 and working as a technical analyst at Merrill Lynch in New York. I said, "Let me begin by mentioning the great appreciation I have for your compositions on the Elliott Wave Principle. Your straightforward and lucid explanations have been a continual source of reference for me. And may I add that amidst all the hogwash written by most self-professed followers of the E.W.P., your work stands with Elliott's and Bolton's as definitive." From that time, we became regular correspondents. While we sometimes had different near term interpretations, our letters confirmed, as Frost said in his first reply, that "We all agree that a new primary bull market started in 1974 and when it is over, it should complete the Supercycle from 1932."

A few months later, John Brooks of the Market Technicians Association called and asked if I would invite Frost to speak at the MTA's annual conference in May. While I was excited at the prospect, I explained that I really didn't know him; we had just written each other a few letters. "You know him better than anyone else around here," said John. So I invited A.J. to speak, and he quite graciously accepted.

A.J. and I first met on Thursday, May 12, 1977 at Skytop Lodge in Skytop, Pennsylvania. We hit it off instantly despite a difference in our ages of 41 years. We spent several hours talking "Elliott" face-to-face in A.J.'s room. It was the first time I had met someone as interested in the subject as I was. That weekend, A.J. participated on a panel moderated by William DiIanni called "Kondratieff, Elliott and Economic Waves" along with economist S. Jay Levy and cycle historian David Rosenau. The soon-to-be-famous Joseph Granville was also a speaker. The conference ended on the 15th. Upon returning home, I sent A.J. a copy of *Nature's Law*, which I had obtained from microfilm at the New York Public Library.

One of the things we discussed at Skytop was the fact that we were each beginning a book on the Wave Principle. A short time earlier, Richard Russell had asked Frost to write a short piece on Elliott for inclusion in a booklet he was writing on technical analysis. A.J. had declined the offer, as he was too busy in traveling across Canada hearing tax appeals and writing judgments. "I rather regretted this decision," said Frost, "as not too long afterward, I found I had more time on my hands than I expected." His additional free time had come about by a decision to present his judgments directly from the bench whenever possible instead of writing them out. This change, combined with frequent adjournments, left him with free time. "This situation," he said, "prompted me to fill in my time by writing notes on my favorite subject: the EWP." It was then that the recollection of Russell's offer grew into a desire to write a book.

As Frost began writing a basic introduction to the theory, I was working on explaining its application. We kept in touch on the subject, and in August 1977, he wrote, "I think someday a sequel will be written to my Elliott book. It will be much better ... and you will be the one to write it." A quick change of fortune changed that scenario. A.J. later recounted the story:

> Writing a book and being introduced to Wall Street are two different things, and I felt I needed help on both scores. Thereupon I contacted Dick Russell, who readily agreed to be my coauthor. Following this decision, I started to send him chapters in draft form. As the work progressed, Dick realized that he had let himself in for a considerable amount of work. In a letter to me, he asked to be excused. His letter did not reach me, and at the time he wrote it, I was in Vancouver with a few weeks to spare so had decided to motor to La Jolla, California to discuss the progress of the book personally. I was surprised to learn upon arrival at Dick's office of his change in commitment. However, he did reconsider the matter and confirmed to me that he would do the work, provided that Ian McAvity was employed to do the chart work. Frances and I then visited Ian McAvity in Toronto to discuss the book, with no concrete results. Subsequently, Dick again changed his mind, so I simply said "Thank you."

Thus, the busy schedules of these two established market mavens caused an opportunity to arise. That September, A.J. and I decided to pool our efforts and write one comprehensive book. I visited him in Manotick late that fall, where we roughed out our respective responsibilities. I spent a delightful time driving around Ottawa for several hours with A.J. and Frances as they talked about his projects while Chairman of the National Capital Commission. I brought my camera, and we took the original back cover photo with the number on the door partially covered to produce a simple "5," the key Elliott Wave number, neatly placed between us.

A.J. Frost signed his final judgment on January 19, 1978, his last official act with the Tax Review Board. At age 70, he retired. Thereafter, his earnings from executing a multimillion dollar estate provided some retirement income and a source of occasional financial gifts to his daughter Joan and his granddaughter Margaret.

With time to spare, A.J. arranged for the two of us to visit Charles Joseph ("Joe") Collins and his wife on the weekend of February 11-12, 1978 at their winter retreat in Indian Rocks Beach, Florida. Collins and his wife talked about having R.N. Elliott as a guest in Detroit in 1938 while they wrote *The Wave Principle* together. The couple portrayed Elliott as gentlemanly but crusty and determined, which he probably had to have been to continue an adventurous life despite the terrible affliction of anemia. (For details, see the biography in *R.N. Elliott's Masterworks.*) It was an absolutely delightful weekend. During the visit, we asked Collins to write the foreword to our book, and he agreed.

Writing and compiling the book was a huge job because my only free time was on weekends, holidays and on the commuter train to and from New York. Our friend, renowned technical analyst Arthur Merrill, suggested we publish the book ourselves, which we did. I had to design all the charts from scratch, and my wife Robin diligently spent the entire spring of 1978 tracing them out. We photographed all the charts in Arthur's basement. I typed the book into a Wang word processor and printed it out, the end result being, to our knowledge, the first book ever typeset that way. I mailed A.J. a final draft in late July. Only the illustrations remained unfinished. After some final editing and paste-up, the book went to the printer in September. Said A.J., "I am like a rooster dancing on a very hot griddle awaiting the 'masterpiece.'" In November, we finally received the finished copies. Our first ad for the book appeared in *Barron's* the same month. After the book came out, Frances said, "You two have made history, I have no doubt." That may have been generously overstated, but as A.J. added, "I feel success is almost assured. Elliott will never die, at least not now."

Over the next ten years, we got together often. The next time was in May 1979, when A.J. and I both spoke at the annual MTA conference. We signed and sold books for a few hours at a table outside the main room.

In the summer of 1979, I flew up to meet A.J. in Manotick. He had sold his house following retirement and was distributing belongings he no longer needed. At that time, he gave me a file of Bolton-Collins correspondence that he had managed to obtain for posterity, as well as his collection of old BCA Supplements. The next day, we drove to Montreal to visit the headquarters of the BCA, which was then run by Anthony Boeckh. There I met Bolton's secretary, Claire Chartrand, as well as Denise Cuirot, who had been in charge of advertising, distribution and production while Hammy was there. Frost said that "Hammy's girls," these efficient and reliable co-workers, were the ones that "really took care of Hammy." Ms. Chartrand still worked at the firm and had kept Hammy's old files intact. I asked her if she felt it would be all right for me to have Hammy's personal copies of R.N. Elliott's two famous books, as I knew no one else who would care to have them. She said, "If Mr. Frost and Mr. Bolton's brother agree to it, it's fine with me."

From Montreal, A.J. was on his way back west to Victoria, and I arranged to drive with him on the first leg, to Toronto. Everything he now owned, he said, was in the trunk of his car. "You're not truly free," he said, "until you can pack all of your belongings in one trunk." On the way, we stopped for an hour to visit one of Jack's friends, who was a retired justice of the Supreme Court of Ontario. That night, Joan made dinner for us, and the next day, I flew home while A.J. continued west to Frances' home in Victoria.

Upon returning home, I wrote Bolton's brother, who graciously consented to letting me have Hammy's books. When I called Ms. Chartrand to provide some instructions on how to courier them, she said, "They're already in the mail." I conveyed my thanks but secretly shuddered to think of these books in the hands of the Canadian Post Office, which always added ten days to the delivery of any letter we sent and sometimes beat up our boxes of books beyond recognition. Weeks passed with no arrival of Hammy's books. The day after I gave up hope, the nearly demolished remnants of a thin manila envelope arrived containing both priceless pieces of financial memorabilia, which had miraculously suffered no damage at all despite being partly exposed. I smiled upon noticing that Bolton's copy of *The Wave Principle* was numbered #144, the most stately of Fibonacci numbers.

In April 1980, I published *The Major Works of R.N. Elliott* (now *R.N. Elliott's Masterworks*) and dedicated it to A.J. Frost. In May, I picked up him and Frances at Kennedy Airport in New York, and we drove to Chatham on Cape Cod for another MTA conference. That summer, I flew him down from Toronto, where he was visiting Joan, to visit me at my parents' house in Atlanta. In November, I traveled to Victoria for the first time, staying in Frances' lovely home and enjoying a few brisk walks with her around the neighborhood. On that visit, I met Frances' daughter Barbara and her physician son-in-law, Glenn. I also took an improved back cover photo for the book, for which we wore matching ties.

Perhaps my fondest memory is of our second visit with Joe Collins, in the summer of 1981. I flew to Detroit, Michigan, and A.J. drove from Toronto. We spent the weekend at Collins' home in Grosse Pointe, where R.N. Elliott had stayed 43 years earlier. On Saturday, we were guests at Collins' country club, and on Sunday morning, we rose early to find Joe in the kitchen cooking us eggs and bacon. Collins was a gracious and brilliant man and extremely energetic for his age. Having the three of us together, spanning the Elliott generations, provided an experience I will always cherish.

I then joined A.J. and Joan on their annual trip to Breaker's Lodge, which was in Southampton on Lake Huron. Now closed, this was A.J.'s lifelong favorite vacation spot. Being near his childhood home of Hanover, it is where he first went to the beach in 1914 at age six. It was an isolated spot and rather chilly, with no phone or heat on the premises. There was little to do but sit in a chair on the beach.

Nevertheless, entertainment was provided by our company, so all in all, it was a pleasant stay.

I visited the Frosts in Victoria again in November, 1984, after giving a speech in Vancouver. A.J. was already involved in affairs of the area, sitting on a couple of boards and as a member of the Rotary Club. One afternoon, we had lunch in the ballroom of the Empress Hotel, at the club's headquarters. A.J. also routinely met a group of friends weekly for coffee at a diner, and I was fortunate enough to join in one morning on their usual topic, the markets. I also had the pleasure of meeting Frances' lively daughter Catherine and some of the Frosts' local friends.

A.J. kept busy throughout this period. He gave an interview for the May 1979 edition of Investor's Hotline. In 1980, he spoke for the seventh time to the Institute of Insurance Appraisers. In the mid-1980s, he spoke several times for the Canadian Society of Technical Analysts, including three years in a row in 1985, 1986 and 1987. On September 17, 1985, he was made the CSTA's first ever Honorary Member. In 1986, the CSTA's Vice President said that the tape of his speech was a "best seller." Even famed trader Eli Tullis took a trip to visit him.

A.J. was fond of saying that I was the one designated to get Elliott "out there." Occasionally, the complexity of the theory provided an impediment to that task, but its inherent attraction overcame all obstacles. We soon could not help but notice that the Wave Principle's publicity was changing in a big way. For years, A.J. had recounted Hamilton Bolton's observation in 1960 that "For every 100 people who know Dow Theory, only one has ever heard of Elliott." In August 1986, he called to say, "The tables are finally turning."

After speaking for the Canadian Society of Technical Analysts in June 1987, I visited A.J. at Joan's in Toronto. Having come prepared, I sat him down for an hour to recount his life story for my tape recorder and took a photo for the occasion.

I visited the Frosts in Victoria for the last time in October 1989. That Friday night, I went to bed early while Jack and Frances stayed up to watch the *Wall Street Week* TV show. The next morning, they were talking about Bob Nurock's comment that he "mildly disagreed" with host Rukeyser's stock market opinion, as if it had been an event. "That doesn't seem like a big deal," I said. It must have been, they replied, because Rukeyser had looked highly annoyed about it. I called Bob that morning, and he told me that after the show, he had actually been ordered by the enraged producer never again to disagree with Rukeyser on the air. After all these years, he had had enough and was composing a letter of resignation. A week later, after receiving the letter, Rukeyser, in a screen-filling close-up, announced that *he* had *terminated* Nurock for bad market calls. (Nurock in fact was the show's best performing panelist and the #1 ranked forecaster by *Technical Trends* at the time.) The Frosts, who knew the real story, never looked at Rukeyser the same way again.

At this time, my friend A.J. was receiving the most publicity of his life. It had developed because he had called for new highs in wave ⑤ after the 1987 crash while I preferred the case for a "B" wave rally in a bear market. This variance of opinion led a few writers to portray our differences as a feud. To us, it was mostly amusing, although we did get annoyed at the occasional invention of quotations. When I sent A.J. a disparaging comment attributed to him in an article, he wrote to the reporter: "Bob Prechter and I are long time friends, and although our Elliott counts are different at present, our long-term counts are in substantial agreement. I never made the remark attributed to me, nor would ever dream of so doing. Please retract." In a written response denying the request for a retraction, the reporter attempted to justify his fabrication by saying that he could *imagine* Frost having said it.

In full support of A.J.'s position and increasing notoriety, I gathered together the letters he had written to me about the market, asked him for a few more paragraphs, and published "A Philosophy of Markets, and the Outlook for Stocks, Gold and the Economy" by A.J. Frost in September 1989. (This book includes the contents of that monograph.) His fame, already waxing, skyrocketed.

Benefiting from a wave of adulation in the press, he did another segment on Investor's Hotline in November and spoke at the Florida XII financial conference in January 1990. Around this time, he began providing weekly market commentary to Financial News Network. I warned him of what the consequences might be, but A.J. loved the opportunity to comment on the market and was quite fond of the attention as well. By September 1990, as the market was selling off roughly in line with his forecast for a top, telephone calls to his house became so frequent and bothersome that he had to get an unlisted phone number.

As 1991 got underway, things changed. Except for a brief period in 1983-1985, A.J. had maintained a bullish stance on gold ever since the 1980 high, and it wasn't moving up. Like me, he also began calling too many stock market tops that were subsequently penetrated. As a result, the hosannas began to cool. The historic stock mania was stronger than either of our analytical abilities during the first half of the 1990s, and eventually, he retired from his stint on FNN. To this day, we agree unequivocally, in line with our wave labeling originally presented in *Elliott Wave Principle* eighteen years ago, that the market is topping out in Cycle wave V and that the biggest bear market in nearly three centuries is nigh.

## RENAISSANCE MAN

What kind of person is A.J. Frost? Physically, he's a tall 6'4". Very thin early in life, he later became quite a large guy and, with his white hair, looks an apt "Jack Frost." A.J. is always formally dressed in suit and tie, but his manner is informal. He enjoyed golf and taught his granddaughter to play. When in his early fifties, he studied yoga. Besides analyzing the stock market, his favorite pastime has always been driving. He often cruised around town just for fun. In fact, each year after retiring, he drove the full distance from Victoria to Toronto and back to visit Joan and her family for extended periods.

Though ambitious most of his life and always desirous of being "at the peak of his professions," A.J. is an exceptionally approachable person, very open and friendly, with a good sense of humor. "Under the Judges' Act," he once wrote, "I am entitled to be addressed, 'His Honorable Judge,' etc., but I never use it and do not want to do so. One day in court, a French lawyer was calling me 'my lord.' Finally, I said to him that if he didn't stop, I would likely get judges' disease. He stopped."

One way A.J. gets a conversation going is to pull out of his suit pocket a brown, wrinkled rock-hard something about the size of a silver dollar and ask people what they think it is. They never guess that the object is the dried-up remains of a potato that he has kept there for years. Once an old German lady told him that a potato placed in the pocket will absorb a person's infirmity. The result is a dried-up potato and a healthy person. He doesn't accept this medical theory, but he loves the resulting conversation piece.

Jack is also somewhat of a flirt. If a pretty woman is nearby, he will go into his palm-reading act as an excuse to hold her hand. When asked about his progeny, he often says coyly, "I have one registered child." Years ago, during one of Jack's camping trips on Georgian Bay as a teenager, he perpetrated what is now known as "the snake incident." Here is how he reminisced about the story years later in a letter to the minister's daughter Betty, who was the victim of said incident:

I recall that Irving and I decided to go swimming. You came down to join us to do some wading. You were wearing a khaki blouse and shorts. As you dipped your toe in the water, you saw a water-snake, which frightened you. I grabbed the snake and held it up in front of you. You ran back to your father's tent, somewhat shaken if I recall correctly. ["She was screaming her head off," he explained later.] Your father came down immediately to "see me," and I could hear my Aunt Ethel in the background. Your father lectured me briefly: It was quite all right for boys to pick up snakes but never to frighten little girls. He said girls were different from boys, a fact that I had surmised a few years earlier. I apologized and promised never to do it again. Surprisingly, your father gave me a most gracious smile, and there endeth the lesson.

Frances agrees that it was Jack's charm that attracted her. For one thing, he enjoys conversing in mild jest, which is always entertaining. Along that line, market prognosticator P.Q. Wall published this tale in June 1992, showing that Jack can match anybody in the kidding department:

### *JACK FROST IS 84 —*
### *UP TO MORE DEVILTRY THAN EVER BEFORE*

Wisdom is never solemn; in fact, it has often shown a strange alliance with mischief. The Scottish poet Robert Burns expressed it in a line about Solomon: "The wisest man the warl' e'er saw, he dearly loved the lasses, O." I bring this up because there are evidently strange rumors circulating in Jack Frost's country club in Victoria that Jack still secretly sends five Christmas cards to ex-girlfriends. This kind of thing could bring Wall Street activity to a screeching halt. Of course, some say the rumors were started by Jack himself. Bitter with disillusionment, I finally reached the Taoist sage and asked him in a simple and calm manner if these rumors were true. "Fifteen years ago, there were two hundred,' said Jack defiantly. "They're dying like flies on me." P.Q.: "If this gets back to Frances, she'll carve you a new one." Frost: "Send your wife up here, P.Q. She needs a vacation."

One day shortly after their marriage, Jack asked Frances to tell him some personal stories about her life. She recounted some of her memories and began to tell about the time in 1945 that she was taking daily walks from a friend's home to Christie Street Military Hospital in Toronto to visit her first husband, who was dying of wounds suffered in battle in World War II. "I noticed that a man with a mustache drove past me each morning for three days. On the fourth day, he stopped and asked if I would like a ride." She was expecting a child at the time and must have looked like she could use a ride, though actually she enjoyed walking for the exercise. "After getting in the car, I became concerned that I might have done something foolish, but the man was merely being helpful and politely dropped me off at my destination." Upon hearing the story and realizing an amazing coincidence, Jack looked at Frances and said, "You were wearing a yellow maternity dress, and I am the man who picked you up."

Whether this story is true or Jack told it for amusement is not entirely clear, but it does show that whichever is the case, he enjoys delighting women. He also likes to be waited upon, sometimes to the point of exasperating his wife. His favorite women are his daughter Joan and granddaughter Margaret (Magi), of whom he is exceptionally proud for graduating from Queen's University and Yale. The happiest time of his life, he said, was when Joan was growing up. As late as 1993, he mused in a letter, "I still love the ladies and love to watch them go by and wonder about my wicked past. However, it was fun, so I shouldn't complain."

As a result of his engaging personality, A.J. Frost has always been a raging social success. When he was with the trust company, he joined a number of organizations for both business reasons and personal enjoyment. He continued the practice throughout his life. In the process, he met many fascinating people. One of his friends was General Findlay Clark, former Chief of Staff of Canada's Armed Forces, who had previously run the NCC. Another acquaintance was Lord Kenneth Thomson, member of the House of Lords in England and owner of over 200 newspapers, including the *Times* of London and the Toronto *Globe and Mail*, as well as Canada's two largest retail department stores and several oil and gas companies. In fact, this distinguished man critiqued the first draft of our book. As a result of A.J.'s connections, the Chancellor of Victoria University got an early copy and had "high praise" for it, as did the former Controller of the Treasury of Canada, a professor of medicine at the University of Kansas, and a professor of philosophy at Victoria University. He sent copies to senators, judges, and the Under-Secretary of Monetary Affairs under Ronald Reagan, Beryl Sprinkel.

A.J. served on two university councils and on the boards of several corporations, a number of which have been mentioned in this story so far. He was a long time Rotarian, the president of a realty company and a Fellow of the Institute of Chartered Accountants. He also earned a title as an Honorable Life Member of Ottawa Historical Society. After serving on the board for a number of years, Frost even became an Honorary Life Member of the Victorian Order of Nurses, a private entity that provided low-cost home-based nursing. For years, A.J. was a trustee for the Boy Scouts of Canada's pension plan and an Honorable Vice President of the BSC's National Council. He was awarded the silver acorn for 25 years of "especially distinguished service to scouting." In 1993, he received perhaps his greatest honor: the Commemorative Medal for the 125th Anniversary of Canadian Confederation for years of distinguished service in business, government and academia.

A.J. is an armchair philosopher and fairly widely read on religion. Back in 1980, I wrote to him, "I think we should have a nice, relaxed little volume called 'Thoughts on the Wave Principle,' with some of our ruminations." This idea finally came to fruition with *Prechter's Perspective* and Frost's "Reflections" section in this book. As far as I am concerned, his most astute observation is the similarity between (1) the Taoist belief that existence is a natural rhythm of contrary forces that achieves harmony and (2) the Wave Principle's revelation that sociological change follows a natural rhythm of contrary forces that produces the pattern of collective human progress. Frost likes to mention that his U.V. philosophy professor friend called the Wave Principle "applied Taoism." As for proficiency at it, he said, "Although it is an *objective principle*, one must develop a *sensitivity* to it." And there, he might say, endeth the lesson.

## CLOSURE

My long association with A.J. Frost has been a joy in all respects, as we share a deep interest. As A.J. said in 1981, "Like you, *I live Elliott.*" In October 1983, I made a suggestion, to which A.J. replied, "It's a date. We toast Elliott, Collins and Bolton on the very day the Grand Supercycle peaks! Locale? 833 Beacon Avenue, Los Angeles, California. If the porch is still there and the sun is shining, we should rent a rocking chair and take a few pictures, owners willing, which they should be if they knew the background." Unfortunately, the bull market has outlasted A.J.'s stamina, so we won't be meeting in California.

The last few years have been a bit rough on Jack Frost. Though amazingly healthy, he has become an extraordinarily sedentary man and, despite the urging of doctors, has taken virtually no exercise in two decades. Asserting from time to time that "age is not a function of years, but the number of breaths you take," he has seemed determined to keep that number to a minimum. As a result, advancing age has been particularly hard on his mobility and sometimes, understandably, his mood. In 1989, Frances observed, "Some days Jack manages pretty well (especially when the market does well), but most days now he is in the dumps, even though he gets calls from people telling him what a legend he is!" In 1993, Jack moved back east to spend his remaining years with Joan's family. He often complains, "Bob, never get old. I've nothing to do but moan and groan."

"The book" is a different matter. Every time he picks it up, he smiles. "We did it, Bob," he says. "We got Elliott out there."

Today Jack is staying at the Castleview-Wychwood nursing home, where Joan visits him daily. Though wheelchair bound, A.J. moves around the city occasionally on a special tram run by the Toronto Transit Commission. He often gets out to Joan's or Magi's for dinner and sometimes visits the Royal Canadian Yacht Club with Magi, who is a member. His spirits are up as he reflects on his wide-ranging life, which has covered ministry, business, finance, public speaking and government. He affirms, "I've had a wonderful life." He ends our conversation saying, "I think of you as first in everything," to which I reply, "That's the way I think of you, and soon the world will know it."

Two years ago in August, upon sensing on the phone a noticeable reduction in his general level of energy, I arranged to visit A.J., assuming it might be for the last time. I notified a mutual Elliottician friend of Jack's to meet me there, and flew up to Toronto to spend the afternoon. A.J. took a few minutes getting through the house with his walker but was soon sitting on the back patio, chatting and twinkling, his old self. Our friend had brought along his young, attractive wife. Upon introduction, Jack flourished his potato, told her the story behind it, and within minutes was holding her hand and reading her palm.

Robert R. Prechter, Jr., October 1996

**A Youthful Frost**

Called To The Bar

JOHN FROST, of Toronto, who was called to the bar recently. He is a graduate of Queen's University and a member of the Institute of Chartered Accountants.

**1937**

RECEIVES APPOINTMENT

A. J. Frost, son of Mrs. E. M. Frost of Hanover, who was recently appointed Comptroller of the Toronto General Trusts Corporation.

**1939**

Saturday, January 28, 1956 THE OTT

**Brother, Can You Spare A Dime**—It seems that some of the "Men Who Broke the Bank at Monte Carlo" are now broke themselves. It was all a part of the fun viewed by the hundreds of Ottawans who attended the May Court Ball yesterday evening. Looking for a handout and getting sneers instead are, left to right, Alec Craigie, John Deutsch, Jack Bankes, Jack Frost, George Wevill, Ted Royce, Denis Coolican and Bill Meek.

—Photo by Newton

1956

THE OTTAWA JOURNAL FRIDAY, NOVEMBER 7, 1958

AT BETTER BUSINESS BUREAU ANNUAL.

Lawrence Ritchie, left, immediate past president of the Better Business Bureau of Ottawa and Hull, congratulates his successor as president, A. J. Frost, right, at last night's 21st annual meeting. Beaming his approval is James A. Roberts, associate deputy minister, Trade and Commerce, who was speaker at the banquet.

—Journal Photo by Dominion Wide

## Better Business Bureau Elects A. J. Frost Head

A. J. Frost was elected president of the Better Business Bureau of Ottawa and Hull last night at the group's 21st annual meeting held in the Chateau Laurier.

1958

**BRAIN TRUST.**

Panellists in last night's discussion of "Fundamentals of Accounting—Taxes" in Rotary Club's five-lecture executive refresher course are chartered accountants, left to right seated, Hamilton Quain; Jack Frost of Toronto General Trusts; J. F. Harmer, taxation division, revenue dept.; and standing left to right, R. F. Burns, and D. A. Ross.

(Journal Photo by Dominion Wide)

**Circa 1959**

WHO'S WHO

IN

**Canadian Investment and Finance**

ALFRED JOHN FROST

Approved 1962

1962

B-6 THE GLOBE AND MAIL, TUESDAY, JAN. 22, 1963 — REPORT on BUSINESS

—Wallace R. Berry.

Advisory council, School of Business, Queen's University, Kingston, meets for January conference with director and faculty in boardroom. Clockwise from lower left are: K. E. Kennedy, New Toronto; Howard I. Ross, Montreal; O. H. Barrett, Montreal; Wesley F. Cook, Toronto; Dr. F. D. Barrett, executive program chairman; Professor L. G. Macpherson, director of school; John Macdonald; advisory council chairman, Mount Royal; A. J. Frost, Montreal; J. R. M. Wilson, Toronto; Professor W. G. Leonard; Professor F. W. Judge; W. D. Small, Montreal, and W. H. Poole, Toronto.

1963

# THE OTTAWA JOURNAL

home delivery 50 cents weekly. Ottawa, Monday, January 22, 1968 Phone 236-7511

## Jack Frost New NCC Chairman

By PETER JACKMAN
of The Journal

Ottawa businessman A. Jack Frost is to be the new chairman of the National Capital Commission.

He now is vice-chairman and has been acting-chairman since the retirement last year of Lt. General S. F. Clark.

Appointment of a new chairman was promised this week by Prime Minister Pearson. Works Minister McIlraith said he would be named toward the middle of the week.

Mr. Frost, executive director of the Association of Canadian Better Business Bureaus, was named to the commission in 1966 and became vice-chairman after the retirement of Professor Anthony Adamson.

1968

1968

(Photo Champlain Marcil)

**PLANTATION MASSIVE** — La Commission de la capitale nationale a planté 15,000 bulbes de tulipes dans le parc Jacques Cartier, à l'ouest de l'édifice Woods. Ces tulipes hollandaises sont un cadeau au peuple canadien de la "Netherlands Flower Bulb Institute". Le projet vise à rehausser la beauté de la région de la capitale nationale en dotant la pittoresque rive nord de l'Outaouais d'une belle floraison printanière. MM. Marcel D'Amour, maire de la Cité de Hull, à gauche, et John Frost, président de la CCN, avaient été invités lors de la mise en terre des bulbes. Comme on peut le constater, ils n'ont pas hésité à mettre la main à la ... terre. La CCN estime qu'en 1969, un million de tulipes combleront les terrains fédéraux en plus du million de tulipes que planteront les particuliers.

Circa 1969

Retiring after three decades of helping to forge the National Capital Region, Douglas L. McDonald, 2nd left, Assistant General Manager Planning, receives a symbolic anvil with stainless steel replica of the Region in place. With Doug are three chairmen of N.C.C., past and present, Jack Frost, at left, Douglas Fullerton, at right and Edgar Gallant.

46

Prenant sa retraite après avoir contribué pendant trois décennies à l'aménagement de la région de la Capitale nationale, M. Douglas L. McDonald, le deuxième, à gauche, directeur général adjoint de l'Urbanisme, reçoit une enclume symbolique sur laquelle est reproduite une réplique en acier inoxydable de la région actuelle. Avec M. McDonald figurent deux anciens présidents de la C.C.N., MM. Jack Frost, à gauche, et à droite, Douglas Fullerton, et le président actuel, M. Edgar Gallant.

Circa 1970

Saturday, May 8, 1971 The Ottawa Journal 21

# 2 Ottawa Men Get Top Scout Awards

Two Ottawa area men received one of scouting's highest awards Friday at the 57th annual dinner meeting of the Boy Scouts of Canada held at the Chateau Laurier.

A. J. Frost of Manotick and Lt.-Col. Frederick Reesor of 3014 Hyde Street, Ottawa, were presented with the Silver Acorn by retiring Deputy Chief Scout Jim Harvey.

The award was granted to the two men in recognition of their many years service to scouting by Governor-General Roland Michener, Chief Scout of Canada.

1971

Working on our book (1977)

Our first dust jacket photograph (1977)

A.J. and Frances (1977)

A.J. at his favorite pastime (1977)

Collins in Indian Rocks Beach (1978)

Our book on display in New York City (1978)

An outtake for the dust jacket (1980)

Collins, Prechter and Frost in Michigan (1981)

Joan and Maggie (1981)

A.J. Frost
(1987)

RIDEAU HALL

THE SECRETARY TO THE GOVERNOR GENERAL
AND HERALD CHANCELLOR

LE SECRÉTAIRE DU GOUVERNEUR GÉNÉRAL
ET CHANCELIER D'ARMES

February 22, 1993

Dear Mr. A. John Frost,

On behalf of His Excellency The Right Honourable Ramon John Hnatyshyn, I am pleased to inform you that you have been awarded the Commemorative Medal for the 125th Anniversary of Canadian Confederation.

This award is being made to those persons who, like you, have made a significant contribution to Canada, to their community, or to their fellow Canadians. The decoration is a reminder of the values of service, individual respect, and community effort on which Canada was built and on which its quality of life will always depend.

Enclosed is the citation in respect of the Medal, as well as a brochure explaining the protocol according to which orders, decorations and medals are worn; the Commemorative Medal for the 125th Anniversary of the Confederation of Canada is placed after the Queen Elizabeth II's Silver Jubilee Medal.

As you may know, miniatures of medals are available; these can be ordered according to the information enclosed.

His Excellency asks me to extend his congratulations to you on receiving this honour, to which I add my own cordial best wishes.

Yours sincerely,

J. A. LaRocque

Judith A. LaRocque

Mr. A. John Frost
3465 Beach Drive
Victoria, BC
V8R-4K8

Enclosures

1 SUSSEX DRIVE 1, PROMENADE SUSSEX
OTTAWA, CANADA K1A 0A1

**THE COMMEMORATIVE MEDAL FOR THE 125TH ANNIVERSARY OF THE CONFEDERATION OF CANADA IS CONFERRED UPON**

**LA MÉDAILLE COMMÉMORATIVE DU 125È ANNIVERSAIRE DE LA CONFÉDÉRATION DU CANADA EST CONFÉRÉE À**

***Mr. A. John Frost***

*in recognition of significant contribution to compatriots, community and to Canada*

*en reconnaissance de sa contribution significative au bien-être de ses compatriotes, sa communauté et au Canada*

**1867 – 1992**

*Gouverneur général du Canada*

*Governor General of Canada*

## *ROBERT PRECHTER ON*

# *RICHARD RUSSELL*

### PERSONAL MEMORIES

Richard Russell was my stock market hero. My father was a joint subscriber to *Dow Theory Letters* with a friend of his, and he would often forward an issue to me after he had read it. I learned a lot about technical analysis from Russell, who is one of the few writers who consistently takes the time to explain his indicators and methods clearly. Russell has made many exceptional market calls. He recommended gold stocks in 1960, called the top of the great bull market in stocks in 1966 and announced the end of the great bear market in December 1974.

A devoted reader of the *Bank Credit Analyst,* Russell became intrigued with the Wave Principle. He met and then corresponded frequently with A. Hamilton Bolton and, after Bolton's death, with A.J. Frost. In 1964, he began publishing occasional wave analyses of individual stocks. After Bolton died, there was a void of Elliott Wave commentary, so Russell began writing from time to time about the Wave Principle as applied to the averages. His handling of the 1966-1975 period, which until 1974 was a bear market that was masked to the average investor until its final two years, was consistent and brilliant. About a week after the low in December of that year, he turned bullish. His reasons why were clear as a bell to me, and the market's response vindicated his approach.

Although I have always been interested in finance, it was probably Russell's letters that most influenced my decision to join the market analysis profession. I wrote my first letter to Russell on March 31, 1976, four months after starting out at Merrill Lynch. "I have been a great fan of yours for several years," I began, "and have recently become fascinated by Elliott." A few weeks later, I attended the first-ever annual conference of the Market Technicians Association in Massachusetts that May, which featured Richard Russell as a speaker. Our meeting was brief and cursory, as Russell was surrounded by interested parties. I figured I would get my chance another day.

Russell and I corresponded off and on about the Wave Principle for three years. From day one, he was supportive. He called my Elliott work "scholarly" and asked if he could mention it in DTL. You can imagine what a thrill it was for me to get this response. When Frost and I decided to write *Elliott Wave Principle* together, Russell was again supportive. We quoted one of his passages in Chapter 8, and he was the first to give the book a terrific write-up. When I designed the front page of *The Elliott Wave Theorist,* I copied the placement of his name before the title. Soon afterward, we arranged a complimentary exchange of newsletters.

Over the years since then, we have gotten together several times while "on the circuit" at seminars and conferences and occasionally call each other about the market. To this day, I only bother to read a few market letters, and his is one of them.

In 1993, I called Dick and told him that his Elliott Wave material from the 1970s deserved to be published. He consented, and with this book, here it is.

**BIOGRAPHY**

Richard Russell was born on July 22, 1924 in New York City. His father was a civil engineer, and his mother was a novelist and short story writer who had four published books and many magazine stories to her credit.

Russell graduated from Horace Mann School in Riverdale, New York. He spent one year at Rutgers and then enlisted in the army during World War II. After taking basic training in the infantry, he transferred to the Army Air Force and saw combat as a bombardier on B-25 medium bombers with the 12th Air Force in Italy. After the war, Russell earned a B.A. in English from New York University. He was always good at art and got his first job as a textile designer.

An uncle who had committed suicide just after the 1929 crash had left young Richard a fair sum of money, and about this time, he decided to figure out how to handle that "gift." He spent months in the New York Public Library reading everything he could on the market and finally came across Robert Rhea's brilliant *Dow Theory Comment* advisory service. Reading those analyses sold Russell on Dow Theory. Because of his design background, he quickly became adept at reading stock patterns. In studying the averages, he became so bullish after the correction into late 1957 that he invested all his money in the market.

In 1958, Russell started writing a mimeographed market sheet as a sideline and sending it to friends. As Russell says, "After a few months, people I didn't even know started asking for the sheet, which I called *Dow Theory Letters*." Russell contacted *Barron's* editor Robert Bleiberg about writing a bullish article. Bleiberg accepted, and within two weeks of the publication of Russell's first article, he had hundreds of subscribers to his service. "The market boomed," he recalls, "and my advisory business grew so rapidly that I quit my design job. At the same time, my brokerage account kept heading north. My new career was underway." His first subscribers paid $30 a year for biweekly commentary on the stock market, bonds, precious metals, economics, and Russell's observations on life. In 1961, Russell moved to San Diego, California, and in 1967, he moved to La Jolla, where he currently resides.

In all, Russell wrote some 25 articles on Dow Theory and technical analysis for *Barron's* from the late 1950s through the 1970s, which gained him wide recognition. As a service to subscribers, he also published a reference chart book of daily Dow prices and reprinted three classic texts on Dow Theory that had become lost to most investors.

Russell's only professional setback occurred in March 1977, when he consented to S.E.C. sanctions for having bought and sold stock he had recommended in his letter. It was a technical rule, and his violation was of no consequence to his subscribers or anyone else. One of the S.E.C.'s demands was that he give subscribers two free months of DTL, which, if anything, appears to have been a ringing endorsement of his publication by the Commission.

Since starting in 1957, Russell has never missed an issue of *Dow Theory Letters*, making it today's longest-running market publication continuously written by one person. Says Dick, "I have written through a heart attack, a quintuple bypass and a motorcycle crash." He has ridden motorcycles ever since 1945 and still rides his Harley, which he muses, "makes me also one of the oldest or longest-riding bikers in the nation."

Russell has been married three times. He has one son and four daughters, aged 15 to 40. One daughter is autistic. His wife, Faye, is a corporate lawyer. In 1995, Russell and a partner started a new business, West Coast Options Fund, which has been successfully writing options for investors. At age 72, he's still going strong.

*The Elliott Wave Theorist*, December 30, 2013

**TRIBUTE**

Richard Russell wrote every full issue of *Dow Theory Letters* for a Fibonacci **55** years, from 1958 to 2013. He began publishing at age **34** and is substantially retiring at age **89**. He still provides commentary but has turned over the bulk of the work to two new writers. If anyone deserves a little time off, it's Dick Russell.

*The Elliott Wave Theorist*, December 18, 2015

**RICHARD RUSSELL (1924 - NOVEMBER 21, 2015)**

It's no secret that Richard Russell's *Dow Theory Letters* was my inspiration to enter the market analysis profession. My high school guidance counselor did not mention "market letter writer" as a professional option, but reading DTL in the late 1960s and especially the early 1970s influenced my decision to follow that path. As a novice I learned a lot about technical analysis from Russell. I still have the three books—one by Russell and two by earlier Dow Theory pioneers—that Russell published over half a century ago.

I wrote Russell a letter on March 31, 1976, after starting out at Merrill Lynch the previous year. Two months later, I attended the first-ever annual conference of the Market Technicians Association in Massachusetts, where I met Russell, the featured speaker. Russell was always gracious to fellow writers, and it was a thrill when a few years later he mentioned EWT in his letter. Out of curiosity, I did a count of how many times I mentioned him in return; I found that while he lived I typed Russell's name exactly **55** (Fibonacci) times into *The Elliott Wave Theorist*, spanning the time from inception in 1979 to December 2013, when I wrote a short tribute.

Most people wait until someone is dead to celebrate them, and I didn't want that to happen to Russell. In April 2003, I arranged to present a "Lifetime Achievement Award for Original Market Research" to him. The award was sponsored by Martin Truax's Atlanta Investment Conference, which was an annual charity event held in Clayton, GA for the benefit of the Friends for Autism Foundation. I showed eight slides in a PowerPoint presentation titled "Richard Russell on the 1973-1974 Bear Market" and then interviewed Russell by phone as his voice filled the room. It was a great day.

In April 2009, John Mauldin and several colleagues hosted a tribute to Richard Russell in San Diego to celebrate the 50th anniversary of *Dow Theory Letters*. The place was packed with friends, presenters and admirers. I was invited to speak and also gave away a box of copies of a book I had put together years earlier titled *The Elliott Wave Writings of A.J. Frost and Richard Russell.*

In October 2010, Doug Casey and David Galland hosted a conference in San Diego, where I got to chat with Russell and my long-time friend Ian McAvity. Here's a picture of us on that weekend.

Many financial professionals have fond memories of Richard. McAvity recalled attending a conference in 1971 featuring Russell as the keynote speaker. The event was part of the genesis of the Market Technicians Association, which formed two years later. He also recalls a time when a direct mail marketing specialist told him in the 1970s, "Russell won't last very long trying to build his business on $1 trial subscriptions." Not a great call. Gary Alexander noted, "He was also a great jazz fan. I discussed big bands with him. He stood in line for the famous Sinatra/Dorsey shows in 1942 and hung out on the 52nd Street jazz scene in NYC in the 1940s." In 2009, Mark Skousen and John Mauldin put together a booklet of Russell's writings titled "Fifty Years of Wall Street." Skousen plans to dedicate a room to him at his 2016 FreedomFest conference.

A few of my favorite quotes from Russell are:

<u>1958-60</u> (from *The Dow Theory Today*): "There is little or no relationship between one bull market and another, either in duration or extent. There is, however, a relationship between a bull market and the bear market which

directly follows. History shows that the more inflationary and speculative the former, the more drastic the latter."

[date missing] "Successful writers display several factors, including (1) competence, (2) honesty and (3) a unique vision. The market letters which fail to find the limelight or a large readership usually lack one of these factors. Those that flounder near the bottom, despite all the hype they can deliver, often lack them all. What few of them understand is that getting subscribers, as difficult as that is, doesn't cut it. Keeping them is a requirement for success, and that demands a dedication to delivering value through the three factors listed above. And if you want to start a market service and believe you can offer all three factors, you must still be patient and persistent. No one becomes acknowledged overnight. The prospective buyer wants to see you perform for a while."

1986: "A blow-off is when the market goes up big and you were bearish the whole rise."

1991: "The last thing the bear wants to kill is hope."

2011: "Almost everything I read about the stock market is based on current fundamental economic news. But the stock market does not operate on current news. Very few advisors are strict market followers. They ignore the news and are strict market technicians. Bob Prechter of Elliott Wave and Joe Granville of the Granville Market Letter are two of such advisors, and you can add Richard Russell."

2012: "I'm my own man, and I've been writing about Dow Theory on my own for over half a century."

Links:

http://www.elliottwave.com/wave/1512DTL

http://dowtheoryletters.com/Content_Free/richard-russell-passes-at-91.aspx

# *A.J. FROST ON MARKETS*

## *1962 - 1974*

## *AN UNPUBLISHED PAPER*

**December 1962**

Elliott discerned definite characteristics of movement in stock prices, which developed, after careful research, into a rational theory of market behaviour. The fundamentals of Elliott's theory (he claimed it was more than a theory and insisted upon his precepts being called a principle) have remained substantially the same since he first announced them until his death in 1947, and no one since then has endeavoured to change any of his basic tenets. A. Hamilton Bolton, in his book *The Elliott Wave Principle — A Critical Appraisal*, disagrees with some of Elliott's interpretations and demonstrates that the theory is not the precise tool Elliott claimed it to be, but significantly, Bolton, who is the leading exponent of the Principle, does not attempt to change Elliott's rules or introduce any new concepts. The problem with the Wave Principle would appear to be not so much a case of trying to throw new light on the subject but applying Elliott's rules to fit market behavior in a realistic way.

Elliott was a stickler for detail and earned the reputation of being a solid purist. His matter-of-fact handling of specific problems, however, as indicated by his interpretative letters, would lead one to think of him more as a pragmatist than a purist. He made unorthodox counts, broke his own rules, constructed his own average to better illustrate the Wave Principle, and from time to time changed his mind about previous interpretations. This is all to the good, but it might have been better if Elliott hadn't created the impression of being such a fussbudget. It is only common sense to realize that the Elliott rules of market movement only deal with underlying tendencies of the stock market to perform in certain ways. The stock market can do anything pattern-wise, and occasionally does. What looks like an Elliott pattern in the process of development sometimes turns out to be a non-recognizable movement and remains so even in retrospect. Instances of this nature, however, are rare, and most stock market movements (no matter how minute) are subject to reasonable interpretation under the Wave Principle.

An interesting case in point as to the amazing propensity of the stock market to reflect Elliott patterns occurred recently in our office. The posting of our hourly DJIA chart fell behind three days (18 postings including the unofficial 3 o'clock figure); in bringing the postings up to date, the hourly figures were scrambled, with the last day posted first. The resulting curve was a jumble until the error was noticed and corrected. The new pattern was a clear-cut Elliott Wave of sub-minute degree. The probability of such a pattern developing on an hourly basis for 18 consecutive periods is roughly equivalent to calling correctly the toss of a coin 18 times in a row — a 256,000-to-1 shot. This demonstrated that hourly trends exist in the stock market and that hour-to-hour movements do not conform to the laws of chance willy-nilly.

Elliott used hourly figures especially in fast-moving markets in order to get a better picture of minor subwaves. The advantages of an hourly chart over a daily closing chart can be seen in Figure 1 [see Figure 3 on page 110], which charts the move in mid-1962 from June 25th to July 10th. The hourly chart is a much clearer presentation of movement than the daily chart and is a big help in recognizing Elliott patterns.

Elliott made extravagant claims for his Wave Principle. He said that the principle, in effect, was a law of nature and applied to all social-economic activity, of which the market was only one expression. The stock market to him was a sort of psychological entity similar to other phenomena and followed an ordered sequence. In fact, Elliott claimed if there were no law behind the market, there would be no market. He said anyone who understood the principle he had "discovered" could be independent of all other investment services. Elliott was not the master of understatement.

## CYCLES PRIOR TO 1929

Elliott's views concerning his Wave Principle, published in the *Financial World* in 1938, as applied to the stock market from 1857 to 1929, are depicted in Figure 2. This diagram shows Elliott's concept of what he believed was a Supercycle wave (he concluded shortly before he died that this wave was No. 3 in the Grand Supercycle), breaking down into five cycle waves. With respect to cycle V, Elliott changed his mind in 1946 and revised his wave count. This modified interpretation is also shown in Figure 2.

On examination of Elliott's interpretations, as shown in Figure 2, we note the following technical difficulties:

(a) as to the Supercycle:

(i) Wave II and wave IV both appear to be flats, which is contrary to the rule of alternation.

(ii) Wave III, which is usually the largest wave, lasted only 4 years compared with a total of 71 years for the entire cycle. This is against the rule of normal proportions. A cycle wave of only 4 years would mean that the five primaries composing it would average less than a year each. This seems almost incredible. Elliott stated that wave 3 should not be shorter than either wave 1 or wave 5. It is arguable whether he was referring to amplitude or time or merely length as such. The length of a line drawn on a chart depends on the amplitude (number of points in a swing) and the time it takes. It may be that Elliott was simply thinking of length in the ordinary sense of normal proportion.

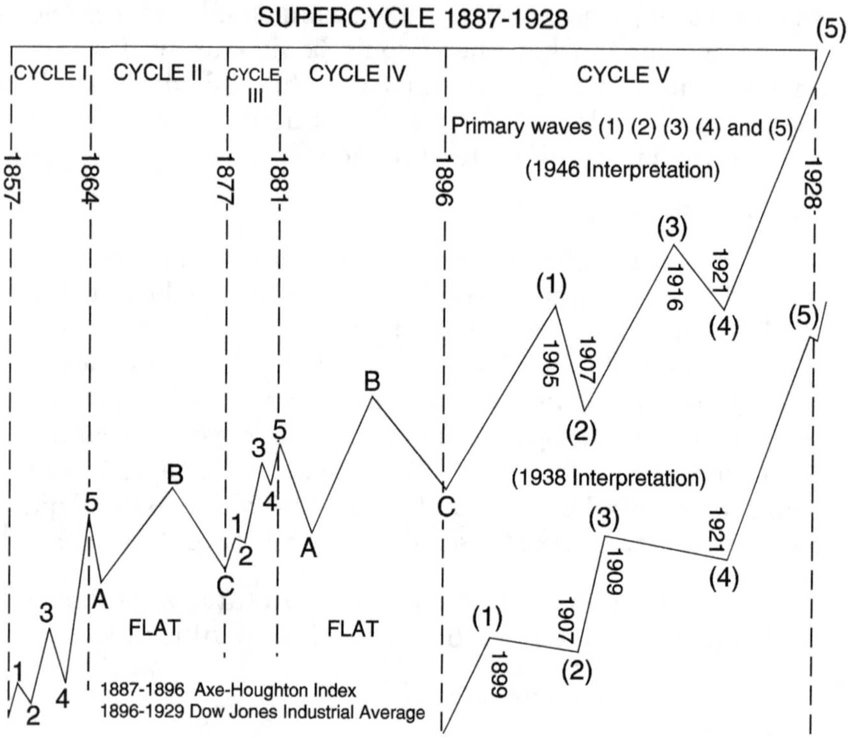


*Figure 2*

(iii) The Supercycle does not come close to Benner's concepts of fixed periodicity (see page 108) — not that it needs to.

(b) as to Cycle V (1946 interpretation):

(i) Wave (3) lacks normal proportion.

(ii) Wave (2) lasted 8 years compared with 3 years for wave (1) and only corrects a fraction of the previous rise. It is disproportionate.

(iii) Wave (4) is even more disproportionate, taking twelve years to correct about 20% of the two-year rise from 1907 to 1909.

(c) as to Cycle V (1946 interpretation):

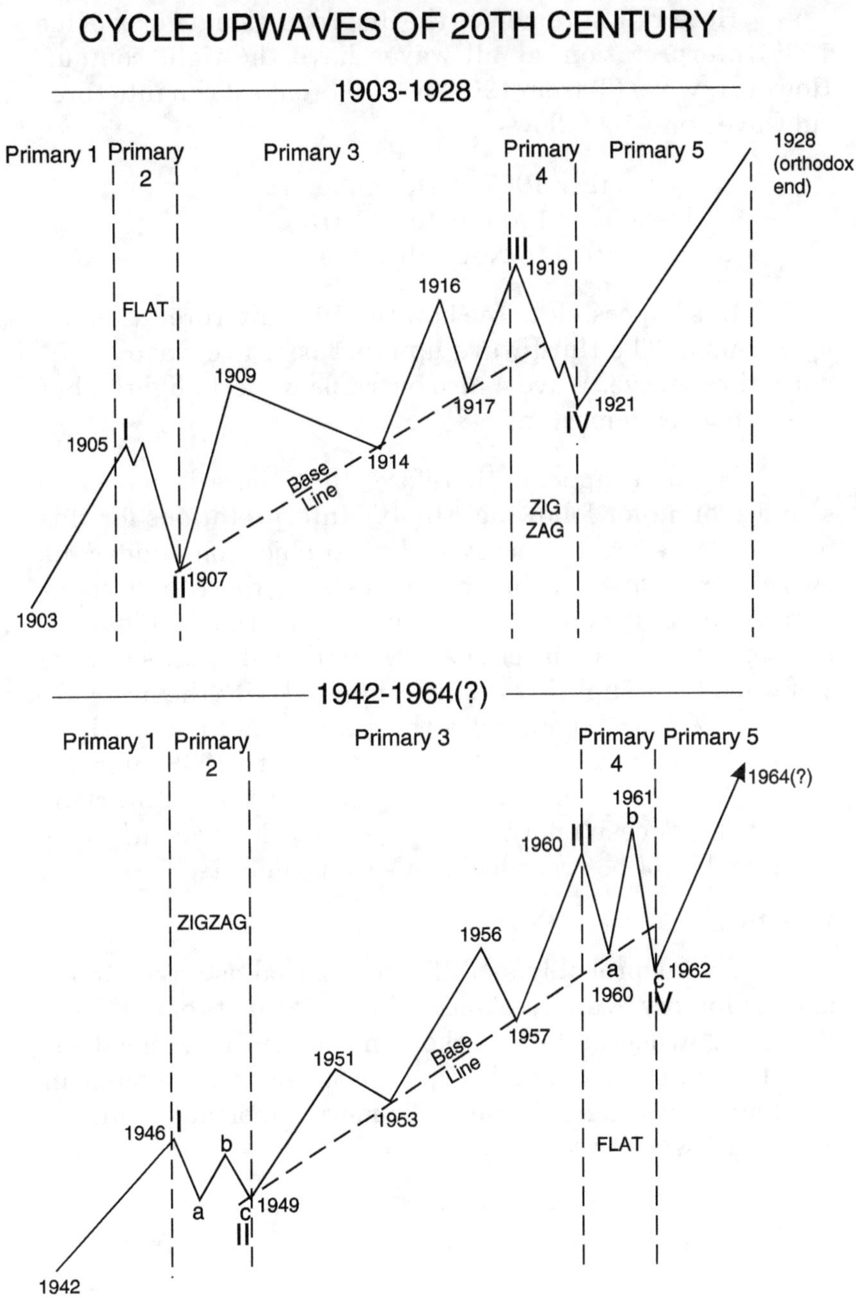
CYCLE UPWAVES OF 20TH CENTURY
1903-1928
Primary 1
Primary 2
Primary 3
Primary 4
Primary 5
1928 (orthodox end)
FLAT
III
1919
1916
1909
1917
1921
IV
I
1905
1914
Base Line
ZIG ZAG
II
1907
1903
1942-1964(?)
Primary 1
Primary 2
Primary 3
Primary 4
Primary 5
1964(?)
1961
b
1960
III
ZIGZAG
1956
a
1960
c
1962
IV
1957
Base Line
1951
1953
1946
I
b
FLAT
a
c
1949
II
1942

*Figure 3*

Here Elliott remedies the disproportionate look of his 1938 Interpretation, as all waves have the right contour. However, wave (3) from 1907 to 1916 breaks down into three subwaves only as follows:

November 1907 to December 1909
December 1909 to June 1913
June 1913 to November 1916.

It is impossible to see how the 1946 interpretation can be accepted. The third wave up must be a five-wave affair, not a three-wave. Wave 4 also overlaps wave 1 slightly, but this is not too important.

It would appear, therefore, that there is no really sound ground for following Elliott's interpretations for this period. There are too many technical objections under his own theory. On the other hand, revising the Elliott count to fit Benner, as depicted in the upper diagram in Figure 3, has some technical objections as well, namely that subwave 2 of wave III is slightly too long compared with the first subwave — 3½ years compared with 2 years — but not nearly so disproportionate as waves 2 and 4 in Elliott's 1938 interpretation. Another technical objection is that wave 4 overlaps wave 1. This doesn't normally happen, but it frequently does and should not be regarded as a serious defect.

**1929-1942**

This is probably as difficult a period as any in stock market history to analyse under the basic tenets of the Wave Principle. Swings in stock market sentiment were tremendous, resulting in confused and erratic patterns of movement in the popular averages. Some of the more important events in retrospect were as follows:

1. Investor psychology of 1929.
2. Market recovery on increasing volume from November 1929 to April 1930.
3. Worldwide depression.

4. F.D.R. election.
5. The Bank Holiday.
6. Enactment of AAA and NRA.
7. Closing of the stock exchange.
8. U.S. off the gold standard.
9. Devaluation of the U.S. dollar.
10. Occupation by Hitler of the Rhineland.
11. Spanish Revolution.
12. Invasion of Austria.
13. Munich.
14. World War II started.
15. Fall of France.
16. Dunkirk.
17. Pearl Harbor.

Under Elliott's theory, each completed wave forms part of a wave formation of higher magnitude, and, in turn, is composed of smaller waves of lesser degree. The Principle as applied to the stock market is one of continuous sequence, expanding and contracting to meet the exigencies of world and national conditions. Nothing pleases the Elliott theorists like the spectacle of minor and intermediate waves expanding into distinct waves of higher magnitude. The fact that the market responds with terrific velocity to the sudden shock of world events, making interpretation difficult on occasion, isn't as significant as the fact that, despite all, reasonable interpretations can be made for any period in market history.

Elliott concluded that the 1929-42 period depicted a 13-year triangle of Supercycle dimensions, correcting the rise from 1857-1929. In studies of proportionate analysis, each wave being 62%, approximately of the previous one, than by the strict observance of his own rule that a triangle must be composed of five waves breaking down into three subwaves. Unfortunately, the 13-year triangle interpretation, wave 3 from March 1937 to March 1938, is a distinct five which offends against the rule of triangles. Elliott never recanted.

Bolton, the leading authority on the Wave Principle, accepted Elliott's hypothesis until two more waves of primary dimension unfolded and then advanced the argument that a 21-year triangle from 1928-1949 was technically more acceptable, as each wave could be subdivided into a three. For these two interpretations, see Figure 4.

The writer suggests that neither the 13-year triangle nor the 21-year triangle may be the best interpretation for the cycle period following 1929 for these reasons:

1. The first wave is probably a five, not a three. Most analysts view the drop from the 1929 high to July 1932 as a three-phase affair, with the third phase breaking down into eight or nine legs. A close examination, however, of the two intermediate waves subsequent to July 1932 indicates that the wave to September 7, 1932 subdivides into three minor up waves of the 5-3-5 variety, and the next move down to February 27, 1933 is a five. Thus the primary wave down from 1929 (or 1928 to take the orthodox high) to July 1932, was incomplete at this point. The move up to September 7, 1932 was a rally in the great bear market of this period, which was only completed on February 29, 1933. The fact that February 27, 1933 did not establish a new low is not objectionable, technically under the circumstances. It is a legitimate failure under Elliott's rules. A further argument in favor of February 1933 as the true low is the fact that the entire move from 1929 down to this point is contained by the base line drawn above the price curve of the averages. This is well hugged, indicating that the underlying trend continued down for several months after the July 1932 low.

2. Triangles are rare and should only be accepted if no better interpretation is available. Most students say that triangles are most apt to occur in small formations. Triangles are common in charts of individual stocks — not so with the averages. A condition precedent to the acceptance of a triangle interpretation would appear to be a clearly delineated contour, with both boundary lines well hugged. This is not true of either the 13-year or the 21-year interpretation.

3. Wave IV from 1942-46 in the 21-year triangle can be interpreted as a five, and this was Elliott's hypothesis

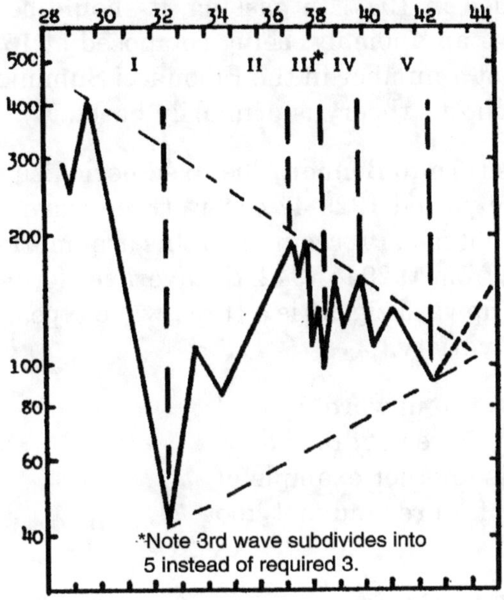


BREAKDOWN OF ELLIOTT 13-YEAR TRIANGLE

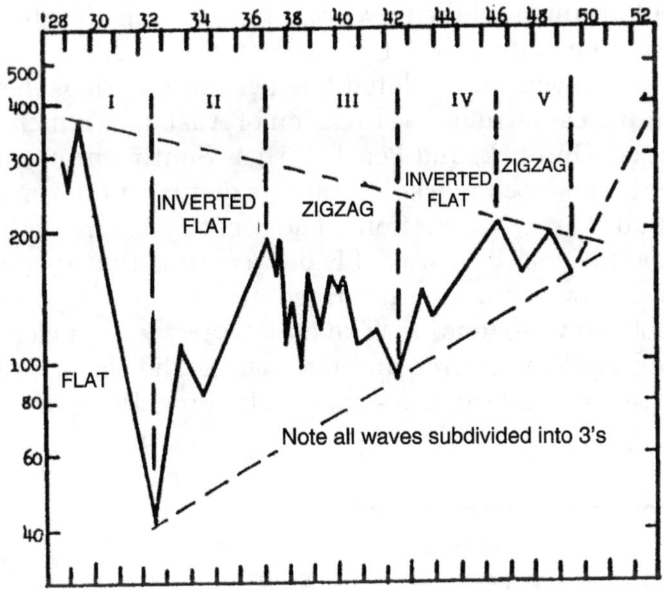


THE TWENTY-ONE YEAR TRIANGLE

*Figure 4*

before he died in 1947. In passing, it should be noted that triangles are an anomaly, being composed of 15 subwaves. Fifteen is not a number in the Fibonacci Summation series, on which Elliott's theory is primarily based.

Let's turn to Benner. The fixed periodicity of Benner suggests the period 1929-42 covers three waves of primary dimension, not five. Proceeding on this assumption, it would appear that from 1929 to 1942, the averages form an upward zigzag.[1] An upward zigzag is a three-wave type of correction of the 5-3-5 variety.

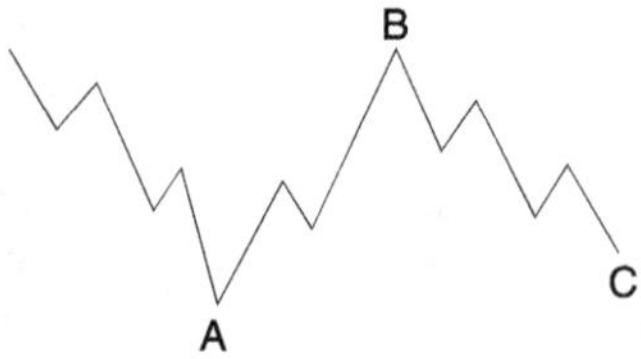


an upward zigzag

The term "upward" is used when wave C does not drop below wave A. It is another example of a technical failure and not too uncommon.

We have already seen that wave A, the first primary wave, is a five to March 1933. Once this conclusion is reached, wave B becomes a clear-cut three without argument, leaving wave C from March 1937 to April 1942 to be counted. Unfortunately, this is a hectic period. War preparations stimulated business in an atmosphere of impending catastrophe — Invasion of Austria, Munich, Fall of France, Dunkirk, and Pearl Harbor. Sentiment naturally ran high and stock market gyrations distorted the time and amplitude of wave formations. The best that can probably be said for this period by way of Elliott count is that it appears to break down into nine intermediate waves with possibly the third wave extending. The cycle starts with a clear-cut five and ends on a three and five count. The waves are not proportionate and there is some overlapping. However, April

---

[1] Frost's objections to Elliott's and Bolton's counts are valid, but he offers an equally distorted interpretation. He and Bolton later joined Collins in marking 1932 as the orthodox bottom and the 1937 high as wave I of the new Supercycle.

1942 is the low point for the period and the downward drift over the five-year period is contained by the base line. Dates of the intermediate waves composing the primary appear to be as follows:

| | | |
|---|---|---|
| March '37 | to | March '38 |
| March '38 | to | November '38 |
| November '38 | to | April '39 |
| April '39 | to | October '39 |
| October '39 | to | June '40 |
| June '40 | to | November '40 |
| November '40 | to | May '41 |
| May '41 | to | September '41 |
| September '41 | to | April '42 |

**1942 TO DATE**

If we accept the interpretation that 1929-42 is a corrective wave composed of three primaries and Elliott's conclusion that April 1942 was the point of culmination (Elliott seems right for the wrong reasons), then we have a new cycle wave up from 1942. Under Benner, one would be inclined to say that the next five primaries should break down as follows:[2]

1942 - 46
1946 - 49
1949 - 56
1956 - 57
1957 - 64 (?)

Benner is not a fine tool like Elliott and can only be used as the broadest indication of what may happen on the basis of fixed cycles. Elliott is a delicate instrument, difficult to understand and apply, and can easily land the interpreter in trouble if his approach is too technical. The

---

[2] This is correct and prescient. Frost later shifts to a different count, but returns to this one eventually.

theory of extensions is an essential part of the Wave Theory, so in any set of primaries, one of the waves is apt to be much longer than the others. This is where Benner and Elliott may diverge temporarily, but nevertheless always seem to be able to get back into juxtaposition as the averages move forward.

Elliott indicated that the move from 1942 would be a thrust, which proved true. The low of April 1942 was 92.92 on the Dow, and every correction through to January 1960 was subnormal in magnitude and normal with respect to the time element. The primary waves are as follows.

#### WAVE I, 1942-46

Elliott analysed this wave into five intermediates. It was a long, sustained advance, bringing the Dow to the 212 level.

#### WAVE II, 1946-49

This wave corrected wave I and lasted 37 months. The contours indicate a zigzag starting with an irregular 5, then a 3 up, followed by a 5 down to the 161 level.

#### WAVE III, 1949-60 - an extended third wave

| | | |
|---|---|---|
| '49 - '51 | Primary III | (a) |
| '51 - '53 | Primary III | (b) |
| '53 - '56 | Primary III | (c) |
| '56 - '57 | Primary III | (d) |
| '57 - '60 | Primary III | (e) |

This is the big wave of the post war period. It is the post war bull market, but it is not of cycle dimension, as the current wave of cycle dimension started in 1942 and is still in force. The advance from 1949 to 1960 hugged its base trend line (on a logarithmic basis) drawn through the lows of 1949, 1953 and 1957. Each wave in the series is of normal proportions and has the right look. The second wave is a flat and the fourth a zigzag, in accordance with Elliott's rules.

This long wave was terminated on January 5, 1960 and the base trend line is broken decisively by the fourth wave, which later climaxed with the Cuban crisis.

There is one minor technical difficulty in reading this long extended wave from 1949 as terminating in January of 1960. The last subwave from September 1959 to January 1960 isn't as clear cut a five-wave pattern as one would like to see. However, it is closer to a five than a three, allowing for a minor overlap of about 1%.

### WAVE IV, 1960-62

In broad outline the market from January, 1960 to October, 1962 is a flat of the same degree and magnitude as wave II (1946-49) in the cycle advance from 1942. This is as it should be under Elliott's rules. Wave II is a zigzag, and wave IV is a flat. Both waves II and IV are of normal proportions and tie in with the market picture very neatly. The whole rise from 1942 is a vindication of the Wave Principle after the rough carriage of the 1929-42 period.

The analyst generally looks for the detailed confirmation of subwave movements to support interpretations of larger wave formations. Here the situation is in reverse, and one would like to skip the subwaves because the general contour of the primary wave formation is so clear cut. The breakdown of intermediate waves for this period is as follows:

| | |
|---|---|
| Intermediate wave A | January 1960 - October 1960 |
| Intermediate wave B | October 1960 - November 1961 |
| Intermediate wave C | November 1961 - October 1962 |

Wave A is a flat with wave C subdividing into five parts. Wave B is an inverted zigzag with a clear cut run up to May 1961. At this point, the waves form a confused pattern and become open to different interpretations. The interpretation we like best is a minor decline to June and a five up to November.

From November 1961, the count is five down to January 28, 1962. The first subminor isn't too clear, but the second is almost perfect and on an hourly basis is a tidy subminuette breaking down into a 13 sub-sub-count. The fourth subminor overlaps wave I, which isn't too important technically when the fifth wave extends. Time and again, fifth wave extensions are preceded by "irregular" fourth waves. Here the fifth subminor expanded, which was followed by a double retracement, the first wave of which carried the market back to 727.14 on March 15th and beyond the point where the extension started (714.60).

From March 15th to June 25th the count is five down with the third wave extending into waves of equal degree, forming in effect a nine-wave pattern. Nine-wave patterns as third-wave formations are vicious and have a tendency to create freak lows. The situation in the spring of 1962 was in Elliott's terms similar to what happened during the great bear market of 1929-32, only the degree and circumstances were different. The decline ending in July 1932 was a nine-wave movement of intermediate degree whereas the decline ending in June of 1962 was the nine-wave movement of minor degree. Both created artificial lows and both were followed by three-wave rallies, but neither was the end of their respective trends.

From the low of June 25th, the market rallied very quickly to July 10th. Figure 5 shows the breakdown of this rally into five subwaves. Most moving averages are too slow to be of much significance under the Elliott system. However the 55-hour average (approximately 10 days) is short enough to move in gear with subminor waves and yet retain its smoothness. The longer the period covered by a moving average, the less helpful it is in delineating waves.

The 55-hour average (55 is a Fibonacci number) appears to be an ideal tool in analyzing and counting minor

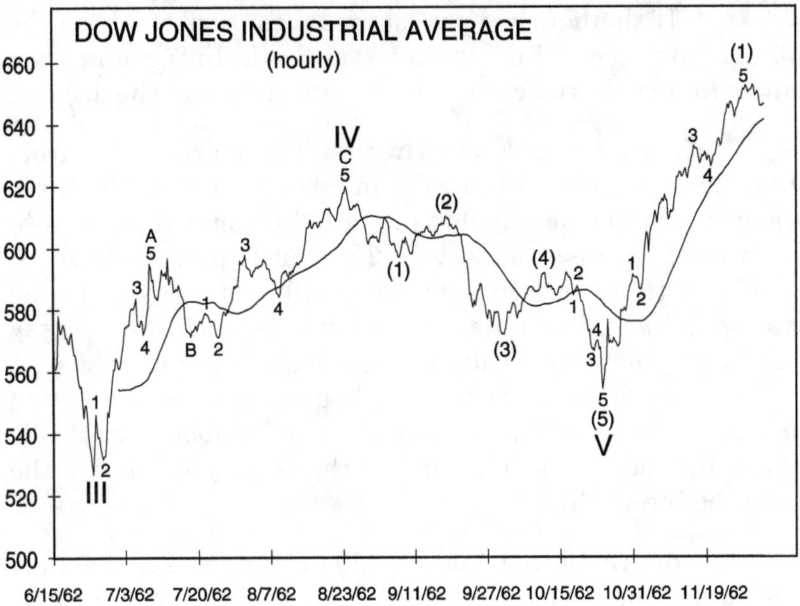


*Figure 5*

waves under the Elliott system. The following rules, though not Elliott, are also helpful in this respect.

1. If the 55-hour average flattens or advances following a drop and is penetrated by the hourly line on the upside, this is an indication of a minor advance.

2. If the hourly curve approaches or falls below the 55-hour average while the average is advancing and then starts to move up, this is a confirmation of the advance.

3. If the 55-hour average flattens or declines following a rise and is penetrated by the hourly curve on the downside this is an indication of a minor decline.

4. If the hourly curve approaches or rises above the 55-hour average while the average is declining and then starts to turn down again, this is confirmation of the decline.

Figure 5 shows clearly that the market rise from June 25 to August 23 is a rally in a bear market. The three waves up can be subdivided into a 5-3-5 count (labeled a-b-c), forming an inverted zigzag. The third subwave deploys, that is, it thins out, giving a wedge-like appearance to the run-up. Elliott didn't refer to wedges as such but did say that deployment generally carried bearish implications. (A wedge is a formation with rising boundary lines converging on a point, or apex. The breakout is usually about two-thirds of the distance to the apex and on the downside through the lower boundary line.)

From the minor high of 620 on August 23, the market turns and forms a pattern of five waves down. This move does not penetrate the previous low of June 25 and is in Elliott's terms a failure, carrying strong bullish implications. The stock markets of Japan, France, Germany, Italy, the Netherlands and Sweden all hit new lows during the week of October 22, as did the Value Line Composite Average based on 1,100 American and Canadian stocks. It is the opinion of the writer that under the basic tenets of the Wave Principle, October 24 was the orthodox end of the primary bear market (flat) from January 1960 and the beginning of a new bull market of primary dimension which will ultimately terminate the cycle advance from 1942 and *will not extend.*

## LOOKING AHEAD

No one knows the future. However, there are clues which tend to foreshadow coming events both in fundamental and technical studies. The business of forecasting is legitimate, and no forecaster worth his salt will fail to have opinions about what is likely to happen. Besides, it is good fun, especially if one does not take himself to seriously, regardless of how serious the job itself may be.

Forecasting should be viewed objectively, having due regard for immediate past history. There is no place for personal prejudices or fixed preconceived ideas. Perspective and due weight are essential ingredients of sound judgment. The forecaster must take into consideration every important development as it occurs and be prepared to change his analysis and admit his error if necessary.

The Wave Principle is an odd approach to the market, especially in terms of Elliott's philosophy. The striking thing about Elliott is his contention that all that happens in the market is regulated by the law of the market. This smacks of esotericism, meant only for those initiated into the secret doctrines of the occult. However, let's not forget that there is a great deal of "common" market sense in the Wave Principle and that it deals with observed psychological phenomena over many years.

Analyzing Elliott with a Benner bias, it would appear that currently the market is in its final primary wave of the cycle advance from 1942. We are in the first of the fifth, and still have some way to go before a major top is reached. On the basis of the 8-9-10 yearly pattern for tops, mid-1964 could be it. In this event, the final run up from October 1962 might be a 21-month bull market. This would appear to be a relatively short period, having regard for expanding credit conditions on a world wide basis and the efforts of most countries, especially the United States, to stimulate their economies by revising tax structures, tariff adjustments, increased spending, etc. 1964 is a long way ahead to predict or even suggest favorable market conditions, but under Elliott and general credit conditions, it doesn't seem too unreasonable.

Beyond the next high, which will top out the cycle movement from 1942, the averages should correct in three waves of primary dimension over a period which in time should roughly correspond with the 1929-42 period. This cycle, on the basis of alternation, should be a flat (1929-42 was a zigzag), so that the correction as a whole may not be too severe. A flat is a 3-3-5 movement, and the first primary could also be a flat. If this should prove to be the case, an "irregular" top could develop within a year after the orthodox high, say in 1965, and a further top several years later when the second primary wave B reaches maturity.

The guessing department is now working overtime, so we will quit at this point. We may have to eat crow.

## CORRESPONDENCE

### LETTER TO BOLTON

**December 10, 1964**

Dear Hammy:

Now that we are well along in the current period of economic expansion and gradually becoming vulnerable to changes in investment sentiment, it seems prudent to polish the crystal ball and do a little hard assessing. In appraising trends, I have every confidence in your bank credit approach except when the atmosphere becomes rarefied. I cannot forget 1962. My feeling is that fundamental tools are for the most part low pressure instruments. Elliott, on the other hand, although difficult in its practical applications, does have special merit in high areas. For this reason I have kept my eye cocked on the Wave Principle and what I see now causes me some concern. As I read Elliott, the stock market is vulnerable and the end of the major cycle from 1942 is upon us.

As you know, I have always accepted unequivocally Elliott's view that 1942 was a major turning point based on my own independent study of the subject and Benner's observations regarding the fixed periodicity of primary cycles. Never having met Elliott or even having been aware of his existence during his lifetime, I would prefer to agree with you rather than disagree on the 1942 vs. 1949 issue. However, the point is so important that I don't see how Elliott can be successfully applied as a theory of market action until 1942 is recognized. To me, 1949 distorts most subsequent counts.

If you will bear with my pigheaded nonacceptance of your view, I shall present my case to the effect that we are on dangerous ground and that a prudent investment policy (if one can use a dignified word to express undignified action) would be to fly to the nearest broker's office and throw everything to the winds.

The third wave of the long rise from 1942, namely June 1949 to January 1960, represents an extension of primary cycles. In the current primary wave from October 1962, the first cycle is an extension of intermediate waves. No more extensions can now take place of either primary of intermediate significance under Elliott's rules. The only possible extension from June 8, 1964 would have to be of minor or subminor degree. This precludes the market from rolling on and on as it did in the late 1920s. If the move from the entire cycle from 1942 may have reached its orthodox culmination point and what lies ahead of us now is probably a double top and a long flat of cycle dimension.

Based on the real possibility that 1929-42 was an upward zigzag[1] and applying Elliott's theory of alternation, the next three primary moves should form a flat of considerable duration. It will be interesting to see if this develops. In the meantime, I don't mind going out on the proverbial limb and making a 10-year projection (Figure 4) as an Elliott theorist using only Elliott and Benner ideas. No self-respecting analyst other than an Elliott man would do such a thing, but then that is the sort of thing this unique theory inspires.

Rather than spell out all the details, I will use diagrams and charts to support my contentions. We can argue details later.

---

[1] I.e., a truncated zigzag, one in which wave C does not travel beyond the end of wave A.

Figure 1. This chart of DBS Investors Price Index (monthly) indicates that the cycle from March 1937 to April 1942 was a five-wave affair, being wave C of an ABC correction of cycle dimension from 1929.

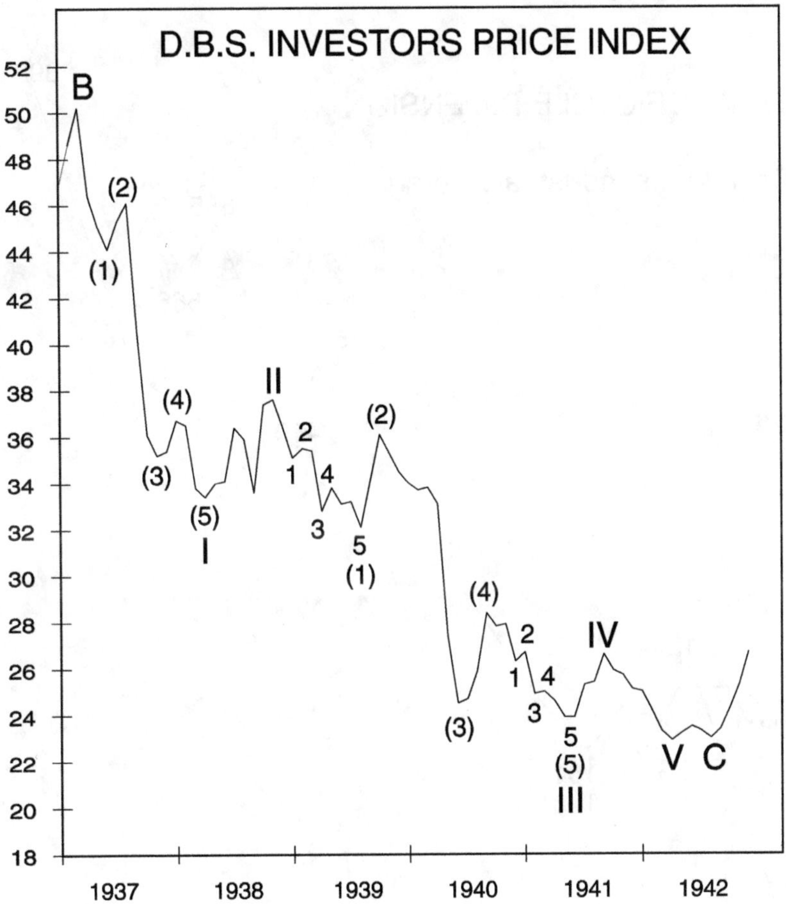


*Figure 1*

Figure 2. This shows the major bull market from 1942-64 according to my count.

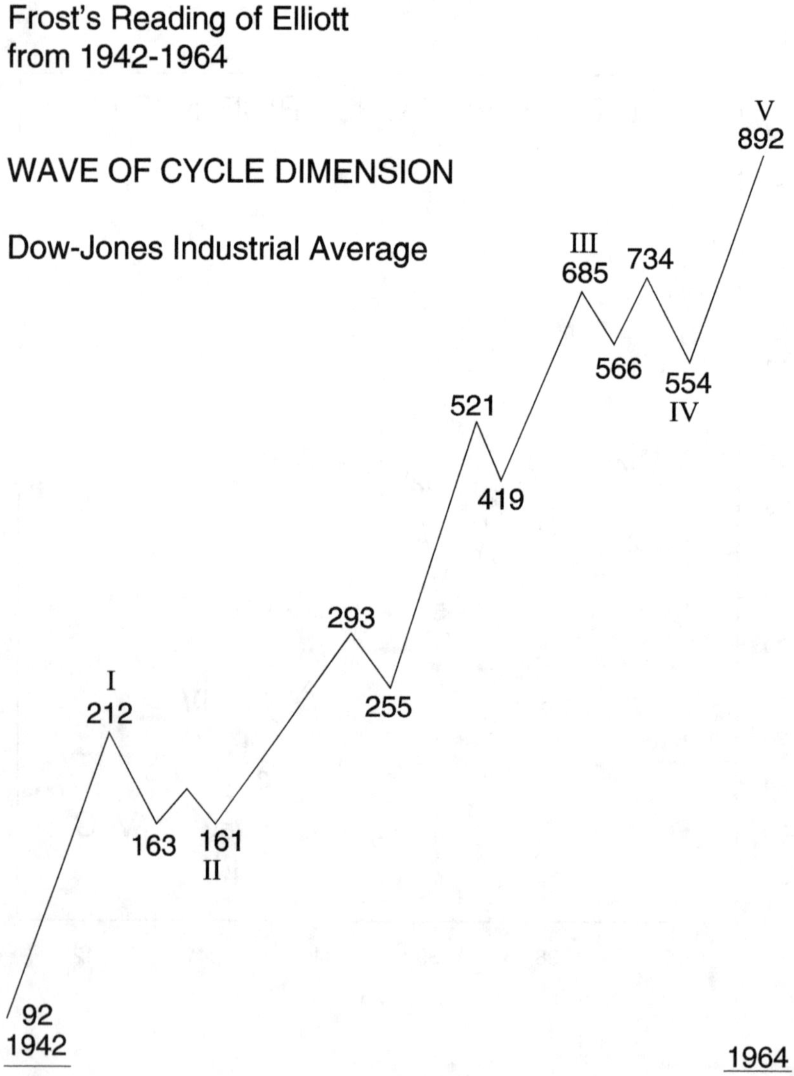


*Figure 2*

Figure 3. "The fifth wave" from 1962.

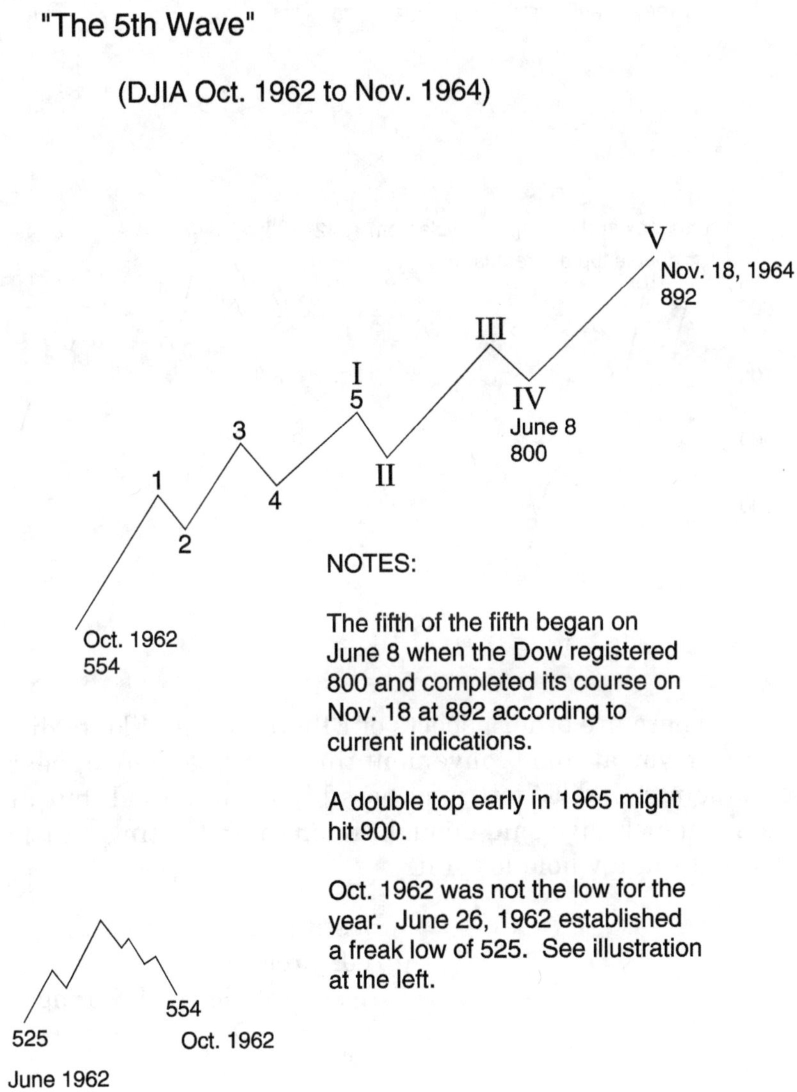


*Figure 3*

Figure 4. The writer's view of Elliott in prospect.

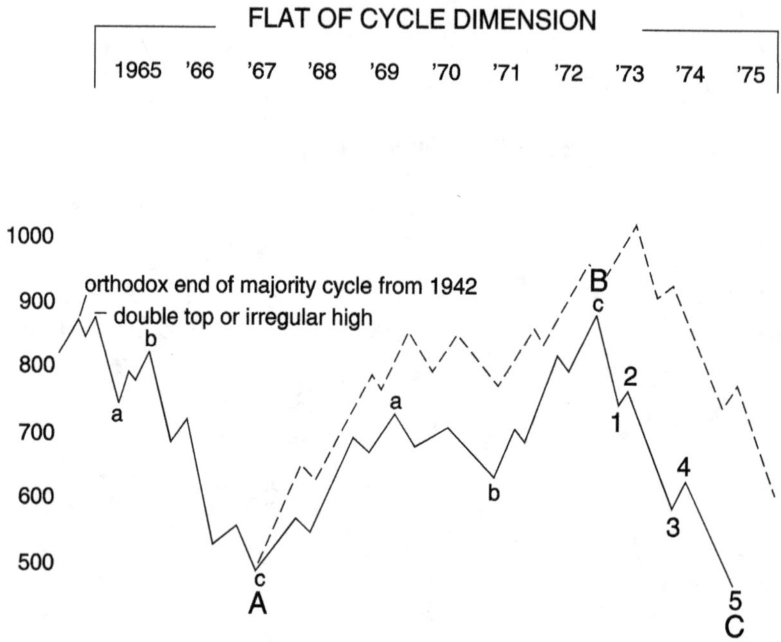


*Figure 4*

There are other aspects of Elliott I would like to discuss with you at some convenient time because there appear to be points that Elliott may possibly have missed, but at the moment I have said enough. I don't mind eating a little crow but not a whole lot of it.

Best to you,
A.J. Frost
Assistant General Manager

## *LETTER FROM BOLTON*

**December 15, 1964**

Dear Jack,

Thanks indeed for all the trouble you went to, to convert me, but I don't really think you expected me to succumb, being the orthodox Elliott "high priest" that I am!

I don't really care where one starts counting the waves, i.e., in 1932 (Collins) in 1942 (Frost) or in 1949 (Bolton). All of us agree we are now in the terminal phase of either wave 3 from 1932 (Collins) wave 5 from 1942 (Frost) or wave B after wave 5 from 1949 (Bolton).

I'd like to make a few comments, however.

1. Is it cricket to use the DBS Canadian average to prove there were five waves down from 1937-42? You cannot find any five wave pattern down in the DJIA, in the S&P, in New York Times, or in Herald Tribune Averages. It is only from the 1939 high that you can count a five-down to 1942. So 1937-42 has to be a three wave and probably 5-3-5. Elliott broke his own rules of triangles when he called 1928-42 a triangle, and I don't see how you can call 1928-42 a three wave unless the last part (1937-42) can be made into a five down, which it can't in any of the U.S. averages. Collins overcomes this by saying 1932 was the bottom. I, by taking 1949. I'm quite happy to let you take 1942 if you feel like it because of the tie-in with Benner, even though it is one year out in timing.

2. Neither Collins nor I could get 685 in 1959 to come out as a five-up; so we had to settle on the end of the fifth wave in 1961. However, again it does not matter since we both have a three-down in 1961-62.

3. Collins thinks that the whole 1957-62 market may have been an irregular correction ending at the bottom in

June 1962, and he tends to agree to the possibility then that wave V began in 1962, but in June, not October.

4. I won't argue about 1962 prior to the Cuban low; it doesn't really make much difference.

5. My interpretation that 1961 completed V (Collins agrees, with however his alternative as a possibility) is consistent with what I wrote in my book in 1960. Wave A under this was complete in three waves in June and we are under this interpretation in wave B. So? All we have to do is to find out when my wave B, or Collins' wave B, or your wave V or Collins' alternative wave V end. Simple, isn't it?

6. This brings me to your Figure 3, which takes the count from Oct. 1962. We (Collins and I) find no evidence to support your extended 1st wave. What you seem to show as five-up to apparently June 1963, we classify as three-up only with early December 1962 to February 1963 as an irregular correction. Since June 1963, therefore, we are in wave 5, and it looks as if the November 1963 lows and the June 1964 lows terminated waves 2 and 4 thereof. Thus we are since June 1964 in wave 5 as you agree. Because of the fact that you have an extended wave in I, you are caught in not allowing your wave V to exceed wave III nor to be able to extend. So you have to call 892 as the end of wave V, but of course you can't count out five waves from June! Actually, we are clearly only in the third wave from June, which we may have completed at 892. The NY Times average has an identical pattern as does S&P. Only the Tribune average shows a possible wave completion of five-up from November 1963 in July 1964 (not November). Anyway, we don't seem to agree that 892 was the end of wave V, so time will tell.

7. Looking at your Elliott-Benner cycle projection, I think it agrees pretty well with my own cycle projections which call for 1965-68 to be down markets and 1968 to 1973 up markets. However, the chances are, from my cycle studies, that my wave C from whatever top in 1964-65 will be

completed by sometime in 1968, and that a new Cycle wave of the Supercycle will start in 1968 and go through to 1973 about and probably will land the Dow Jones Industrials in the 3000-4000 area if they don't split it!

I have two cycles that I am relying on here. One is the occurrence every 36 years of 3 years of "chaos". You can track this back as far as records go, for instance 1929-32, 1893-96, 1857-60, 1822-25, etc. This cycle in itself is always followed by 4 to 5 years of up-markets, i.e., 1932-37, 1896-1901, 1860-65, 1825-29, etc. But what makes 1968-73 look even more dynamic is an approximate overlapping 4-5 year segment of a cycle of about 45-46 years duration which in all stock market history has created great up trends. This cycle runs from 1969-73 or almost a perfect overlap. In the past, this part of the cycle has taken place in 1922-27, in 1878-82, and in 1832-36. If you look at what happened to stock prices in these periods you will see what I mean. They were all new era markets, i.e., taking averages generally to about double what the previous peaks had been.

The combination of these parts of the 36 and 45 year cycles have never in the last 200 years coincided before. So I expect what we will see is extreme monetary inflation starting sometime in 1968. Perhaps this will result out of a worldwide devaluation of currencies.

So, here endeth the lesson according to St. Bolton! Seriously though, as 1965 progresses we ought to compare notes.

Best regards,
A.H. Bolton

## *LETTER TO BOLTON*

**December 18, 1964**

Blessed Bolton,

The idea of your canonization gives me a great spiritual lift. Even your name has the esoteric quality of a beatitude! It may be that I am blest to be the Devil's Advocate appointed in your case (*SOB*) despite the imposition of the ecclesiastical law now requiring me to continue in this capacity until the year of Grace 1975 when Heaven shall advise us who is right about the Elliott Wave Principle. This shall be your confirmation, B.B., or lack of it, B.B.

A saint, however, should not ask "Is it cricket?" when dealing with the law. The law (Elliott) was made for the Dow, not the Dow for the law. The Dow reflects very imperfectly the manifestations of the principle and has no claim upon it. The writer read 1937-42 to be a five-down in his long epistle of December 1962. This count always seemed a bit shaky until the DBS Industrial Average dropped the scales from the writer's eyes.

Let us look at June 8, 1964 (Dow 800) to November 18 (Dow 892, intra day high 897) — is it a five-up? B.B. says no, D.A. says yes. My information, direct from the disembodied Elliott I'll have you know, has it that the last minor, November 11-18, was truncated by shock at the mundane level. The Law saved the day, however, by causing a sudden fast rise which brought the intra day high to 897, being 161.8% of the hourly low at the time of the Cuban crisis. The Heavenly Ratio, B.B., — succumb, succumb, succumb.

I rest now because I have a little trust work to do.

Wickedly yours,
A.J. Frost
Devil's Advocate within the Law

## *LETTER TO MR. J.W. BERRY,*
### *PRESIDENT, CENTRAL OFFICE*
**June 28, 1965**

RE: Stock market

Dear Mr. Berry:

It has occurred to me that following yesterday's market action, our markets may be in much worse position than realized by most analysts. Personally, I was expecting the averages to form a base for a reasonably strong summer rally despite the fact the four long-term indicators I have the most confidence in (banking figures, momentum, breadth and pattern) have already given advance notice that the stock market and the economy are in for serious trouble.

It seems to me that the short term indicators, which have been reasonably strong, are on balance likely to be restricted by the long-term outlook. At best, I feel we can only expect temporary relief, which may be insufficient to allow investors an opportunity to realign positions.

Economically speaking, the basic monetary climate is deteriorating so rapidly that I feel we may be seeing the beginnings of a recession of greater magnitude than anything we have seen since 1937 when our markets dropped 49%. I would like to see us take a defensive position in the V.I.F. — Equity Section. If we do this, I feel it would have a salutary effect on the growth of the Fund and keep us on top for years to come.

Yours very truly,
A.J. Frost
Assistant General Manager

*A Supplement to*

*The Bolton-Tremblay*

# *BANK CREDIT ANALYST*

## THE ELLIOTT WAVE PRINCIPLE of Stock Market Behavior

1967 SUPPLEMENT

It is a pleasure to write the 1967 Elliott Wave Principle Supplement. Fortunately, I discussed the Principle at some length with Hamilton Bolton in February. Our counts varied in detail, but we were much closer to agreement than at any time in the past. Both of us felt that once the baby bull market had exhausted itself, the next leg of the bear market would probably match in time and amplitude the 1966 drop.

I trust that the observations made here will be of interest to those subscribers who have been following the Wave Principle and for those unfamiliar with it. I also hope to offer a new basic approach and a new philosophy.

There is a little bit of truth in everything.

A.J. Frost
B. Com., FCA, CFA
Associate Editor of
*The Bank Credit Analyst*

May 25, 1967

# *ELLIOTT'S WAVE PRINCIPLE 1967*

## *FOREWORD*

Many analysts consider the Elliott Wave Principle to be an authentic approach to market analysis; others have no use for it. It is a theory which some ancient Roman might have characterized as attracting arrows to the breast. Certainly, the theory is not without its detractors.

Elliott's thesis has many valuable tenets. He observed or, as he said, discovered, a number of basic principles of stock market behavior which he developed into a rational method of analysis. Elliott's basic patterns are just as much in force today as they were at the time of his death, and just as useful. Elliott did not know all there was to know about the Wave Principle, nor is anyone ever likely to fully comprehend its significance or know its causes. The analyst can only hope for greater knowledge of its characteristics.

After years of study, R.N. Elliott observed a *tendency* of the market to form rhythmic patterns and noted that in an expanding economic climate, the stock market advances in a series of waves with corrections in between. When five waves have run their course, the series becomes a completed subwave of a big wave, which in turn has to be corrected. The big wave also consists of a series of five waves which are larger in time and amplitude than the first series, and so on. Elliott, in his first monograph (1938), offered no explanation of this phenomenon, but in the second monograph (1946), he endeavored to provide a rationale via the Fibonacci Summation Series, which he called *Nature's Law*. This mathematical recursive sequence can be found in Mendel's

Law of Heredity, the architecture of the Great Pyramid, Greek sculpture, music, plant life, occult speculations and in branches of science and physics. The series is also embodied in the Expo '67 symbol, which is an ancient symbol denoting the Unity of Man. Elliott's over-enthusiasm for the Fibonacci sequence of numbers as a law of nature influencing stock market trends alienates and frustrates many students who might otherwise be willing to accept the Wave Principle as a useful stock market concept. What started out as a relatively simple theory based on empirical observations developed into a principle of immutability. Elliott obviously pushed his theory too far. There is no doubt, however, that the stock market does tend to follow the Fibonacci series, but it is only a *tendency*.

For some time, it has been felt that Elliott's rigid tenets needed to be restated. Hamilton Bolton recognized the need, and had been planning to do something about it before his death. There is no doubt that there is much in Elliott that needs refinement, and some of the statements he made and interpretations he offered are not correct. Possibly the simplest question of all to ask about the Wave Principle is, "What is a wave?" This question has never been satisfactorily answered as far as identifying a wave of any particular degree is concerned. Also, the rule of alternation and the various rules regarding extensions need clarification. Restatement based on scientific research could be a most rewarding project for the analyst who has sufficient interest to give the Wave Principle the consideration it deserves.*

---

*Frost and Prechter fulfilled these goals with *Elliott Wave Principle* in 1978.

## *ELLIOTT'S BASIC TENETS*

Basic rules relate to:

1. Impulse and corrective waves
2. Extensions
3. Rule of alternation
4. Proportionate analysis
5. Volume
6. Failures
7. Time element
8. Thrusts
9. Tenets of investing

### (1) IMPULSE AND CORRECTIVE WAVES

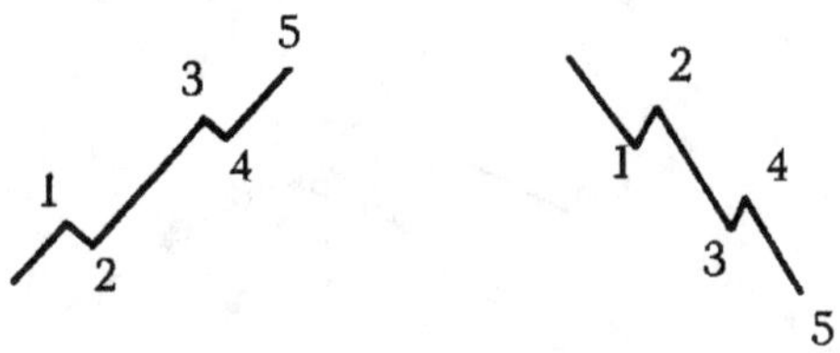


The main trend up or down is composed of five waves: three in the main direction and two counter to the main trend. Waves 1, 3 and 5 are known as impulse waves and are generally of an accelerating nature.[1] Each successive wave carries the market into new territory. Waves 2 and 4 are corrections or consolidations. A correction which moves horizontally rather than diagonally is sometimes thought of as a consolidation because of its underlying strength.

Corrective waves are normally composed of three waves: drop, rise, drop, or rally, drop, rally, depending on

---

[1] Actually, most impulses accelerate up to their midpoint and then decelerate.

whether the main trend is in a bull or a bear cycle. The first and third waves are in the direction of the correction and the middle, or second, wave is counter to it.

The most fundamental of all tenets of the Wave Principle is that each wave forms part of a larger wave formation and, in turn, can be subdivided into smaller parts, or waves of lesser degree. Thus, the Elliott system recognizes patterns of fives and threes in alternating wave sequences subdividing and expanding into further patterns of fives and threes. At the top of any wave, five subwaves spell the end of the movement, and the next five subwaves of the same degree, but in the opposite direction, indicate the beginning of the next wave in the opposite direction.

In a typical stock market cycle, the pattern according to Elliott is:

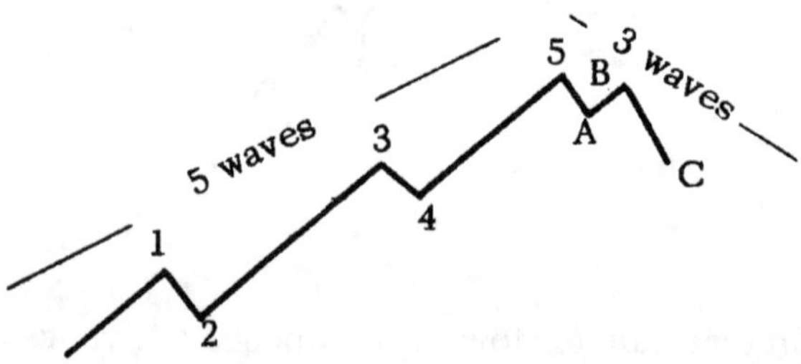


= 8 waves

This pattern then subdivides as follows:

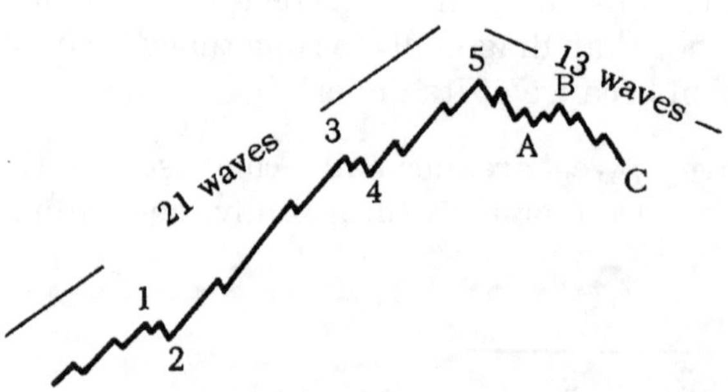


= 34 waves

The next breakdown produces 144 waves, as in Figure 1.

BREAKDOWN OF STOCK MARKET CYCLE

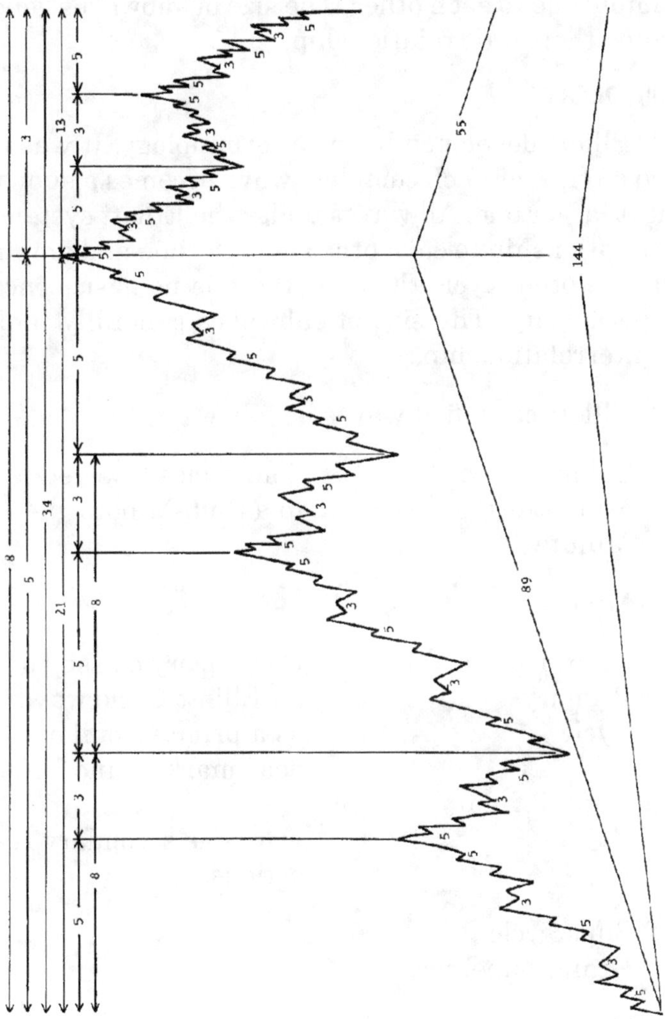


*Figure 1*

Once a wave has run its course, it automatically becomes a subwave of the next larger wave. The subwaves of a wave of any degree usually bear some relationship in time and amplitude to each other. The size of subwaves generally indicates their interrelationship.

## TERMINOLOGY

Elliott developed his own terminology. It was necessary to do this, as each complete wave becomes a subwave of the next larger one. All waves under the Elliott system have some relationship to each other in both time and amplitude, but unlike other cycle theories, there is no basic concept of fixed periodicity. The size of subwaves generally indicates their interrelationship.[2]

Elliott classified waves as follows:

| | |
|---|---|
| Subminuette<br>Minuette<br>Minute | Sometimes referred to as sub-Minors |
| Minor | |
| Intermediate<br>Primary<br>Cycle | Dow theory classifies an Elliott Cycle wave as a primary bull or bear market, and Intermediate and Primary waves as secondary reactions. |
| Supercycle<br>Grand Supercycle | |

Thus, a wave of Primary degree will subdivide into waves of Intermediate degree and an Intermediate degree wave will break up into Minor waves.

---

[2] Frost added this paragraph to this same discussion in the 1970 Supplement, where we have omitted the repeated section.

As a general proposition, a main trend wave composed of five subwaves (or nine, as we shall see later) is easier to identify than a correction composed of three waves. Corrective waves, especially in bull cycles, tend to develop irregularities and in any event are not necessarily three-wave affairs. *It follows, then, that if a wave cannot be subdivided into a five according to Elliott's rules, it must be a corrective wave.* In analyzing waves, more latitude is permissible in making an Elliott count of corrective waves than in counting the impulse waves. By their very nature, impulse waves tend to be clean-cut affairs, as if the waves were moved to action by sudden impulse. Impulse waves are frequently so well delineated that it is almost impossible to misinterpret them (like the perfect shot in golf, so easy that it keeps the duffer's interest up).

Given any distinct set of waves of recognizable magnitude, it becomes theoretically possible under the Wave Principle to forecast the next wave or series of waves. As each wave works itself into the fabric of the market structure, it has its effect on successive waves. This is the Elliott philosophy, and it is this characteristic which sets the Wave Principle apart from other technical approaches to the stock market. Each wave enters into the chain of causes which makes the market what it is at any given time. In Elliott terms, the principle behind the market is one of continuity and form.

Impulse waves tend to develop the following characteristics:

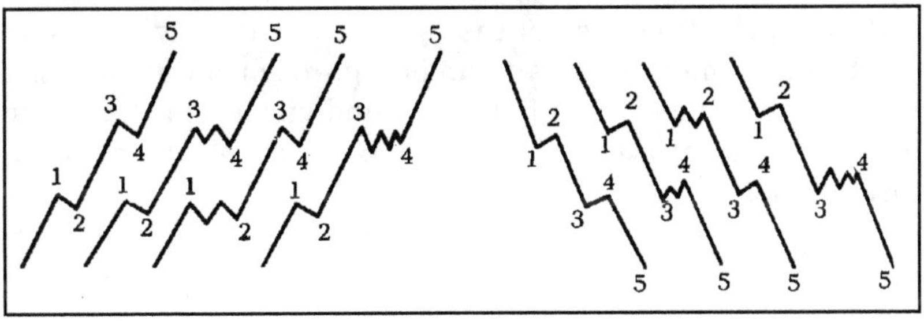

Spotting these formations in the Dow gives the analyst clues as to future probabilities.

A few rules of some practical importance have been formulated which are most helpful to the analyst:

(a) Wave 4 should not overlap or drop below the top of wave 1;

(b) Wave 3 is often the longest wave in a series, but seldom the shortest;

(c) Fifth waves and corrections may deploy or spread out, giving a wedge-like appearance to the move. This characteristic of stretching of waves indicates a strong or a weak market depending on whether they appear in an upward or downward movement;

(d) first waves of five-wave patterns and A waves of ABC patterns are usually relatively short;

(e) first and fifth subwaves of a "C" wave are often about the same magnitude.

In dynamic bull cycles, corrective waves tend to be profuse and erratic. A satisfactory count may be difficult despite the fact that the wave is obviously corrective. In a bear market, corrective waves are usually quite regular and easy to count. Elliott classified corrections into three main categories, as shown on the next page.

A zigzag is a three-wave affair of the 5-3-5 variety. A flat is a three-wave affair of the 3-3-5 variety.

Subwaves of Minor waves do not always subdivide, or if they do, the time element is so thin that the division may not be too apparent. As a triangle approaches its apex, the latter waves may not subdivide. Subdivision is a tendency at all times, not a certainty, especially in sub-Minor wave formations.

A flat tends to be more of a horizontal correction or consolidation, while a zigzag is usually a correction in depth with a diagonal slope. *The B wave of a flat is frequently higher than the beginning of wave A (in a bull cycle), thus making a new high.* Since B belongs to the corrective wave, the new top is considered irregular or unorthodox, although there is nothing really irregular or unorthodox about such a formation under Elliott.[3]

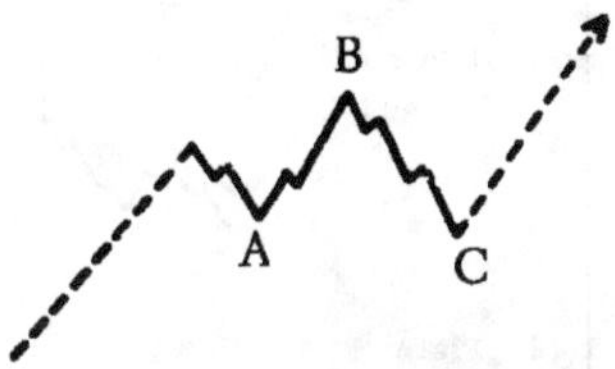


B is called an irregular top, and because of the frequency of flats, irregular tops are common.

Triangles and horizontals[4] are composed of five legs, which tend to subdivide into threes depending on their size. This type of formation is rare and found only in fourth wave formations, according to Elliott. Triangles, like flats and upward zigzags, are usually followed by strong subsequent action, or a "thrust" movement. (See chart on next page.)

## (2) EXTENSIONS AND DOUBLE RETRACEMENT

Extensions frequently appear in one of the three impulse waves of the five-wave type movement. They never appear in corrective waves, which are normally composed of three subwaves. Extensions on the downside are rare, but not on the upside.[5] If an impulse wave expands, that is, breaks down into a further five-wave pattern, the extended wave is generally much longer than the other waves in the series.

---

[3] Quite true. That's why *Elliott Wave Principle* calls these flats "expanded," rather than "irregular."

[4] Elliott called these "double threes" and "triple threes." In the preceding diagram, the label "upward zigzag" means one with a truncated "C" wave.

[5] Frost added this sentence to this same discussion in the 1970 Supplement, where we have omitted the repeated section.

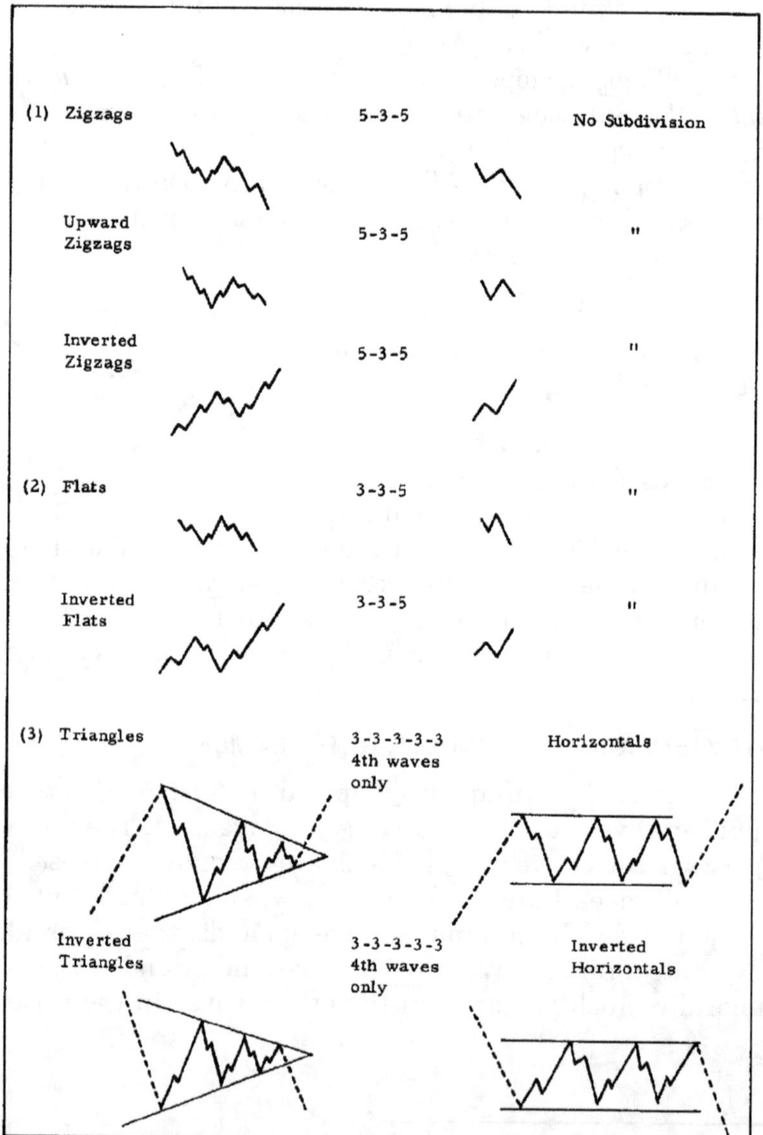
(1) Zigzags
5-3-5
No Subdivision
Upward Zigzags
5-3-5
"
Inverted Zigzags
5-3-5
"
(2) Flats
3-3-5
"
Inverted Flats
3-3-5
"
(3) Triangles
3-3-3-3-3 4th waves only
Horizontals
Inverted Triangles
3-3-3-3-3 4th waves only
Inverted Horizontals

Extensions seldom appear in more than one of the impulse waves. The effect of an extension is either a five-wave pattern with one long wave or an elongated wave composed of nine parts of about the same degree. The following diagrams illustrate extensions.

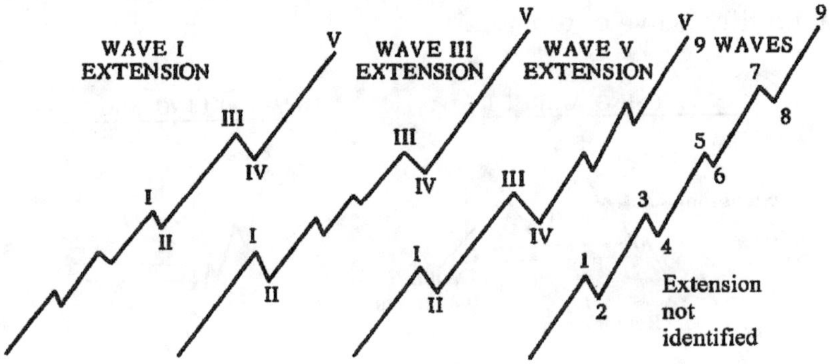


Extensions can develop in any impulse wave, but they usually appear in the third or fifth wave. Sometimes when all waves are about equal, it is often difficult to identify the extending wave. Under these circumstances, a count of nine is equivalent to a count of five. This is another practical analytical guide.

We now have in the direction of the main trend:

(a) Five waves of normal proportions;
(b) Nine waves of normal proportions;
(c) Five waves with one wave extending.

Analysis of impulse waves is comparatively easy compared with corrective waves.

Fifth wave extensions are of special significance. Elliott claimed that an extension is never the end of a cyclical movement, and from this observation he formulated the rule of double-retracement. The practical importance of this rule is that it gives the analyst a clue as to what is likely to happen next. If the ground covered by an extending fifth wave is to be retraced twice, it indicates that a flat will probably emerge, with both the A and B waves covering most of the territory of the fifth wave.

The figures below show a double retracement following a fifth wave extension.[6]

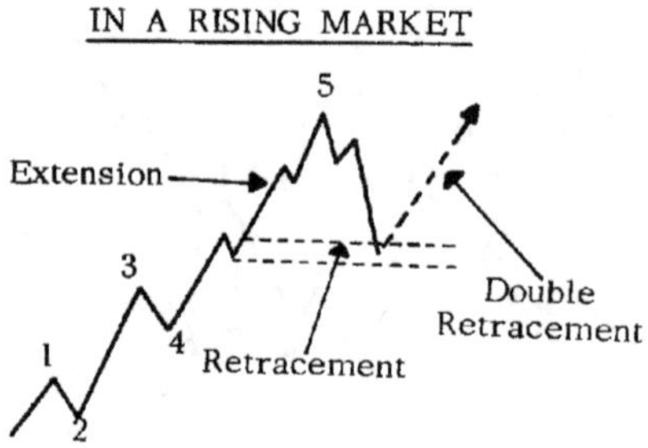


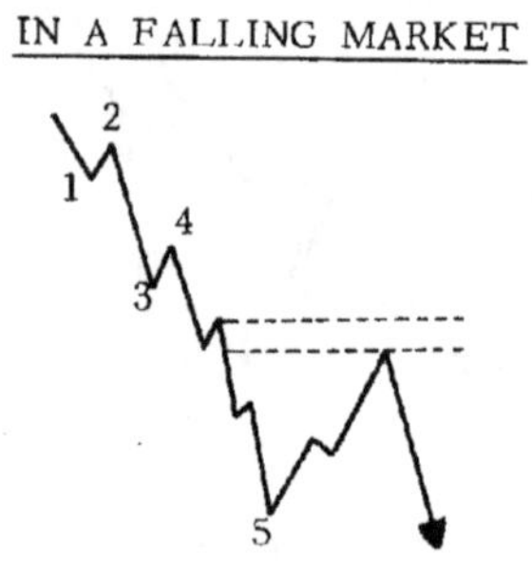


The first retracement carries the market back to the point where the extension began. The second retracement carries the market beyond the extension and produces an irregular top. Flats generated by fifth wave extensions invariably produce irregular tops, i.e., a top in the corrective series which goes above the orthodox end of the preceding five-wave movement.

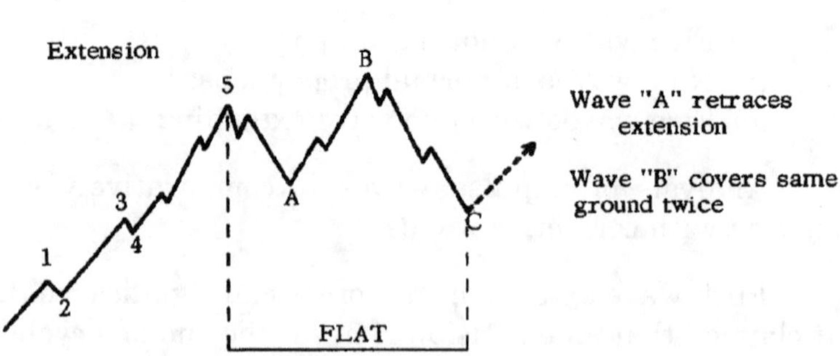


[6] Frost added these figures to this same discussion in the 1970 Supplement, where we have omitted the repeated section.

An extension may occur in any of the impulse waves, but only fifth wave extensions are doubly retraced.

### (3) RULE OF ALTERNATION

Elliott's rule of alternation has a number of applications, the most obvious being that the market unfolds in alternating patterns of fives and threes. The next application of importance is that second and fourth waves take turns at complexity. If the second wave is simple, the fourth will be complex, or vice versa. A pattern which is easy to read is often followed by one which is difficult to interpret.

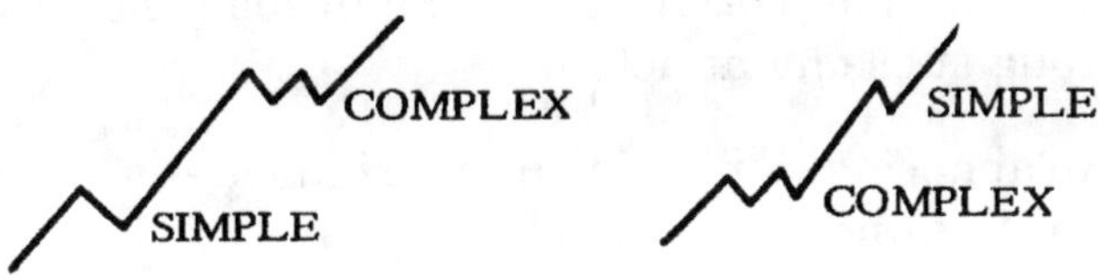


If the second wave is a zigzag, the fourth will be either a flat or a triangle. Flats and triangles have, according to Elliott, the same technical significance except that triangles do not appear as second waves.

Under Elliott, this rule of alternation serves to place the analyst on constant notice to expect different twists with regard to patterns of movement as the market unfolds.

### (4) PROPORTIONATE ANALYSIS

Elliott used proportionate analysis in forecasting the probable extent of waves, and with some success.

The basis of proportionate analysis is the ratio 1:1.618, or 61.8%, of which we shall later spell out a little more. Since a bull cycle is composed of five waves and the ensuing correction three waves, the normal correction in time and amplitude would be 3/5 of the previous rise and 3/5 in time. However, as things never work out quite so nicely in practice as in theory, it might not be unreasonable to conclude that a normal correction is where either the amplitude ratio or time ratio is 62% or thereabouts, and a substandard correction is where both price retracement and time duration ratios are less than 62%.

Amplitude and time ratios are usually calculated as follows:

$$\frac{\text{Number of points in correction}}{\text{Number of points in previous advance}} = \text{Amplitude Ratio}$$

$$\frac{\text{Number of days to correct}}{\text{Number of days in previous advance}} = \text{Time Ratio}$$

A subnormal correction in amplitude generally indicates strong subsequent action.

An abnormal correction in time indicates an extended base for a sustained movement.

When amplitude and time ratios are in conflict during a correction, the amplitude or price ratio takes precedence. The "right look" is more important than the time element, and should always be given the greater weight.

It is not our intention in this supplement to deal at any length with this subject. *The Elliott Wave Principle — A Critical Appraisal* gives background information. We would point out, however, that the rise from the October 1966 low to the end of the rally in May 1967 is a normal amplitude ratio, but the time ratio is an overcorrection, providing an inverted time base for a sustained bear market.

**(5) VOLUME**

Volume received some attention from Elliott, but not as much as most analysts would give it. His views on volume are orthodox, but related to wave sequences to provide further clues on possible future trends. According to Elliott, volume on the third wave (presumably waves of Intermediate degree and less) is generally the greatest. If the fifth wave registers higher volume than the third, it is an indication that the fifth wave is going to extend. As long, therefore, as volume increases with successive impulse waves, another impulse wave is due. However, under Elliott's theory, volume rolls over prior to the orthodox end of a bull cycle. Once volume drops on the fifth, or any extension of it, the end of the movement is in sight. In a bear cycle, the exact opposite is true[7], with the final wave ending on dullness. Volume should therefore expand or contract, generally speaking, with the trend until, with prices still rising, volume registers less than on the previous subwave. A new high on decreased volume spells trouble. A new low on decreased volume is favorable.

Analyzing volume is difficult, as there are so many degrees of waves to which to relate it. Volume can be deceptive, and this may be the reason why Elliott didn't give it much space in his writings.

Elliott's views may be presented graphically, as follows:

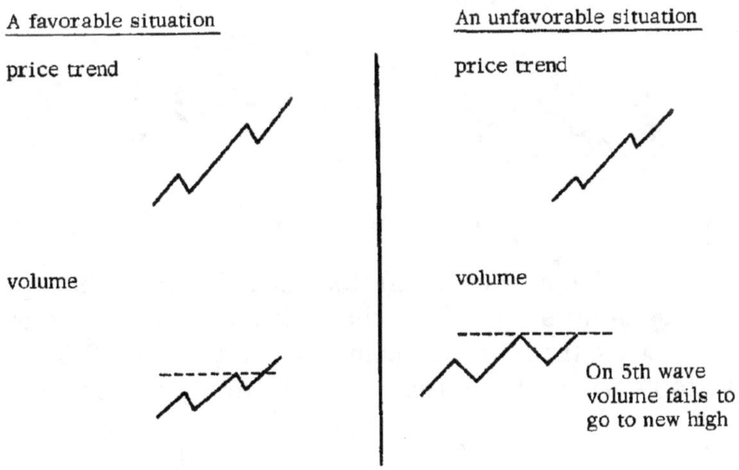


[7] Frost's discussion implies that he means that the same is true, so the implication is the opposite of bearish. However, in the 1970 Supplement, he makes a case that low volume in a bear market is bearish.

## (6) FAILURES

Failures are not uncommon, and give warning to the analyst of impending strength or weakness of stock prices, depending on whether the failure occurs in a bull or a bear cycle. In a bull situation, a failure occurs when wave 5 fails to penetrate the top of wave 3, or in the case of a bear cycle when the fifth wave fails to go below the previous low established by wave 3. The effect of a failure is that *the next wave borrows two waves from the preceding movement.*[8]

Failures can readily be detected by observing the subwave breakdowns. For example, June 25, 1962 was the terminal point of the third wave down from the 1961 high. The next move was a 5-3-5 affair, followed by a 5-3-5-3-5, which lends strong credence to the argument that the *orthodox low of the 1962 spring collapse did not come until October 24th.* This thesis is also supported by the fact that many of the stock exchanges of the world did not touch their lows until October, as did the advance-decline line.

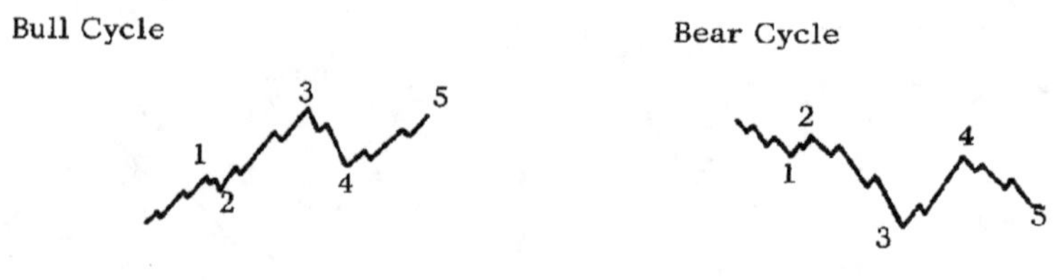


It should also be noted that the July low of 1932 presented a similar situation, in that this low was followed by a 5-3-5 up wave (rally in a bear market) and a 5-3-5-3-5 down wave to February 1933, the end of the great bear market.[9]

---

[8] He simply means that the ensuing rise or fall is enhanced by this event. The number of waves in each form does not change.

[9] This statement is highly debatable.

Failures have been ignored by most students of Elliott, yet the Wave Principle becomes a hodgepodge on occasion without it. It changes a five into a three and the ensuing three into a five, thus producing baffling situations in Elliott's terms, unless of course the failure is recognized.

### (7) TIME ELEMENT

The stock market is replete with Fibonacci time periods, which coordinate with wave patterns. A few examples will suffice to illustrate.

**Duration in years (approximately)**

| | | |
|---|---|---|
| 1907 to 1962 | = | 55 years |
| 1921 to 1942 | = | 21 years |
| 1949 to 1962 | = | 13 years |
| 1921 to 1929 | = | 8 years |
| 1932 to 1937 | = | 5 years |
| 1929 to 1942 | = | 13 years |
| 1937 to 1942 | = | 5 years |
| 1928 to 1962 | = | 34 years |

**Duration in months (approximately)**

| | | |
|---|---|---|
| August '21 to November '28 | = | 89 months |
| September '29 to July '32 | = | 34 months |
| July '32 to March '37 | = | 55 months |
| July '32 to July '33 | = | 13 months |
| July '33 to July '34 | = | 13 months |
| March '37 to March '38 | = | 13 months |
| May '46 to October '46 | = | 5 months |
| September '53 to August '56 | = | 34 months |
| January '60 to October '62 | = | 34 months |
| December '57 to October '60 | = | 34 months |
| April '56 to December '57 | = | 21 months |
| November '61 to October '62 | = | 13 months |
| February '66 to October '66 | = | 8 months |

While time periods appear to coordinate with wave patterns, reliance cannot be placed upon them for forecasting purposes. There is no way of telling in advance whether a change of direction will occur at the end of any period.

Elliott felt the time factor was of some importance because, as he said, it "confirms and conforms" to the pattern. Although time periods don't seem to have definite forecasting value, they do have the advantage of placing the analyst on notice.

### (8) THRUSTS

A thrust is a dynamic move pushing the market up from a solid base. Corrections within the thrust are, for the most part, subnormal in character, giving further impetus to each successive subwave up.

Corrections frequently provide clues as to the strength or weakness of subsequent action. Elliott said a thrust flowed naturally from a triangle and that triangles and flats had similar technical implications. The reason for this is probably nothing more than that these two types of corrections tend to be subnormal in amplitude, but not necessarily subnormal in time. In other words, if a market won't go down during what one might expect to be a normal period of correction, it may be foreshadowing strong subsequent movement. This would appear to be a reasonable concept and should in theory indicate that a weak zigzag would also carry a similar warning of strong action, whereas an ordinary zigzag would indicate ordinary strength. A flat, on the other hand, in which the end of wave C was no lower than the top of wave A, would indicate unusual strength.

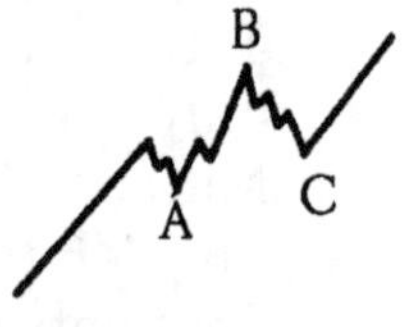


The same reasoning applies in reverse to bear markets, where the corrections are usually clearer. A short term trader should be able to operate more effectively in a bear market than a bull market using the Elliott system.

### (9) INVESTMENT TENETS

Elliott always kept in mind the basic principles of his philosophy and applied them in a reasonably consistent manner. His hypothesis was that the Principle he "discovered" worked best when applied to the averages rather than individual issues; hence he adopted as a cardinal investment rule the thesis that the best approach was to select issues which moved in harmony with the averages. Elliott also stressed marketability and soundness. His main rules were as follows:

1. Buy stocks which tend to move in harmony with the general averages.

2. Choose stocks which are active, well-seasoned and in medium price range.

3. Diversify, for purposes of stability.

## *ELLIOTT AND BANK CREDIT*

Over the years there has been a remarkably consistent relationship between monetary conditions and the stock market cycle. A. Hamilton Bolton, in his new book, *Money and Investment Profits,* leaves the reader in little doubt on this point. Other analysts, such as Beryl Wayne Sprinkel, economist at Harris Trust and Savings Bank, have underlined the importance of monetary change in relation to stock market trends. The Federal Reserve has also noted in its publications that "the total flow of money in a nation is an important indicator of the level of business activity, and changes in the flow may well reflect the trend of coming economic events." It is also the writer's view that the monetary condition of an economy is the dominant factor affecting equity values and that an examination of money factors can give the analyst dependable clues as to future trends in equity values. Money and money changes have predictive power and often point to developing conditions, which in turn affect the stock market cycle.

The monetary history of modern capitalism has been one of almost continuous credit expansion. Long term economic patterns tie in with the Elliott concept of *growth.* Bear markets, or corrective patterns in Elliott's terms, seldom exceed in amplitude the upward wave patterns they are supposed to correct.

## THE CURRENT OUTLOOK

The upward market thrust from 1942 on reflects Elliott's philosophy and the economic facts of life. Since 1966, the market appears to be consolidating in the form of a large flat, with wave C still to run its full course. Although the culmination of this wave could carry the Dow below the Cuban crisis low of 554, it need not be considered calamitous. There is little room for long term pessimism. The Wave Principle hints at short term caution and is in accord with bank credit analysis, which suggests that before the stock market and the economy enter an expanding phase, *a period of bank credit liquidation is a must.*

The bank credit cycle affects the stock market cycle, but beyond giving notice as to whether the climate of investment is favorable or unfavorable, it does not reflect the cyclical position. Elliott Wave patterns, on the other hand, tend to reflect the cyclical position of the market as a whole. The bank credit approach tells the investor whether or not he is *onside,* and the Wave Principle gives details as to position. The two approaches are complementary.

From both an Elliott and bank credit standpoint, it is too early to become optimistic about the outlook for the stock market. When this time does come, we hope and expect these two basic tools will spell out the message in clear large print, but for the present, we advise a policy of caution. By the time the market has completed its long consolidation from 1960, the monetary climate will likely have changed and we will be standing on the threshold of a *Cycle wave of great speculation.*[10]

## *ELLIOTT AND CYCLE THEORIES (BENNER)*

The Elliott Wave Principle is a wave theory, not a cycle theory. The Principle does not hinge on recurrent time periods. Waves may expand or contract in time, giving a high degree of flexibility to the length of waves of all degrees, including corrective patterns. Fives may extend, and threes may double up. Waves do, however, have a tendency to unfold within the framework of the Principle.

Well-known cycles are the 17-week cycle, 9-year cycle, etc. A less known cycle was developed about 1875 by Samuel T. Benner, who wrote a book entitled, *Business Prophecies of the Future Ups and Downs in Prices.* Benner observed that the highs of business tend to follow a repeating 8-9-10 yearly pattern, but lows tend to follow two series of time sequences, suggesting that recessions (bad times) and depressions (panics) tend to alternate.

Rules of fixed periodicity for anticipating changes are mechanical, and do not allow for any assessment of economic factors. Benner, however, did make a number of economic forecasts of great accuracy, and built for himself an enviable reputation as an analyst. He had previously failed in business as an iron works manufacturer. An application of Benner's rules as he might have applied them to the stock market from 1902 on are shown in Figure 2.

---

[10] I.e., the 1980s-1990s bull market.

**8 - 9 - 10 CYCLE THEORY (BENNER)**

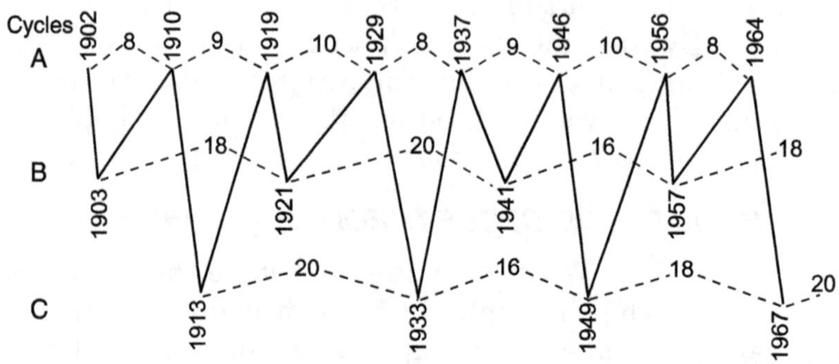


Cycle A 8 - 9 - 10 years and repeat
Cycle B 16 - 18 - 20 years and repeat (8 - 9 - 10 multiple)
Cycle C 16 - 18 - 20 years and repeat (8 - 9 - 10 multiple)

No two cycles repeat themselves within a span of 54 years. This is close to the Fibonacci number 55.
Cycle C segments taken in pairs approximate the Fibonacci number 34.

*Figure 2*

As a matter of interest, it should be noted that the 8-9-10 series bears a loose relationship to Fibonacci numbers:

| 8-9-10 | Selected Subtotals | Closest Fibonacci Number | Difference |
|---|---|---|---|
| 8 | 8 | 8 | 0 |
| 9 | | | |
| 10 | | | |
| 8 | 35 | 34 | + 1 |
| 9 | | | |
| 10 | 54 | 55 | - 1 |
| 8 | | | |
| 9 | | | |
| 10 | | | |
| 8 | 89 | 89 | 0 |
| 9 | | | |
| 10 | | | |
| 8 | | | |
| 9 | | | |
| 10 | | | |
| 8 | 143 | 144 | -1 |

## *AIDS TO INTERPRETING ELLIOTT*

There are three aids which are very helpful in applying Elliott theory to stock market trends, namely: 1) hourly charts, 2) a 55-hour short term moving average and 3) an 89-day medium term moving average.

### HOURLY CHARTS

Elliott used hourly figures in charting the DJIA in fast moving markets. Since the Wave Principle applies to short term movements just as much as it does to cyclical movements, hourly figures are often significant. They indicate the subdivision of larger moves and train the eye to detect Elliott patterns in miniature. Patterns are repetitive and often bear a family resemblance to patterns many times their size in time and amplitude. Many serious students of Elliott maintain an hourly chart of the Dow. Two examples of hourly charts are shown in Figures 3 and 4. The hourly chart shown in Figure 3, from June 25 to July 9, 1962, a period of approximately 10 days, shows a number of Elliott patterns, and to the trained Elliotter such patterns represent at critical junctions a possible change of direction. The closing prices, on the other hand, for the same period, taken by themselves, are without any particular significance. The second hourly chart, Figure 4, shows price changes in the Dow from March 23 to April 10, 1967. Here again, we see a number of clear-cut patterns.

The large pattern is an ABC Minor corrective wave. The A wave subdivides and re-subdivides showing three different degrees of waves. The C wave, on the other hand, only shows a five-wave breakdown. All told, there are five different waves which subdivide into fives, three waves which subdivide into threes, and one three which doubles up to form a seven. The undivided waves or legs total 330. It should be noticed that in four of the five-wave patterns, the third wave is the longest. In no series is the third wave the shortest. When the analyst gets used to an hourly chart as a tool of interpretation, he can observe hundreds of waves of varying degrees over a relatively short period of time, many

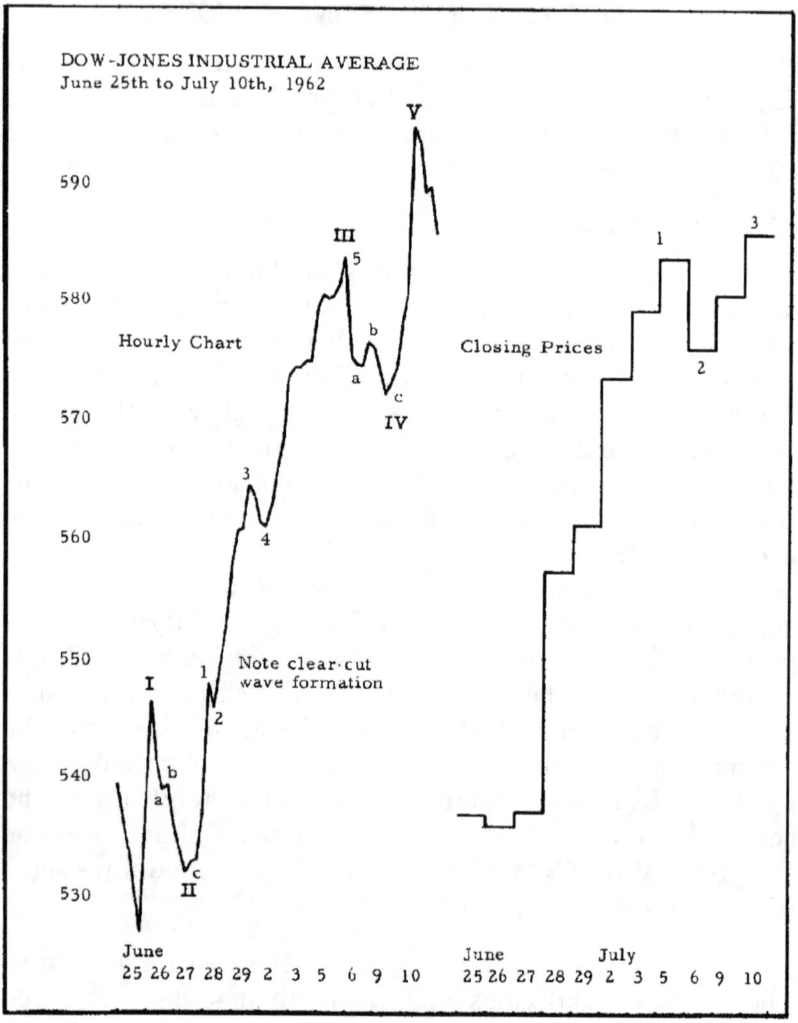


*Figure 3*

of which can be fitted into larger and more significant waves. Reading subminors gives the analyst a "feel" for waves of higher degree. With enough experience, the analyst will avoid the pitfall of manufacturing wave counts to fit some fixed preconceived idea of what ought to be.

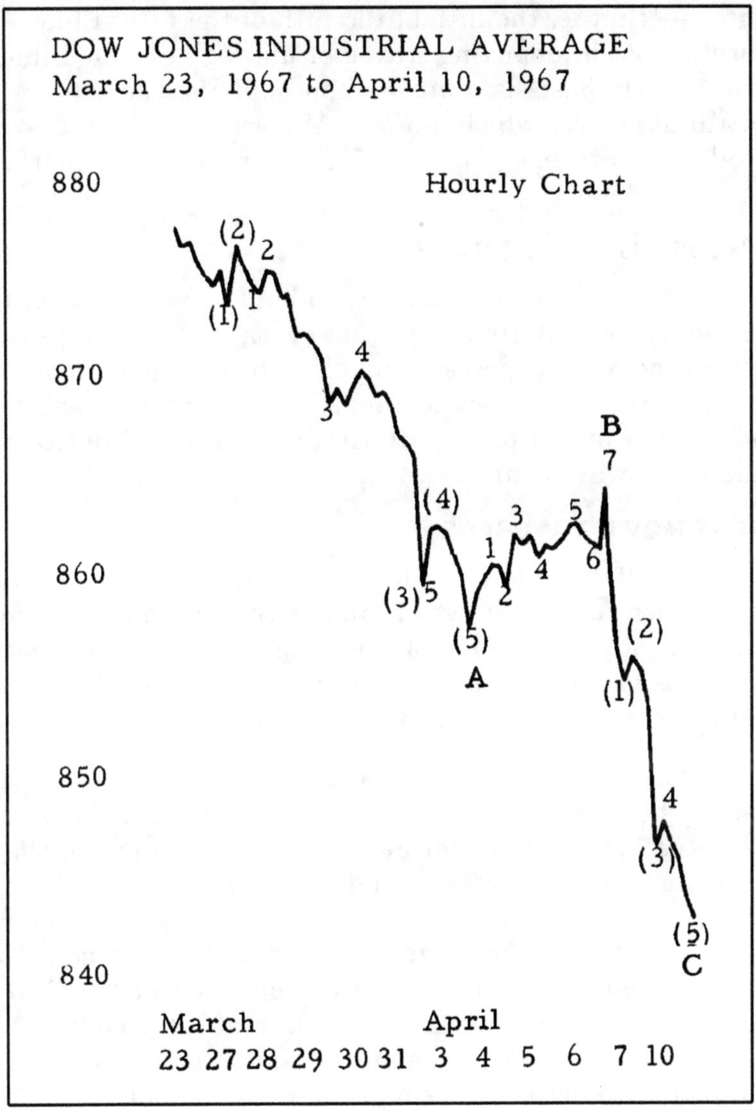


*Figure 4*

Clear-cut fifth waves of the third degree often signify the end of a movement. These can readily be spotted on an hourly chart. The Cuban crisis low in October 1962 and the low of October 1966 are examples of fifth waves of third degree — that is, the fifth of the fifth of the fifth. Elliott is a useful tool in depicting waves of all degrees, but Elliott on an hourly basis is a *must* when applying the theory to the Minute waves which compose Minor waves. Elliott is an excellent mental exercise even if one's interest in the market is only academic.

### 55-HOUR MOVING AVERAGE

55 is a Fibonacci number. 55 hours are equivalent to 10 trading days. A 10-day moving average of closing prices is, for practical purposes, equivalent to a 55-hour moving average. Such an average tends to eliminate sub-Minor fluctuations in the price pattern and is a useful device in making subwave counts.

### 89-DAY MOVING AVERAGE

An 89-day trading period approximates the 17-18-week cycle of fixed periodicity, which is one of the recognized market cycles. A moving average of this length tends to delineate the waves of Intermediate duration and assist in the count of subwaves composing Primary movements.

The above averages seem to work well together, possibly because they tie in with the mathematical base of the Wave Principle. In terms of the Wave Principle, they delineate wave structures and provide a good starting point for more detailed wave analysis. *Whenever the moving average trends cross, it is an indication of a possible change in market trend.* Usually such crossings indicate the beginning of a new wave formation of Intermediate or higher degree. In corrective patterns, it is most important to wait for an actual crossing from above to below the intermediate moving average trend rather than rely solely on a count of waves. Corrective patterns are often complex, and patience pays.

## *WHERE ARE WE IN THE STOCK MARKET CYCLE?*

### BOLTON'S VIEW

Subsequent to writing[11] the 1966 Supplement, Bolton concluded that June 1962 to January 1966 was a fifth Cycle wave of a Supercycle, and that February 1966 started a major bear market in Wave Principle terms which would correct or consolidate the entire rise in the averages from either 1942 or 1949. He also felt that five waves down had been completed on October 7, 1966, and that the move up from that date should form a B wave to be completed in three subwaves. He projected 900 on the DJIA as a possible recovery top because of heavy volume and the possibility of a 62% correction of the 1966 decline. This view implies that, A being a five down, B will be a three and C will be a five to end the bear market.

Bolton saw little possibility of the market regaining the 260 points lost in 1966[12] and said, "We face a fairly long period of stock market unrest."

### ANOTHER VIEWPOINT

Viewed in relationship to the major market swings from 1942, the long advance from 1949 to 1960 looks like a real third wave extension of Cycle dimension (see Figure 5). Usually the third, a middle wave, is the longest, with the first wave of the series the shortest. Fourth waves tend to alternate in complexity with second waves and are not infrequently longer. On balance, fourth waves are the most troublesome.

If the above statements are a reasonable premise for Elliott interpretation of wave sequences, then the following pattern would appear to be unfolding: Cycle I: 1942-1946; Cycle II: 1946-1949; Cycle III: 1949-1960; Cycle IV: Incomplete.

---

[11] "Subsequent to writing" should read "In".

[12] Actually, in his 1966 Supplement, Bolton discussed Collins' idea that the 1966 top would be followed by an irregular correction.

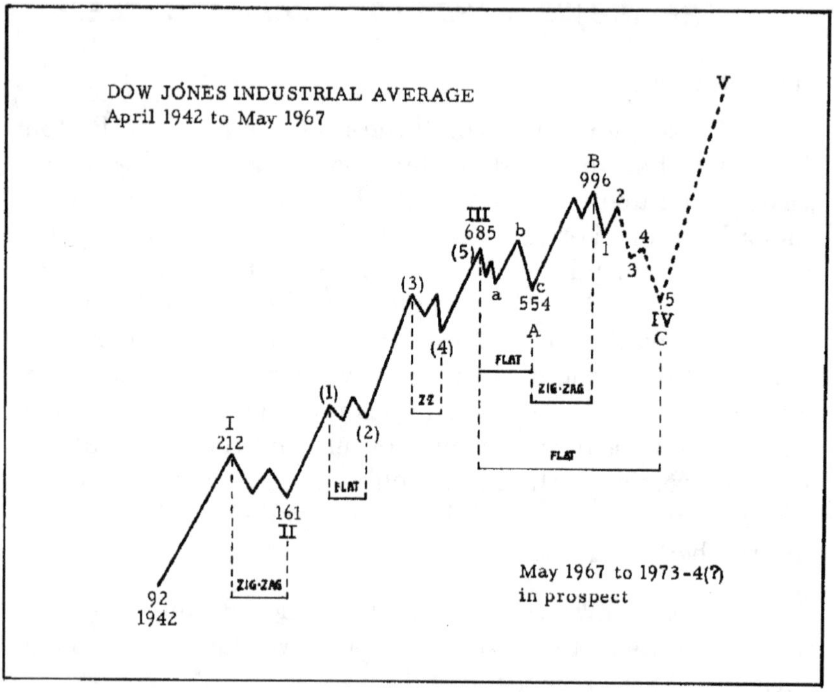


*Figure 5*

Most of Cycle IV from early 1960 has run its course. It could be over, but we don't think so. As we see it, the five-wave down in 1966 is only the first leg. It is not big enough to be the whole of the final phase. It is of Intermediate rather than Primary dimension. The breakdown of Cycle IV to date comprises two completed Primaries, as follows:

| | | |
|---|---|---|
| Primary A | – | January 1960 to October 1962 (Cuban crisis) |
| Primary B | – | October 1962 to February 1966[13] |
| Primary C | – | Incomplete |

[13] Frost has returned to Bolton's old idea that the advance from 1962 was a B wave, which he later rejected in favor of calling it wave V. In Figure 5, the 1962 low should be labeled wave IV and the 1966 peak wave V. Frost returns to this view in the 1970 Supplement.

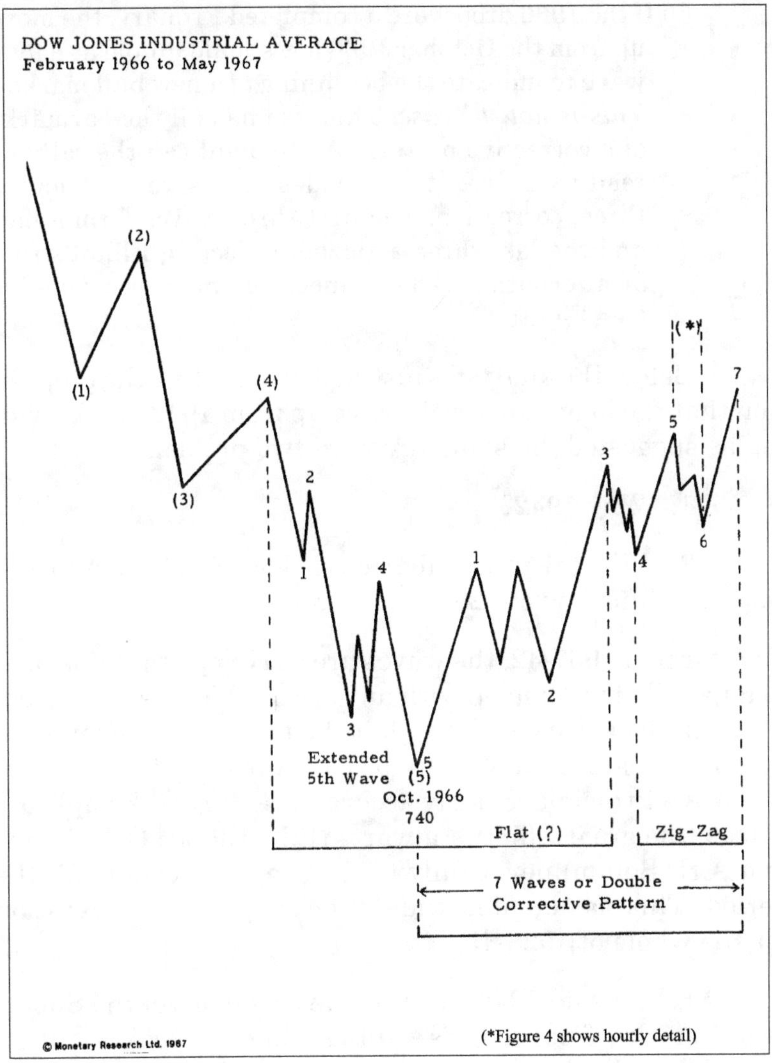


*Figure 6*

Other reasons for concluding that there is more to come:

(a) The fifth wave of the 1966 decline extended (Figure 6), and calls for double retracement.

(b) The fifth wave did not come down to the start of wave A, the January 1960 high of 685 (Figure 5).

(c) If the 1966 drop were a completed Primary, the move up from the October 1966 low should unfold as a five-wave to indicate the beginning of a new bull market. *This is not the case.* This rise has all the earmarks of a corrective pattern. At no point can the rally be read as a five. It subdivides as a seven, or double three, correction. The first three waves form a flat, and the last three a zigzag, reflecting Elliott's rule of alternation. The connecting wave is a sub-five (see Figure 6).

Before the analyst is justified in accepting the proposition that the long Supercycle wave up from 1942 is subdividing as suggested, he should resolve two problems:

1. Why 1942?

2. Why take the Cuban crisis low of 554 DJIA rather than the June low of 525?

From 1937-42, the waves are so choppy that it is next to impossible to come up with any acceptable interpretation. The right look does not exist, but the time period of approximately 5 years from March 1937 to April 1942 in terms of the Wave Principle is fairly accurate. To further complicate things, the great Elliott stalwarts (R.N. Elliott, C.J. Collins and A.H. Bolton) never fully agreed on wave counts for the period. This has created wide differences of interpretation for the whole of 1928-49.

Elliott said 1942 was the starting point of the Supercycle. Viewed from today's vantage point, it looks as if he was right, albeit for the wrong reasons. The writer views the Cycle drop from 1929 to 1933 (not 1932), the Cycle rise to 1937 and the subsequent drop to 1942 as subwaves of a Supercycle correction in its broad outline. The details are irregular. Events shape the details rather than the big swings of the market. It is probable that Hitler, the Spanish revolution, the invasion of Austria, Munich, World War II, the fall of France, Dunkirk and Pearl Harbor may have disturbed investment sentiment.[14]

If it is necessary to characterize the 1929-42 period, an upward biased zigzag is probably as close to reality as any interpretation. The 1932 low was a freak. From the low in July of 1932, the Dow moved up in a 5-3-5 and down again in a five-wave sequence to February 27, 1933 at 50.16, indicating that the July 8, 1932 low was an unorthodox low and February 1933 the true low. From February 1933, the market moved up in three Primary waves to a high on March 10, 1937, from which point the market moved down irregularly to April 1942, touching 92.92, which can be read in various ways. One Canadian index, the DBS Investors Price Index (monthly), is a five-wave down (see Figure 7). On balance, it would appear that 1929-42 is a Supercycle ABC correction.[15]

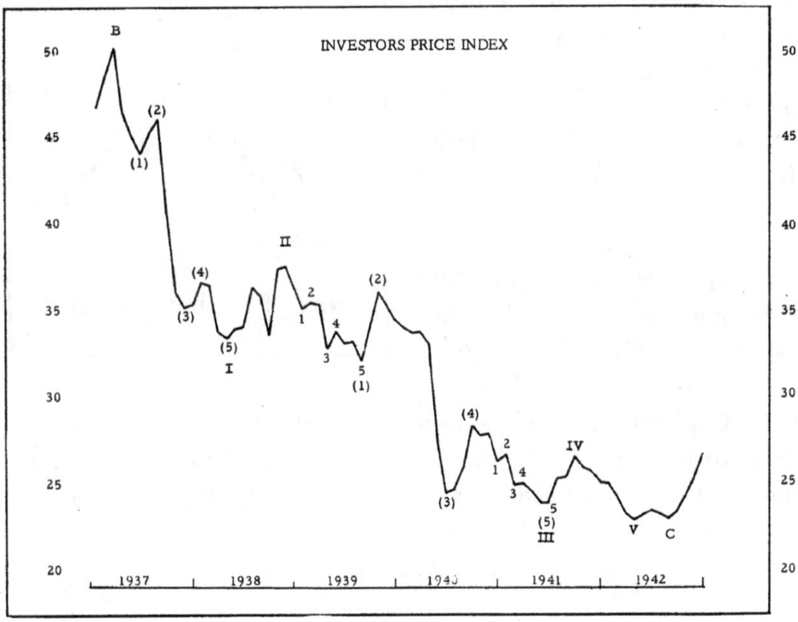


Source: Dominion Bureau of Statistics

*Figure 7*

---

[14] My opinion is that sentiment is the underlying cause of events, not vice-versa. The pattern comes first, so cannot be "disturbed" by events.

Apart from Elliott, there is support for the view that 1942 is the terminal point. The Supercycle in (1) interest rates, (2) time/demand ratio, (3) loan/deposit ratio and (4) money velocity ratio (*The Bank Credit Analyst*, May 1967) is cogent enough for both the economist and analyst to assert that 1942 is the Supercycle low, in cyclical terms, of both the stock market and the economy.

Another question of importance is the Cuban crisis low of 554 vs. the actual June low of 525. The sharp, nervous decline in the spring of 1962 resulted in an overextended trend, establishing a DJIA June low of 525.

A FAILURE PATTERN

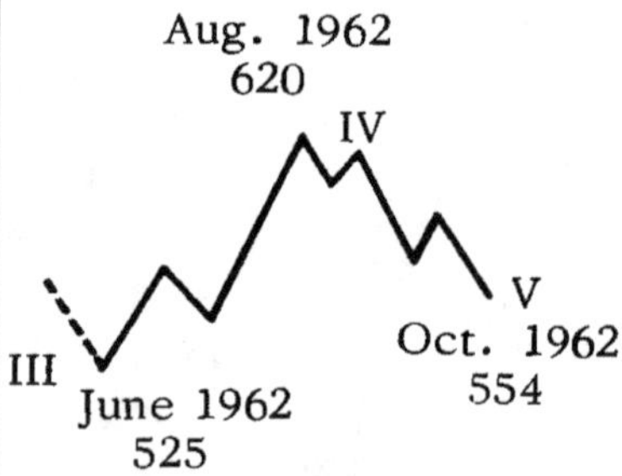


Waves IV and V from Nov. 1961

The market rose to August and then declined to October 1962 in a clear cut five-wave move. (See illustration.) If one accepts the Cuban crisis low as the orthodox low of the 1962 decline, then the count must be a five-wave affair down from November 1961, and the move up to almost 1000 in February 1966 can be read as a three-wave affair. Thus, the entire move from January 1960 to October 1962 becomes an ABC of Primary dimension, followed by a Primary "B" wave up from the Cuban crisis to February 1966. Despite the fact that this wave B

[15] While not impossible, this view makes a simple pattern appear complex. The paragraph that follows, however, does point out facts that reflect the wave count in the inflation-adjusted DJIA, which traced out a perfect triangle from 1929 to 1949, with subwave C, the third and therefore most intense subwave, ending in 1942.

appears to travel too far[16] in relation to the start of wave A in January 1960 (685), the rise can be accounted for by the sustained growth of Dow-Jones earnings during the period. From the high of 996, we now appear to be approaching the middle impulse phase of Primary wave "C". C waves, like thirds in five-wave series, are often violent. The shake-out phases of 1932, 1937 and 1962 were middle impulse waves in terms of the Wave Principle, two of which generated unorthodox lows.

### CURRENT OUTLOOK ACCORDING TO ELLIOTT

*Intermediate Trend:*

> Down to 620-650 zone by fall based on the rule of Elliott that middle waves are usually the longest. Intermediate wave 3 of Primary wave IV of Cycle C should, therefore, exceed in magnitude the 1966 drop from the high of 996 in February to 740 in October.

*Primary and Cycle Trends:*

> Since the market, according to our interpretation, is in its final Primary wave of the long Cycle trend from January 1960, these two trends now coincide, and will automatically terminate together at the same point. In terms of the Wave Principle, this point should be normally below the Cuban crisis low of 554 DJIA. The market could go lower, or it could accommodate to a basic improvement in fundamentals without damaging the wave count, but our expectation is that the decline will be normal and carry down to at least 554 in 1968.

Figure 5 shows the wave details and our views in prospect.

---

[16] True.

## *MATHEMATICAL BASIS OF WAVE THEORY*

It is recorded that a famous Italian mathematician by the name of Leonardo da Pisa was born about 1175. During the Dark Ages, man's knowledge retreated following the decline of the Roman Empire. Leonardo da Pisa, or Fibonacci as he is better known, was one of few men who helped keep alive man's knowledge of mathematics at a critical time in history. Fibonacci was the son of a mercantile businessman of Pisa, Bonaccio. Because of his father's commercial interests, Fibonacci gained an early interest in arithmetic, and in trips to Egypt, Sicily, Greece and Syria, he became acquainted with the Eastern and Arabic mathematics of the day. He wrote three major works, *Liber Abaci, Practica Geometriae* and *Liber Quadratorum*. In the *Liber Abaci*, a problem was posed, as follows:

How many pairs of rabbits can be produced in a year from a single pair, if every month each pair begets a new pair starting with the second month?

MR. RABBIT'S FAMILY TREE DIAGRAM

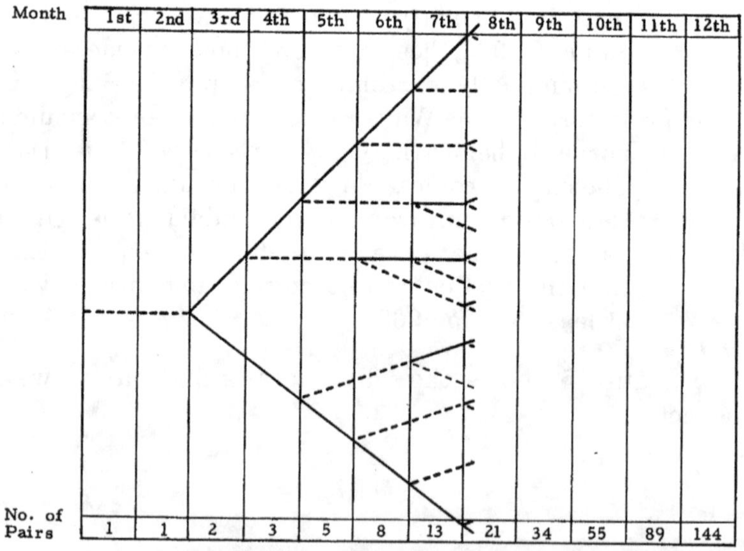


———— Solid line represents a pair 2 months old or older

-------- Broken line represents a pair 0 to 2 months

(A pair of rabbits is not productive until 2 months old)

*Figure 8*

The answer is 144 (see Figure 8).

The summation series in the rabbit problem bears the Fibonacci name:

1, 1, 2, 3, 5, 8, 13, 21, 34, 89, 144, etc.

This series has a great many important properties:

(1) The sum of any two consecutive numbers forms the number above it. Thus, 3 plus 5 equals 8, 5 plus 8 equals 13, 8 plus 13 equals 21, etc.

(2) The ratio of any number to its next higher is 61.8 to 100 (after the very early numbers, which of course are rounded).

(3) The ratio of any number to its next below is 161.8 to 100.

(4) The ratio of each number to the second below is always 261.8 to 100. (Note: 2 plus .618).

(5) Each number divided into the second above it goes 2 times, with a leftover of the exact number below it. Thus, 34 goes into 89 twice with 21 left over. And 5 goes into 13 twice with 3 left over, etc.

(6) This summation series has been classified as being related, each number to the number before by the formula:

$$\tfrac{1}{2}(\sqrt{5} + 1) \qquad (1.618)$$

and each number is related to the number above by the formula:

$$\tfrac{1}{2}(\sqrt{5} - 1) \qquad (0.618)$$

It is most interesting that the square root of the number 5 (2.236) is the dominant factor in the formula.

(7) The ratio 1.618 multiplied by the ratio 0.618 equals 1.

The stock market waves follow the Fibonacci series. Thus, in a bull market, there are five waves; in a correction, three. Breaking down the five waves into 5-3-5-3-5, we get 21 waves of lower degree; in a correction, 5-3-5 or 13 waves. Each of these, of course, are Fibonacci numbers. In a bull market of greater detail, we have 21-13-21-13-21, which totals 89 waves, and the correction is 21-13-21, or a total of 55. The perfect bull and bear cycle will comprise five plus three, which equals eight waves. Of next lower degree, the total will be 21 plus 13, or 34, and the next lower degree will be 89 plus 55, which equals 144. And so on ad infinitum.

The ratio of 61.8 to 100 and 100 to 161.8 became a central part of Elliott's theories in regard to both *time* and *amplitude.* See *The Elliott Wave Principle — A Critical Appraisal.*

### FURTHER NOTE ON FIBONACCI NUMBERS

The advantage of the Fibonacci numbers as a mathematical basis of the Wave Principle lies in the fact that it deals in finite whole numbers, not in a concept of growth involving infinitesimal increments or differentials such as in the case of calculus. In other words, it is a method of analysis which takes into account the characteristics of the data available.

## *GOLD AND DROSS*

Q. Can we have another 1929?

A. Not in this cycle, or in the foreseeable future.[17]

---

[17] Exactly.

Q. Which is more important, when to buy or what to buy?

A. Stocks are like sex; timing is everything.

Q. Is the market a random walk?

A. No. A recursive mathematical sequence is not random.

Q. Is investing an art?

A. Timing is an art. Selection is a science. Elliott tends to turn timing toward the scientific.

Q. Do many analysts use Elliott?

A. Only a few high priests.

Q. Does Elliott mesh with Dow theory?

A. Beautifully. An understanding of Elliott helps delineate secondaries under Dow's great theory and makes the theory more meaningful.

Q. Are Elliott's tenets absolute?

A. No. There is only a tendency of the market to follow Fibonacci sequences. No general average can ever be developed to reflect Elliott adequately at all times. The Dow is the best general average for Elliott purposes.

Q. What about Benner's 8-9-10 year concept?

A. Let's keep an eye on it. It could be helpful.

Q. Does Elliott tend to keep abreast of changing economic conditions?

A. Yes.

Q. Have you used Elliott to advantage in other fields?

A. Yes, horse racing.[18]

Q. Why not use bar charts for interpreting the waves?

A. If you can't take two or three minutes per day to post an hourly chart (use a pencil), add a few figures and use your calculator to divide by 10, you have no real interest in Elliott.

Q. Under your interpretation, is not an intraday top of 1000 too high for wave B in relation to the start of wave A?

A. A very good question, indeed. Elliott measures both prices and confidence. The rise from the Cuban low of 554 DJIA to 1000 in 1966 is due mainly to the rise in corporate earnings[19] from 1962 from $30.00 to $56.00, a whopping 80% increase in Dow-Jones earnings (see Figure 9). The price-earnings ratio also follows an Elliott pattern (see Figure 10)[20], and fits in with the interpretation that the period from January 1960 to date is a long period of consolidation from which will emerge a tremendous bull market starting in a year or two.

Q. Does the Dow move in increments of its square root?

A. I don't know. The Fibonacci Summation Series has square root aspects, and a few analysts do follow square roots as a useful device in gauging stopping points. Sometimes it seems to work, but I would not rely upon it.

---

[18] At one time, Frost oversaw the receivership of a bankrupt racetrack. He plotted gross receipts and profits and observed that the bankruptcy occurred after a substantial A-B-C decline and that a recovery had begun upon receipts tracing out five waves upward.

[19] Earnings bear little relationship to price movements in the averages, and when they do, they lag.

[20] A labeled chart appeared in the Walter White section, which will be reprinted in an upcoming book.

Q. Can you get extensions in successive waves?

A. The general rule is only one extension of the same degree in any five-wave move. You can not be 100% sure of Elliott's extensions rules. An extension can split or double.[21]

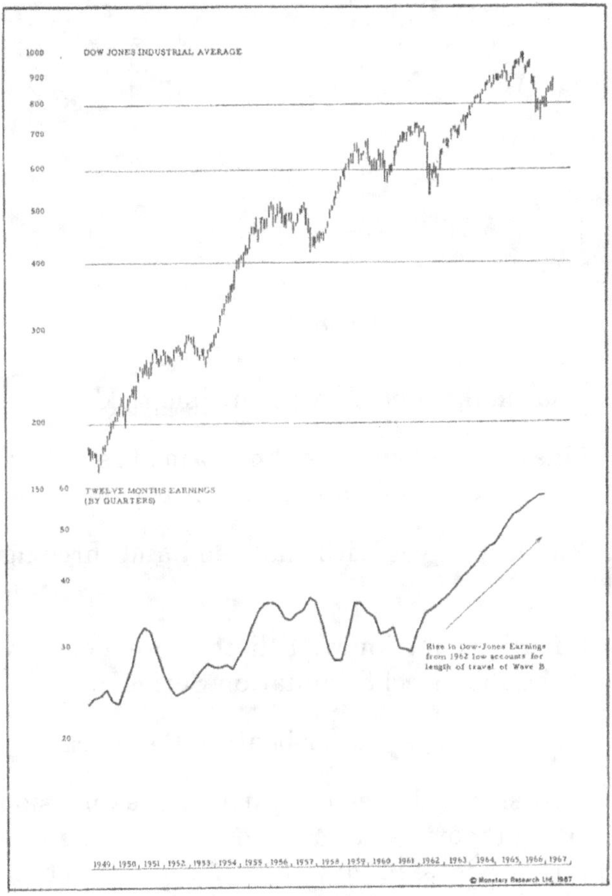


*Figure 9*

---

[21] "Split" is unclear. "Double" presumably means, for instance, that the fifth wave of an extended fifth can also extend.

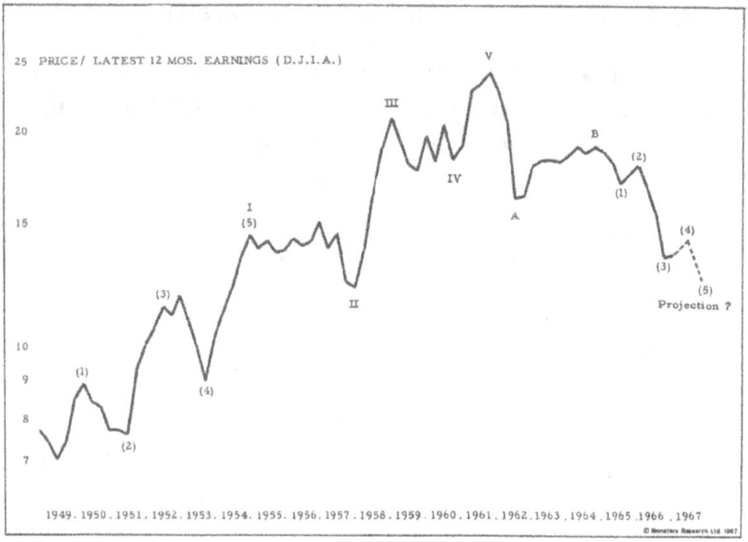


*Figure 10*

Q. What makes the Wave Principle tick?

A. Mass psychology takes the form of repetitive patterns which are predictable and measurable.

Q. Why five waves with the trend and three against the trend?

A. I really don't know. Elliott contended it was a reflection of the Fibonacci Summation Series.

Q. Is Elliott a system for beating the market?

A. I get sick and tired of hearing the expression that such-and-such a theory is not a system for beating the market. The market will skin you alive if you are not careful, so why not have a system? Elliott should help you to keep abreast and ahead of the market. The problem with Elliott is to believe what you see. Fixed preconceived ideas are what beat you, not the market. Study Elliott.

Q. You regard the period from January 1960 as a fourth wave from 1942. Why not a second wave?

A. You seldom see such a complex wave in a second position. This is a sound Elliott argument for considering 1942 as the real starting point of the Supercycle.

Q. Did Bolton change his wave analysis before he died?

A. Yes. For some time he felt the market was in a "B" wave up from June 1962. When a fourth and fifth wave were added, bringing the market close to 1000, he changed his count to a five. Other Elliotters who took their count from the Cuban crisis low of 554 started with a five up, which became a sub-five when two more waves were added.

Q. Did Bolton rely on cycles of fixed periodicity?

A. No, but he never overlooked them. Bolton's main study was bank credit. The Elliott Wave Principle and cycle studies were his avocations. In one of our friendly market vendettas back in 1964, he did comment on two cycles.[22]

Q. When wave C has run its course, will we see a new bull market of Cycle dimension?

A. Yes.

Q. Any ideas on timing?

A. Possibly 1968. A look at the future can never be too accurate.

Q. Do you think Elliott will have a definite message when a bottom is finally reached?

A. The balance of probabilities favors it. I recall a remark of Bolton's made on February 10, 1967, when we were discussing the October 7, 1966 bottom of the market.

---

[22] See "Letter from Bolton" of December 15, 1964.

He said, "I was in Europe at the time, but if I had been here, I think I would have caught it." Markets usually end on a clear-cut five-wave pattern. If you have a five series of well subdivided waves with the middle waves the longest, it is not too difficult to catch the fifth of the third degree of a Primary wave. Try it. An hourly chart is a must. Elliott is a lot of fun. You can look so wise or so foolish in the eyes of your friends.

Q. How high should the next Cycle go?

A. As I interpret Elliott, the next Cycle wave will be a fifth from 1942, with a long supporting base in the form of a series of flats and zigzags, indicating great technical strength. This is usually a blow-off situation, and the Dow could double its previous high of 1000. Monetary inflation and world wide devaluation of currencies combined with a protracted cycle of optimism could perform this magic.

Q. You must like crow?

A. I've eaten it before.

Q. Do you rely solely on Elliott?

A. Never. Elliott does give market perspective better than most theories, but it is only one tool.

Q. Did Bolton change his views respecting 1949 as the starting point of a Supercycle wave?

A. I don't know. He always recognized 1942 and 1932 as possible starting points, but preferred the count from 1949. After modifying his count of the wave 5 up from the low of 1962, he might have become partial to 1942. We always argued over that one.

Q. Sometimes it is difficult to interpret the waves.

A. We all have that problem. If the market doesn't conform to any recognizable Elliott pattern, don't be too concerned. The market may give the answer later in retrospect, but it may not. If you are a serious student of Elliott, research another general average. If this adds to your confusion, then forget about it.

Q. Are there long important periods which would clarify the Elliott Wave Principle if one could be certain about the reading?

A. You can never be certain about anything in market analysis. We know lots for maybe, but nothing for sure. In the game of chess, there are 169 billion billion billion patterns of possible play in the first 20 moves. The stock market is slightly more complicated than chess.

Q. You did not answer my last question.

A. I know. The answer is "yes," but a "yes" isn't really an adequate answer without going into detail.

Q. Some analysts contend that the stock market reached a new high in May of this year. Do you agree?

A. No. Both the economy and the stock market have been in a bear trend for some time. We are not out of the woods. To see the forest, one must take a position above the trees. Looking at the Dow averages is the best way to view the jungle. The picture isn't bullish. Some analysts are overly optimistic and a few of the younger New York boys seem to be very much impressed with their own importance. A little knowledge is a dangerous thing, and so is a little experience.

Q. Did you know Bolton well?

A. Yes.

Q. What characteristics impressed you the most?

A. His incisive mind and humour. He developed the bank credit approach as an area of study which will influence market analysis indefinitely, and he preserved the Elliott Wave Principle for future research.

Q. What about his humour?

A. This is an excellent note on which to end. A lady analyst recently told of this exchange involving herself:

Lady Analyst: Mr. Bolton, if you were shipwrecked and alone on an island in the Southern Seas, what would you desire the most?

Bolton: *Barron's.*

*A Supplement to*

*The Bolton-Tremblay*

# *BANK CREDIT ANALYST*

## THE ELLIOTT WAVE PRINCIPLE of Stock Market Behavior

1968 SUPPLEMENT

This year, in the 1968 Elliott Wave Principle Supplement, we are pleased to present a mathematical analysis of the Wave Principle by Walter E. White, a mathematician with Atomic Energy of Canada, Limited. As far as we are aware, Mr. White's research constitutes the first major mathematical contribution to the study of the Wave Principle for many years.

This Supplement also contains a review of the current market interpretation based on Elliott Wave theory, by Russell L. Hall[1], investment analyst in Ottawa. Mr. Hall is associated with a well-known investment firm and has over twenty years background as a market student and analyst.

The Editors
June 21, 1968

---

[1] Frost co-produced this Supplement.

## *ELLIOTT'S WAVE PRINCIPLE*
## *1968*

### *SUMMARY OF CONCLUSIONS*[2]

1. Considerably more to come on the downside between now and 1970. Probably a bear slide at least equal to the 1966 decline of 256 points.

2. The move up from October 1966 does not appear to be the beginning of a bull market of Cycle degree. It does not have the right look or count under Elliott's rules to be classified as other than a move against the main trend.

3. The next Cycle bull market needs a base. A base has not been completed, as the 1966 decline was a five-wave affair and therefore only the first wave of a larger pattern. A full corrective pattern is never a five.

4. The low of the market should form below the 740 DJIA level, and quite conceivably could reach the 554 level registered at the time of the Cuban crisis.

5. The current up wave is expected to exhaust itself below 1000[3] DJIA, since the down wave in 1966 was a five. In other words, the first wave of a zigzag.

---

[2] This list provides an excellent perspective on the future.

[3] The final high in December 1968 was 985.21.

6. Based on mathematical projection and pattern analysis, a target date of 1970 is indicated the bottom of the bear market correction and the commencement of the next Cycle wave bull market. The next upward Cycle wave should more than double[4] the old high of 1000 DJIA.

## *HISTORICAL DEVELOPMENTS*

During the middle thirties, R.N. Elliott developed a principle of stock market behavior based on a tendency he observed, or "discovered," of the market to move in rhythmic patterns. The basic patterns consisted of wave series which could always be divided into smaller wave series and subdivided again into still smaller series, within the framework of certain basic rules.

Elliott first published his theory in 1938 in a monograph entitled *The Wave Principle*, which was followed later by a more extensive publication in 1946 entitled *Nature's Law*.

After Elliott's death in 1947, there was little interest in the Wave Principle until a book was published by A. Hamilton Bolton in 1960, entitled *The Elliott Wave Principle — A Critical Appraisal,* a result of his series of annual reviews started in 1953. This publication has been followed each year by an annual supplement updating the Elliott outlook, based on market developments.

Elliott considered that wave I of a Grand Supercycle started in approximately 1800 and that the period from 1857 to 1928 comprised Grand Supercycle wave III.[5] On this assumption, Grand Supercycle wave IV started in 1928 and was composed of either three waves or a five-wave triangle.

---

[4] Today the Dow is six times its 1966 high in nominal terms.

[5] Like Collins, Hall uses "Grand Supercycle wave III" when he should mean "subwave III of the Grand Supercycle," i.e., Supercycle wave III.

Previous supplements have outlined various interpretations with respect to this period, as follows:

1. Three waves ending in 1932 (Elliott, 1938; Collins, 1966).

2. Three waves ending in 1942 (Frost, 1967).

3. Triangle ending in 1942 (Elliott, 1946).

4. Triangle ending in 1949 (Bolton, 1953).

These interpretations agree on one major point, namely that a Grand Supercycle impulse wave (Grand Supercycle V) started from the depths of the depression. Since this wave will probably run for many years, its duration is not of great practical importance at this time. What does concern us are the subdivisions of this wave and the investment implications. The commencement date of Grand Supercycle V is therefore of some importance because it provides a bench mark from which to interpret the intervening waves.

The chart [on page 143] depicts on logarithmic scale the fluctuations of the market as shown by the Dow-Jones Industrial Average from 1928 to 1968. An examination of this chart shows a major drop from 1929 to 1932, a rally from 1932 to 1937, and a decline from 1937 to 1942. The whole movement from 1942 is contained between two parallel trend lines, or a "channel," in Elliott terms. From the chart, it is obvious that 1932 and 1942 are major bottom reversal points, and it is fairly easy to accept either date as the commencement of Grand Supercycle wave V. 1949 appears to be a part of the 1942-1966 movement. We shall comment later on the subject of channelling and the significance of 1966 as the terminal date of a Supercycle from 1942.

## WHERE ARE WE IN THE STOCK MARKET CYCLE?

Students of the Elliott school have difficulty in agreeing with each others' interpretations but generally agree with respect to the basic concepts of stock market behavior as enunciated by Elliott. Elliott is not a science, as the "principle" tends to accommodate itself to man-made decisions, especially over short time periods. For this reason, wave movements tend to develop intricate patterns, and it often becomes difficult for the student to be sure of his count and the wave degrees involved in his analysis. Let us take an example of these differences and consider their practical application to the current outlook for the stock market under Elliott's rules. The best example we can think of is Bolton vs. Frost. A.H. Bolton wrote his last Elliott supplement in 1966 and A.J. Frost wrote the 1967 Supplement. Frost, as have most students, acknowledged Bolton's preeminence in the field.

In the 1966 Supplement, Bolton concluded that February 1966 probably terminated a Supercycle (wave I), which paralleled Collins' interpretation of a Supercycle termination (wave III) at the same time.

At the time of his death, Bolton held the view that the 1966 decline was the A-wave of a major bear market, which would eventually correct or consolidate the entire rise of the Supercycle. This view implies that since A was a five-wave down, B will be a three and C will be a five to end the bear market.

Under this interpretation, the next bear market will be a *big* five-wave down, sufficient to be classified as a wave of Cycle dimension. It may be that we are soon to see the start of this wave and that, when it has run its course, a new bull market of Supercycle dimension will start, probably in 1970 or late 1969[6], and keep going for several years (see diagram).

---

[6] The market's patterns always seem to take a lot longer to develop than wave analysts anticipate. Time forecasting is nearly impossible, but the *form* is always true. Still, the next diagram calls the drop into the 1970 low and subsequent recovery perfectly.

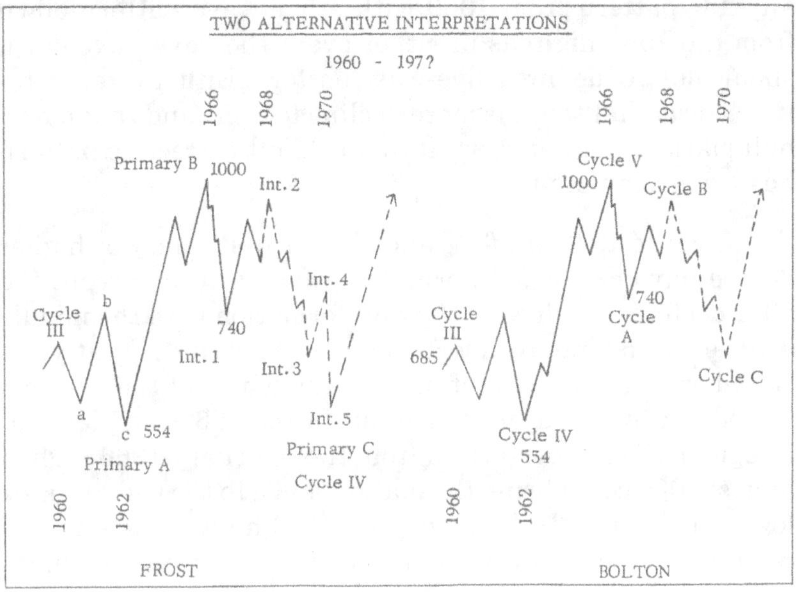


## FROST'S VIEW OF ELLIOTT

Frost queried Bolton's count from the low of 1962 to the high of almost 1000 DJIA in 1966 and contended this rise was a three-wave affair, making a giant B wave in a long consolidation which began in 1960 (see 1967 Elliott Supplement). Under this interpretation, the move down from the 1966 high should form a five-wave pattern before the next bull market gets underway. Bolton's C wave, counting down from 1000 DJIA, a five, will be Frost's third wave of wave C counting from 1960, also a five. In other words, both agree that the next bear market wave should subdivide into a five-wave pattern, but Frost warns that there may be more to come on the downside even after the next five-wave down has run its course.

## AUTHOR'S VIEWPOINT

As third waves in bear markets are usually the most bearish, it does not make too much difference for the time being whether the market is going to follow an ABC zigzag pattern down from the 1966 high, with the C-wave breaking into a five, or whether the correct Elliott interpretation is an ABC pattern from 1960 with a five-wave pattern down from the 1966 high, as in either event the next wave down should subdivide into a five-wave pattern. Either interpretation *warns* that there is more decline to come and that a new bull market will not start until an Elliott corrective pattern has been completed.

Since 1942, all flats and zigzags of Primary or higher degree have developed normal C wave patterns except the 1962 decline, which was a C wave formation with the middle wave establishing an unorthodox low in June of that year. Based on Frost's assumption that the whole of the '60s is a period of consolidation, as set out in the 1967 Supplement, a regular C wave correction from the February 1966 high of almost 1000 could bring the market down to the Cuban crisis low of 554 DJIA. If, however, the 1966 high is the end of a Supercycle wave up from 1942, then the next bottom might not reach such an extremely low point[7], but in any event it should be well below the October 1966 low of 740.

In connection with the comment earlier about the difficulty of differentiating between wave degrees, the difference between these two interpretations should be noted.

If 1966 is the end of a Supercycle, it must be followed by a Supercycle correction composed of three Cycle waves. Therefore, February 1966 to October 1966 must be classified as a Cycle, the rise from 740 (October 1966) to the next peak is a Cycle, and the ensuing bear market must also be a Cycle composed of five Primaries. So far, this pattern, and particularly the A wave from February 1966 to October 1966, appears too small for waves of Cycle degree. If so, the only alternative is that the current three-wave correction from 1966 will turn out to be only the A wave of a much larger Cycle movement.[8] We do not know whether Bolton had any thoughts in this respect or not.

---

[7] An accurate forecast.

[8] This is what happened.

Frost, on the other hand, considers the period from 1960 to be Cycle wave IV of a Supercycle, which makes his C wave from February 1966 a Primary, and the decline from the peak near 1000 to the October low at 740 the first Intermediate, composed of five Minors.

Here, then, we have a situation where the same waves (for example, February 1966 to October 1966) are Cycles in one case and Intermediates in the other. As a result, the implication of Frost's Cycle wave IV is for a larger decline than is projected by Bolton's Supercycle wave IV.

On the basis of proportionate analysis, using the Fibonacci ratio of 161.8:100 or 161.8%, and applying this ratio to the 1966 decline of 256 points, we get a figure of 414. A drop of 414 points from the 1967 high of 946 would mean a low of 532 DJIA, or a point somewhere between the orthodox and unorthodox lows of 1962. Proportionate analysis conforms to Frost's pattern analysis, but caution suggests that this reading may not be the correct one. The odds at this juncture do not appear to warrant such drastic deterioration of market values.

The 1966 drop was a five-wave pattern with the fifth wave extending. On this point Bolton and Frost agreed, and as 5th wave extensions call for double retracement, Bolton's C wave should move down below the 740 level and Frost's third wave plus his two additional waves to follow should easily go well below this target.

In any event, the Elliott message appears to be that we are in a Cycle or Supercycle bear situation of some duration and magnitude. Elliott is a valuable tool in the investment decision making process and, despite some differences in interpretation, its message is loud and clear — *be cautious at this time.*

## *CHANNELLING*

To identify wave formations, Elliott made extensive use of channelling. For full details, the reader is referred to Part III of *The Wave Principle* by R.N. Elliott. The next chart shows the DJIA from 1928 to date with trend lines and channels marked. The following points are of interest:

1. The wave from 1942 to 1966 contains five up trends with four corrections (assuming 1960 to 1962 to be corrective). This is consistent with a concept of a completed Supercycle from 1942 to 1966, made up of nine Cycle waves.

2. The whole movement from 1942 to 1966 is contained between two parallel trend lines, or a channel. These lines are closely approached or contacted in 1946, 1949, 1956, 1960 and 1962. The contact points in 1946, 1949, 1960 and 1962 are the terminal points of waves I, II, III and IV (assuming wave III from 1949 to 1960).[9]

3. A trend line joining 1937 and 1966[10] is touched by the 1960 peak, which is also a contact point on the 1942-1966 channel.

4. The 1966 peak fell well short of the top of the channel, but terminated on an extension of the line joining 1937 and 1960, thus creating a strong three-point trend line from 1937 to 1966.

5. A trend line parallel to 1937-1966, using 1942 as a starting point, is currently somewhere about 450 DJIA and would cross 500 during 1970.[11]

---

[9] This is the proper analysis of 1942-1966 and builds upon Collins' work in the 1966 Supplement.

[10] The upper line remains valid today as resistance for wave V.

[11] This trendline, expertly drawn according to Elliott's rules, stopped the market with precision at the 1974 low of 572.

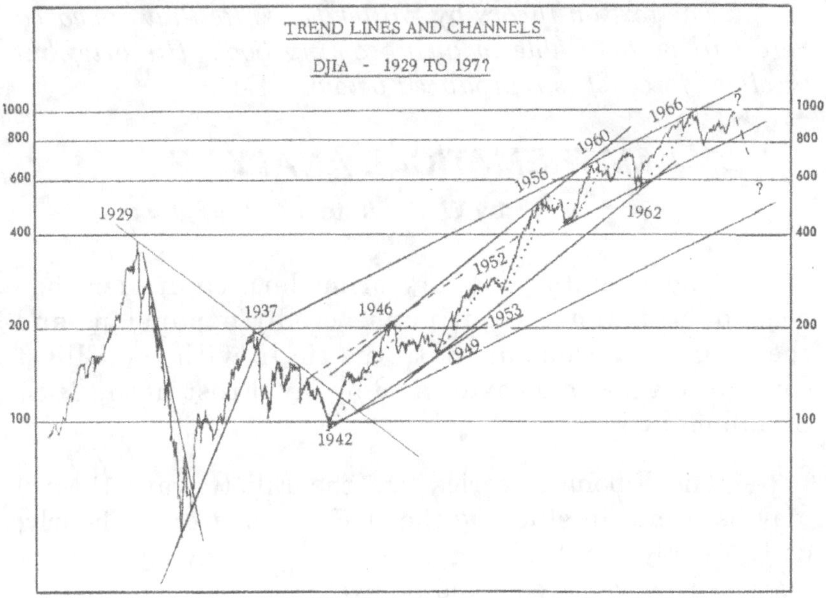


6. A three-wave corrective pattern from 1966 of the same magnitude as 1937-1942 could contact the bottom of a 1937-1966, 1942-? channel in approximately 1970 at approximately 500 DJIA.

Using the channelling technique, it would appear that February 1966 was the orthodox end of a Supercycle dating from 1942. The waves from 1932 to 1937 and 1937 to 1942 could be either Supercycle I and II of a Grand Supercycle, making 1942 to 1966 Supercycle III, or they could be part of the corrective pattern which started in 1928, thus making 1942 to 1966 Supercycle I. The correction which started from February 1966 should be composed of three waves, with the third and final downwave terminating in about 1970.

*The text on theory by Walter E. White that appeared here will be available in an upcoming book. His brief but excellent forecast is reproduced below.* – Ed.

## MATHEMATICAL ANALYSIS

**by W. E. White**

The monetary history of modern capitalism has been one of almost continuous credit expansion, and the long term economic patterns tie in with the Elliott concept of growth as explained by Mr. Frost in the 1967 Supplement.

The Fibonacci series (i.e. the Elliott wave theory) may be useful in studying the stock market on an hourly, daily, weekly, monthly or annual basis. In studying the stock market, however, we should realize that:

1) The wave theory does not imply a fatal determinism. Elliott's original work was done many years ago when oscillations were of much greater magnitude. The performance of the stock market during the past twenty years suggests that the magnitude of the oscillations has been limited by the Banking Act of 1935, the Employment Act of 1946 and the Cold War.[12] The slopes of the trend line connecting important turning points were:

| | | |
|---|---|---|
| 1942 - 1946 (high) | 17% | per year |
| 1949 - 1957 (low) | 9% | per year |
| 1957 - 1966 (low) | 6% | per year |

Some analysts believe that the 6% figure is relatively modest, and that this slope may be maintained, or possibly exceeded, during the next two or three decades.[13] The 6%

[12] Actually, the magnitude of the oscillations has been limited by the smaller degree of the waves.

figure may be exceeded if the annual rate of inflation increases from about 1½% to 3% per year as some studies forecast.[14]

2) The economy of the United States is now the strongest economy in the world and may remain the strongest for decades and, possibly, centuries.[15] Thus, comparisons with Supercycles in the nineteenth century may not be of much value. Rates of annual growth of the gross national product and of population were about equal for two hundred years between 1700 and 1900, and the 1929-1932 depression may have been due, in large part, to the fact that the economy was not yet adjusted to the slower rate of population growth during the present century (about one-half the rate between 1700 and 1900). This adjustment has now been made by large expenditures on science and on engineering development.

3) Conclusions should not be drawn from studies of the Dow Jones Industrials alone. This average is no longer representative of the whole market, and wave studies should be made on other averages and on other indices such as advance-decline plots, point and figure charts, momentum and volume series, etc. If the Elliott studies are broadened in this way, a better perspective is obtained and many anomalies become less disturbing.

4) We should expect shocks to have a greater effect during speculative markets when a higher percentage of stocks are in weak hands.

5) Information is available which may be used to determine the trend of the market without reference to the

---

[13] This decreasing upside momentum signaled the end of the Cycle degree bull market, so the opposite conclusion should have been drawn.

[14] Inflation soared over the next 12 years, and stocks went nowhere. Inflation does not drive the stock market.

[15] The comments in this and the next three paragraphs are highly debatable.

Elliott Wave theory. The theory is useful as an auxiliary tool which adds to the perspective.

The next important low point may be in late 1969 or 1970. Note the following Fibonacci numbers:[16]

| | | | | |
|---|---|---|---|---|
| 1949 | + | 21 | = | 1970 |
| 1957 | + | 13 | = | 1970 |
| 1962 | + | 8 | = | 1970 |
| 1965 | + | 5 | = | 1970 |
| 1966 | + | 3 | = | 3 months before 1970 if we count from the 1966 low point. |

In addition to the above, the 89.5-year cycle indicates a probable drop in the market in 1970.

In the 1960 handbook, *The Elliott Wave Principle -- A Critical Appraisal*, Mr. Hamilton Bolton asked, "Is the principle fact or fancy?" and said that "We suspect that the principle has more fact than fancy."

On page 102 of this same book, the chart on Libbey-Owens-Ford Glass contains the question, "End of Bull Market in 1959?"[17] Can we afford to ignore a method which pinpoints turning points with such accuracy?

W.E. White
June 21st, 1968

---

[16] An excellent call, and without any fundamentalist ruminating.

[17] In late 1959, Libbey-Owens-Ford Glass began a 15-year bear market.

**February 5, 1969**

Mr. Charles J. Collins
800 Buhl Building
Detroit, Michigan 48226

Dear Mr. Collins:

It appears to me that Elliott is presently tracing out a pattern that is very clear — in fact one interpretation seems so clear that I wonder if there are cogent alternatives which should be obvious, yet which I do not see. I cannot help but notice the similarity between the present picture and that of 1938-1939 when another "B" wave was formed.

If one accepts the early 1966 top of DJI 1000 as a terminus of great significance, should there not follow an A-B-C type correction?

If the A wave of the above was complete in the fall of 1966 at DJI 740, can one assume that everything since then is part of the B wave?

If the B wave in itself is a 3 part affair (a,b,c,), can it not be assumed that a completed at DJI 952 and b at DJI 820? Furthermore that the c and last part is at an advanced stage with possibly 4 out of 5 minor waves complete? Is this all to "pat"?

I always am very grateful for your replies and hope you will again see fit to favor me with an answer. Any comments or observations you may offer would be sincerely appreciated.

Very sincerely,
Max L. Resnick

P.S. On page 12 of the 1966 Bolton Tremblay Elliott supplement, you speak of correspondence with claimants of "infallible" methods or systems for forecasting the stock market — which in most instances went haywire.

Then you state, "Elliott was one of three notable exceptions." Would you care to say who were the other two?

**February 10, 1969**

EIGHT HUNDRED
BUHL BUILDING
DETROIT, MICHIGAN 48226

Dr. Max L. Resnick
330 Blue Hills Parkway
Milton, Massachusetts, 02187

Dear Dr. Resnick:

I am returning your sketch. You have numbered the Elliott Wave movement exactly the same as I have, so I see no need to comment on this.

I am leaving the city at this time, but will reply to your postscript on my return in late April.

Very truly yours,
Charles J. Collins

April 27, 1970

*BARRON'S*

# Market Ebb Tide

## Elliott's Wave Theory Suggests That the Lows Are Still to Come

By Charles J. Collins

There are various methods, formulae, timing studies and equations, not to mention intuition, by which the stock market's course is gauged. I watch a score or more of indices in this connection but, as I stated in a recent interview, I wouldn't bet my thumb on any one of them. Paraphrasing Sweet William of Stratford on Avon, "Stock market, thy name is fickle."

All the same, this does not say we should shut our eyes to economic, timing, and technical factors that relate to stock prices. Among the technical approaches, one of the best that I have come across is the Elliott Theory. I knew Elliott intimately, wrote his first book for him, and continued in correspondence and personal contact until his death. At this juncture in the market, when earnings and business activity seem headed downward and the credit factor seems to be improving, thus raising a serious question as to the primary direction of stock prices over the months ahead, let's, for what it is worth, see what Elliott's approach is saying.

**How Now, Mr. Dow?**

Let me first pay tribute to Charles H. Dow, Founder of Dow Jones & Co. and father of the Dow Jones averages. With little of the historical or factual material available to present day analysts, Mr. Dow advanced a number of fundamental theories of stock market behavior that have stood the test of time and been of inestimable help to students of market action.

One of Dow's observations was that a market swing generally develops three important impulses in the main direction. In a cyclical upswing, or so called bull market, for example, prices first rebound from the over-pessimism of the preceding bear swing. Then, as the second impulse toward higher price levels, comes the market's adjustment to the improving economic conditions that the initial market upswing has sensed. The third upward impulse is created by the overoptimism that, as the British economist Pigou has since demonstrated, generally characterizes the closing phase of a forward movement and, incidentally, proves the movement's undoing.

A student and admirer of Dow's teachings, R.N. Elliott developed Dow's "three impulse" observation into a rather complex and fine-tuned science. Working with the Dow Jones averages from 1897, he demonstrated the correctness of Dow's observation and found that it applies as well to hourly, daily, weekly, yearly and decade-to-decade swings of the stock market. He traced a Grand Supercycle running from 1857 to 1929 (or late 1928 to be exact; the abortive upmove in 1929 was the second wave of a three wave correction that ended in 1932.) In brief, Elliott showed that every market movement, regardless of size of importance, develops Dow's three impulses in the primary direction, impulses No. 1 and 3 being separated by secondary or corrective swings in the opposite direction. Elliott found that the corrective swings consisted of only three impulses, two tending to correct the previous trend, separated by a counter-impulse.

**Changes Nomenclature**

Elliott buffs will note that I have departed somewhat from his nomenclature in designating the various types of waves, which is only a matter of semantics. Thus, Elliott would have called the bull market of 1962-66 an "Intermediate";[18] I have called it a cyclical[19] movement. By so doing, I adhere more nearly to the widespread non-Elliott market terminology, identifying bull and bear markets with the cyclical swings in business which these market moves often parallel. Under my nomenclature, the great wave which is made up of five cyclical waves in the main direction, or three against the main trend, is termed a Supercycle. The lesser waves that, together, make a cyclical wave are termed Intermediates.

Now, let's get to the practical matter of what Elliott's theory currently is saying. Toward the end of 1965, I wrote an article for the Bolton-Tremblay annual Elliott Survey in which I took the position that, according to the theory, the market was ending its third Supercycle since the 1932 bottom, and that we were faced with a protracted period of irregularity, to be characterized by two down-waves of cyclical proportions, with an intervening cyclical up-wave. This reading is diagramed in Chart I (semilog scale). The Roman numerals indicate the three Supercycle swings between 1932 and 1966. Within each Supercycle the Arabic numerals indicate the cyclical swings that, collectively, constitute a Supercycle.

The degree of any correction, according to Elliott, must correspond with the degree of the wave

[18] Primary, actually.

[19] Collins did this in the 1966 Supplement as well.

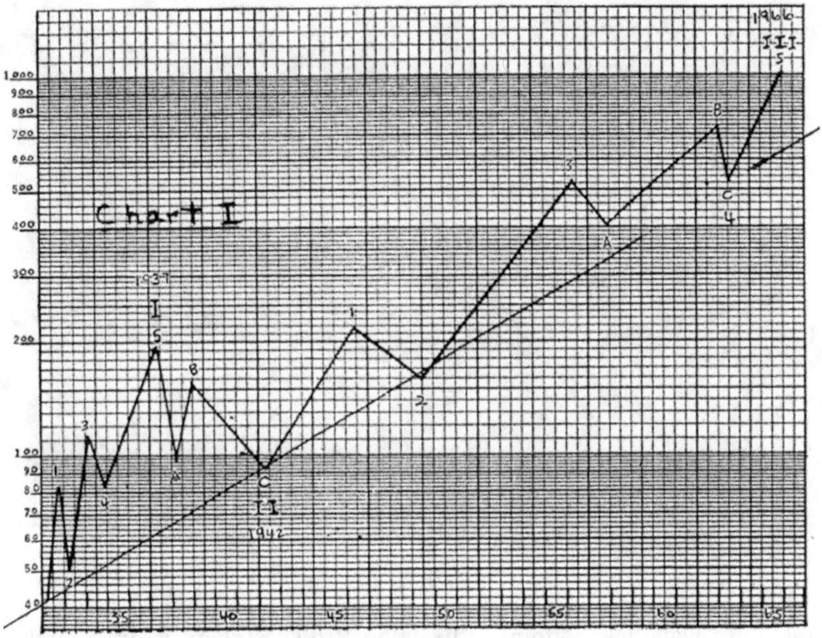


*Chart I*

it is correcting. Stated otherwise, an upmovement of bull market or cyclical proportions should be corrected by a down movement of somewhat equivalent nature, partially cancelling the upswing. This may be effected in price, or in time, or in a combination of both. It will be noted that the Supercycle correction that followed Supercycle I (1932-37) took four years[20] to work itself out, and, as I postulated in the aforementioned 1965 article, the ensuing correction consists of three waves of cyclical extent.

An up-wave that ran for nearly 24 years (thanks to the inflationary policies of the federal government, with tandem support from the Federal Reserve) as did Supercycle III (1942-66) could not be corrected overnight, as was the case in 1962, when an upmove (1957-62) of only cyclical proportions was being corrected. Thus, in 1965 I foresaw a Supercycle correction to be made up of three waves (two down, one up), each of cyclical dimensions. To date, the pattern is working out as projected.

The corrective process from the early 1966 peak is shown in Chart II (arithmetic scale). So far, there have been two completed waves of cyclical length, and the third, or culminating, cyclical wave is in progress. When

[20] Five, actually.

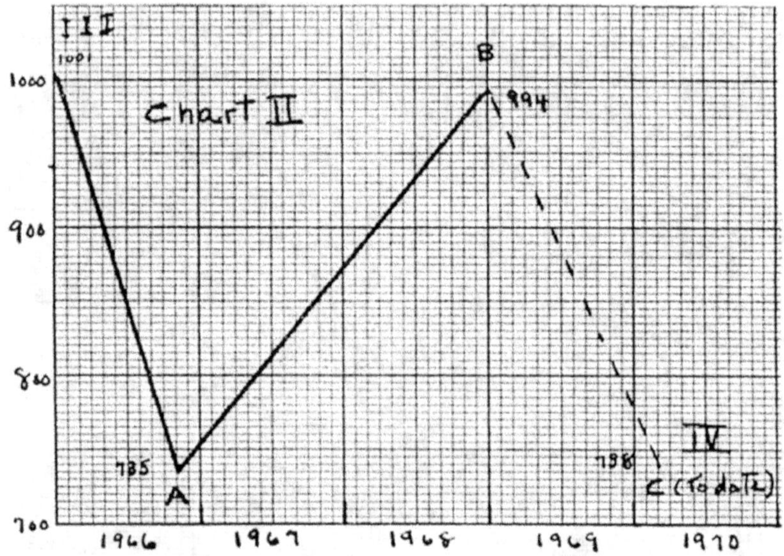


*Chart II*

this third wave has bottomed, the entire corrective process to Supercycle wave III (1942-66) will have been completed. The three cyclical waves, taken together, will then constitute Supercycle wave IV, to be followed by Supercycle wave V, an upswing running over a number of years and being made up of five waves, each of cyclical measurement, with three up-waves being separated by intervening downwaves.

**New Upsurge Ahead?**

Americans, generally speaking, think and plan in terms of yearly intervals, the English in terms of decades, the Chinese in terms of centuries. The American stock market, while frequently breaking down into one or two year cyclical moves, in its wider swings seems to favor the British system; it often starts one of its major moves around the beginning of a decade, i.e. 1921-29, 1932-37, 1942-66.

There is logic to this habit. Over the 18 decades that this country has been a nation, all but two have witnessed material growth in U.S. wealth. The exceptions were 1811-20, and 1931-40. In the first instance, Britain was blockading Napoleon, thus cutting badly into our essential raw material exports to Europe. The second occasion was to the accompaniment of a worldwide deflation in credit. With 16 out of 18 decades showing progress, the expectancy for the 'Seventies is for another great upsurge in wealth and share prices of leading American corporations (Supercycle V, that is), provided we escape such imponderables as the atomic bomb, complete socialization of our society, or a radical inflation.

At the moment, however, the main question is: Has the stock market's period of irregularity of the past four or more years (Supercycle IV) ended, or is there further downside movement ahead? Since Elliott's Theory is the substance of this discussion, what does Elliott say? To begin with, the cyclical down wave in 1966 (wave A on Chart II) was made up of five intermediate waves. Elliott termed this type of formation a zig zag, as opposed to an A wave made up of three intermediate waves, which he termed a "flat." The significance of the zigzag formation is that the following B up-wave should not go as high as the commencement point of the A wave, while the succeeding C downwave should go below the bottom point of the A wave. Since the A wave dropped to 735 (intra day) on the Dow, and since the present C wave has dropped, so far, only to 738, Elliott would seem to call for further downside movement in due course.

**Beware of C Wave**

There is, however, another Elliott approach to the question. This has to do with the character, or makeup, of a C or third corrective wave. Elliott maintained that this particular wave, unlike the A wave of a correction, had to consist of five waves. As an exception, or rare occurrence, nine waves could develop, but this would be merely an extension of one of the three main waves into a five wave movement.

Let us now examine the C wave from late 1968 to date. The price movement, in terms of the daily range of the Dow Jones industrial average, is shown in Chart III. What we are looking for, under Elliott, is five waves (three down, two up), each of Intermediate proportion. I have numbered these waves on the chart as I read them under Elliott's rules. Wave 1 ran from early December 1968 into January 1969. There followed an A-B-C correction (three waves) to March 1969, all of which constituted wave 2. Wave 3 carried to late July 1969. Following wave 3 there was an advance, or corrective wave into November 1969; this could have completed wave 4, but not necessarily so, as shall be seen.

So far, we can feel assured that the C wave from the November 1968 peak of 994 on the Dow has completed three of its essential five waves. From this point there are three ways the market can "fluctuate" (to use the well-known J.P. Morgan observation) to complete the remaining and necessary two intermediate waves. As a first hypothesis (Chart IV), the assumption can be made that Intermediate wave 4 was completed at 871 in November 1969, that waves one, two and three of concluding intermediate

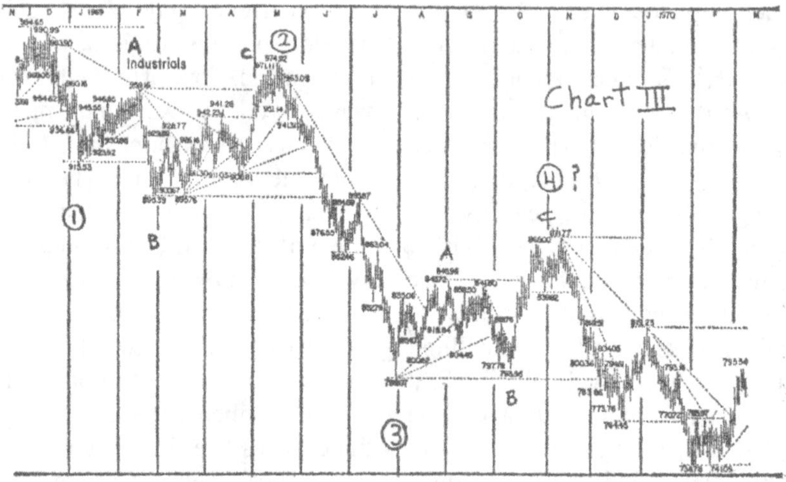


*Courtesy of R.W. Mansfield Co.*

*Chart III*

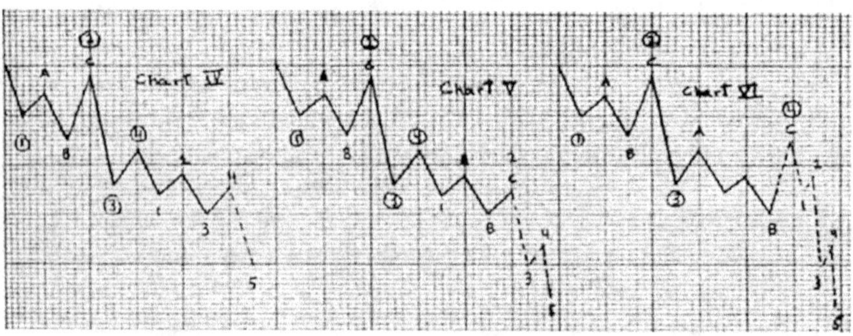


*Chart IV* *Chart V* *Chart VI*

wave 5 have been registered, that the January-March rally was all, or a segment of the fourth wave, leaving one further plunge into new low ground to be accomplished.[21]

**Alternate Hypotheses**

Second (Chart V), it can be assumed that the first wave of intermediate wave 5 was concluded in December 1969 and that the rally

[21] That's what happened.

into January, the drop into February and the rally into March are all part of an A-B-C correction, the total of which will continue the second wave of intermediate wave 5. This would call for another down wave to below the early February 1970 support point, an ensuing rally of sizable dimension, and then a last plunge into new low ground.

The third assumption (Chart VI) based on possibly improving credit conditions, would be an extension of the February-March 1970 rally well beyond the 800 level on the Dow, possibly to or above the November 1969 peak. In that event, the entire movement from the July 1969 bottom of 788 on the Dow to the aforesaid rally peak would have to be classified as an extended A-B-C correction or intermediate wave 4, still leaving Intermediate wave 5, carrying below the early February 1970 low point, to be consummated.

It is a trite saying, but one that merits repetition, that the stock market will not be hurried. Regardless of which of the three formations discussed above takes place, the gist of this lament is that under Elliott's theory the market bottom for the correction that began in early 1966 is still ahead.

*Mr. Collins, now retired, has been as investment counselor in Detroit since 1919. A former NYSE member, he is also the author of a book,* Fortune's Before You *(Prentice-Hall, 1937) and numerous magazine articles on investment theory.*

*A Supplement to*

*The Bolton-Tremblay*

# *BANK CREDIT ANALYST*

## THE ELLIOTT WAVE PRINCIPLE of Stock Market Behavior

1970 SUPPLEMENT

We are pleased to present, as a supplement to *The We are pleased to present, as a supplement to The Bank Credit Analyst*, the 1970 Elliott Wave Principle of Stock Market Behavior.

Mr. A.J. Frost, B. Com., F.C.A., C.F.A., wrote this supplement. The author is one of the leading students in North America of the Elliott Wave Principle and has been a contributor to *The Bank Credit Analyst* on this subject on numerous occasions in the past. He authored the 1967 Elliott Wave Supplement and was associated with the late A. Hamilton Bolton for a number of years during the period when Bolton made major contributions to the Elliott concept.

The Editors.
May 26, 1970

# *ELLIOTT'S WAVE PRINCIPLE 1970*

## *SUMMARY OF CONCLUSIONS*

The Industrial average has been in an overall major bear market since February 9, 1966 when the DJIA peaked out at approximately 1000.[1] The decline since December 2, 1968 is only a phase of this overall decline. The market in all probability will continue to drop until September or October of this year, bottoming out above the 1956 high of 524 DJIA. It may go lower, but in any event should hold above the 1929 high of 381. The Cycle bear market (i.e., since 1966) under Elliott's tenets is correcting or consolidating the long rise from 1942 to 1966. A new bull market could get off the ground this fall and register new highs above 1000 in the Dow Jones Industrial Average within a period of a few years. Figure 1 shows five Minor waves down from April 9 and reflects what appears to be the balance of probabilities under Elliott's Theory for the remainder of the current bear market.[2]

## *ELLIOTT WAVE PRINCIPLE*

### BACKGROUND INFORMATION

It is an accepted fact of life that the stock market and the economy experience wide pendulum-like swings. The upward and forward movement of the market usually

---

[1] Frost returns to the proper view of the 1966 top in this supplement.

[2] The market actually took four more years to reach its low.

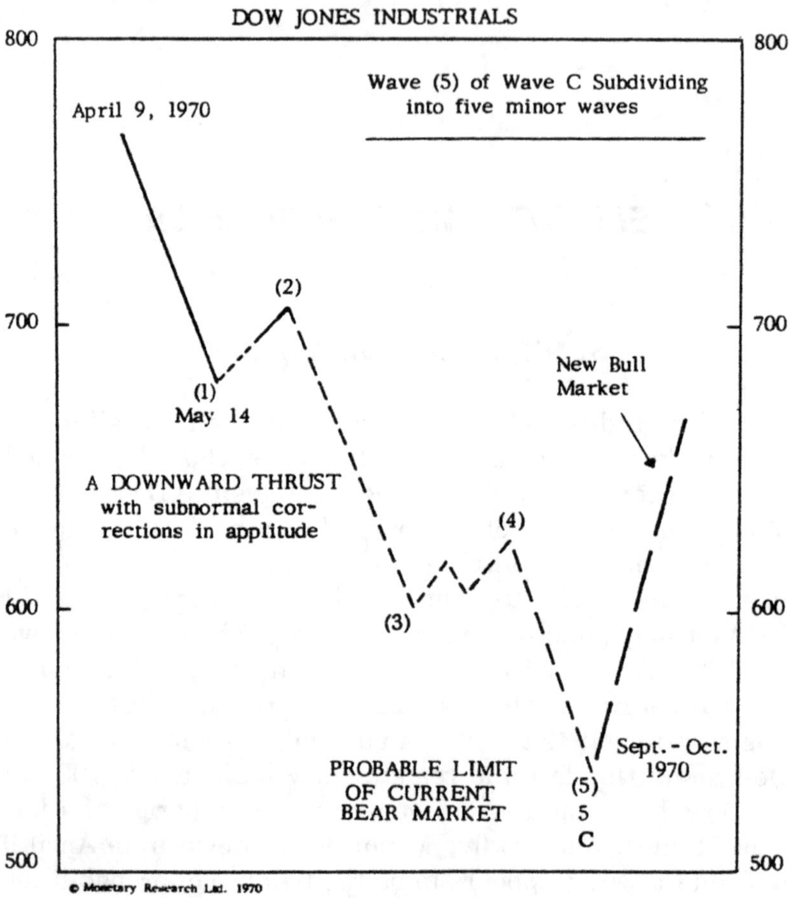


*Figure 1*

develops in a series of waves until the breaking point is reached and the entire movement is reversed. Recurring periods of prosperity and depression have existed from the earliest of times. In Genesis, Joseph, in interpreting the Pharaoh's dream about seven fat cows being eaten by seven lean cows, cautioned, "During the seven prosperous years, gather and bring together all you can." Joseph predicted a depression. Today, we still have the problem of "gathering in" during prosperous times and of guarding against reverses. *The business cycle is not dead.*

The Railway Panic of 1893 and the Rich Man's Panic of 1907 touched off for the first time in history an intensive study of monetary conditions in the United States. In 1908, Congress established a Monetary Commission which led to the enactment of the Federal Reserve Act in 1913. Prior to this time, the money supply of the United States could not be readily expanded or contracted to meet the needs of the economy on a national basis. Before 1914, the investor operated in a boom and bust atmosphere. Every few years, a credit panic would develop. Funds would find their way into the stock market, causing a sharp rise in prices, only to be later withdrawn to meet the demands of business. The banking system of those days was so inflexible that in 1907, Bernard Baruch withdrew $150,000 in cash from the vault of the Manhattan Company in New York and shipped it to Salt Lake City to meet the pay roll of a company he was interested in. Money in those days could not be easily transferred from one place to another, and credit could not be expanded or contracted to meet the requirements of business.

In those early days of spasmodic booms and sharp credit panics, Charles H. Dow, editor of *The Wall Street Journal*, observed that a primary bull market comprises three phases:

1. The first phase develops out of depressed conditions, when the market rebounds to known values.

2. The second phase is usually the longest phase, as the market rises in response to improving business conditions. This is the steady "mark-up" phase (Dow's second phase and Elliott's third wave).

3. The third phase is the blow-off period when speculation tends to raise the price of stocks to comparatively high levels, and the market advances on "hopes and expectations."

Dow referred to the primary trend as an all-engulfing tide composed of three forward impulse movements, with intermediate declines, or secondary reactions, interrupting the main trend. He did not regard daily fluctuations or minor movements of any great importance. This anatomy of the market first observed by Dow was further analyzed by the late R.N. Elliott, who observed that there was a rhythmic regularity to the market. He discerned that the stock market tended to unfold according to basic patterns, and that Dow's three impulse waves, with secondary reactions in between, could be subdivided and re-subdivided into waves of smaller degree and that each complete primary wave of three impulse waves up was a subdivided part of a larger wave formation. Elliott concluded that waves were not simply of the order of primary, secondary and minor, but of a much wider spectrum. He also advanced the theory that following an upward wave of any degree, a correction of the same degree will follow, and that this wave will be composed of five waves of lesser degree, thus completing the Cycle.

## CORRECTIVE PATTERNS

The correction (down and up)

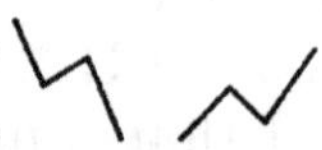

Normally composed of three waves. The first and third wave are in the direction of the correction, and the second counter to it.

Corrective waves are of two main varieties:

FLAT

ZIGZAG

A *flat* is a 3-3-5 affair, and a *zigzag* a 5-3-5 affair. A flat is usually a horizontal correction, while a zigzag is frequently a correction in some depth, with more of a diagonal slope. The B wave of a flat tends to move higher than the beginning of wave A in a bull cycle, and lower than the beginning of wave A in a bear cycle, e.g.:

Because of the frequency of flats and inverted flats, irregular tops and bottoms often appear in wave sequences, making wave counts more difficult.

Triangles and horizontals are composed of five legs,[3] which tend to subdivide into threes depending on their size. This type of formation is rare, and found only in fourth wave formations according to Elliott. Triangles, like flats, are usually followed by strong subsequent action.

On February 9, 1966, the great bull market of Cycle dimension from 1942 peaked out at 1000 DJIA (peak V, Figure 2.) This peak also marks the beginning of a Cycle wave of correction, which is still current. Waves of Cycle dimension subdivide into three Primary movements. The first major subdivision was the Primary bear market of 1966, which chopped 256 points off the Industrial Average before terminating in October 1966 (point A, Figure 2). The next wave was a Primary bull market which carried the market back to 986 (point B, Figure 2), terminating on December 2, 1968. Since then, wave C has taken over, and is developing into a vicious bear market. What we are concerned with now

---

[3] Triangles yes, but not double or triple threes.

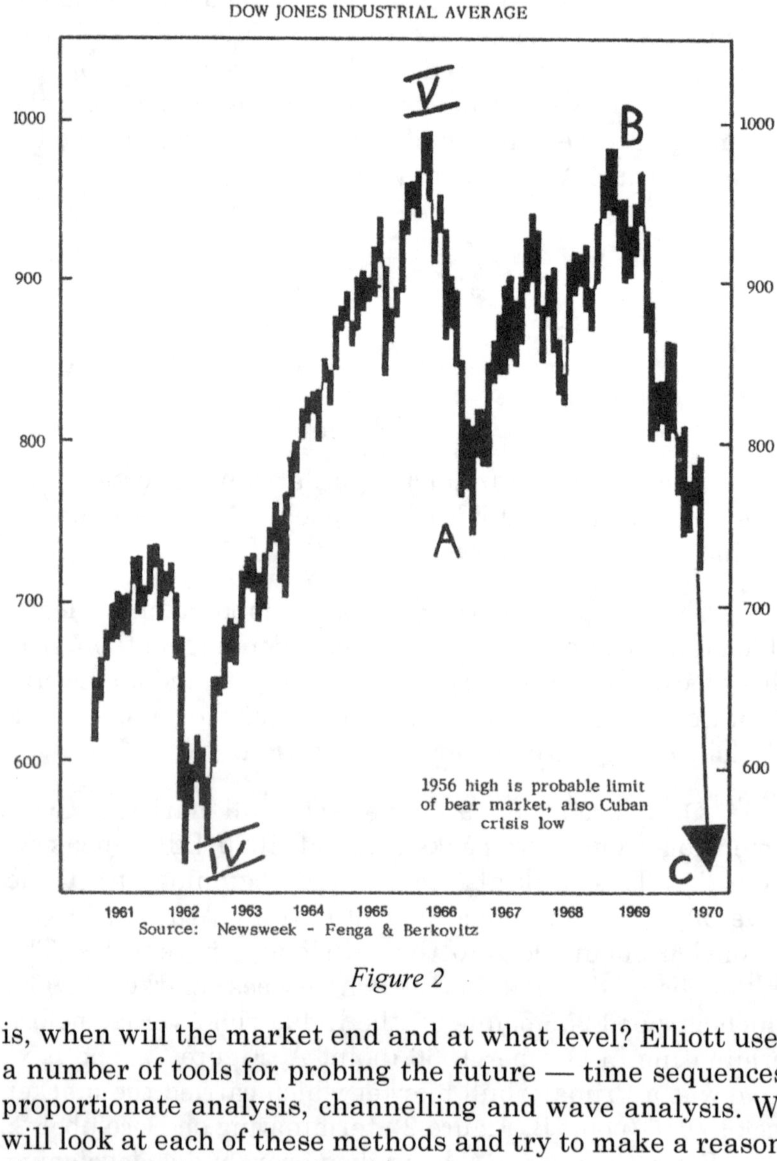


*Figure 2*

is, when will the market end and at what level? Elliott used a number of tools for probing the future — time sequences, proportionate analysis, channelling and wave analysis. We will look at each of these methods and try to make a reasonable forecast based on them.[4]

[4] Inserted just after this section was a repeat of the introduction to the Wave Principle that Frost presented in the 1967 Supplement. For this book, we incorporated the few additions into the 1967 version.

As markets tried to rally on May 11, 1970, the *Globe and Mail* of Toronto, Canada, carried the following headlines on May 12:

"New York Trading Pace is Slowest in Years"
"TSE Volume at Low Point in Almost Eight Years,"

thus indicating at that time that the bear market had not developed selling pressure, but was still very much a bear.

## PROPORTIONATE ANALYSIS

Leonardo da Pisa, known as Fibonacci, was an Italian mathematician who helped keep man's knowledge of mathematics alive during the Dark Ages.[5] He visited Egypt during the early part of the 13th century and came back with a *Summation Series*, which bears his name:

1-1-2-3-5-8-13-21-34-55-89-144, etc.

Elliott claimed that this number series was the basis of the Wave Principle. Walter E. White, a Canadian mathematician, has developed the subject, and this was originally published in the 1968 Elliott Wave Supplement.

At this point, it is probably sufficient to say that the sum of any two consecutive numbers gives the next highest number, and that the ratio of any number to the next below is 161.8 to 100. This relationship, 1.618:1, is a central part of the Wave Principle.

A. Hamilton Bolton in May 1960 said, "Should the 1949 market to date adhere to the Fibonacci formula, then the advance from 1949 to 1956 (361 points in the DJIA) should be complete when 583 points (161.8% of the 361 points) have been added to the 1957 low of 416, or to a total of 999 DJIA."

---

[5] Actually, he started a revolution in Western mathematics in the high Middle Ages by introducing Arabic numerals with place values in 1202.

This forecast was made almost six years before the great bull market peaked at approximately 1000 DJIA.

Applying the same formula to determine the extent of the current bear market, we get a number of possibilities, each indicating that a severe market lies directly ahead. Probing future possibilities is always a useful exercise.

A drop of 61.8% from the recorded high of 1000 DJIA would bring the Dow back to 381, its 1929 high. This doesn't seem probable, but on a Supercycle wave analysis basis, the current Cycle wave from 1966 should not overlap the 1929 high. Under the Elliott system, it is theoretically possible to have the current down thrust bounce off the 1929 high.

Should the current C-wave from December 2, 1968 (DJIA 986) drop 414 points (161.8% of the 1966 A-wave decline of 256 points), the market would bottom out at 572.[6]

If the same number of points (414) are deducted from the high of May 15, 1969, then the decline should be complete at 554, the Cuban Crisis low. If we take the drop of 176 points from May 15 to July 30 of 1969 and apply the formula, we have a possible drop of 285 points from any of a number of peaks:

| | |
|---|---|
| August 25, 1969 | 839 - 285 = 554; |
| September 2, 1969 | 839 - 285 = 554; |
| September 23, 1969 | 836 - 285 = 551; |
| November 10, 1969 | 861 - 285 = 576; |
| April 9, 1970 | 794 - 285 = 509. |

The 1956 high of 524 DJIA is the probable limit of the current bear market. It was at this level that the 1962 decline ended, and under Elliott's theory it represents a

[6] The hourly low for the Cycle wave IV bear market was 572.20 on December 9, 1974.

logical reversal point. This high is the terminus of wave (3) from 1949 to 1959, which was an extension of the move up from 1942 to 1966 (Figure 3).

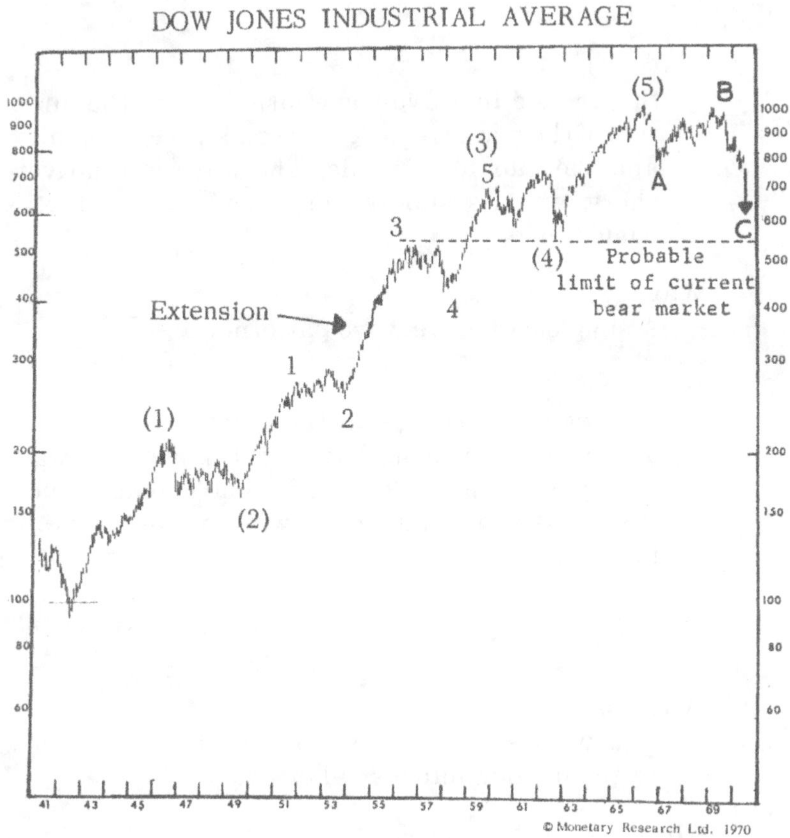


*Figure 3*

## ***ELLIOTT IN ACTION***

On April 9, 1970, the DJIA touched 794 and then declined to 677 by May 14, 1970, a drop of 117 points. This movement appears to be a complete wave of Minor degree, which under Elliott's rules will, in all probability, form part of the final five-wave pattern of Intermediate degree of wave C from December 2, 1968.

As this series of wave formations affords an excellent opportunity to study Elliott's rules in some depth, we have posted the hourly moves (Figure 4), and numbered the sub-Minor waves in order to scrutinize wave formations in minute detail.

Wave (1):
: Subdivided in a five-wave formation in the direction of the main trend. The second wave is complex, and the fourth is simple. The wave is relatively short, and its subdivisions conform to Elliott's basic tenets.

Wave (2):
: A simple corrective wave pattern.

Wave (3):
: This wave is the longest of the series, and is a perfect downward extension. Wave 2 is complex and wave 4 simple. Wave 3 is longest in time and amplitude, and breaks down into a five-wave pattern with the fifth extending.

Wave (4):
: A volatile ABC.

Wave (5):
: This wave subdivides as a five, with the first wave re-subdividing into a smaller five.

All waves in the above series conform to the Wave Principle and demonstrate the basic rhythm in the market — 134 hours of continuous trading without a flaw, reflecting that indefinable something which Elliott called the law of the market. In *The Wave Principle* (1938), he said, "The market has its law. Were there no law, there could be no center about which prices could revolve and, therefore, no market."

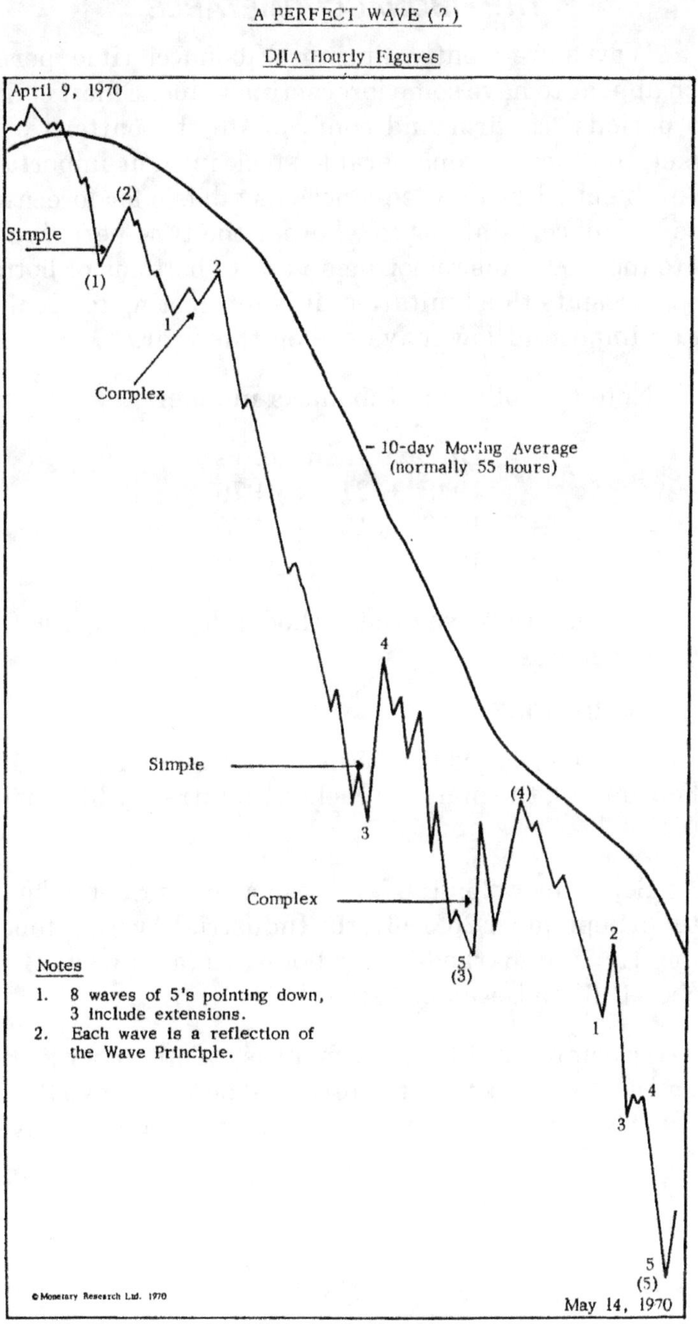
A PERFECT WAVE (?)
DJIA Hourly Figures
April 9, 1970
(2)
Simple
(1)
2
1
Complex
10-day Moving Average
(normally 55 hours)
4
Simple
3
(4)
Complex
5
(3)
Notes
1. 8 waves of 5's pointing down, 3 include extensions.
2. Each wave is a reflection of the Wave Principle.
2
1
4
3
5
(5)
©Monetary Research Ltd. 1970
May 14, 1970

*Figure 4*

## THE FIBONACCI TIMETABLE

Waves frequently fit into Fibonacci time periods, which appear to have some forecasting value. Elliott claimed time periods "confirm and conform" to the pattern of the market, and he put considerable stock in their importance. The problem with time sequences as a basis for forecasting is the lack of certainty as to whether the time periods cover tops to tops, bottoms to bottoms, tops to bottoms or bottoms to tops. Despite this limitation, it is interesting to speculate that an important low may develop this year.

Note the following Fibonacci numbers:

**Duration in years**
1949 + 21 = 1970
1957 + 13 = 1970
1962 + 8 = 1970.

October 1962 was the orthodox low of the 1962 Primary bear market.

### DURATION IN MONTHS

February 9, 1966 + 55 months = September 9, 1970. On February 9, the market reached an intraday high of over 1000.

September 26, 1967 + 34 months = September 28, 1970. On September 26, 1967, the Industrial Average touched 947 hourly, and marked the end of wave (a) of wave B from October 1966 to December 1968.

December 2, 1968 + 21 months = September 2, 1970. December 2 appears to be the terminal point of wave B, DJIA 986 hourly, and from this point, the big decline (wave C) started.

July 30, 1969 + 13 months = August 30, 1970. July 30 saw the end of a 176 point decline from May 15, 1969.

December 18, 1969 + 8 months = August 18, 1970. On December 18, the market started to rally, following a decline of almost 100 points. This rally ended January 5, 1970.

January 5, 1970 + 8 months = September 5, 1970.

April 9, 1970 + 5 months = September 9, 1970. April 9, 1970 is important, as it marks the end of a large inverted flat from July 30, 1969 to April 9, 1970, and appears to be the beginning of the end of the great bear market which started in February 9, 1966 at 1000 DJIA.

## ON CHANNELLING

Stock prices have a habit of hugging or following a base line. When considering an upward movement, the base trend line is drawn below the price curve connecting exposed reversal points, and in a bear market the base trend line is drawn above the price curve. To channel a movement, a parallel line is drawn above or below the base line connecting a reverse point or points, thus containing the trend within two parallel lines. A cycle move tends to travel within parallel planes, and may persist for years. After the completion of a fourth wave, channelling becomes quite significant.

Figure 5 shows the Industrial Average travelling within a comparatively wide channel. The hugging of the base line indicates strength of movement. A throw-over appears probable around the 550 level. Eventually, when prices break out of the channel on the upside[7], strong evidence will exist that the bear market (wave C) has been laid to rest.

---

[7] This is Frost's "stop" on his bearish opinion.

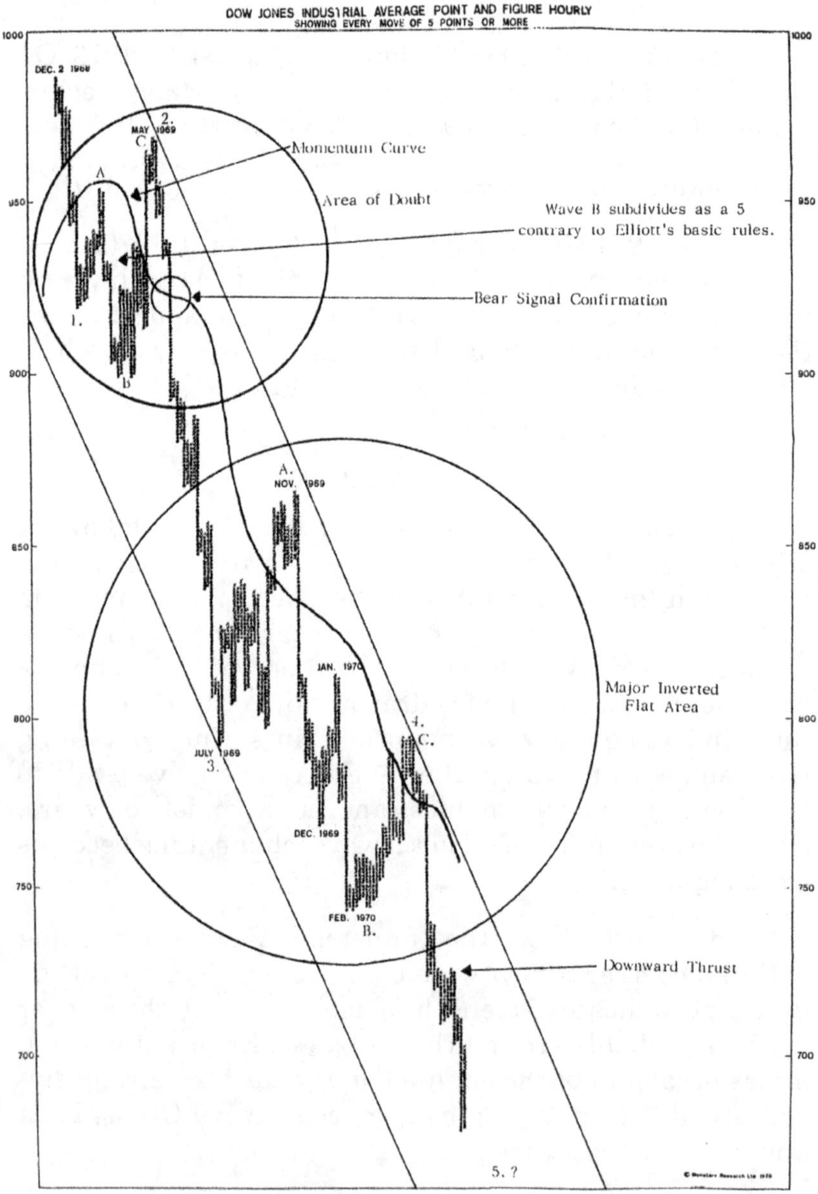

DOW JONES INDUSTRIAL AVERAGE POINT AND FIGURE HOURLY
SHOWING EVERY MOVE OF 5 POINTS OR MORE
1000
950
900
850
800
750
700
DEC. 2 1968
MAY 1969
2.
C
A
1.
B
Momentum Curve
Area of Doubt
Wave B subdivides as a 5 contrary to Elliott's basic rules.
Bear Signal Confirmation
A.
NOV. 1969
JAN. 1970
JULY 1969
3.
DEC. 1969
FEB. 1970
B.
4.
C.
Major Inverted Flat Area
Downward Thrust
5. ?


*Figure 5*

## *WAVE ANALYSIS - WAVE C IN PARTICULAR*

Under Elliott's rules, the market has been in a Cycle bear market since February 9, 1966. Wave A ran from February to October 1966, when wave B took over and ran to either December 1968 or possibly May 1969. The termination of wave B is in some doubt (Figure 5), as the decline from the December high subdivides as a 5-3-5 and the move up to May 15, 1969 resembles a five-wave pattern. Because of the failure of these waves to subdivide properly, doubt exists as to when wave B terminated. December 2, 1968, the actual high of 986 DJIA, has a better look than the final May 15, 1969 peak of 968, and is supported by the wave formations of Standard and Poor's 500-stock Index. Although we have some reservations about it, we are accepting 986 DJIA as the orthodox high and terminal point of wave B.

Although it was difficult at the time to determine when and where wave C started, the fact that the averages penetrated the momentum curve on June 9, 1969, appears to confirm the view that the market has commenced its final Primary descent.

Wave C from December 1968 to date is shown in Figures 5 and 6 on a point and figure hourly basis, showing all moves of five points or more. The Intermediate waves have been numbered to indicate the wave formations under Elliott's rules. Wave C is the final wave of the ABC wave of Cycle dimension, and accordingly should subdivide into a 5-3-5-3-5 pattern, with the fifth wave also breaking down into a 5-3-5-3-5 series of Minor waves. What to watch for now is the fifth wave of the fifth wave from April 9, 1970.[8]

---

[8] This is an excellent and accurate conclusion of the market's structure. The "fifth wave of the fifth wave" was underway and about to terminate. It did so at 631.16 on May 22, 1970. His target, however, wasn't met for another 4½ years.

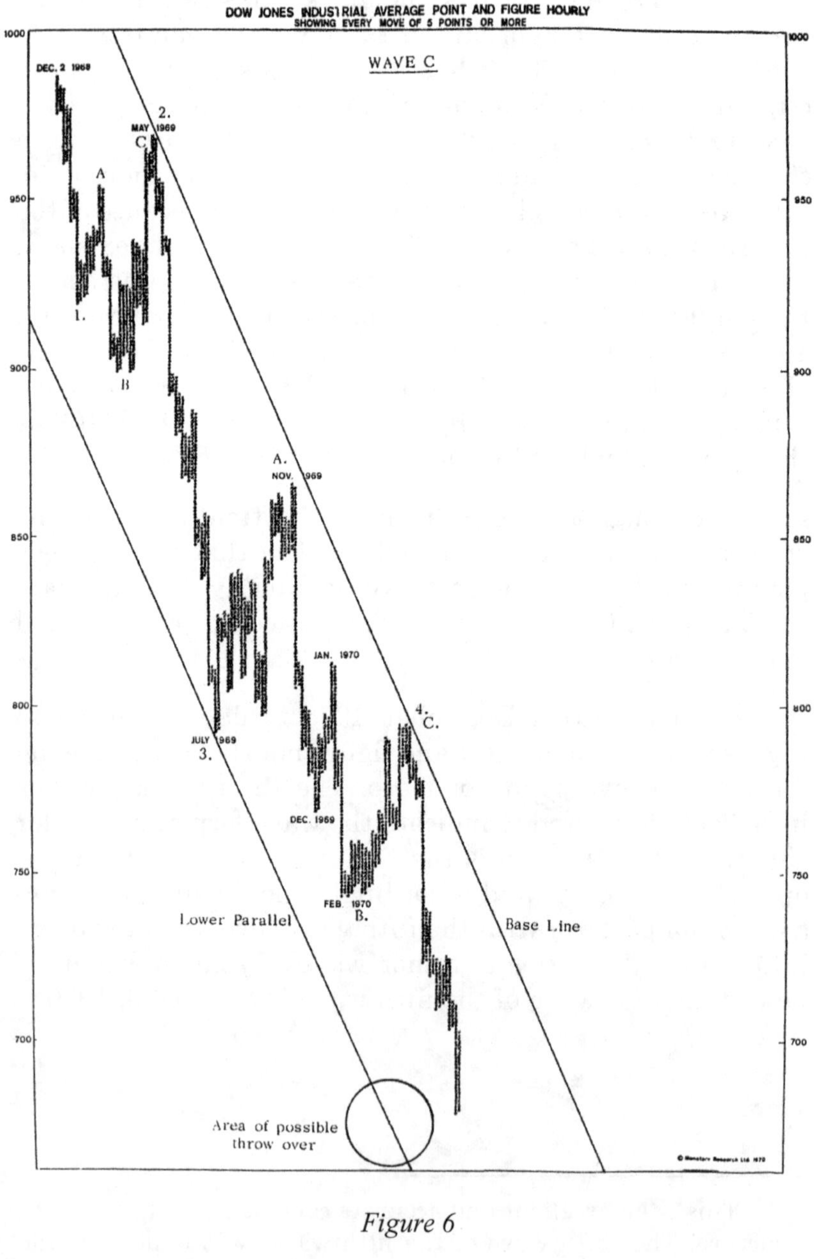
DOW JONES INDUSTRIAL AVERAGE POINT AND FIGURE HOURLY
SHOWING EVERY MOVE OF 5 POINTS OR MORE
WAVE C
1000
950
900
850
800
750
700
DEC. 2 1968
1.
A
B
C
2.
MAY 1969
3.
JULY 1969
A.
NOV. 1969
DEC. 1969
JAN. 1970
FEB. 1970
B.
4.
C.
Lower Parallel
Base Line
Area of possible
throw over

*Figure 6*

Wave C has subdivided to date as follows:

| WAVE | FROM | TO |
|---|---|---|
| 1) | 986 December 2, 1968 | 920 January 8, 1969 |
| 2) | 920 January 8, 1969 | 968 May 15, 1969 |
| 2a) | 920 January 8, 1969 | 952 February 14, 1969 |
| 2b) | 952 February 14, 1969 | 899 February 26, 1969 |
| 2c) | 899 February 26, 1969 | 968 May 15, 1969 |
| 3) | 968 May 15, 1969 | 792 July 30, 1969 |
| 4) | 792 July 30, 1969 | 794 April 9, 1970 |
| 4a) | 792 July 30, 1969 | 860 November 10, 1969 |
| 4b) | 860 November 10, 1969 | 743 February 3, 1970 |
| 4c) | 743 February 3, 1970 | 794 April 9, 1970 |
| 5) | 794 April 9, 1970 | ? |

## *THRUSTS*

A flat formation is generally followed by dynamic market action, which Elliott called a thrust. Within a thrust, corrections are usually subnormal in character, giving impetus to each successive move up or down. Inverted flats are followed by downward thrusts. Triangles have the same technical implications as flats in generating strong market action.

One of the most potent inverted flat formations in stock market history developed between July 30, 1969 and April 9, 1970 (Figure 5). This correction is subnormal in amplitude, but of more than eight months duration. The current downward thrust stems from this unusually strong bearish formation and implies that the market should continue on its downward course for a few more months.[9]

---

[9] Frost's comments about the inverted flat implying downside power were true, as the market literally crashed thereafter. That crash denied his expectation of "a few more months" down because the market in its final days covered immense ground in a brief period. In fact, it bottomed the day after the publication date of this Supplement. The spike low, however, nicely fulfilled the "possible throw over" comment on Figure 6.

## *RULES TO REMEMBER*

A few guidelines are sometimes of great help in assessing market behavior and in determining wave counts. The main rules are:

1) Wave 3 is usually the largest in any series of impulse movements. It is seldom the shortest.

2) Wave 4 should not drop below the top of wave 1.

3) The first wave of a series (including corrective series) is usually the shortest.

4) Frequently the first and fifth waves of wave C are about equal in time and magnitude.

5) Waves may deploy or stretch out. All waves are highly flexible.

6) In a bull market, corrective waves tend to be erratic and difficult to count. In a bear market, corrective waves are usually quite regular and easy to count.

## *QUESTIONS AND ANSWERS*

Q. Is Elliott's theory an authentic approach to market analysis?

A. Yes. The Wave Principle has a mathematical base. Post an hourly line chart of the DJIA and you will observe hundreds of significant Elliott patterns over a period of several months. Many technical patterns, such as "Head and Shoulders," are Elliott patterns, and their significance depends on its basic tenets, not on technical analysis. Below is an illustration.

**HEAD AND SHOULDERS**

For example, breaking the neck line will not necessarily be followed by a decline. The exact opposite may be true, although technical analysis will call for a further drop after a pull back to the neck line.

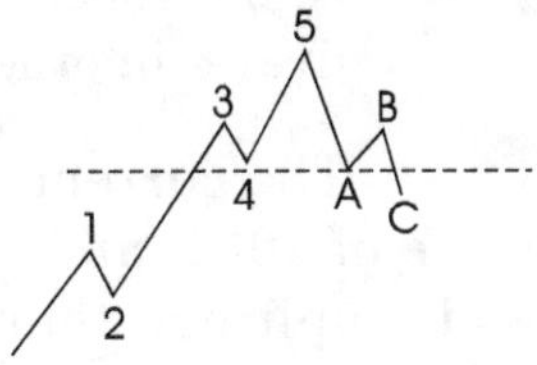


Q. Any comments on the mathematical principle?

A. Walter E. White, who is both a mathematician and an economist, has concluded that the long-term economic patterns tie in with the Elliott concept of growth (see the 1968 Supplement).

Q. Has Elliott been right about the market?

A. Yes. The 1966 slide of 256 points has been consistently recognized as the first phase of a Cycle bear market. The Elliott conclusions reached in the 1968 Supplement, dated June 21, 1968, were as follows:

> 1) "The move up from October 1966 does not appear to be the beginning of a bull market of Cycle degree. It does not have the right look or count under Elliott's rules to be classified as other than a move against the main trend."
>
> 2) "The next Cycle bull market needs a base. A base has not been completed, as the 1966 decline was a five-wave affair, and therefore only the first wave of a larger pattern. A full corrective pattern is never a five."
>
> 3) "The low of the market should form below the 740 DJIA level, and quite conceivably could reach the 554 level registered at the time of the Cuban crisis."

4) "The current up wave is expected to exhaust itself below 1000 DJIA, since the down wave in 1966 was a five — in other words, the first wave of a zigzag."

The current wave C is one degree above the small c wave of 1962, and therefore should be more severe in time and amplitude than the 1962 bear market. It should also be greater than the 256 point drop of wave A of 1966, its companion wave in the current cycle. The first wave of any series is usually the shortest in time and amplitude.

Q. If the fifth wave of a series extends, will the fifth wave of this extension also extend or subdivide into a five?

A. Yes, it is possible. One never knows about extensions. Volume will sometimes give a dependable clue, but not always. For example, if volume increases in the fifth wave and keeps on increasing with each new impulse, the span of the fifth wave will usually increase and theoretically keep on until exhausted. Elliott illustrated spans of the fifth wave of several degrees in a diagram published in *Financial World* in 1939.

SPANS OF THE 5th WAVE
OF THE SEVERAL DEGREES INDICATED

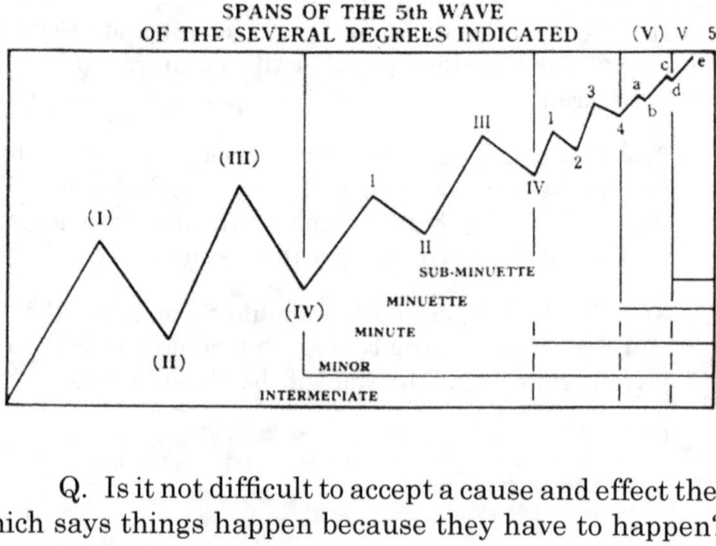


Q. Is it not difficult to accept a cause and effect theory which says things happen because they have to happen?

A. Yes, indeed. Esotericism is difficult to comprehend. Elliott seems to join esotericism with mathematics and empirical evidence. Let us not forget that there may be a little bit of truth in everything. It is pointless to sweep something under the rug because we do not comprehend its rationale.

Q. Would you rely solely on Elliott?

A. Elliott theory is only one tool, but it gives better perspective than most market tools.

Q. What market tool would you rank second?

A. Technically speaking, breadth.

Q. Where does Dow Theory fit?

A. Dow Theory and Elliott theory have certain similarities. Dow Theory, by its very nature, is a late indicator while Elliott is an on-the-spot indicator. Dow Theory is more significant within an Elliott context. Both are wave theories or trend theories, call them what you will. The prudent investor should not disregard the implications of Dow Theory, and the same applies to Elliott. In explaining his theory, Dow used the simile of the tide and the waves which rolled over the beaches, and how each wave would move up a little further until tidal action (the Primary trend) retracted. This is also the basis of the Elliott Wave Principle, which Elliott developed into a rational method of analysis.

Q. Charles H. Dow adopted as a fundamental tenet that any signal, to be authentic, must be confirmed by two averages, the Industrials and the Rails. Is confirmation essential?

A. Elliott theory does not depend on a confirmation of two averages. Confirmation is an integral part of Dow Theory, and it is in this area that Dow Theory can be helpful to the Elliott theorist. No one average consistently reflects the underlying tendency of the market to subdivide into Elliott patterns. Elliott, at one point, tried to develop his own average, but the records do not seem to be available. As the perfect index will never be developed, the analyst should apply the Elliott Wave Principle to other averages for confirmation, and he should regard both Dow Theory and Elliott theory as different methods of studying the same ocean and its engulfing tides.

Dow developed his theory under inflexible credit conditions. Elliott developed his theory under much more favourable circumstances. If Elliott's theory had been developed prior to Dow's studies, the chances are that Dow would have added to Elliott's basic tenets rather than develop a separate theory of market action. Apart from confirmation, Dow Theory is a splinter concept of Elliott. On the other hand, if Dow hadn't preceded Elliott with his basic analysis, the Elliott Wave Principle might never have been "discovered."

Q. When are Dow signals most effective?

A. When the second wave is of Primary or Intermediate degree, using Elliott's terminology, Dow sell signals of 1929, 1937, 1962 and 1966 were most effective. Signals were less effective in 1953 and 1957. Elliott and Dow are complementary wave theories. Reading the two theories together can prevent a whipsaw.

Wave B of wave II within the general context of waves will almost invariably be followed by a five-wave down, but the resulting wave C may not produce enough of a correction[10] to allow the investor to sell and get back in. Elliott counts should be followed closely by the investor to assess the weight to be attached to Dow Theory signals, and, by the same token, Elliott theorists should have due regard for the basic tenets of Dow Theory.

---

[10] "...below the low of wave A to allow the Dow Theory investor..." is what he means.

Consider the following diagram:

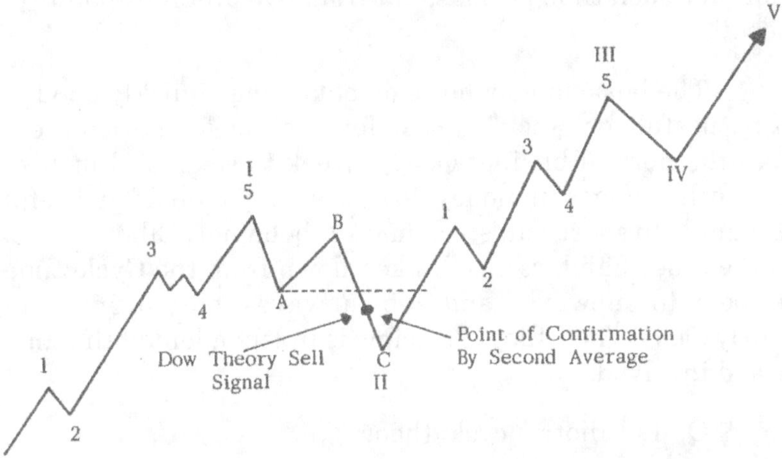


Q. The current bear market is the most severe since 1929. Is there any special reason for this?

A. The current phase is a once in a generation situation. The Cycle from 1966 relates to the entire movement from 1942 to 1966, and is of the same degree under the Elliott system. The carnage of the 1966-1970 bear Cycle should build a base for a long upward movement. The present situation will not likely be repeated for many years to come.

Q. Is investing an art or a science?

A. Security analysis is mainly scientific, but market analysis is more of an art. Elliott theory is a blending of both.

Q. Does Elliott theory tie in with bank credit analysis?

A. In many ways, yes. Bank credit analysis is a study of the cyclical and super-cyclical forces of money and credit which underlie the basic cyclical and supercyclical movements in stock prices. The Elliott Wave Principle has a cyclical and supercyclical counterpart of these same forces. Empirically,

Elliott Wave and bank credit analysis have tied in extremely well over such time periods, but from two different points of view.[11]

The basic money flows do not change quickly enough to be useful for stock market forecasting for periods less than the normal business cycle. Week-to-week and month-to-month changes in money flows are not particularly useful as a guide to short-run stock market behavior. Elliott Wave, on the other hand, can be broken down from the Cycle time period into subwaves and sub-subwaves, etc., even to an hourly basis. The Elliott Principle is independent of the time period involved.

Q. Is Elliott a cycle theory?

A. The Elliott Wave Principle is a wave theory, not a cycle theory. Waves have a high degree of flexibility. The Principle does not depend on periodicity. Five-wave patterns may extend, and any phase of a three-wave correction may expand or double up.

Q. Is it necessary to keep hourly charts?

A. Yes. It is the only way the analyst can study the Principle and read its minor subdivisions. If a wave does not subdivide properly or in the manner anticipated, it places the interpreter on notice that something may be wrong with his count. The Elliotter should also keep hourly point and figure charts and a short-term moving average (10 days, or 55 hours). For instance, it was most difficult to read the hourly moves from February 2 to April 9 of this year, but the hourly moving average indicated a five-up and the probable end of the large inverted flat from July 30, 1969. Hourly figures are helpful.

---

[11] Bank credit is probably extended for the same reason the stock market rises: an increase in general optimism.

Q. If the DJIA penetrates the 1956 highs, what then?

A. Under the tenets of the Principle, the Industrial Average should go lower, but the Dow should hold above the 1929 high of 381. On a Grand Supercycle basis, the current bear market should not overlap the Supercycle high of 381.

Q. When a new bull market starts, where do you think it will end?

A. Considerably above its 1966 high of approximately 1000, possibly as high as 2000 by 1973 or 1974. It will depend on the monetary climate.

Q. Do you see any grounds for optimism over the next few months?

A. Technically, no. Fundamentally, no.

Q. I am holding disaster stocks on margin. What should I do?

A. I hope the message is clear by now. Elliott Wave theory is telling us that the market is probably going to go a lot lower.

Q. Can Elliott stand on its own feet, independent of other tools?

A. Technically, I believe it can, but fundamentally, it offers the best answers when combined with other tools, such as those developed and published in *The Bank Credit Analyst*.

Q. Is the stock market a random walk?

A. The market is random to those who do not understand it. Randomness is peculiar to our own limitations, not that of the stock market.

Q. Will the stock market turn up ahead of the economy?

A. I think so. Possibly the lead will be greater this time. It could be as long as 12 months.

Q. Do you anticipate that the market will bottom out quietly?

A. No. We are in a downward thrust in Elliott's terms. The market may be trying to reach the point it would have reached had it not been for the massive injection of credit following the abandonment of restrictive policies after the 1966 bear market. Thrusts are not dull, and do not end on dullness.

Q. Will a selling climax clear the air?

A. Between March 15, 1962 and May 29, 1962, three selling climaxes developed, with each climax going deeper into oversold territory. The first selling climax marked the end of an Intermediate wave down. The low of the market did not occur until late in June 1962. I expect the end of wave C will be climactic[12], and the best way I know of detecting the final bottom is to keep hourly charts. Hourly charts help one to get the feel of the market. The Cuban crisis low was a fifth wave of the third degree, as was the 1966 low. Hourly line charts and point & figure charts only take a minute a day to post. They are worth their weight in gold. Bar charts are not very helpful.

Q. I note that Elliotters occasionally change their wave counts. Any comment?

[12] It certainly was.

A. Oliver Cromwell once said, "You must believe that you may be wrong." The Elliott Wave Principle is a fantastic tool, especially when the market is moving impulsively, although one can never tell for certain when a wave will extend or subdivide in some unexpected way. It is easy to count in retrospect, and it is not too difficult to identify major turning points *at the time.* Intermediate counting is always difficult because of the flexibility of wave trends.

Q. Of what value is Elliott so far as individual stocks are concerned ?

A. Very slight value, but on occasion, wave analysis can be helpful.

**April 6, 1974 The Financial Post**

# Trick is to spot that Elliott wave

*Peter Brimelow*

*Nature and her Laws lay hid in night*
*God said, Let Newton Be, and all was light*

A.J. Frost is far too judicious to apply Pope's epigram to R.N. Elliott's work on the stock market.

But he does say Elliott's theory that a certain regularity, or "wave," underlies all nature is "fascinating, almost a philosophy." And he shakes his head sympathetically as he tells you that: "Poor Elliott became obsessed with it, started seeing it in everything."

Frost, of Manotick, Ont., has been described as "the greatest living interpreter" of the Elliott Wave Theory by one of its famous U.S. exponents, Richard Russell, publisher of the *Dow Theory Letter*.

Elliott's theory applies only to the U.S. Dow-Jones Industrial Average. Among Frost's predictions made in conversation with FP some weeks ago[13]: Another market break is imminent, parallel to last fall's 200-point drop on the Dow from its high 900s.

A ragged, zigzag pattern in 1974 will be interpreted as summer and year-end rallies.

The U.S. stock market is in a five-wave downward move from the Jan. 11, 1973, high; this downward move could go below the May, 1970, low of 627.5 sometime in 1975.

But then the market will move upwards until probably 1983, breaking 2,000 on the way. This will be the fifth, upward wave of the dominating sequence which began in 1932 (see chart).

Why?

Because that's the way it is, reply Elliott wave theorists.

The idea that the universe follows certain patterns which can be expressed numerically is ancient, going beyond Pythagoras to the builders of the great pyramids. It was after a visit to Egypt that the 13th century Italian mathematician Fibonacci developed his sequence of numbers in which each is derived by adding the two preceding – 1, 2, 3, 4, 8, 13 – so that the ratio of each to the next tends toward the "golden ratio" of 0.618.

**Nature study**

This relationship surfaces in many aspects of nature – the structure of seashells, the rhythm of seed germination, and (according to Elliotters) the apparently inexorable nature of the economic cycle.

R.N. Elliott, writing in the 1930s, claimed to have perceived the Fibonacci sequence in stock-price movements.

---

[13] The Dow made its high for the year the previous month.

# Where we are in the 'supercycle'

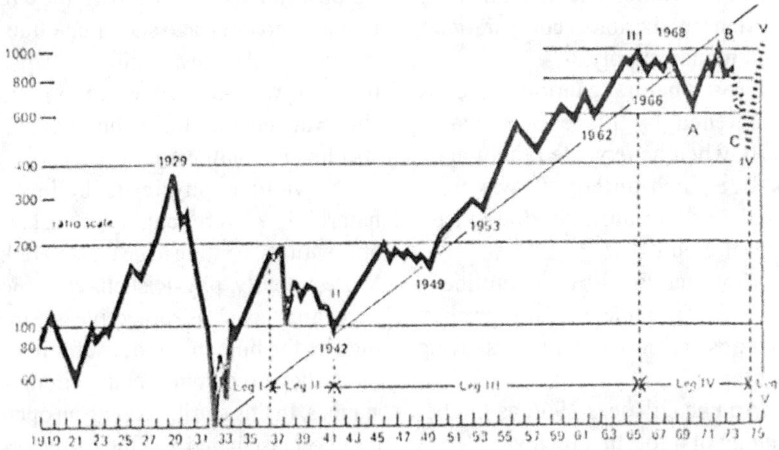


He expressed this as a five-stage rising movement, the first, third and fifth of which go up, joined by the second and fourth which go down. After this comes a downward thrust of three stages, the middle one being a recovery.

But the theory is much more complicated, since each wave is subdivided, and the subdivisions in turn are subdivided – sometimes. So that although Elliott followers are inclined to talk about "supercycles" which last for decades, in fact they regard hourly price movement charts as indispensable for watching how the waves divide.

"Elliott is not a fixed-periodicity theory," Frost says. He means that the waves are of varying length. There are also a host of other possible difficulties, such as "extensions" and "inverted flats," which mean that Elliott followers have to be constantly revising their views.

Frost, however, is quietly confident. He says he's made a considerable amount of money following it, and that it enabled him to pick out "to the hour" the low in the Cuba crisis crash of 1962.

Frost can afford to be confident. His own approach involves extensive use of other technical aids, especially market breadth, and although he's enough of a technician to assert flatly that "the stock market is not a random walk," he prefers fundamental and technical factors to confirm each other before he buys.

Frost was also a vice-president with the Montreal investment counseling firm of Bolton, Tremblay & Co. at a time when the late Hamilton Bolton, who first interested him in the theory, was developing the bank credit-money supply approach still followed by the widely respected *Bank Credit Analyst* service that Bolton founded.

The vagaries of credit policy, in fact, make life very difficult for Elliott followers. The original work was done in a period of comparatively fixed money supply.

Frost's natural caution is greatly heightened by his experience in 1970, when he expected the market to slide much further. "It was truncated," he explains, "by the expansion of credit."

However, Frost's basic outline in 1970 remains intact – he was predicting a possible move to 1,000, starting that fall.

And he still sees 1966 as the beginning of a fourth, downward leg, a view that the current market certainly hasn't put to rest.

One advantage of Elliott Wave Theory is that it encourages an extremely long investment perspective. The supercycles cover lifetimes, and students like Frost follow it as much out of artistic interest as for trading purposes. This may be why they're prepared to envisage such huge fluctuations – the devastating collapse of 1929, whose relative proportions show up on our logarithmic scale, still haunts them.

Newtonian physicists believed nature's laws were actually unmistakable entities, waiting to be discovered. More recently, physicists have come to regard "laws" as subjective groupings by the human mind, useful in as far as they predict in specific circumstances. In this spirit, keeping an open mind yet fascinated by Elliott's underlying vision, Frost continues to keep his hourly charts. He talks to other members of the Elliott community, but is shy of publicity and pursues a successful career far removed from the fluctuating market.

*Elliott Wave theorist A.J. Frost traces the current stock market "supercycle" back to the lows of 1932. The first upward move ended with the Dow-Jones industrial average peak at 196 in 1937, and was followed by a second, downward move to the low of 1942. The third, upward move culminated in the 1966 high – exceeding 1,000 on an intraday basis – and the fourth, downward move is still in progress. Frost regards the Jan. 11, 1973, peak (B) as a peculiarity of a "flat" three-stage correction, in which the second peak sometimes exceeds the original high. That the Dow is still in a bear cycle can be seen from the fact it has shipped below the long-term trend line. For clarity, subdivisions have been omitted from this chart, with the exception of the characteristic three-stage correction (A, B, C) which Frost says is shaping up within the fourth move.*

# *THE ELLIOTT WAVE PRINCIPLE IN RICHARD RUSSELL'S DOW THEORY LETTERS*

## *1964 - 1980*

# *RUSSELL ON STOCKS & BONDS*

**July 2, 1964**

On June 30, Burroughs rose a whopping 10%, pushing above the base-like rectangle pattern which has contained the stock for the past 7 months. The breakout was accompanied by heavy volume and a definite reversal to the upside in the stock's relative strength. One point of particular interest in BGH is the fact that the collapse since the 1962 high has taken the form of five distinct legs (as marked on chart). This

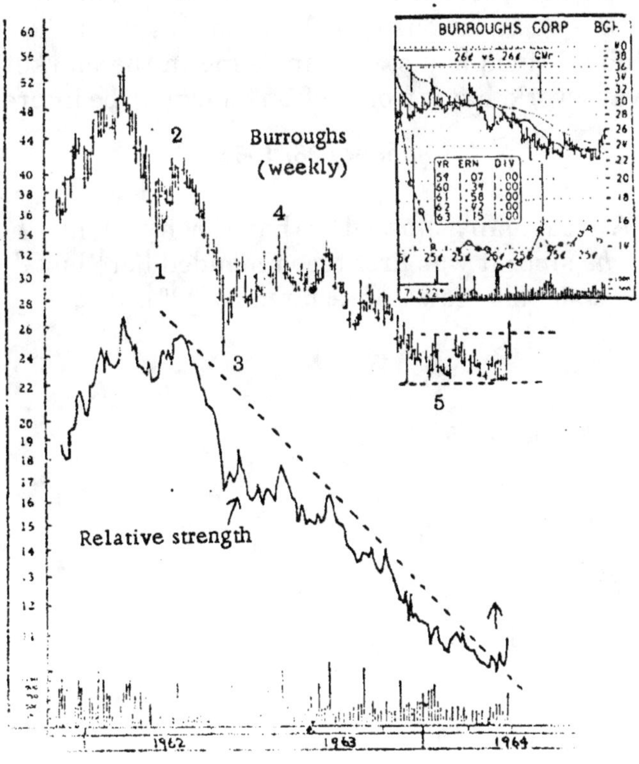

five-leg pattern is often associated with the *completion* of a major movement in a stock and it is, for instance, the formation which appeared in the Bucyrus-Erie decline. While such observations are, of course, strictly theoretical, it is possible that BGH has completed a major bear market of its own and is now ready to embark on a new bull phase. At worst, last week's breakout from point 5 suggests that a major (upward) correction in BGH is now underway. If such a correction succeeds in retracing only half of the ground lost since the 1962 high, it could take BGH to the 38 area. I continue to view purchases in BGH as an intelligent speculation.

**July 14, 1964**

Many readers expressed interest in last week's discussion of "five major legs" as the probable completion of a major movement (see Burroughs in the last Letter). This, of course, is from the observations of R.N. Elliott back in the 1930s. The Elliott Principle (as with anything in the market) does not always work, but it works often enough to be interesting.

**January 28, 1965**

A great many subscribers have been patiently holding *Burroughs* since it was first recommended here last June at 24. This issue has now appreciated by 33%.

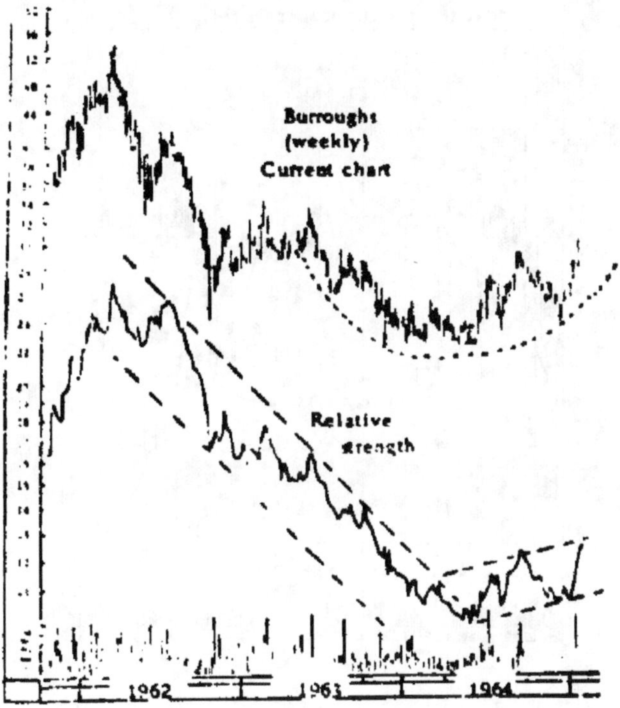


**May 4, 1965**

Back [on July 2, 1964] when I first started recommending Burroughs, I included a long-term (monthly) chart. This chart traced a major *five-step decline*. At that time I wrote (BGH was 24): "One point of particular interest in BGH is the fact that the collapse since the 1962 high has taken the form of *five distinct legs* (as marked on the chart). This five-leg pattern is often associated with the *completion* of a major movement in a stock, and it is, for instance, the formation which appeared during the Bucyrus-Erie decline." BGH subsequently rose 50%.

Obviously the action in BGH does not necessarily have to repeat in other issues. However, one stock which I have been watching with great interest is Fansteel Metallurgical Corp. FNL has undergone one of the most perfect five-leg collapses on the board (see monthly chart). FNL during early

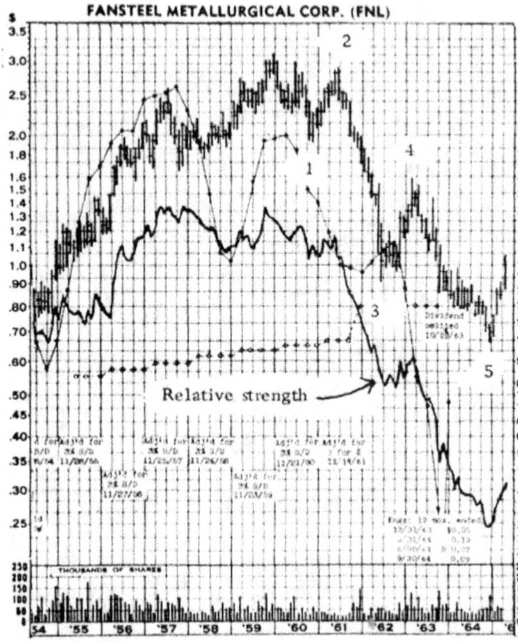


1965 touched what was probably its lowest level of market "popularity" (relative strength) in history — as seen on the chart. In other words, FNL is a stock which has to all purposes completed a major bear market and dropped to an extreme in unpopularity. Between 1959 and 1964, in fact, FNL lost almost 80% of its market value.

**May 13, 1965**

*Fansteel*, recommended in the last Letter, jumped a full 10% (!) on April 11 to a new high. The stock needs a rest, but it acts as if it wants to keep going.

**March 20, 1968**

I have often[1] referred to the Elliott Wave Theory. This is the theory which holds that all markets occur in

---

[1] He *used* it often, as he says later, but he had referred to it only a few times up to this point.

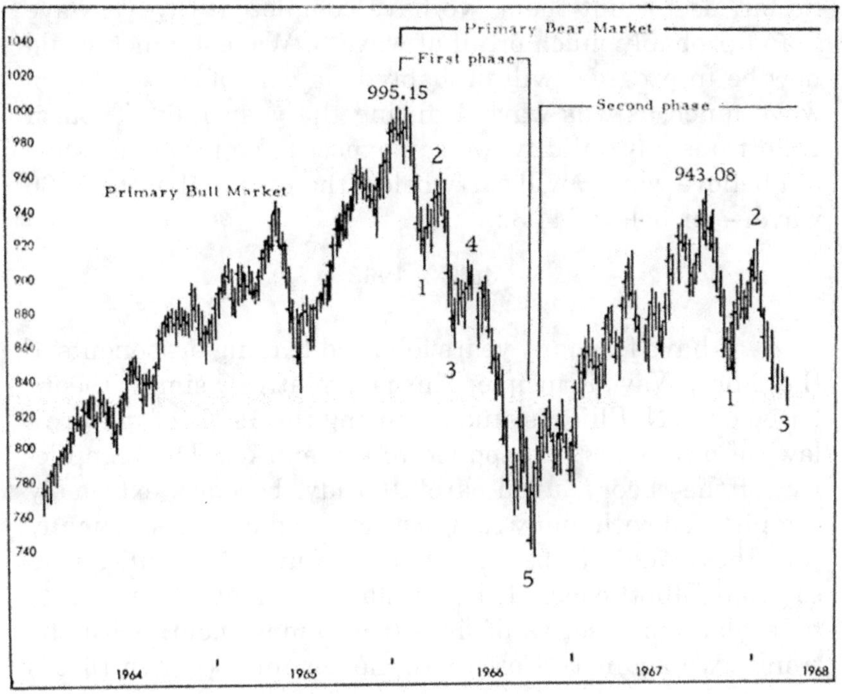


five waves. Three waves in the direction of the main trend and two waves counter to the main trend. Although Elliott considered his five-wave thesis to be an immutable rule, I would prefer shying away from any fixed rules as applied to the stock market. Nevertheless, the five-wave pattern does repeat so often in stock market movements that it is worth taking up at this time.

Note that the first phase of the bear market was completed in five definite waves. I have numbered these five waves on the chart. The fifth wave ended at the 744.32 low of October 1966. The resultant correction to the 1967 high took the form of a very complicated three wave correction and extension.

Now note that I have drawn the movement down from the 943.08 1967 high in the form of three distinct waves.

So far, as I count them, we have completed wave 1, wave 2 and probably much or all of wave 3. Wave 4 which could now be in progress will probably be a sort of consolidation wave much as was wave 4 during the year 1966. Then, if Elliott has any validity, we can expect to go into final wave 5. I believe wave 5 will carry below the terminal of the 1966 wave — or below 744.32.

**July 3, 1968**

I have for many years followed leading proponents of the Elliott Wave Principle. This is a relatively simple theory based on R.N. Elliott's studies during the 1930s of "nature's law" of movements as applied to the market. The "simplicity" of the theory, upon careful study, becomes extremely complicated with many ramifications and nuances, so many that they could not begin to be taken up here. Suffice it to say that Elliott concluded that major (primary) movements take place in a series of fives (three movements with the trend, two against). Corrective movements occur in threes (two with the trend and one against the trend).

I had correspondence with Hamilton Bolton regarding the Wave theory prior to that brilliant man's death a few years ago. I also had some correspondence with one of Elliott's most brilliant successors, A.J. Frost.

Bolton believed that a major upward cycle ended in 1966 at 995.15 (closing) on the Dow. He then expected a full downward correction (bear market) from the 1966 high to some future low point perhaps in the 550 to 700 area. Bolton felt that the 1966 decline represented wave A, that an upward corrective wave B would follow (B is perhaps just now being completed). Then a final downward C wave would complete the bear market. The final C wave (which could now be beginning) would take the form of a five-wave: three downward waves and two correcting upward waves. This final C wave should be of greater extent than the first A downward wave (i.e., greater than the 1966 decline).

A.J. Frost differed with Bolton in interpretation. Frost believed that the great bull market started in 1942 (Bolton thought 1949). Frost believed the first bull wave ended in 1946 at 212, then a corrective wave took the Dow back to the 1949 low of 161. Wave 3 then carried to the 1960 Dow high of 685. From the 1960 high, Frost believed that a complicated, "consolidation" wave (wave 4) was in progress. The A part of Frost's wave 4 took the Dow from the 1960 high of 685 to the 1962 low of 535. The B part of this irregular correction took the Dow to the 1966 high of 995.15. From the 1966 high, Frost expected a final C wave down, a C wave broken into five parts which might take the Dow back to the neighborhood of the 1962 low (i.e., the mid-500s on the Dow). Following this completion of corrective wave 4, Frost expected a final great fifth leg up, and this fifth leg or wave would complete the bull market.

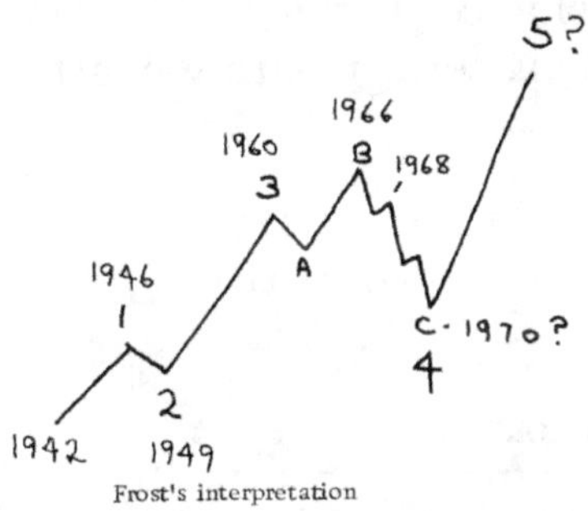

Frost's interpretation

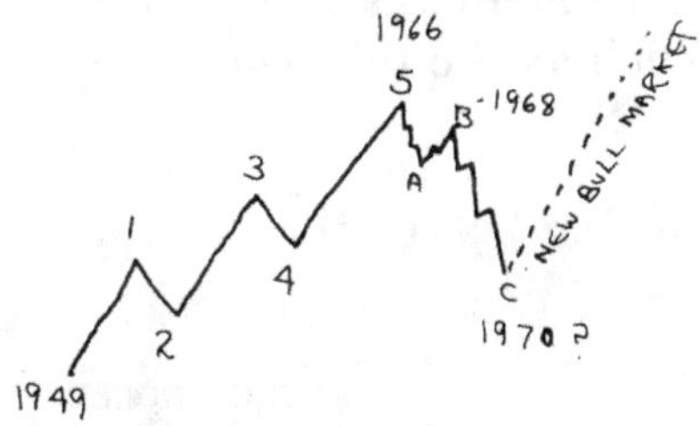

Bolton's Interpretation

The difference between Bolton's and Frost's interpretation is that Bolton expected the next C wave down to complete the bear market (Bolton felt that the bull market ended in 1966), and that following the next major wave down from here, a new Supercycle bull market would begin.

From the practical standpoint, both Frost and Bolton are now pointing to danger in that both would expect that we are now seeing an important corrective wave. Frost would say that we are about to see the end of corrective wave 4, leading to the final upward bull wave 5 (completing the whole bull market which started in 1942). Bolton would say that we are about to see the final part of the bear market which started in 1966, and that following this we will begin a totally new bull market.

## November 15, 1968

I have often referred to the Elliott Wave Principle, a theory of pattern which Elliott believed had a basis in the very nature of things. Elliott noted that a great many upward movements could be divided into five waves (three waves up known as the 1, 3 and 5 waves and two waves down known as the 2 and 4 waves). Conversely, down movements could be divided into three waves (wave 1 and 3 down and wave 2 up).

In my own experience, this type of action is seen too often to be discounted as mere chance. Often the Elliott movements can be seen best on long-term monthly charts such as the two below.

On Anchor Hocking, we see a long wave 1 and a *complicated* correction for wave 2. Usually if corrective wave 2

**ANCHOR HOCKING GLASS CORP.**

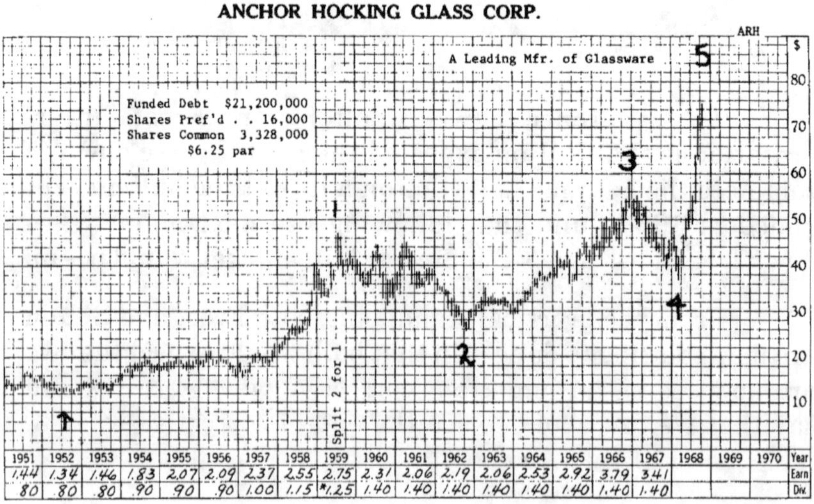

is complicated, the wave 4 correction can be expected to be simple, and if wave 2 is simple, wave 4 will be complex. To continue, upward wave 3 took ARH to the 1966 high, whereupon a simple wave 4 correction was seen. Wave 5 up is now in progress and as Elliott observed, the last or 5 *wave* is likely to be the *speculative* one. There is little doubt of the speculative intensity of the current wave 5 in ARH.

Commercial Solvents produced a wave 1 up starting in 1957. The corrective wave 2 was rather complex. A wave 3 up took CV to the 1961 high, and a simple corrective wave 4 plunged CV to the 1962 low. The final wave 5 started out conservatively enough, but after backing off in 1965, wave 5 ended with a typical wild speculative explosion. Following wave 5, CV entered into a major bear market, and between 1966 and 1968, CV dropped from 79 to the mid-20s.

This study is particularly interesting since it shows two stocks currently at very different stages of their cycle, one in the (probable) final blow-off stage and one in a major bear market collapse.

**COMMERCIAL SOLVENTS CORP.** ★

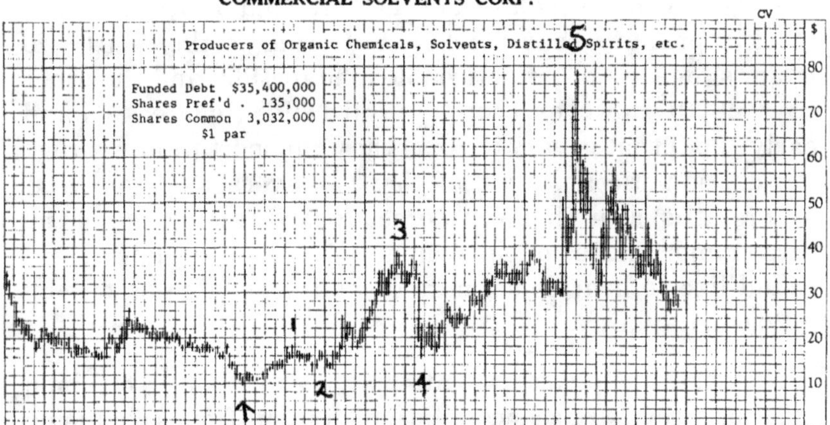


| 1952 | 1953 | 1954 | 1955 | 1956 | 1957 | 1958 | 1959 | 1960 | 1961 | 1962 | 1963 | 1964 | 1965 | 1966 | 1967 | 1968 | 1969 | 1970 | 1971 | Year |
|---|---|---|---|---|---|---|---|---|---|---|---|---|---|---|---|---|---|---|---|---|
| .52 | 1.01 | 1.01 | 1.31 | 1.07 | .53 | .52 | 1.02 | 1.70 | 1.90 | 2.00 | 2.00 | 2.24 | 2.21 | 2.05 | 1.42 | | | | | Earn |
| 1.00 | 1.00 | 1.00 | 1.00 | 1.00 | .93 | .28 | *.25 | *.50 | *.65 | *.80 | .83 | 1.10 | 1.20 | 1.20 | 1.20 | | | | | Div. |

* and small stock div.

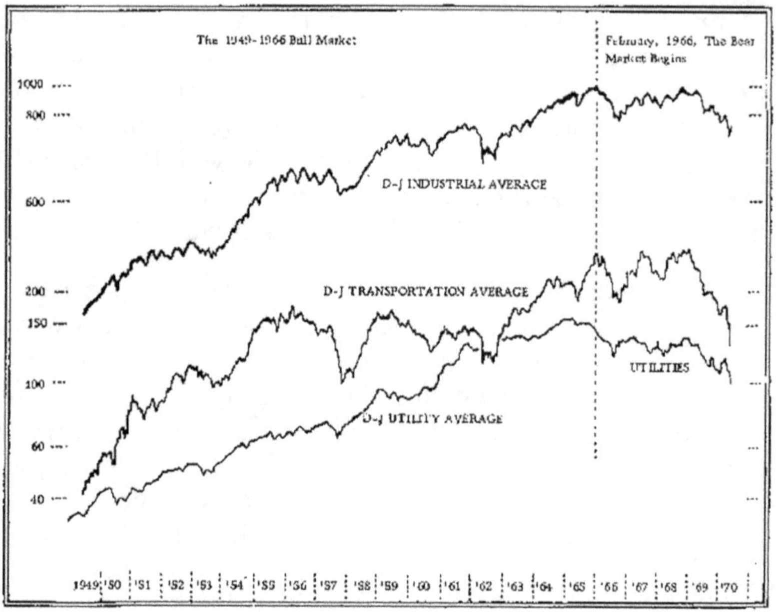


**September 16, 1970**

Last week, I received a letter from a gentleman at a large New York bank, and the letter raises an important question which deserves answering here. He writes: "I have been particularly interested in your comments to the effect that we now have seen two of the three major declines that mark a primary bear market. Referring to the chart two major slides are quite noticeable (one in 1966 and the other in 1969-70). However, there is a third slide (in late 1967 and early 1968) that is very clear in the Transportation Average but not so noticeable in the other two averages. From your letters, it is clear that you do not regard this as one of the three major phases of the primary bear market; however, I would like to hear some more of your reasoning as to why it does not qualify."

Now I believe this gentleman is expressing a common misconception, a misconception which stems from a confusion between Dow Theory and the Elliott Wave Theory. Let me attempt to clarify. Elliott (writing in the 1930s) believed that bull movements occurred in a five-step series of upward zigzags, three rising waves and two declining wave corrections. He believed that bear movements occurred in a three-step, downward zigzag, two declining waves separated by a single corrective rising wave.

The fact is that Elliott's observations regarding the wave theory have been borne out so many times in actual practice that they must be taken seriously. The problem is that most amateurs do not know how to break the waves down correctly. Each Elliott wave may break down into many subwaves, and a mere glance at a chart and a cursory dividing of a structure into three-wave and five-wave patterns is usually so far from a true Elliott analysis as to be more deceptive than useful.

Hamilton Bolton (founder of the *Bank Credit Analyst*) did some remarkable work on Elliott, and Bolton's research and interpretations have been carried on by the present editor, Donald Storey. Storey believes that the first wave of the current bear market started for the Dow Industrials in February, 1966. The first wave ended at the October, 1966 lows. The second wave (and this was the major corrective wave) carried to either the December 1968 peak or possibly the May 1969 peak. From there the third leg (which was again a downward leg) began, and Storey believes we are continuing in that leg now. He feels that this leg will ultimately approach or break the 1970 lows, going perhaps as low as the 1962 Dow low (535) or the 1956 and 1957 peaks (520).

**May 2, 1973**

I am taking up most of this report with one of my "secret" pet studies, the Elliott Wave Principle and its application to the market and individual stocks. I feel that this is a good time to present the study. My subscribers are out of this horrendous market, thereby avoiding crushing losses. They are in the gold shares, which means that they are participating in a once-in-a-lifetime (or in two lifetimes) bull movement in the "king of metals." Yet there is no rest for the market student, and that little voice is saying, "Russell, get on that typewriter. If your subscribers are out of the market and in gold shares, they're probably happy and receptive enough to do some real work." Consequently, I give you Elliott.

Anyone who spends a decade or so around the stock market eventually hears the expression, "Elliott Wave Principle." Yet, not one in a thousand has any useful understanding of the Wave Principle. In 1939, *Financial World* published a series of articles by R.N. Elliott in which Elliott (on the basis of studies of 80 prior years of market action) formulated certain theories regarding "natural movement." Elliott began his series with the following sentence, "Since the beginning of time, rhythmic regularity has been the law of creation." Elliott then went on to describe these rhythms or cycles, and in his studies, he demonstrates that these natural rhythms occur in the "tides, the heavenly bodies, cyclones, day and night, even life and death!"

Following Elliott's death in 1947, a few intrepid students continued the studies formulated by Elliott. One of these men was Garfield Drew (of odd-lot fame). In his book, *New Methods for Profit in the Stock Market,* Drew outlines Elliott's theories, and I want to say while I am at it that Drew's book represents one of the milestones in stock market literature (Jeff, take a bow, because I don't feel you have ever received the real credit you deserve for that book).

Hamilton Bolton, founder of the authoritative *Bank Credit Analyst* (and a brilliant market student) was an avid follower of the Wave Principle. In 1960, Bolton published his classic volume, *The Elliott Wave Principle.* I have been interested in the Wave Principle since the mid-1950s, and I had been corresponding with Bolton prior to the publication of his book. Naturally, I was most pleased to have that book, and I think I spent a solid month literally memorizing every line in it. (Ham Bolton died a few years ago, and with his passing went the leading student of Elliott.)

I have not mentioned Elliott very often in these reports; I did in 1968 when I called for a breaking (by the Dow) of the 1966 low, and I did in 1964 when, with the help of Elliott, I picked Burroughs as a buy near its extreme low of 20. Since 1968, I have revised many of my interpretations of Elliott and the market (Elliott revisions are necessary at times), and I have been wanting to present the whole fascinating Elliott Principle again. But it is such a difficult and massive study, that I have simply been putting it off. At any rate, I do want to familiarize my subscribers with the Wave concepts, so here goes (remember, this is, of necessity, a very simplified and abridged presentation).

I will start by saying that Elliott ties in with an extraordinary numerical series, a series which is seen repeatedly in nature. This is the *Fibonacci* series, so named for a famous 13th century Italian mathematician. The Fibonacci series is computed as follows: Start with 1 and add the next number to get the total or Fibonacci number. Thus, 1 and 2 equals 3, 3 and 2 equals 5, 5 and 3 equals 8, etc....all of which gives us the Fibonacci series 1, 2, 3, 5, 8, 13, 21, 34, 55, 89, 144, etc. These numbers appear so often in nature that we must conclude it is far beyond mere coincidence; for instance, *one* God, 5 limbs of man (head, 2 arms, 2 legs), 5 openings in the face (two eyes, two nostrils, mouth), we knock 3 times, 5 continents, 21, the age of maturity, trees always branch from the base in Fibonacci series, on and on. It's simply amazing!

So much for the numerical series. Elliott discovered that stocks advance in broad *bull markets* composed of *5* legs as shown on the chart, and they correct in bear markets composed of *3* legs. Furthermore, each of the 5 bull market waves break up into 21 subwaves. A bull market is composed of 5 subwaves up, a three-wave correction, a second five-waves up, a three-wave correction, and a final five subwaves up (see chart).

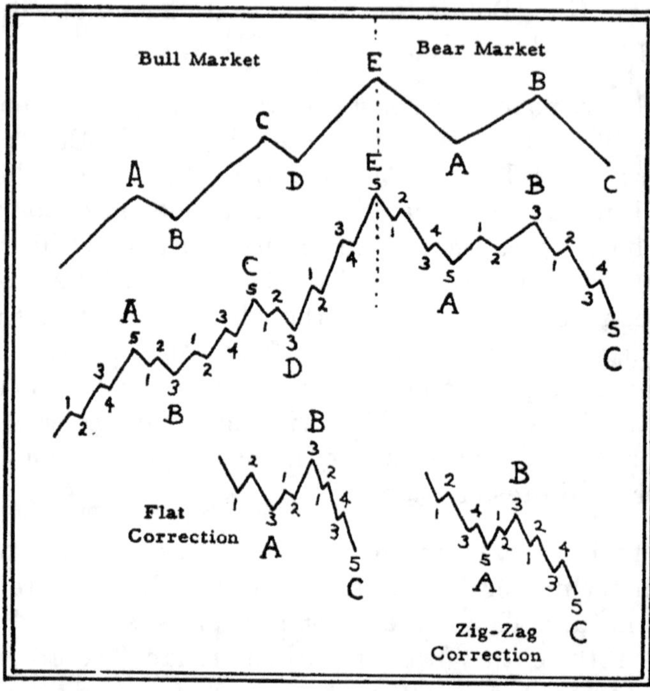


There are many complexities in the Wave Principle, and it is now necessary to explain one of them. It is the Elliott interpretation of *corrections.* There are two kinds of corrections (or bear markets) following a bull movement. One correction is termed the *zigzag* (see chart), and the other is called the *flat.* A zigzag is made up of five subwaves down, three up and five down. By definition, the peak of the leg B is *below* the start of leg A, and this means, of course, that zigzags are the most severe kind of correction. The flat is three subwaves down, a three up and a five down. Usually the peak of wave B is near or even above the start of wave A, so that flats tend to be *milder* corrections than zigzags. They are also (fortunately) much more common.

This whole concept provides us with many valuable principles. In order to explain some of these principles I am going to use actual charts. I find the most useful are monthly graphs showing very long-term movements (in logarithmic and arithmetic scale). Actually, there are instances when log charts will show Elliott movements best, at other times arithmetic charts will provide best results.

Remember, Elliott is *not a magic way* of beating the market. Using Elliott correctly may require years of study. Not all charts will show anything on a wave interpretation basis. Often a stock will appear *unanalyzable*, but an examination of other stocks in the group may provide hints. In general, I do not "force" Elliott interpretations. There are always a number of near-perfect charts for interpretation, and I use them while *avoiding the "undecipherable" ones.*

Back to the practical principles.[2] Let's take the chart of J.P. Stevens (STN). Note that STN has collapsed from its

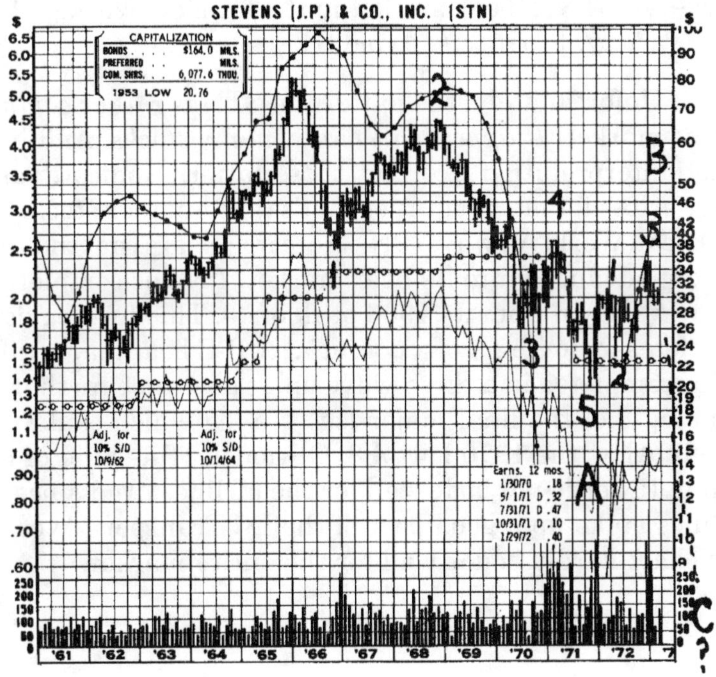


2 The examples that follow are a brilliant application of "Elliott" and provided an unbeatable perspective on several stocks and the market as a whole.

1966 peak of over 80 in a series of five distinct waves. The fifth wave took STN to a 1971 low of 20, a total loss of about 80% of its peak value. Now, what do we know? We know that the Wave Principle states that bear market corrections take the form of three waves down. But there is no way we can get a three count out of the 1966-70 collapse in STN; it occurred in five waves.

This suggests that the 1966-70 five-wave collapse in STN was not a completed bear market, that it was all *wave A* of a huge three-wave bear market which I have marked A-B-C. Furthermore, it appears that the A wave was completed (in 1970), the B wave is about over (B was a 1-2-3 which ended around January, 1973). We should now get another five-wave decline, which will be major leg C in the major A-B-C bear market in STN, a bear market in the form of a zigzag of the 5-3-5 variety. Prognosis: Avoid STN.

Unfortunately, the pattern in STN is rather *common* in this market! *It appears in many, many stocks.* And if my Elliott interpretation is correct, those patterns indicate vastly lower prices for many equities. Let's take another stock, Pan American World Airways (PN). Here it appears that the stock is more advanced into its bear market. PN has completed a five-wave down from its 1966 peak of 40. This five-leg down completes major leg A of a potential A-B-C bear market. Leg B was completed in a three-wave up. It now appears that PN is on leg 3 of the final major leg C, a leg which could take it well below the 1970 low of 8. Obviously, this kind of pattern in PN does not bode well for the airlines. And since the airlines make up a good part of the DJ Transport Average, this chart hardly bodes well for the entire market.

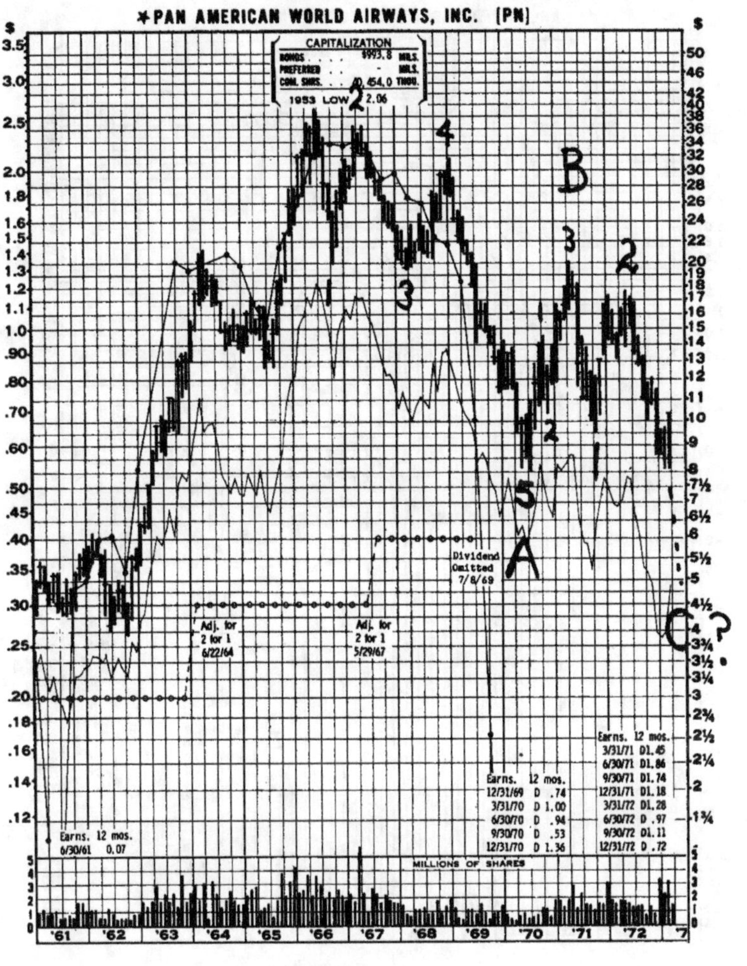


Let's take a third example, Arlan's Dept. Store (AAD). Here we see a disastrous cave-in from the 1969 high of 40 to a 1973 low of 2. It appears that we have a full bear market smash here, a completion of a giant A-B-C pattern in the form of a series of 5-3-5 waves down. What happens next at AAD? Well, based on the chart and the situation of the company (running at a deficit), I would have to say that either the bear market is over, or it's about all over for AAD. The stock can't

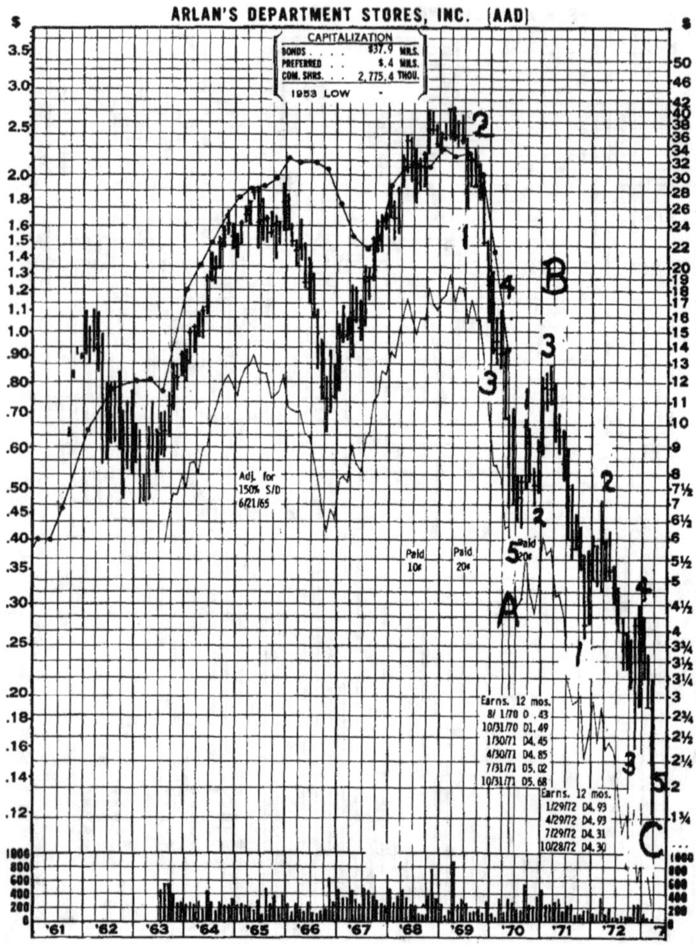


get much cheaper, and the company will either start a new life, merge, or go out of business. Those who followed Elliott would not possibly have ridden this stock down.

Should one take a chance and figure the worst is over for AAD? Should one buy it here at this price? That's a whole different story. For that I would want much varied evidence that the company will survive, that this is the final bottom, etc.

Let's turn to Standard of California (SD). Here we see that SD completed a perfect major three-wave bear market during 1966-70. A new bull market took SD to an all-time high of 90 this year in three distinct waves. What can we say of SD now? It would seem that we could now be in a corrective wave 4 in SD, and following this correction a final wave 5 should take SD to new highs. Furthermore, it would seem that wave 4 should hold above the peak of wave 1 or above 65 on any major corrective decline from here. Why is SD so strong in the face of the smash in so many other stocks? There could be a hundred reasons, but Elliott doesn't concern itself with reasons. The Wave Theory couldn't care less whether the chart shown was one of SD or the price of wheat in Kansas.

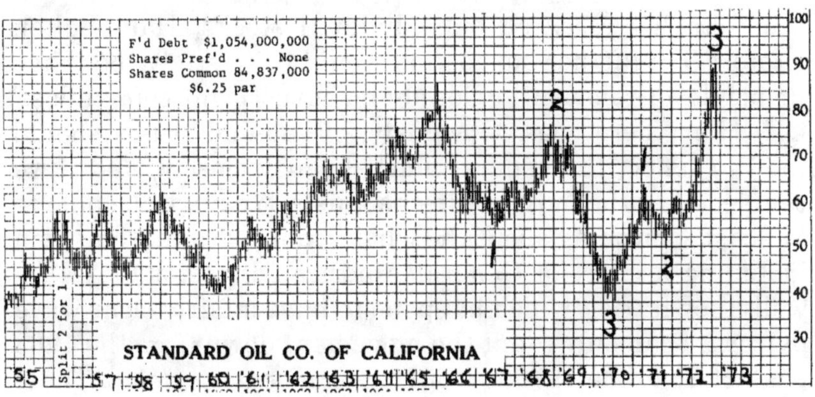


Next I will show Chrysler. I *cannot* get a three-wave count on the decline in Chrysler from the 1973 peak of 73 to the 1970 bottom of 16. If my five-wave count is correct, then the 1968-70 decline in Chrysler constituted wave A of a giant A-B-C bear market. If this is true, then the rise from the 1970 bottom to the present was middle wave B, and I would guess that the B wave is about completed. This suggests that wave C, which should be a five-wave down, lies ahead. Since the bear market in Chrysler is taking the form of a zigzag correction (5-3-5 waves), then leg C should take the stock well under its 1970 price of 16.

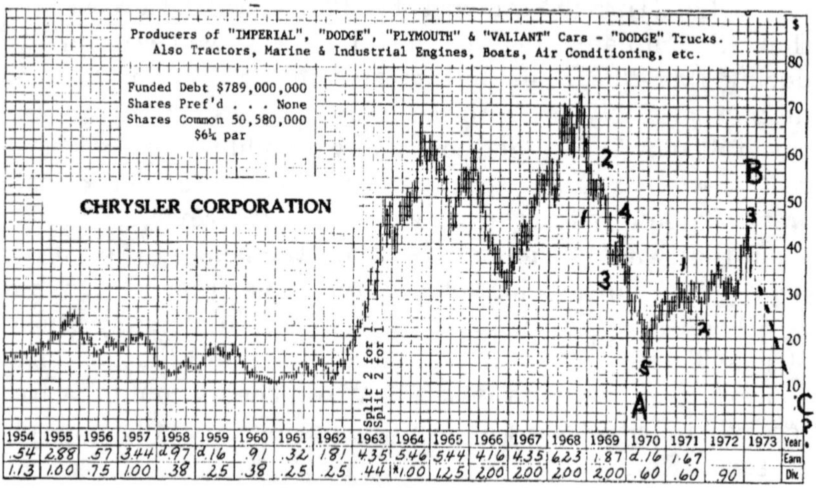


In his research on individual stocks, Ham Bolton wrote, "One further suggestion would be to study the Wave Principle in relation to closed-end investment companies." OK, Ham, here goes. Obviously, closed-end trusts should tend to reflect the general market fairly closely, and if we can decipher the message in the trusts, we might be able to forecast something about the whole "market" situation. I am including a chart of General American Investor (GAM), a well-known trust which happens to have a fairly clear wave pattern. I can only count the movement down from the 1963 peak of 22 to the 1970 low of 9¾ as a *five-wave down*. There is *no way* I can get a three-wave out of that movement (obviously, a three-wave would be more pleasant since it would at least offer hope that the bear market in GAM and on Wall Street in general could be drawing to a close).

Unfortunately, I cannot get an A-B-C count for the 1963-70 decline in GAM. Such a count would imply that a bear market had been completed. Actually, the 1968-70 cave-in took the form of five waves, numbered 1 to 5 on the chart. I have designated these five waves major wave A on the chart. Major wave A should be the first wave of a major A-B-C bear market correction. Next, note the advance to the January, 1973, peak of 20 in GAM. This advance

**GENERAL AMERICAN INVESTORS CO.**

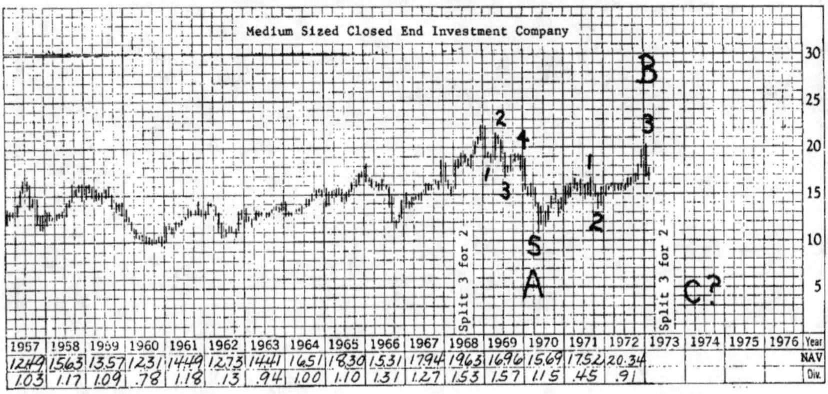


breaks down into three waves, and these should complete larger wave B. So, what do we know overall? We know (or at least guess) that GAM is in a zigzag type bear market which will ultimately be completed in three major waves, A-B-C, of the 5-3-5 subwave series. Downward major wave C (which should be composed of five subwaves) is probably now in progress.

Since GAM is an investment trust, this may tell us something about the general market. Now any idiot knows that the market is composed of many stocks (all in different stages of Elliott Wave patterns), but the broad implication would be that the *majority* of stocks are in patterns corresponding to the pattern in GAM. Thus we can be prepared for a movement in which many, many stocks will decline in the C leg of major A-B-C primary bear markets. If my Elliott Wave interpretations are correct, the warnings are there aplenty.

Next, I want to discuss the Dow itself in Elliott terms. For this I am including my chart of the Dow and the Value Line broad unweighted Industrial Average. I am using the 1966 peak as the point in which the 1949-66 bull market ended for the DJI. This corresponds with my Dow Theory studies, and it agrees with Ham Bolton's studies. Before I go into this I find it necessary to present a few Elliott Wave "rules" or observations.

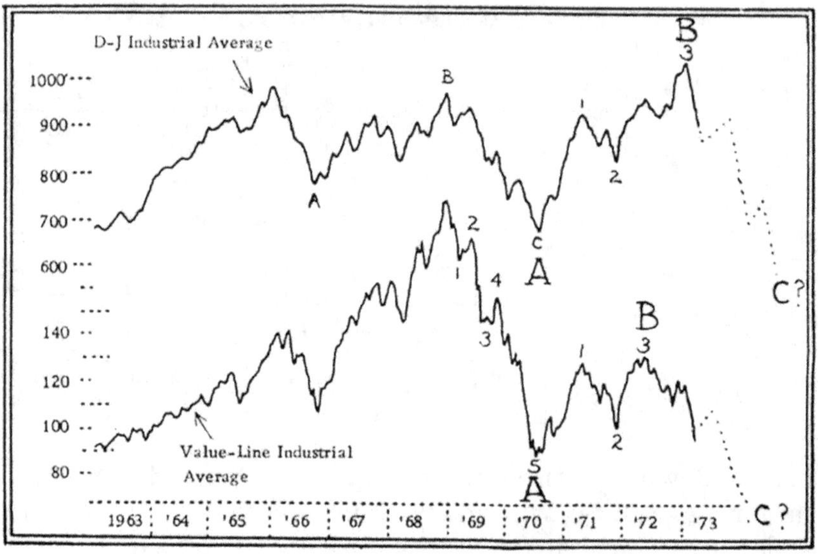


1. Wave 3 is usually the longest wave.
2. Wave 4 should *not* dip below the peak of wave 1.
3. The first wave of a series (even in corrections) is usually the shortest.

Studying the Dow on the chart, one might say that a bear market ended in 1970, in an A-B-C zigzag down (small A-B-C on the chart). If that were true, then it would also follow that a new bull market started at the 1970 low. All right, then the first wave up would be the rise from the 1970 Dow low of 631.16 to the 1971 peak of 950.82 or wave 1 on the chart. Wave 2 would be the 1971 down-wave marked 2 and wave 3 would be the 1973 advance to 1051.50. We would now be in corrective leg 4 with leg 5 still to come, a leg which should take the Dow to new highs.

BUT ... Note that the 1973 leg 4 took the Dow *below* the peak of leg 1 (below the 1971 peak of 950.82). Rule 1 of the Wave Theory states that wave 4 should not dip below the peak of wave 1. Something is wrong. And here is how I interpret the action. I believe that the decline from the

1966 peak to the 1970 low was wave A (large A on chart) of a massive A-B-C wave bear market, a bear market which is assuming the shape of a "flat." The rally to the 1973 peak constitutes major wave B (large B on chart) of the corrective flat, and this wave actually rose slightly above wave A, which is not atypical of flats. These first two waves are the 3-3 waves of a total 3-3-5 bear market correction. We are now in the major downward wave from B to C, a wave that should take the form of a five-wave down. This will complete the bear market, and wave C should terminate below major wave A (or below 631.16 on the Dow).

As for the Value Line Average, I can only get a *five-wave count* for the 1968-70 decline. This suggests that a bear market began in 1968 for the Value Line Industrials, and the first major leg (A) was completed at the 1970 low. A three-wave correction carried to the 1972 peak (completing major wave B), and we are now at the beginning of major down leg C. Note that the Value Line bear market is in the form of a distinct downward *zigzag* and thus will provide a much more severe bear market than the *flat* pattern bear market in the Dow. This would explain the crushing collapses in so many non-Dow stocks, compared with the relatively resistant performances of the Dow Industrials. We should now be in the major C leg of the bear market in Value Line, a leg which will subdivide into five waves (the low for Value Line should be well below the 1970 low).

**July 6, 1973**

*ELLIOTT'S WAVES*: Everyone would love a real "peek into the future," and this is a particular fantasy of stock market students, investors and economists. I tried to provide such a peek in [the issue of May 2, 1973], which offered a lengthy discussion of Elliott's Wave Principle. One of the fascinations which the Wave Principle holds for me is that it offers at least the possibility of a "blueprint of the future" (assuming, of course, that my interpretations are correct).

As a matter of fact, only a "wave" or pure cycle theory can purport to give us a look at the future. For this reason, I try to coordinate Dow's Theory (which is *not* a cycle theory, but must be adjusted to developing market action) with Elliott's Wave Principle, which, like all good wave theories, operates on patterns which are "preordained" and are in harmony with "nature's law of motion." Perhaps because some of my Elliott comments (from May 2) have been coming true, I have received many letters asking me to update the market picture. Here, then, is an update.

I cannot repeat all of the basic Elliott Wave Principles set forth, but again I ask all subscribers to save and file each of these reports so that they can be used for future reference. Mr. A.J. Frost of Canada is probably the greatest living interpreter of Elliott's Wave Theory. Mr. Frost worked with the great Hamilton Bolton (founder of the *Bank Credit Analyst*), and some of Frost's outstanding Elliott analyses have appeared in the *Analyst*. I have had some correspondence with Mr. Frost recently, and needless to say I am always intensely interested in what he has to say about Elliott.

Elliott interpretations of the market require much work, knowledge and artistry. Mr. Frost keeps a good many charts varying from long-range graphs to actual hourly chart of the Dow. It should be borne in mind, however, that Elliott is basically a method for making "sense" out of the market movements, much as an oceanographer might attempt to make sense out of the patterns of the tides.

Elliott students must constantly check, recheck and even change their data and interpretations as the movements of the market unfold. Mr. Frost has at least two possible long-range interpretations of the market, one theorizing that a major bull cycle began in the early 1800s leading to a peak in 1916, a correction (leg 4) to 1942, and then a series of three legs to 1966. Under this way of thinking, we are now in corrective leg 4 which should end perhaps in 1976, prior to a final leg 5 which might end in the early 1980s while perhaps taking the Dow to 2000 or better.

The second Elliott thesis is the one that I personally feel more "at home with." I have drawn a chart which serves to illustrate the second interpretation. This Elliott thesis states that a Supercycle *began in 1932*. The Supercycle was to take the form of five typical but major Elliott waves, three up and two (corrective waves) down. I have labeled these five major legs on the chart with Roman numerals. As we can see, three of the legs are already completed, and we are now in the midst of major Elliott wave IV (which is a corrective or bear market leg, as was major leg II).

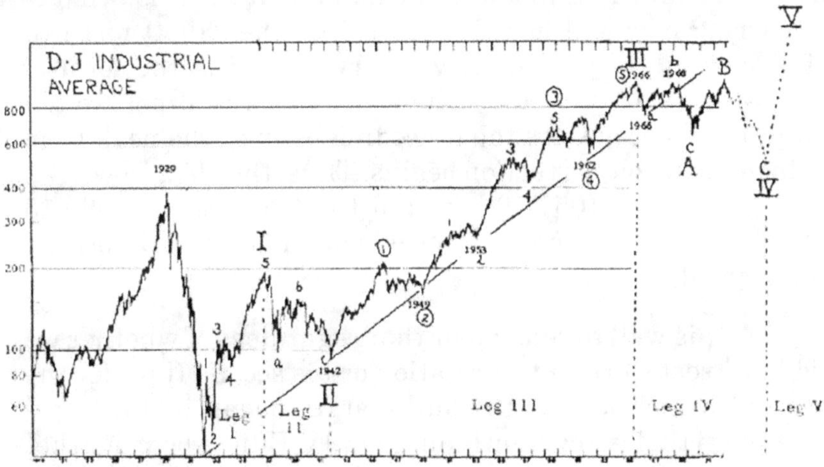


Now let's examine the major Elliott legs. Leg I, the first upward leg, carried the Dow from the Great Depression low of 41 to the 1937 bull market peak of 194 (Roman numeral I on chart). Leg I, which was composed of five smaller legs (three up and two down), was followed by a major but typical three-leg correction. This is shown on the chart by Roman numeral II and it carried the Dow down to the 1942 low of 92.

Major Elliott leg III is identified by the Roman numeral III on the chart. This was an extremely complex leg, containing many smaller bull and bear markets. I have broken leg III down on the chart so that readers may study it. This is the enormous upward leg which contained not only the 1942-46 bull market but the great 1949-66 bull market. Leg III was born during 1942 (in the depths of World War II) with the Dow at 92. It ended 24 years later in the midst of the booming 1960s (1966 to be exact) with the Dow at 995. From there Elliott leg IV began, and this was to be the *second major correction* of the whole Elliott Supercycle since 1932 (the first correction, of course, being the 1937-42 collapse or leg II as seen on the chart).

So much for history. The important thing is: what is occurring now and how does it fit into the Elliott picture? The current major Elliott wave IV is taking the form of an A-B-C "flat" type correction. In flats, the B peak often approaches or betters the preceding peak or the peak from which the whole correction begins. Thus, the 1972 Dow peak (B on chart) of 1051.70 bettered the 1966 peak of 995.15 (995.15 being the point from which the entire Elliott leg IV started).

It is well to remember that regardless of whether we follow Frost's first interpretation or his second (I prefer the second, which is that the bull market began in 1932), we are nevertheless currently in a leg IV Elliott bear market correction. Furthermore, we are now in the third or final (C) leg of the major A-B-C bear market as seen on the chart. Note that the current leg IV Elliott bear market correction has cracked the entire 37-year upward trendline, a trendline which has held since 1932. This is typical of major Elliott corrections, and it demonstrates the *seriousness* of the current descent.

The fact that we are now in an Elliott leg IV correction provides one interesting guideline, and one that I hope we never have to use! In Elliott bear markets, most leg IV declines hold above the peak of leg I. Since the peak of leg

I was the 194 peak of 1937, no decline from here should break 194 on the Dow (is that a consolation?). At any rate, my own guess is that the 520 peak of 1956-57 should act as a very strong downside resistant level for the Dow. Frost writes that C waves tend to be exponential, however, and I have often been fooled by the *power of a C wave* (both of the bullish and bearish variety). Thus, if the 520 area is ever broken on the downside, it would (I feel) be an omen of utter disaster.

**August 8, 1973**

*CHART OF THE MONTH*: The accompanying chart may be telling the most important story of the year. Here we see a monthly chart of the Utility Average with the 1970 closing low of 95.86 labeled. Those who studied my recent Elliott Wave pieces know that major bear markets take the form of an A leg down, a B leg correction (upward) and a final C leg down. Try as I might, I *cannot* show the 1970 low as the completion of a Utility bear market under Elliott. I see the 1965 to 1970 smash as bear market leg A for Utilities. The action since 1970 is part or all of corrective leg B, which was probably completed in late 1972.

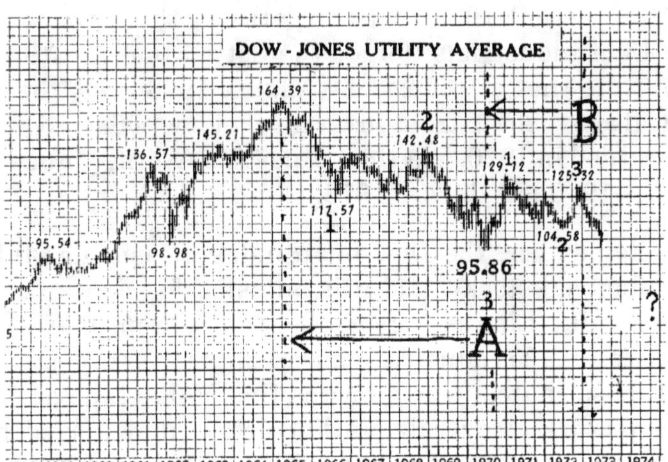

The action of 1973 is probably the beginning of the major leg C down, and if Utilities crack 95.86, I will be fairly certain of this depressing fact. Therefore, if 95.86 is broken on the Utility Average, it will be a most ominous sign suggesting that the predictive Utility Average is leading the way for Wall Street and the nation. If so, that information should be worth the price of a subscription to this advisory ten times over.

### November 9, 1973

Back in [the May 2, 1973 issue] I presented a rather lengthy and detailed study of the Elliott Wave Principle, a phenomenon which I have been interested in almost as long as I have been interested in Dow's Theory. James Dines termed the [May 2] study the first clear and readable explanation he had ever seen on the Wave Principle, and I receive requests every day or so for an updating of Elliott in terms of the current market. Frankly, the interest in Elliott has proved far greater than I suspected (everyone seems to want to look into the "Elliott crystal ball").

I have updated the chart of the Dow Industrials and the Value Line Industrials, which appeared in [the May 2 issue]. The current chart should be of interest even to those who do not follow the Wave Principle. The solid black lines depict the actual 1963 to 1973 paths of the Dow and the Value Line Industrials (forget the dotted lines for the moment). Note that at the recent August 1973 lows, the *Dow held* well above the extreme bear market low of 631.16, which was recorded in 1970. But the Value Line Average broke well below its 1970 low during 1973.

Remember, the Dow is an index measuring 30 blue chip Industrial stocks, and it is adjusted for capitalization. But the Value Line is a geometric average measuring the price action of 425 Industrial shares, regardless of capitalization of those shares (which means that Value Line provides a good picture of overall market action undistorted by a few huge capitalization stocks). The meaning of the chart

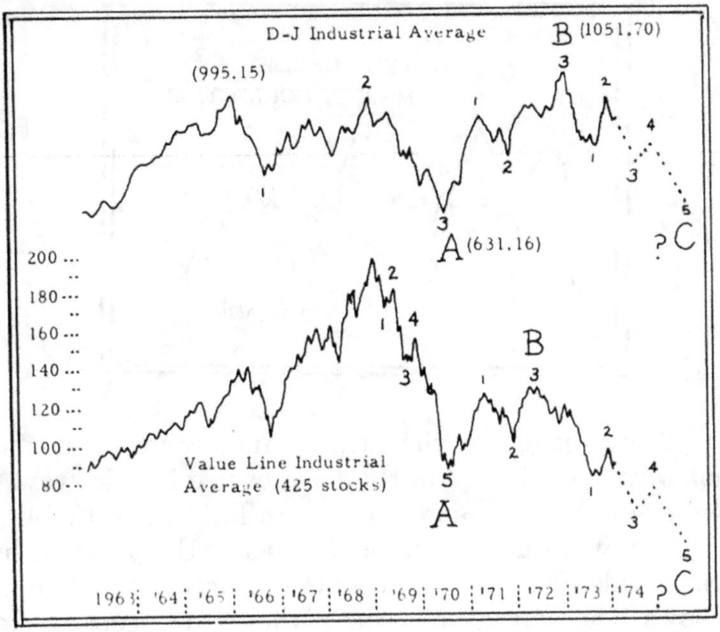


is clear. The *Dow stocks* have, in general, staged a strong comeback from their 1970 bear market lows. They have also held the major portions of their recovery moves, even during the latest decline. Not so the *vast majority* of stocks on the NYSE as measured by Value Line. Value Line shows that the average NYSE stock broke to new lows during 1973, and—just as important—the recovery since the 1973 low has been anything but impressive.

In May, I discussed the *two types of Elliott bear markets*, the mild "flat" correction and the more drastic "zigzag" correction. I include a chart showing these two types. Note that the flat is composed of a major downwave A (containing three smaller legs), a major wave B up (also three smaller legs), and a final wave C down (composed of five smaller legs). In the flat, the peak of the B wave may be near or even above the start of the A wave, and the final wave down to the C bottom may be above or somewhat below the termination of wave A. Thus the flat tends to be a mild correction.

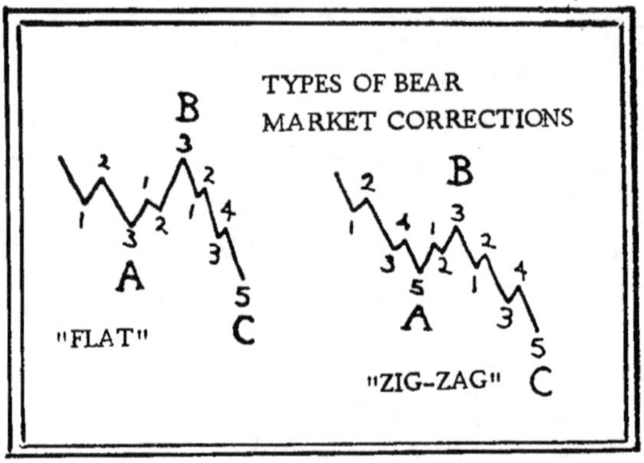


The *zigzag*, on the other hand, consists of three major waves as shown, in the form of five legs in wave A, three legs in wave B and five legs in final wave C. But in the zigzag, wave B terminates well below the previous bull market peak, and wave C takes the structure to important new lows. Therefore, the zigzag is the pattern seen in most drastic bear market declines.

I have stated that the Dow Industrial Average is in a flat correction. Thus, the January 1973 peak of 1051.70 was actually slightly above the major top of February, 1966 (which saw the Dow at 995.15). Note that the Dow completed the first major wave A of the bear market (1966-70) in three smaller legs; it completed the second (upward) wave to B in 1973 in three legs. I believe that we are now in our final major wave down, the C wave, and this should develop in five smaller legs, of which 1 and possibly 2 are completed (we could now be going into leg 3 as shown on the chart.

Where could this "flat bear market correction" under Elliott terminate for the Dow? I would guess probably in the vicinity of the 1970 lows (in other words, somewhere around the 1970 low of 631.16, depending on conditions at the termination of the entire wave).

The Value Line Average is an entirely different story. Value Line, as stated in [the May letter], is undergoing a much more drastic zigzag correction of the 5-3-5 variety, as seen in the pattern on the small chart. Note, in Figure 2-5, that I currently put Value Line's Average in major wave C of the bear market. We should have completed secondary legs 1 and 2 with legs 3, 4 and 5 still ahead. Leg 3 should end below the recent 1973 low for the Value Line Average, and final leg 5 (which should wind up major leg C) should end at drastic *new lows*.

*Conclusion*: According to my interpretation of Elliott, we remain in a primary bear market situation. The bear market could end around late-1974[3] or 1975 with the Dow down below 700 and the majority of common stocks (as measured by the Value Line Industrial Average) at frightening new lows. At that point, however (and here is the bright part) we should be able to exchange our gold shares (which could be sky-high by then) for top-grade common stocks which will (hopefully), at that time represent truly great values.

**November 21, 1973**

*FIBONACCI*: In the last mailing I presented my latest Elliott Wave interpretations. Elliott is based to a large extent on an extraordinary series of numbers known as the Fibonacci series (named by the famous Italian mathematician, Leonardo de Pisa). The series has the following properties, among others.

(1) The sum of any two numbers forms the next number, as follows. 1 and 1 equal 2, 2 and 1 equal 3, 3 and 2 are 5, and so on to 8, 13, 21, 34, 55, 89, 144, 233, 377, 610, 987, etc. Keep these numbers in mind!

(2) The ratio of any number to the next higher number is 61.8 to 100.

---

[3] A great call, accompanying a fantastic analysis.

(3) The ratio of each number to its next lower number is 161.8 to 100.

(4) The ratio 1.618 multiplied by .618 equals 1.

(5) Of interest are the Fibonacci measurements of the Great Pyramid of Gizeh (many believe that the Great Pyramid contains divine messages of revelation). The Pyramid's angle of elevation to its base is 61.8%, and the number of inches in its height is exactly 5813 (all Fibonacci numbers). A pyramid, of course, has 3 sides.

(6) The Fibonacci numbers appear *repeatedly in nature,* five appendages of man (head, two arms, two legs), five fingers, five toes, five senses, five openings of the face (two nostrils, two eyes, mouth), age of maturity 21, beginning of teenage years 13, in music we have the octave made up of 13 keys, 8 white, 5 black, trees always branch from the base in Fibonacci series, etc., etc. These are only a very few examples.

In the stock market, Elliott students know that bull markets tend to develop in series of 3 advancing waves separated by 2 declining waves (total 5). Bear markets tend to develop in two declining waves separated by an upward correction (total 3). Total of major movements in an entire bull and bear cycle is 8.

I have gone into the Elliott interpretations of *movements* in many preceding Letters including the last. But I have not mentioned Elliott *periodicity*, which is a fascinating phenomenon.

I list below a number of Fibonacci *time spans* in years which I feel are beyond coincidence: 1907 panic low to 1962 panic low 55 years; 1949 major bottom to 1962 panic bottom 13 years; 1932 crash bottom to 1937 bull top 5 years; 1937 bull top to 1942 depression bottom 5 years; July 1932 final bottom to March 1937 bull top 89 months. (I could list many more.)

1921 depression low to 1942 depression low 21 years. 1921 bull bottom to 1929 bull top 8 years. 1929 bull top to 1942 depression bottom 13 years. September 1929, bull top to July 1932 final bottom 34 months. January 1960 top to October 1962 bottom 34 months.

Now, for the first time, I want to bring this study up to date. We know under Dow Theory that the last great primary bull market started on July 13, 1949 (notice the 13). According to Dow Theory, the bull market ended in February 1966.

The lowest point of the bear market which began in 1966 was the 631.16 of May 26, 1970. According to my interpretation of Fibonacci dates, the year 1970 was a most important year. Observe these relationships. 1949 (beginning of primary bull market) to 1970 was 21 years. 1957 (end of second phase of bull market) to 1970 was 13 years. 1962 (year of major panic cave-in) to 1970 was 8 years. In my opinion, the recurrence of Fibonacci relationships pointing to 1970 as a key year are too numerous to be brushed aside as mere "coincidence."

Now, from February 1966 (the month of the bull market top) to July 1973 (July was the month when many averages struck bottom such as the NYSE, Amex, Value Line, etc.) was exactly 89 months. Is that another sheer coincidence?

If so, then here is the next coincidence. The Dow hit its August 1973 low at 851 (8, 5, 1 are all Fibonacci numbers). And then the most extraordinary of all. The peak of the recent rally came at 987, which is also a perfect Fibonacci number! (See Fibonacci numerical series at beginning of this piece.)

My conclusion is that 1970 was a very critical year for the market, and that the final bottom will likely be measured in terms of Fibonacci numbers from 1970. Second, I believe that the 987 peak in the Dow (October 26, 1973) was a very important point and probably represented the last top. Next, I am postulating that the final bottom for the current primary bear market could come either *five* years from the critical year 1970, which would make the bottom 1975 — or eight years from 1970, or 1978. If I had to guess, I would say that the final bottom will come in 1975. As to a "Fibonacci guess" regarding the final bear market low for the Dow, I will guess a figure of 61.8 percent of the peak 1051 Dow figure (recorded in January 1973). That figure would be 649, which corresponds roughly to the figure put forth in the last mailing.

### November 30, 1973

I have been doing a good deal of additional thinking regarding the *Fibonacci* timing series as discussed in detail in the last Letter. In that report, I stated that 1975 could be the year of the bear market's end. The following relationships, however, strike me as worth noting. From the bull market top of 1966, a span of *8* years (8 is a Fibonacci number) would take us to 1974. From the May 1970 bear market low (and the outstanding significance of the year 1970 was explained in the last Letter) to December 1974 would be *55* months. The number 55 is also a Fibonacci series. Thus I feel that *December 1974*[4] will be a month well worth watching, as far as Elliott is concerned. Conceivably, the bear market could end there.

### December 12, 1973

*THE TALE UNFOLDS*: I use the *Elliott Wave Principle* in conjunction with the Dow Theory because it helps me in my thinking. It is necessary to revise the smaller Elliott Wave projections, but on the whole, the larger projections stand up.

---

[4] A phenomenal call.

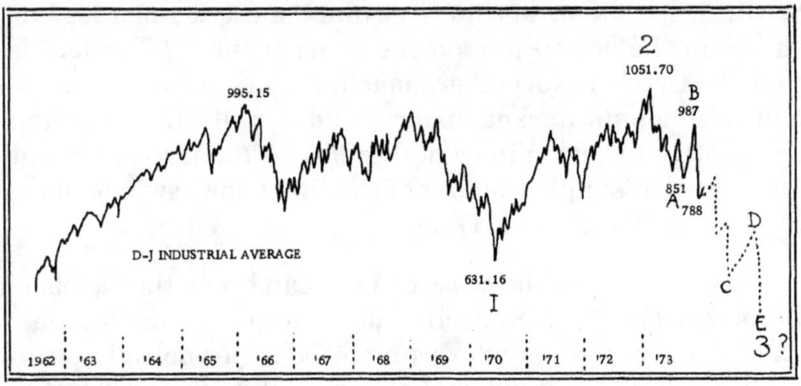


I have included a chart, which *updates* my Dow-Elliott thinking regarding the entire primary bear market to date. As I have explained before, primary bear markets generally take the form of a giant 1-2-3[5] pattern down, with the 1 and 3 waves being the major downswings, and the number 2 wave being the major correction. In a "flat" type bear market correction (which I believe the Dow is now in) the peak of wave 2 (2 is the upward corrective wave) often approaches or even betters the old bull market top (which it did in January 1973 when the Dow bettered the 1966 top).

The first major wave (I) carried from the '66 bull market top of 995.15 to the 1970 low of 631.16. The big corrective wave (2) took the Dow (but little else) up to a 1973 high of 1051.70. All of which brings us to the wave we are now in—the final major downward wave 3.

Wave 3 (or 2 to 3) should break down into five legs in an A-B-C-D-E type pattern as shown on the chart. The first downward leg A has been completed, as has the upward correction, which is leg B. From B, we have dropped a straight-line 200 points to the December low of 788. The question: does the huge drop to 788 represent all of leg C

[5] Russell changes notation from letters to numbers and vice versa, but the concepts are the same.

or will leg C break up into five much more defined legs as shown in the dotted line on the chart (B to C)? The fact is that the October-November smash was one of the most violent declines in market history, and it will take time and perspective to determine whether 987 to 788 is to represent all of leg C or simply the first of the three downswings in leg C (as shown on the chart).

Actually, on the *daily* chart, I can break the October-December (987 to 788) decline down into five smaller legs, and Elliott optimists who want to be super-optimists can claim (at least for now) that 987 to 788 may complete the B-C leg. I'm afraid I'm not that hopeful.

Here is my reasoning. The C leg in an Elliott pattern is generally longer than the A leg. The A leg of major bear market wave 3 took the Dow from 1051 to 851, a decline of 200 points. The C leg took the Dow from 987 to 788, a decline of 199 points. The odds are great, therefore, that the October-December 1973 smash is simply the *first* downward sub-leg in the much larger B-C leg as shown on the chart. Unfortunately, this implies that the bear market will ultimately be very drastic with the termination of the C leg perhaps in the low 600 area, and final leg E even lower (perhaps substantially lower).

*Conclusion*: The A leg of this final major leg 3 was large — 200 points. The second downward leg or leg C shapes up as a big leg, we have already seen 200 downside points. All this points to a big bear market, and I expect the ultimate termination to occur below the 1970 low of 631.16 and most likely well below it. I want my subscribers to prepare for this kind of depressing action. I don't make the market, I simply interpret it as best I can. What I come up with my subscribers know about. But there's no sense dealing in happy pipe dreams in this business when you're getting 200-point downside patterns in the Dow (and remember, the 200 point A leg of wave 3 came before anyone ever heard of the Arab oil embargo).

**August 28, 1974**

You need three things to survive in the stock market and probably four. The three are money, knowledge and guts. The fourth is luck. The only easy thing you can do in the market is lose money. Everything else takes work. I have found the Elliott Wave Principle to be a help to me in investing and understanding the big picture. That's why I have included rather simplified (and I hope understandable) rundowns on Elliott in these reports for the past 12 years.

In [the DTLs of July 6, 1973 and December 12, 1973] I presented reviews of the Wave Principle as I apply it. In [the July letter] I published a very long term chart, showing the interpretation of Mr. A.J. Frost of Ontario, Canada, to my mind the leading Elliott practitioner living today. Frost worked with Hamilton Bolton (founder of the *Bank Credit Analyst*). Bolton did much original and outstanding work on Elliott. I corresponded with Bolton while he was alive, and I have corresponded with A.J. Frost since.

A.J. Frost interprets the Supercycle as follows: We have been in an Elliott Supercycle since July 1932. The first bull wave carried from 1932 to 1937, the (bear) correction lasted from 1937 to 1942. The great bull leg 3 was the rise from 1942 to 1966. Frost believes (as I do) that we have been in wave 4, a major bear or corrective wave since 1966.

Elliott bear market corrections take the form of downward zigzags or flats The downward zigzag is usually the more drastic of the two. In the milder correction or the flat, the middle (B leg) often equals or even surpasses the preceding bull market high, as shown on the chart. This is exactly what occurred when in January 1973, the Dow bettered the 1966 peak of 995.15. Thus, Frost and I feel that we are now (and have been) in a flat-type correction ever since 1966.

The main A-B-C waves in an Elliott flat-bear market break up into a further division of 3-3-5. I have marked the

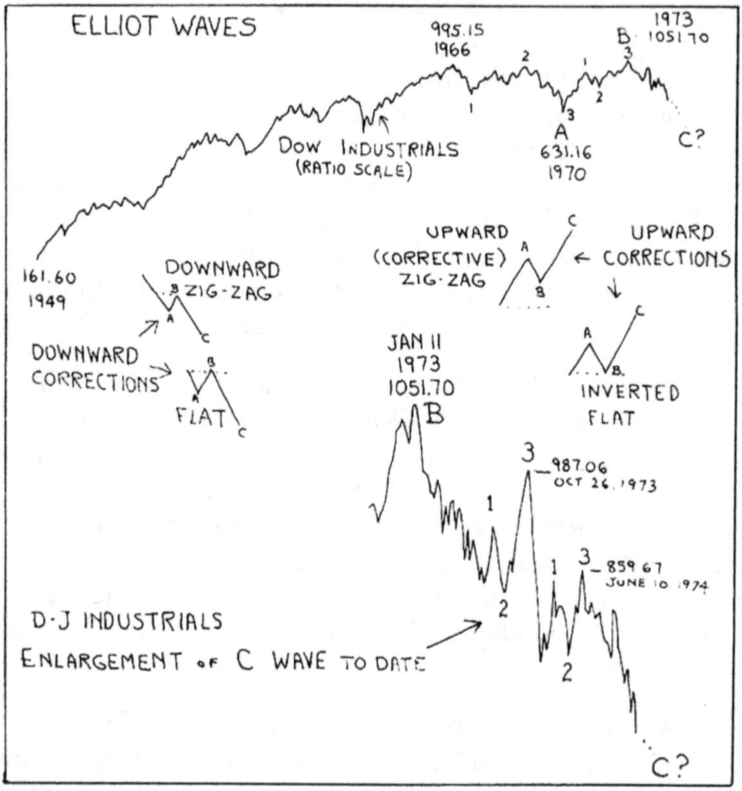


A wave (1966 to 1970) with a 1-2-3 showing the three divisions. I have done the same with the B wave (1970 to 1973) showing the 3 divisions to the 1051.70 peak of 1973. The lower part of the chart deals with the C wave, and this is the major downward wave we are now in. This C wave should ultimately take the form of *five legs* and terminate below (perhaps well below) the 1970 low of 631.16. Frost believes that the bottom of the C wave could be around the 520 area,[6] the level formed by the 1955-56 tops. I do not disagree with this view, but it would not surprise me to see the Dow go below the 520 area; possibly even to the area of the 1929 peak of 381 before this bear market breathes its last.

[6] Frost neglects his forecast of 572, made in 1970.

Many feel that the current bear market could not be more drastic or costly. I take issue with this viewpoint. I would say that it is "lucky" for Wall Street and the world that the primary bear market which began in 1966 has assumed the form of an Elliott *flat* — rather than a zigzag. If the bear were a zigzag, I am reasonably convinced that the downside action would be of much more catastrophic proportions.

Referring to the lower section of the chart, this is simply an *enlargement* of the B to C wave (1973 to the present). It is important to study the two upward corrections which have been numbered 1-2-3, the first correction ending on October 26, 1973, the second terminating on June 10, 1974. These are inverted or Elliott *flat-type corrections* against the main declining trend of wave C. Just as flats in a bull market are milder than downward zigzag corrections, inverted flats in a bear market represent *weak upward* corrections. This is important. It is important for two reasons: (1) inverted flats (such as those of 1973 and 1974) are indications of weakness, and these weak upside corrections usually generate strong subsequent downside action. They have done exactly this. (2) But Elliott corrections tend to *alternate*. Therefore, following these flats, we can probably expect a correction of the (upward) zigzag variety. This should produce some impressive rallying action somewhere ahead.

I realize that the foregoing Elliott material represents "heavy going" for the average reader. I don't know how to avoid that. We're playing the toughest game in the world when we handle our investments. We're competing with the top brains, the biggest money, the coldest calculators. We've got to try to be as smart or smarter than most of them. That's the reason for the hard work and the mind-bending studies.

**September 18, 1974**

I daily rack my brain to try to explain what is happening in the market and the world. A few days ago I received a letter from A.J. Frost, to my mind the foremost authority on the Elliott Wave Principle. I want to include two excerpts from Frost's latest letter to me:

> "Would you agree with me that the market is probably *now* discounting some dramatic and overwhelming event in our history, not apparent to observers of the national scene, such as the repudiation of domestic debt by a world trading nation. It is only a feeling, but my guess is that the market is trying to tell us something that is unknown. The unknown is greater than the known, except to the market. One can almost hear Charles H. Dow whispering from the grave: 'something is up.'
>
> "Hamilton Bolton was a great Elliotter who rescued the Principle from possible extinction. At times he said: 'I would like to sweep it under the rug.' Many of his friends presumed to know that the Principle had no application to stock market behavior without having done their homework. He often became discouraged but never gave up. Shortly before he died in April 1967, we spent a few hours together and talked a great deal about Elliott and banking figures. He said: 'Before this is all over, we are going to see a real lulu of a bear market.' Another thing he said was: 'A cycle of loan liquidation is a MUST.' This was seven years ago!"

There is no doubt about it. We are seeing the great liquidation now. There isn't a man alive who can tell how this thing is going to go — not a soul. The swing could go first to cash (cash means liquidity, and cash at any cost means soaring interest rates). Then we could swing to gold because (1) gold is real money, and the paper monetary system itself may start tottering, (2) it will become obvious that the price of gold *must* be raised, because the current low price of gold will not allow for the coming massive amount of borrowing (against gold) which is needed if the system is to survive.

One way or another, however, I know that no bear market ends and no bull market begins *until the cycle of liquidation is completed*. That will be the painful cycle, the *third phase of the bear market*, the part that will call for all our skill at survival.

**October 30, 1974**

*A REMARKABLE ELLIOTT PROJECTION*: A few days ago, Mr. A.J. Frost of Canada sent me his market projection, based on his unique and brilliant Elliott Wave studies. I have redrawn the chart which Mr. Frost sent me, and I feel that the whole Frost interpretation is so interesting that I want to include it in this Letter.

The chart shows the Dow Industrials in its tremendous upward thrust or bull movement from 1932 to the present. As Frost interprets it, we have seen two major bull waves so far, leg A (1932-37) and leg C (1942-66). We have seen one completed bear leg so far, leg B (1937-42), and we are currently in the second corrective bear leg (leg D), which began in 1966 and is still in force.

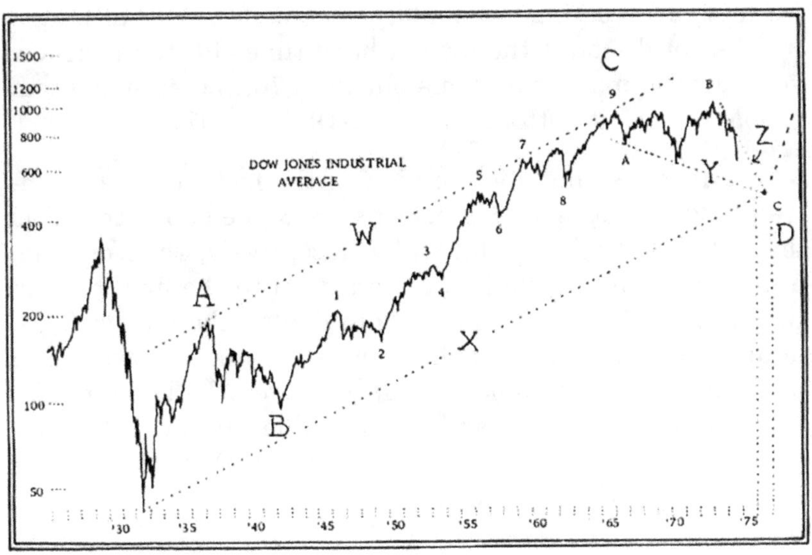

Frost projects current leg D to extend into 1976 (longer than most analysts expect) but to terminate in the area of the 1955-56 highs of around 520 (this is a bit shallower than most of the dyed-in-the-wool bears expect). Frost sees the current bear market (major leg D) as an A-B-C "flat" correction, which should terminate at the point at which three important trendlines intersect. How these trendlines are drawn on this semilog chart is clear enough. The top trendline W of the great channel intersects the 1937 and the 1960 and 1966 peaks. The lower channel trendline X is drawn parallel to trendline W and starts from the 1932 low. A third trendline Y connects the 1966 and 1970 bottoms. And the most recent trendline Z runs through the 1973-74 peaks.

Following the end of the current bear market (leg D), Frost expects a final or fifth upward leg [E, dashed line extending up from D]. Leg E should complete the great supercycle which began in 1932.

The question may be asked, "What do I think of all this?" My answer is only that I think it is fascinating, and if it comes to pass, it is hopeful. It flies in the face of the concept of a coming extended, great depression, although it does not discount the idea of hard times for the next few years (if the market bottoms out in 1976, the economy will probably not hit bottom until late-1976 or 1977).

It is also possible, in view of the fact that many unweighted averages of all stocks have dropped 85%, that this market may back and fill, rally deceptively, then decline, and in general become totally erratic until the final bottom in the Dow. Such action would provide all the players with additional losses, even if the Dow is to sink no lower than an ultimate 520. Business could turn very bad, the public mood could turn black, and it is possible that over the next year or so the majority of stocks could just be sitting, sliding further or slowly building bases.

What could be the basis for the final leg E of the supercycle? Perhaps a giant upward revaluation in gold, perhaps some kind of world agreement on oil, energy, food, etc. But all of this is in the realm of overworking the crystal ball, so I should probably stop here (with many thanks to Mr. A.J. Frost).

### December 20, 1974

*Question*: Russell, what about the panic for cash and the profit collapse which you foresaw for 1975? *Answer*: They may well be coming, and today's prices may have discounted them. But I never argue with the market, and the fact is that the last *confirmed* lows in the Averages were made on October 3 and 4 (Industrials 584.56, Transports 125.93). Both Averages have not been lower since. Industrials have been lower, but that constituted a nonconfirmation.

The extent of the damage brought in by the bear market is shown in this chart. This unweighted chart shows the disastrous story of the last number of years. There's been only one worse collapse in Wall Street history.

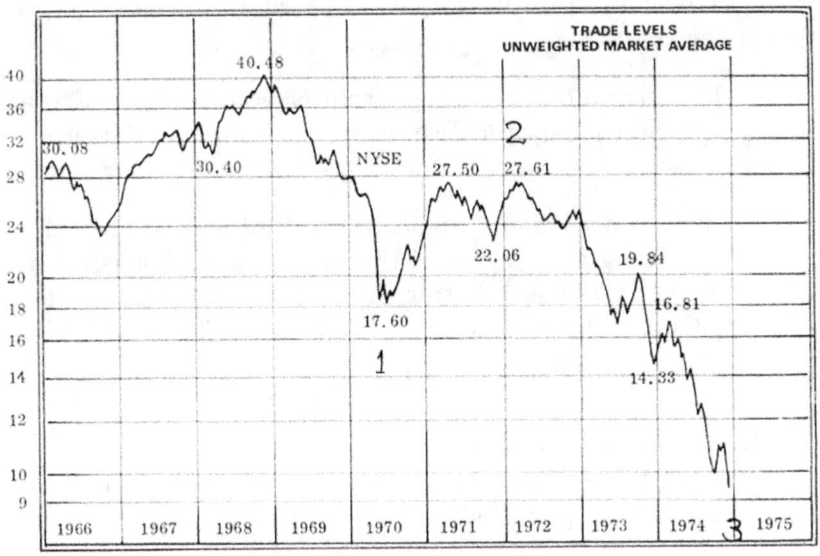

The 1-2-3 notations should be clear to all who followed my earlier discussion of the Elliott Wave Principle. Bear markets come in major 1-2-3 waves. According to the chart, this major downward zigzag could be completed.[7]

**January 2, 1975**

Readers are going to have to indulge me in this one, but I must admit to a personal fascination with *Fibonacci numbers*, so bear with me. Let's update the study.

According to my data, the year *1970* was a very important one. On May 26 of that year the Dow hit a low of 631.16, its lowest point of the bear market (that began in 1966).

From 1949 (beginning of the great bull market) to 1970 was 21 years.

From 1957 (end of the second phase of the bull market) to 1970 was 13 years.

From 1962 (the year of the panic smash) to 1970 was 8 years.

These FS relationships indicated to me that *1970 was a key year.*

Here is an exact excerpt from November 30, 1973, a paragraph that most of my readers have probably forgotten about:

> "I have been doing a good deal of additional thinking regarding the Fibonacci timing series as discussed in detail in the last Letter. In that report I stated that 1975 could be the year of the bear market's end. The

---

[7] One of the greatest market calls of all time, particularly in light of his having previously recognized the long term bearish significance of the 1966 high.

following relationships, however, strike me as worth noting. From the bull market top of 1966, a span of *8* years would take us to 1974. From the May, 1970 bear market low to December, 1974 would be *55 months*. The number 55 is a FS number, as is 8. Thus I feel that *December 1974* will be a month worth watching, as far as Elliott is concerned. Conceivably, the bear market could end there."

Here's an added thought. When the numbers making up 1974 are added, they total 21, a FS number. At any rate, on *December 6, 1974* the Dow dropped to a closing of 577.60, its *lowest level of the bear market*. It would be more than interesting if that low held.

**April 9, 1975**

*HAPPY CYCLES*: True cycle theories entail *periodicity* or time periods. Thus Dow's Theory and the Elliott Wave Principle are not actual cycle theories. Both deal with form, not time. A Dow Theory bull market can take a few years to a few decades. An Elliott Wave form can consume a day or a thirty-year period. But a true cycle has to do with a time period, such as *every* six months, every year or every decade. When a true cycle materializes, it occurs *on time* regardless of news events, an Act of God, psychology or anything else.

**May 30, 1975**

*Question*: You have been saying that from the standpoint of your Elliott Wave studies, you are of the opinion that the bear market is over. Would you update your Elliott studies in the light of that statement? *Answer*: I used Elliott in my bullish Special Report of December 20, 1974. I went into Elliott in some detail on October 30, 1974, and I do not have the space to present a full Elliott Wave discussion here. However, I do want to include this chart of the Dow (weekly)

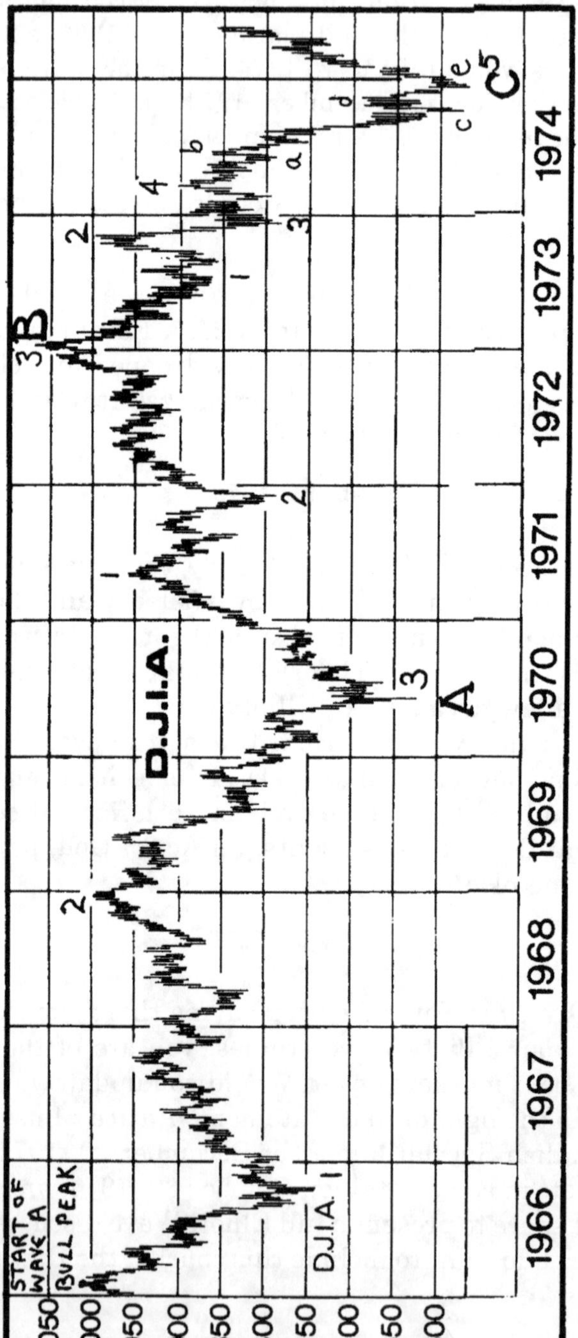
START OF WAVE A
BULL PEAK
D.J.I.A.
DJIA
1050
1000
950
900
850
800
750
700
650
600
1966
1967
1968
1969
1970
1971
1972
1973
1974
A
B
C

covering the years 1966 to the present. I have labeled the chart with figures and letters according to my own Elliott interpretations.

As discussed in previous Letters, I felt that the 1966-74 bear market was assuming the broad form of an A-B-C Elliott "flat." A flat correction differs from the more severe "zigzag" correction in that the flat A-B-C often contains an A-B second leg in which point B carries above the previous bull market top. Following B, a relatively shallow C leg should take the bear market to new lows. Note on the chart that in actuality, point B took the Dow to 1051.70, which was well above the 995.15 of 1966. Following the B leg, the Dow plunged to new lows of 577.60 at C, but point C (577.60) was not too far below the termination of the A leg at 631.16 for the Dow.

Flat corrections take the form of three major A-B-C legs with subdivisions of the three legs usually running as follows: three intermediate waves in leg A, three in leg B and five in leg C. This is known as the 3-3-5 flat correction. Note that I have labeled the chart to show well-defined three-part divisions in waves A and in wave B. Wave C is more complex with four intermediate waves (labeled 1 through 4) and then a 5 wave that breaks up into five smaller waves labeled a through e. Note that minor wave e, intermediate wave 5 and major wave C all ended in December 1974.

*Question*: How do you classify the current rise from the December low, according to Elliott? *Answer*: I classify it as wave A of a new bull market. As I count it, we have completed an a-b-c-d of a five-leg major A advance. The e leg has extended so that we could have one more new high on the Dow (above the 858.73 of May 13) before the current rise ends and a full-scale correction sets in. I have illustrated this by labeling my Elliott count on the Dow (as seen in the accompanying chart of the Dow and the A-D ratio).

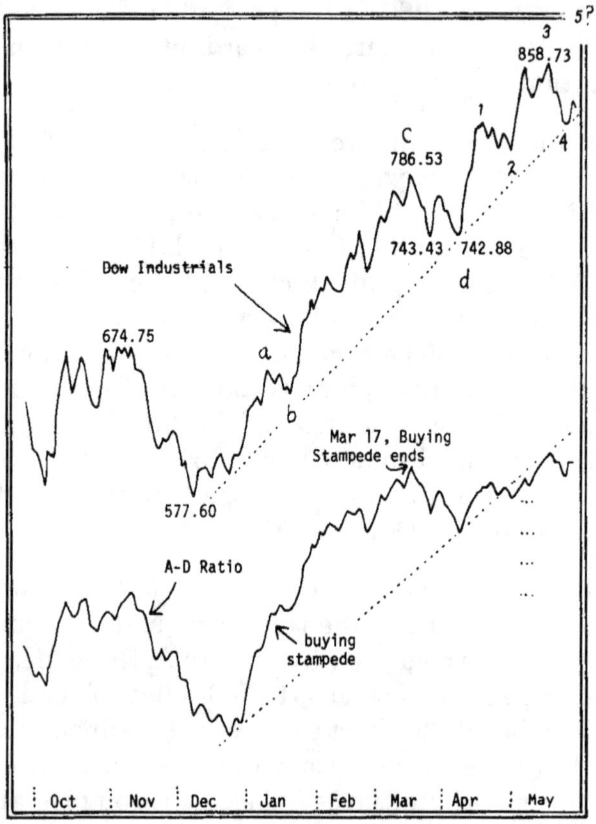


**June 11, 1975**

My Elliott Wave studies imply that we are in a new bull market cycle, and probably the last major upwave of the huge supercycle which began in 1932.

**July 25, 1975**

I just received a letter from Mr. A.J. Frost (of Elliott Wave fame), and he writes that "On balance, I look for a big down-slide this fall." I won't argue with Mr. Frost, but if the Transports continue to resist upside confirmation, I doubt that the correction will hold off until fall. We should also remember that the Elliott Wave study is a predictive technique, whereas Dow's Theory deals more with identification of movements.

**April 14, 1976**

*Question*: How much credence do you give Elliott and the Fibonacci series in your stock market interpretations? As I remember, you used both studies to call the 1974 bear market bottom. And in [the DTL of February 27, 1976] you used Fibonacci in your interpretation of the end of the bear market in gold bullion and Western gold shares. *Answer*: Elliott is based to a large extent on the Fibonacci series, but sometimes I use Elliott, sometimes Fibonacci, sometimes both. As to how much credence I give to these studies, I use them where I think they are meaningful. I almost always use them in connection with other studies or to back up other studies. I try not to "push" either Elliott or Fibonacci; in other words, I don't try to force them to fit a given situation.

The Fibonacci series appears over and over again in nature. Since the stock market is made by the minds and psyches of men, I apply the Fibonacci series to the market at times.

The series appears so often in nature that in my opinion, it is totally beyond coincidence. For instance, five openings in the face (two nostrils, two eyes, mouth) five major bodily appendages (two arms, two legs, head), 13 the first teen age, 21 the age of maturity, one almost always knocks 3 times on a door, the card game of 21, on and on.

If you examine a dollar bill, you will notice the 3-sided pyramid. At the top of the pyramid is an eye (e is the fifth letter of the alphabet) set in another triangle. The eye is known as the Eye of Providence, or the Holy Christian Trinity (again three). The pyramid represents (ancient mythology) the path to heaven. Note that the pyramid is made of *13* layers, standing for the 13 original American colonies. At the base of the pyramid we see the number MDCCLXXVI, the Roman numerals for 1776, the year of Independence. The total of the numbers in 1776 equal *21*. On the right side of the dollar we see the eagle holding a branch with *13* leaves on it. Above the eagle is the circle with *13* stars. In the eagle's mouth is a ribbon with the words "E Pluribus Unum," the latter three words being made up of *13* letters.

Elliott fits into Fibonacci in that the Elliott Wave theory holds that bull markets develop in *three* broad upward waves separated by *two* corrective waves, or *five* waves in all. Bear markets develop in *two* major declining waves separated by *one* major upward correction, three waves in all. The Fibonacci ratio of 61.8%[8] often appears in the stock market in the form of a corrective swing being 61.8% of the preceding movement.

Here is an exact excerpt from November 30, 1973, a paragraph that most of my readers have probably forgotten about:

> "From the bull market top of 1966, a span of 8 years would take us to 1974. From the May 1970 bear market low to December, 1974 would be *55 months.* The number 55 is a FS number, as is 8. Thus I feel that *December* 1974 will be a month worth watching, as far as Elliott is concerned. Conceivably, the bear market could end there."

So there you have it, a "prediction" made in November, 1973, during a collapsing market, pointing to December 1974 as a bottom for the entire bear market which began in February 1966. Was that a pure piece of dumb luck, a shot in the dark based on numerological bunk? I leave it to you.

### April 23, 1976

Followers of Elliott may be interested in the action of the 7¾ notes. The notes advanced from their September low of 96½ in a series of five steps (labeled A, B, C, D, E) to a peak of 101½ in January 1976. From there, the notes corrected in the normal 1, 2, 3 pattern with the low occurring

[8] Actually, 61.8034...%

in March 1976. More recently, the 7¾ notes have rallied over 102 to their highest level on record. This could be the beginning of a second A-B-C-D-E Elliott bull pattern for the notes. If so, the bond market could produce the bullish surprise of

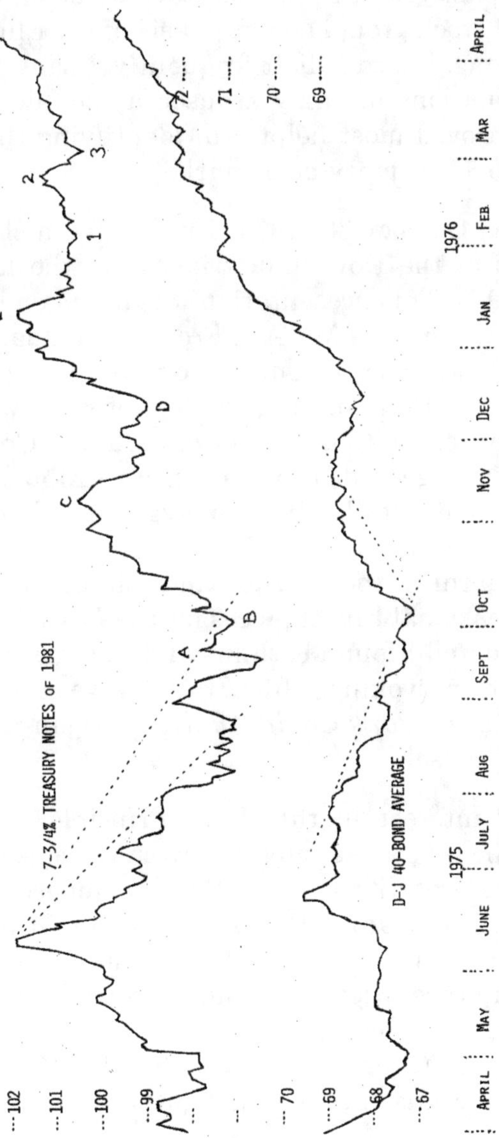

the decade (a confirmed bull market in bonds would prove a greater shock than did the 1974 bottom in the stock market, at least in my opinion).

**October 15, 1976**

In past years, I provided reviews of the market (and occasional stock groups) on the basis of my Elliott Wave interpretations. I used Elliott frequently during 1973-74, and those discussions not only aroused a good deal of interest but they proved most helpful in identifying the end of the great 1966-74 primary bear market.

[On] October 30, 1974, I presented a chart showing the action of the Dow Industrials from the late 1920s to October 1974. This presentation was based on both my own analyses and those of Mr. A.J. Frost of Canada. I personally consider Frost to be the outstanding living exponent of the Wave Theory. Frost did a good deal of work with the late, great Hamilton Bolton, founder of the *Bank Credit Analyst.* Bolton gave a good deal of credence to Elliott and always attempted to dovetail Elliott's Wave Principle with his own work on bank credit. I used to correspond with Hamilton Bolton regarding the market and Elliott. Mr. Frost was writing occasional Elliott pieces for the *Bank Credit Analyst* at the time and I found both his and Bolton's work exciting and thought-provoking. After Frost's wave studies no longer appeared in the *Bank Credit Analyst,* I began corresponding with Frost myself.

My interest in the Wave Principle has continued through the years. As subscribers may remember, I used Elliott interpretations in my Special Report of December 20, 1974, as part of my thesis that the great primary bear market was over. Perhaps due to the success of Frost's and my own interpretations, the Elliott Wave Principle became quite popular during 1974 and early 1975. So contrarian that I am, I stopped using Elliott (at least in Dow Theory Letters) as soon as I realized that it had gathered a following.

Nevertheless, I do continue to study the market in Elliott terms. And because interest in Elliott has now simmered down, I want to review the whole market picture in terms of the Elliott Wave Principle again. I am really doing this for three reasons: (1) Because I believe it may be helpful to subscribers during this very difficult period; (2) Because I just received some very interesting new material from Frost, and (3) Because Dow Theory Letters is the only widely- circulated publication left which discusses Elliott on the basis of A.J. Frost's interpretations (if Ham Bolton were alive, I am fairly sure he would agree with the interpretations included in this mailing).

At any rate, I include a redrawing of a very long-term Dow chart (see next page) which Frost has just sent to me. I concur in Frost's classification and interpretation of the waves and subwaves. Of major importance is the *superwave* concept, which is illustrated on this chart. The superwave premise states that *a giant bull thrust began in 1932*, and that bull movement is still very much *in force*.

Elliott made much use of "*channeling*" in his appraisals of current and future market movements. Channeling is the process of drawing parallel lines through high and low points of market movements, and it is a whole separate study in itself. However, it is an integral part of Elliott.

As you can see, a rising trendline has been drawn connecting the 1937, 1933, 1942 and 1974 bottoms. The fact that the parallel line starting from 1933 does contain the 1974 bottom suggests that the *1974 low was extremely important*, more important, for instance, that any other low in modern memory.

All right, now let's go over the major wave patterns since 1932. The first ascending wave (wave I on the chart) of the great primary bull upthrust was actually the 1932-37 bull market. Wave II was a bear market and developed as a perfect a-b-c pattern, carrying down to the 1942 low (amid the crisis of World War II). Major rising wave III *extended* in

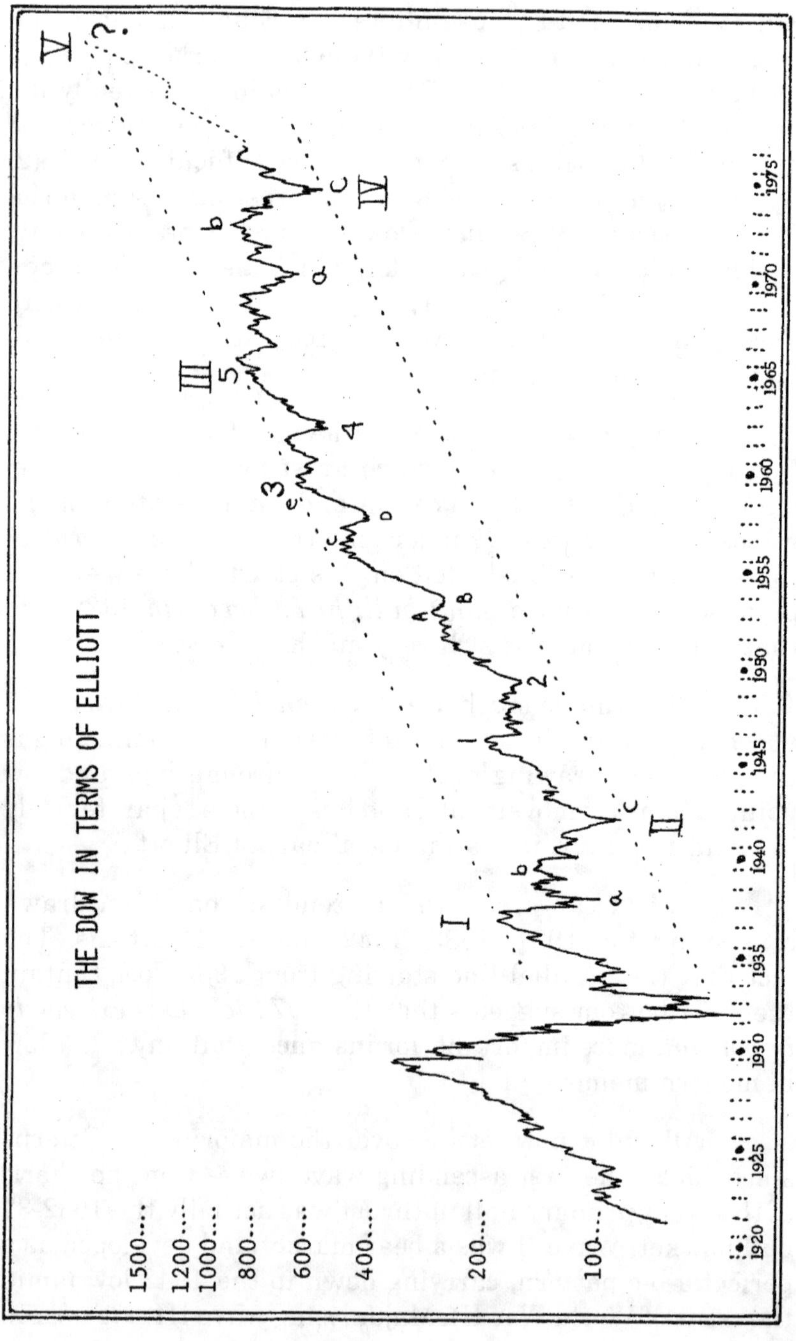
THE DOW IN TERMS OF ELLIOTT
1500
1200
1000
800
600
400
200
100
1920
1925
1930
1935
1940
1945
1950
1955
1960
1965
1970
1975
I
II
III
IV
V
?

the form of five sub-waves (numbers 1 through 5 on chart) to the final 1966 top. This was the point at which I called the termination of the great 1949-66 bull market.

Next came major corrective wave IV, a wave which again assumed the form of a perfect A-B-C bear market. Wave IV carried the Dow down to the historic December 1974 low (577.60). From the 1974 bottom, major wave V is now underway.

From an Elliott standpoint, the most important thing we can perceive at this point is that we are now in the final mighty upwave of the super-bull market which began in 1932. Personally, I like to use Elliott in conjunction with Dow Theory, and, of course, Dow's Theory entails a good many other factors such as yields, values, sentiment, phases, etc. It is my opinion that we are in the earlier stages of a major bull market, a bull market that will (perhaps like the bull market of 1949-66) contain a good many smaller bull and bear swings). But I do think that the late-1974 lows represented a great buying area, and I do think that we will see very much higher prices for stocks before we ever see the 1974 levels again.

What does Frost think now? He believes that the bear market (or major wave IV) ended in December, 1974 and the wave V of the super-bull market began from the December 1974 low. Frost is of the opinion that wave V will be a very big bull market, carrying perhaps to 1500 or even 2000 on the Dow (see upper channel on the chart). He feels that wave V could take 8 years or longer to unfold.

*Now this is very important.* Frost notes that the first leg of a bull movement is usually *shorter* than the second leg. But note that the rise from December 1974 (577 on the Dow) to the July 1975 high (881) was 304 points. But the rise from the October 1975 low (784 on the Dow) to the July 1976 peak (1011) was only 227 points. Thus the second leg of this bull market is (so far) shorter than the first leg. When this happens, it is probable that the second leg is *extending* and what seems like the "shorter leg" is merely the first subwave of a five-leg uptrend. Thus, Frost believes that the second subwave of this bull market (B-C on the chart) is only now getting started!

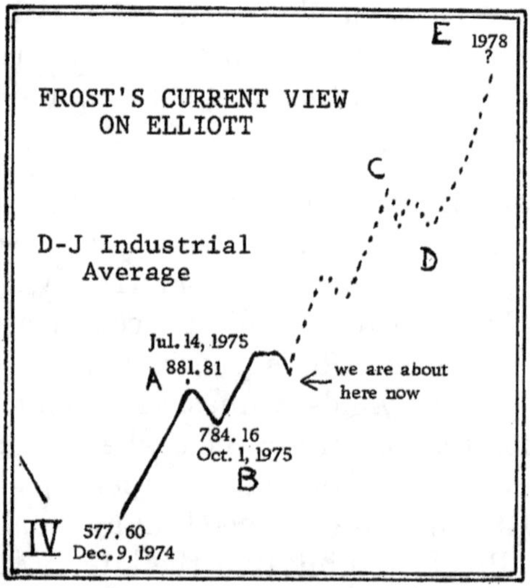


For my part, I quite agree with Frost, and I believe that we are currently probing and stabbing for a very important bottom from which to launch the next bull swing in this early part of wave V. I feel that the frustration, consternation and skepticism being generated now all go a long way toward building a healthy base for the coming rise.

*Question*: What about the elections? How can you draw all these "conclusions" without even knowing whether Ford or Carter will win? *Answer*: Elliott patterns swallow up news events the way an elephant would swallow acorns. Who in this world actually knows whether the market would take a Ford victory bullishly or bearishly, or how it would take a Carter victory? "News goes with *the trend*," runs the old Wall Street adage. And the trend has an extraordinary way of going with Elliott (of course, our problem is interpreting Elliott correctly).

*Question*: Come on Russell, the pound sterling and the British market are collapsing, business here is sloppy, the stock market has been reeling, investors are worried and yield-minded, debt is piling to the sky in the U.S. and the world, and you are presenting us with this Elliott "magic" nonsense. Do you expect us to swallow this stuff? *Answer*: I offer people a look inside my head when I mail these reports. I happen to give Elliott a good deal of credence. In 1974, Elliott was a great help to me. It was also a great help to me in 1966. I follow Elliott, and since I do, I feel my readers would like to know one of the concepts that affects my thinking. I don't expect readers of these reports to "swallow" anything. You can only assimilate what you accept in your guts.

But I think Elliott is a serious study. Many highly intelligent men have followed the study. I don't expect miracles from Elliott. And my interpretations could be wrong at this time. In these Letters, I try to convey to readers my own approach to the market, and of course many readers (who are far more knowledgeable than I) simply read these reports for perhaps a single new idea or merely to check their own thinking against mine.

**November 5, 1976**

*Question*: Russell, I have studied the long-term Elliott projection in your Letter [of October 15, 1976]. It's very interesting, and I assume you believe what you wrote. At any rate, what do you think the Elliott major upwave number V is implying for this nation? *Answer*: I've given a lot of thought to that question. And strangely, I believe the answer came to me while we were visiting the little seacoast town of Encinitas (about 30 miles north of San Diego). It was evening, a few couples were strolling along the main street, enjoying the balmy sea air. A few stores were still open, a health food restaurant, an ice cream parlor, an art supply store, a quaint little antique shop. We had come to Encinitas to see a movie, and we had about half an hour to kill before the picture started. We stopped next door to the theatre, at a bookstore. The bookstore proved to be a center for all kinds of spiritual and psychological books. On the walls were various posters telling of local meetings, folk singing events, art classes, etc. I stopped in my tracks. I could literally feel the "good vibrations" emanating from this bookstore and from this town (which probably doesn't even appear on most maps of California).

I don't know exactly why, but at that moment something in my unconscious seemed to click. I remembered that only three years ago it appeared "obvious" that the U.S. was heading for disaster. It seemed equally clear that the center of world power was moving from the U.S. to Europe. Europe (under the leadership of France and West Germany) was assuming command, while Nixon and gold seemed to be digging a grave for the U.S.

Then I thought, "How the times have changed." Russia is currently having severe economic problems, her credit is endangered, and she may even have to cut her mighty defense budget. Africa is in turmoil, the Mid-East is in flux and Arab money has been moving to the U.S. Italy is on the verge of total collapse, France is staggering under inflation, Britain has become at best a second rate power. But China is turning increasingly to the U.S. for friendship, and it could be that 800 million Chinese know what they are doing.

In fact, of 13 medium-sized and major stock markets including Britain, Canada, Denmark, Japan, West Germany, Australia, Belgium, Holland, Sweden, Switzerland, Italy, Spain and France, only one has outperformed the U.S. stock market since January 1975. That one is Australia, and the relative strength of the Australian market (compared with the U.S.) has been dropping rapidly over the past two months. Those relative strength figures should tell us something.

I believe that the next 10 years are going to see the U.S. reemerge as the spiritual, economic and political leader of the world. I believe that Vietnam, Watergate, the drug scene, the crime explosion, all those many tragic experiences, represented a kind of purging for the U.S. prior to its new emerging period of world leadership. Perhaps the clean sweep of the 1976 Nobel Prizes by the U.S. represented an early vision of things to come. Perhaps the January, 1975 primary bull signal was the trigger that ushered in the "new age" for America. One way or another, I think it is coming.

The "good vibrations" I felt in Encinitas set off this brainstorm of mine. True, the thoughts had been brewing in my head for many months, but it was the feel of this West Coast town that caused all those ideas to jell. Obviously, I could be wrong, and it is possible that nothing may turn out the way I see it. But I believe I am correct, and that's why I'm writing about it now.

*Question*: That's all great, if it happens, Russell, but what about all those huge problems that won't go away? For instance, what about the skyrocketing U.S. debts? *Answer*: The pendulum has a habit of swinging both ways, even though most of us either don't notice the swings (or perhaps we don't know the meaning of the swings). For instance, it is becoming clear that the American people are getting fed up with debt and the manufacture of debt. In a word, Americans are turning rather conservative, and we see it in the sluggish (but not bearish) economic statistics. In an article in the October 29 *Wall Street Journal* entitled "The New Mood in Public Spending," Paul McCracken points to this mood and he also points to new legislation which is calculated to limit spending by law.

A few weeks ago, Nobel Prize winning economist Milton Friedman cited the U.S. need for a Constitutional amendment setting a limit to government spending! As if this thought is not extraordinary enough, think how amazing it is that socialist Sweden (although the socialists have now been voted out) elected capitalist-thinking Friedman to the ranks of Nobel Prize winner.

As the final shocker, which I feel reflects not only growing U.S. conservatism but perhaps even world conservatism, it can now be said that (despite all sorts of official predictions) the world's population growth rate is slowing down. It has been widely known that the U.S. birth rate is sliding, but now we hear that the new trend is spreading throughout the world. Thus, one of the worst fears of the Club of Rome, the demographers and the economists is evaporating. It just could be that this bull market is going to have, as one of its cornerstones, a severe case of "universal sanity." Can you imagine what the market would do if world peace, conservatism and sanity ever "took over?"[9]

**December 1, 1976**

*BOND YIELDS*: The little chart of bond yields is very interesting in Elliott Wave terms. It is interesting because the decline in bond yields (and the rise in bond prices) has come in the form of five subwaves down (as marked on the chart).

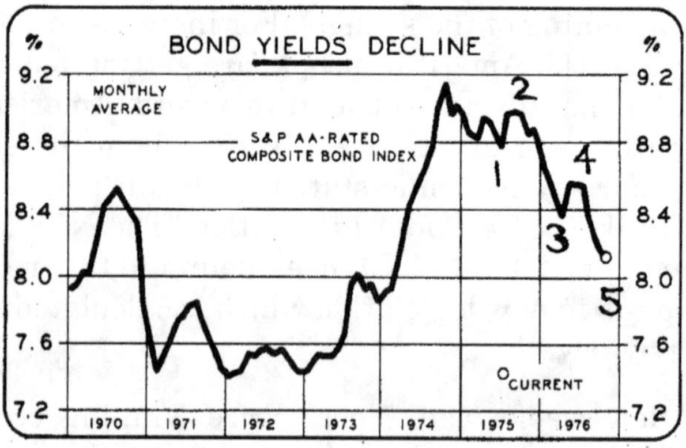


[9] All this good feeling turned out to reflect a peak that was not bettered for six years.

Bear markets (in Elliott terms) do not occur in five-wave down movements, *they occur in three-wave declines.* An Elliott bear market is characterized by a major wave down, an intervening upward correction, and a final major wave which breaks to new lows.

Now note this carefully: Since the decline in bond yields has now formed a five-wave declining pattern, we can assume that the yield decline pattern is *not a completed bear market.* It might have been if it were three waves down, but the five wave decline indicates that what we have here is the *first downleg* (divided into five subwaves) of a major 1-2-3 bear market. In other words, when the current five-leg pattern is completed, we will have an upward correction (which will mean higher yields temporarily), and *then a final leg down* (which will indicate major new lows in yields).

The fact that the decline in interest rates has already assumed a five-wave declining pattern is, by my analysis, very *bullish long term for bonds.* It means that we are seeing only the *first part* of a major slide in bond yields. The first leg has already lasted for two years. The odds are that three years or more will elapse before the declining bond-yield structure is completed.

**January 14, 1977**

The market was quite "overbought" by year end, and there was much puffing and straining in the Dow. The Dow rallied off its November low (see chart) in a perfect Elliott series of five minor waves. Following the fifth leg, in the last DTL, I wrote, there should be an a-b-c-type reaction which would serve to correct the November-December rise.

As it turned out, the fifth minor leg was completed by the time I wrote [the January 5, 1977 Letter]. Consequently, the Industrials greeted the New Year with a resounding little plop (an action which could hardly have surprised any of my

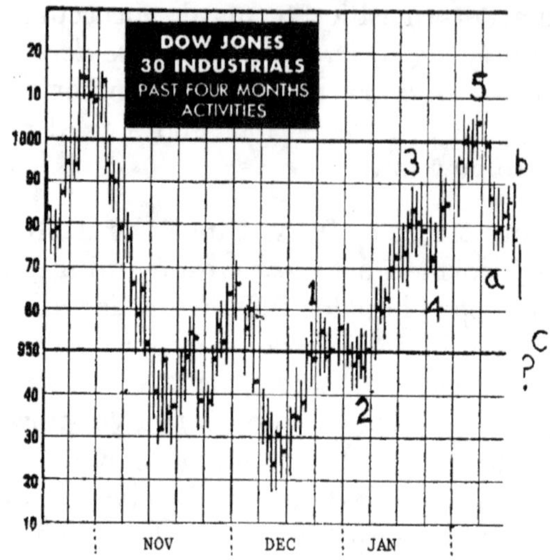


subscribers). The Dow dropped back to 978.06 on January 5, forming "a leg" of a potential a-b-c corrective pattern. It remains to be seen how the pattern will actually evolve. A rally to 983.13 completed the "b leg," and as this is written the Dow has dropped precipitously below leg a. Thus the "c leg" (and hopefully the windup) is now underway.

**January 26, 1977**

*Question*: Russell, I hear what you say, but I'm getting very worried about rising interest rates. Don't you think booming interest rates will kill off this bull market? *Answer*: No, I think rising interest rates could temporarily *hold back* the primary bull trend, but the market will adjust to higher levels of interest rates in due time. People are still "spooked" by the shockingly high interest rates of 1970 and 1974, but I don't see them coming again in 1977. I am updating a chart of bond yields which I included in the December 1st Letter. I noted at the time that interest rates on a long term basis were heading down, but that the decline in interest rates was becoming climactic. I based this on my Elliott reading of the chart, showing the interest rate decline in the 5 wave of a typical Elliott 1-2-3-4-5 pattern.

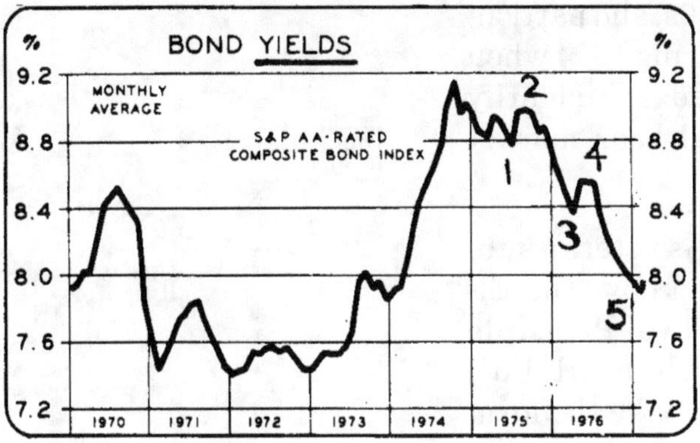


Following the conclusion of the 5 leg, and I think we are there, we should have a normal upward correction. This correction will serve to increase interest rates. In fact, we could see AA-rated bond yields rise from the current 7.9% to about 8.4% (at about point 3 on the chart pattern). After that, I expect interest rates to decline again, to new lows. Nevertheless, rising interest rates could make the market nervous during at least the first part of 1977, thus holding back the primary trend a while longer.

**March 9, 1977**

There are only a handful of men in the world who I consider expert at interpreting the Wave Principle. Charles J. Collins of Detroit, A.J. Frost of Canada, Robert Prechter of Merrill, Lynch in NYC. Recently I received letters from both Frost and Prechter, and putting their thoughts together with my own, I have decided to present another Elliott report to subscribers. I want to stress, however, that the following interpretations are mine, and they do differ in some aspects from those of Frost and Prechter.

Unfortunately, these studies are not easy to follow or to comprehend, and they do require a good deal of thinking. But I feel that Elliott is well worth it. Like any other market study, Elliott can be useful at times and useless at others. Certainly Elliott was invaluable to me all during the 1960s and 1970s, and particularly during 1974 when it helped me identify the final bear market bottom.

As veteran subscribers know, the Elliott Wave Principle states that all bull markets take the form of five major waves, the 1, 3, 5 waves being advan-ces and the 2 and 4 waves being declines or corrective waves. Elliott sees all bear markets as three- wave sequences, with the 1 and 3 waves being declines and the 2 or middle wave being a corrective advance. All of the major waves in both bull and bear markets can be subdivided into many smaller waves, but I want to try to keep this discussion as simple as possible.

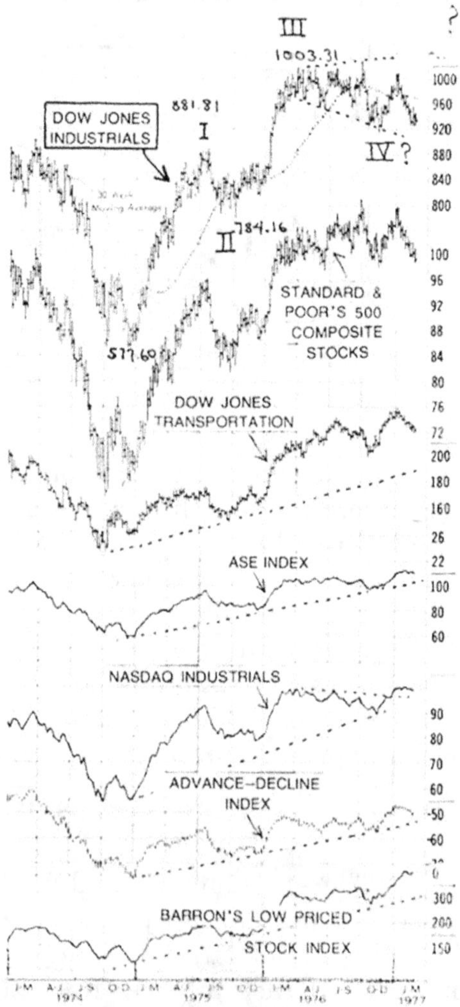


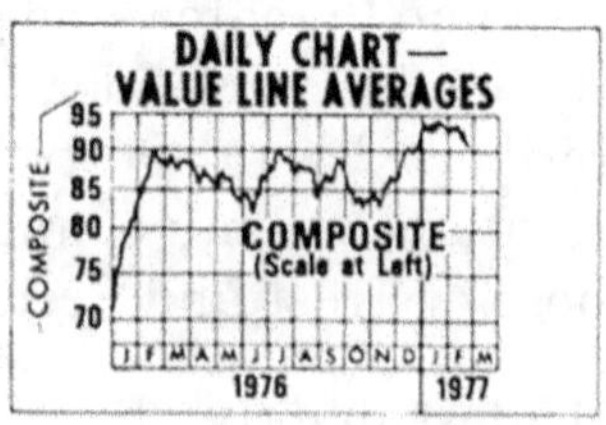


I have included a number of charts here which should help to illustrate where I think the market (actually I am dealing with the Dow Industrials) could be in Elliott terms.

As I see it, the first major wave of this primary bull market began at the December 1974 low of 577.60 (this is labelled wave I on the chart). Wave I carried the Dow to 881.81 in July 1975. Next came a simple correction. This first corrective wave (wave II) took the Dow down to 784.16 in October 1975. Wave III started from the 784.16 low of mid-1975. This wave advanced to the March 1976 Dow peak of 1003.31. Wave III (as I show it on the chart) is somewhat suspect, because an Elliott wave III is almost always greater in extent than a wave I. Therefore, what I have labelled as wave III may ultimately turn out to be only the first leg of a very much larger wave III (a bullish hope, certainly). But only time will tell.

Elliott made a point of the phenomenon of *alternation*, which states that where corrective wave II in a bull market is *simple* corrective wave IV will be *complex* — or vice versa. Note that corrective wave II (during 1975) was indeed simple, and this was one of the reasons why I felt that the market was in for a lot of sideways and complicated action following the late rise into 1976. Wave IV, as you can see on the chart, is far more extended and complicated than was wave II. It is therefore running true to Elliott form.

As I interpret it, advancing wave III ended on March 11, 1976 at 1003.31 on the Dow. What followed was corrective wave IV, a wave that is actually a most fascinating pattern.[10] Elliott alludes to this kind of pattern in this 1939 article in *Financial World* and he terms it a "reverse symmetrical triangle." This is the structure which has been confusing almost every analyst and investor in the nation since early 1976. But as I see it, we have now probably completed the Elliott reverse triangle. The triangle wave-form, I should emphasize, *only occurs during* a wave IV, and thus the triangle of 1976 would appear to fit into my Elliott interpretation.

---

[10] This came from Prechter's reports, which had further concluded the previous month that the fifth wave had ended as a truncation on the last trading day of December 1976.

For the interest of subscribers, I am including the actual diagram (Horizontal Triangles, below) drawn by R.N. Elliott for his article on triangles in the 1939 *Financial World*. In my opinion, there is a good chance that we completed a "D" type triangle at the 924.04 Dow low of November 1976. If so, then the next major Dow move should be wave V, an advancing wave which will either complete the entire bull market which began in December 1974, or complete the first leg of a much larger wave III.

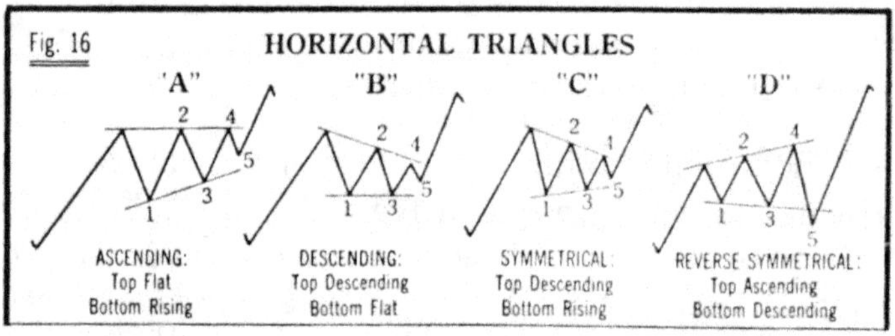


I have also drawn a daily chart which shows the extraordinary Dow reverse symmetrical triangle in detail. Here we see the termination of wave III at 1003.31 (March 1976). Next came the five-point reversal triangle of March to November 1976, terminating with the 924.04 low of November 10.

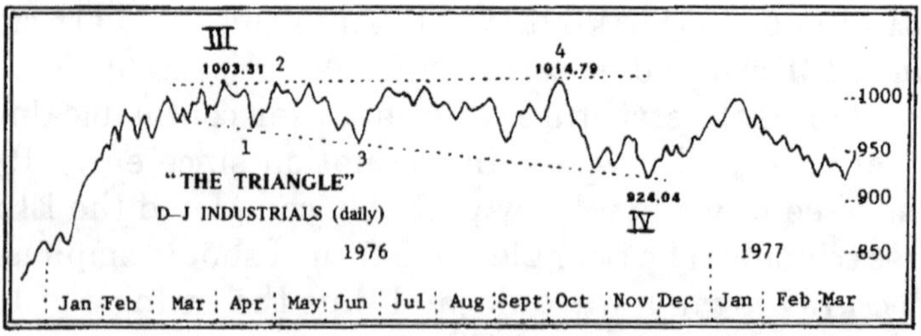


The importance of the 924.04 low (if indeed that is to be the Dow low) should now be apparent to all readers. If 924.04 was THE low of wave IV, then we are currently moving into wave V, which should be the most speculative wave yet seen in this bull market. In order to allow readers to understand why I think that 924.04 "could have been the low," I now want to go into one mathematical aspect of Elliott.

Going back to the chart, the decline represented by wave IV should serve to correct the rise of wave III only (since wave I has already been corrected by declining wave II). The advance of wave III took the Dow from 784.16 to 1003.31, a distance of 219.15 Dow points. If we apply the *Fibonacci ratio of 61.8%* to 219.15, we get 135 points. Adding 135.43 to 784.16 gives us 919.59, a figure which is less than 5 points from the 924.04 low of November 10. This suggests that 924.04 could have been the end of wave IV, or it suggests that there might be one more decline which would take the Dow slightly below the November low of 924.04 (to around 919).

Turning back to the composite chart of the seven different averages and indices, it is interesting to note the possible confirmation of the thesis that wave IV ended in November 1976. On the latest decline, the Standard & Poor 500 held above its previous lows in November. The DJ Transportation Average not only held far above its November low on all the action since, but it never got near its rising bull market trendline. The ASE (Amex) index has held above its bull market trendline and recently moved into new high territory, suggesting that November was the Amex low and that a new Amex rise is underway. The exact same thing can be said of the NASDAQ Industrial Average.

The Advance-Decline Ratio (which tends to act like an unweighted average) has held well above its bull market rising trendline. This is true even though the "buying stampede" of the past four months has ended. Barron's Low Priced Stock Index has pushed into new high ground for the bull market, suggesting that an increasing degree of speculation could lie ahead.

At the bottom of the chart, I have included the broad, unweighted Value Line Index, which includes over 1600 stocks on the NYSE, the Amex and the OTC. Like the A-D Ratio, the Value Line, despite all recent corrective action, is currently near its bull market high. The rise from the November 1976 low on the Value Line Composite has the look of the beginning of an important new rise.

*Conclusion*: If the November 1976 Dow low of 924.04 represented the termination of the wave IV triangle correction, then the next major move of the Dow should be an advance which we will label wave V. Since fifth waves are usually the *most speculative* waves, we should be prepared for frothy action on the next important rise. If successful, wave V should carry above the bull market high or above 1014.79.

The termination of wave V could mark the end of the whole bull market, or it could mark the end of leg 3 of a much larger major wave III. There is simply no way of telling now. But our tactics in either case should be the same. If the end of wave V marks the finish of the current primary bull market, we will sell to avoid what could be a severe bear market. On the other hand, if the end of wave V marks the end of the second rising phase of a huge wave III (obviously, we will label it wave III in retrospect), it will still pay us to move out. This is so because we have been in a mild triangle correction during 1976-77 and the next downside correction is almost guaranteed to be more severe than anything we have seen so far in this bull market.

*Note*: Hamilton Bolton, a great Elliott student, observed that in bull markets, the wave III advance is usually greater (in extent) than the wave I advance. But there are exceptions. The rule of the exceptions is that wave III may be shorter than either wave I or wave V, but wave III is never shorter than both. This rule applies to the current bull market. Note on the chart that wave III of this bull market is shorter than wave I. This indicates that the coming wave

V should be greater than the 219 points of wave III. Or it indicates that wave III, as I have drawn it on the chart, is only the first wave of a much larger five-leg structure, all of which will ultimately be labelled as wave III.

Either way, it is a very bullish concept for the stock market. Elliott is saying that for whatever reason (Jimmy Carter, do you know something we don't?) this bull market is going considerably higher. If, for instance, 924.04 was the low of wave IV and the coming wave V results in a Dow advance of just 239 points (or only 20 points greater in extent than wave III), then the ultimate Dow peak could be 1143. On the other hand, if wave III as shown on the chart turns out (in retrospect) to be just the second rising leg of an extended wave III structure, then the Dow is fated to go higher than even the wildest optimists are thinking about before this bull market breathes its last.

After all that, I suspect the typical subscriber might say, "Russell, I can follow about half of what you're talking about, but so what! What good is Elliott really?" And my answer is that I use Elliott as a more important frame of reference. I believe man's life makes sense, and since the stock market is made by the minds and emotions of men, I think the market should and does make sense. Using both the Dow Theory and Elliott, I feel that I am working in twilight and on some occasions I feel I am actually working in the light. Without Elliott or the Dow Theory, I know I would be operating totally in the dark.

**May 4, 1977**

*FIBONACCI*: I'll admit it, the Fibonacci series as applied to the stock market has always held a great fascination for me. Periodically, I have commented on the Fibonacci series (FS), and these studies have been a great help to me in the past. During 1973 and 1974, I published a number of FS, and I concluded that the final bear market bottom could arrive in December 1974. As fate (or Fibonacci) would have it, that is exactly what happened. And coincidence or not, the events of 1974 only confirmed my belief that there is a "great collective intelligence" which operates in the stock market. That intelligence is a function of millions of minds all reacting, interacting, confirming and even cancelling out each other. FS, I believe, is or can be a prime aid in unraveling the mystery of the market's intelligence. So here I go.

Leonardo de Pisa (called Fibonacci) was the greatest mathematician of the Middle Ages. Elliott, of Elliott Wave fame, was fascinated with Fibonacci's discoveries. In his 1946 monograph, *Nature's Law*, Elliott mentions the FS, and it is clear that he felt that his Wave Principle was based on the FS.

I have been working for the past three months on the FS, trying to uncover something in that mysterious series that might provide us with a key date for the period ahead. I have never mentioned the following to anyone, so here it is for what it is worth.

> 1966 bull market top to 1974 bear market low was *8* years.
>
> September 1976 bull market high (so far) to *October 1977* is *13* months.
>
> December 1974 bear market bottom to September 1976 bull market high is *21* months.
>
> December 1974 bear market bottom to *October 1977* is *34* months.
>
> May 1970 crash bottom to December 1974 bear market bottom is *55* months.
>
> May 1970 crash bottom to *October 1977* is *89* months.

Thus, I have presented a Fibonacci series of 8, 13, 21, 34, 55, 89. It is of interest to me that the high for this bull market (so far) occurred on September 21, 1976 at 1014.79 on the Dow. That high arrived exactly *21* months after the December 1974 bear market low. Rather mysteriously, the high came on the 21st day of September 1976.

It is also of interest that the month of *October 1977* comes up *three times* in my tabulations. It seems to me that October could be a *very important month.* Unfortunately, in working with the FS, there is no way of telling whether the projected key month will be a bottom or a top. We have to watch the market for *clues.*

Let's assume that *October 1977* is fated to be a key month for the stock market. If that comes to pass, what are the forthcoming possibilities? The bullish possibility would be a bottom forming here or somewhere in the next few weeks (or even months), with a new major rise carrying into October.

The bearish possibility, and one that I certainly hope does not come to pass, is a series of weak rallies and stronger declines with the ultimate bottom arriving in October. October is a long way off, and I would hardly relish the idea of the bottom materializing then.

**May 13, 1977**

*MIXED RHYTHMS*: I am including a composite chart of a number of important market averages and indices. I have been studying this chart for some weeks now, trying to decipher the "message" in those various indicators. What we see here is a very mixed but fascinating picture, and I want to review the picture now.

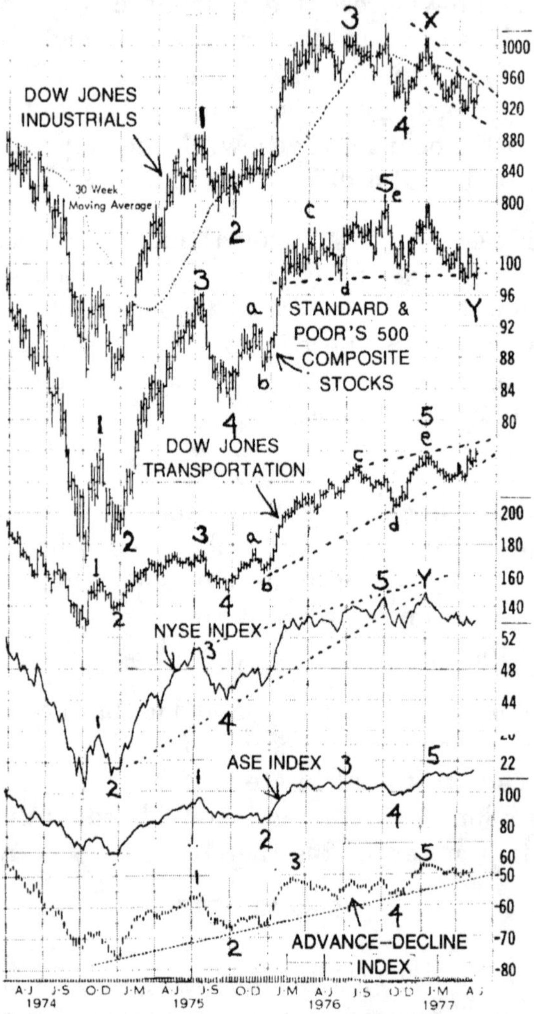


All graphs are drawn on a weekly basis. At the top of the chart we have the Dow Industrial Average. As I see it, the Dow has moved up during this market in a series of three waves (marked 1-2-3 on the chart). A second corrective wave ended at 4, but the ensuing rise ended in failure at point X. Since then the Dow has drifted off in what I would term a "descending wedge." As a rule, the price movement will break out of a descending wedge on the upside.

If this comes to pass, the Dow should push up through the 950-60 area. But the failure at X implies weakness, and I am doubtful as to whether the Dow is capable at this time of making a new bull market high above the 1014.79 high of September 21, 1976.

The S&P 500 seems to be in a different cycle than the Dow. I count three completed legs up to point 3 in mid-1975, a correction to point 4, and then an a-b-c-d-e to point 5 in late 1976. But the whole pattern in the 500 since late 1975 seems to have taken the form of a "head-and-shoulders" top. Two weeks ago the support was broken at Y on the chart. This would seem to indicate real weakness in the 500. I see the S&P 500 as a laggard now, unable to keep up with the Dow on any rise from here.

The DJ Transportation Average has been the "powerhouse" of this bull market. I count a completed five legs up from the October, 1974 low, with the 5 leg "extending" as shown on the chart. The "true top" for the Transports probably came at point 5 (e) on the chart, and the recent action appears to be a possible "false top" or "blow-off" move. Note that the Transports have formed a "rising wedge" pattern, just the opposite of the pattern which shows on the Industrial Average. Any move above the upper rising trendline on Transports should lead to exhaustion.

I see the NYSE Index as also having completed a five-leg rise at the September 1976 peak (marked 5 on the chart). At the January peak Y, I think we saw a "failure," and this led to the most recent weakness. As in the case with the S&P 500, I feel that the NYSE Index is not apt to make a new high from here.

The patterns of the AMEX (ASE), and the Advance-Decline Ratio (NYSE) are all remarkably similar. I count completed 1-2-3-4-5 patterns in both of these. In each case, the price movement is very close to the rising trendlines, and I would say that it would be most important that these trendlines not be violated.

*Conclusion*: After 15 months of generally sideways movement, the various market averages and indices have moved out of synchronization to a remarkable degree. This suggests to me that any rise from here should be ragged and quite selective, unlike, for instance, the rises of early 1975 and early 1976. When a market becomes this ragged, I usually prefer to leave it to the floor traders and the speculatively inclined.

**July 29, 1977**

*FIBONACCI*: Most of my readers know of my interest in the Fibonacci numerical series. I last explained the series in [May 4, 1977], so I am not going to do so again. But I do want to review my findings, and I want to add one new facet.

The series, if you remember, deals with the sum of each two numbers adding up to the third as 1, 2, 3, 5, 8, 13, 21, 34, 55, 89, etc. At any rate, in [the May 4, 1977 Letter] I stated that a truly extraordinary number of dates pointed to *October 1977* as a most important period. I cannot tell yet whether October is fated to be a top or a bottom. But here are the figures.

> September 1976 bull market peak (Dow 1014.79) to October 1977 is *13* months.
>
> December 1974 major bear market bottom to October 1977 is *21* months.
>
> May 1970 crash bottom to October 1977 is *89* months.

And here is the new one I came up with. From September 21, 1976 (the bull market high for the Dow) to the week of October 17th, 1977 would be *55* weeks. So let's see what October may bring. Personally, I'll be most fascinated to find out.

Exactly 20 years ago, by the way, in *July*, the second phase of the 1949-66 bull market ended, followed by the *October* 1957 market bottom — and a great buying area for the coming bull market third phase.

**September 30, 1977**

Using my Fibonacci studies, I have made a case for the second phase bottom to appear in October (next month). Whether the market obliges remains to be seen (obviously, the odds are always overwhelmingly against Richard Russell or any other analyst being able to pick a major bottom down to the last month). At any rate, more important than my picking the bottom in October is the probability that a good bottom does lie somewhere ahead. When we hit it, I'm going to say "buy 'em."

But I'm not going to say "buy 'em" until I am reasonably convinced that we are at THE bottom.

**November 18, 1977**

Many subscribers have written asking what I think of the current market in terms of the Elliott Wave Principle. This seems like a good time to bring the Elliott interpretations up to date.

The last thing I discussed [on May 13, 1977] was a phenomenon which I termed an important "upside failure" for the Dow in late December 1976. That incident was a dramatic failure by the Dow to push above its previous market peak of 1014.79 (September 21, 1976). I wrote: *"But the failure at 'X' on the charts implies weakness, and I am doubtful as to whether the Dow is capable at this time of making a new bull market high above the 1014.79 high of September 21, 1976."*

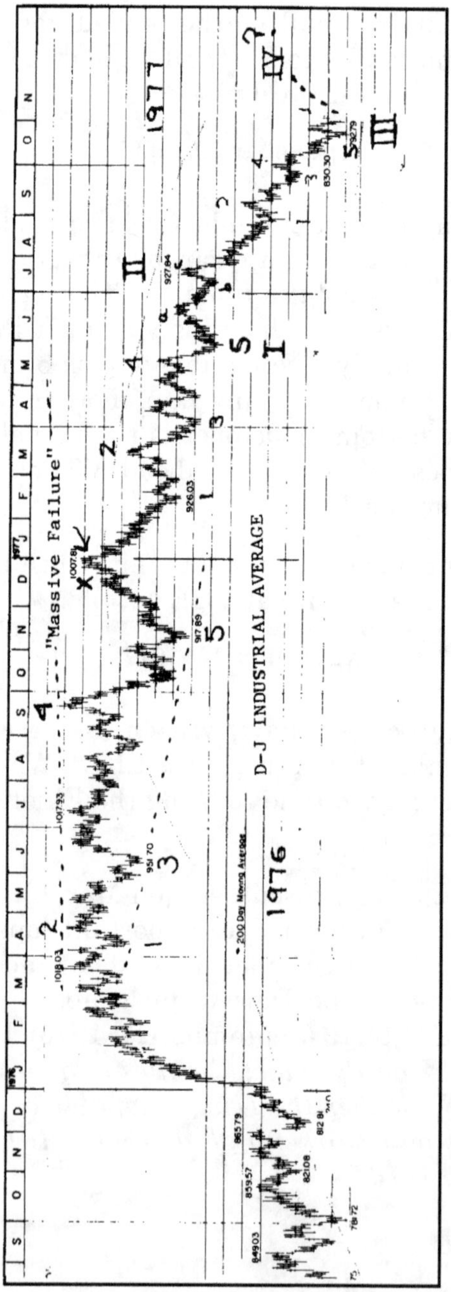
D-J INDUSTRIAL AVERAGE
"Massive Failure"
1976
1977
200 Day Moving Average

I have included an updated chart of the daily Dow action, and I think the whole situation is beginning to take form in Elliott terms. During 1976, we had a giant "consolidation/correction" which took the form of a one-year triangle. This triangle (a triangle is always a corrective pattern) is shown on the chart as a five-point triangle, and the triangle is contained by the two dotted trendlines.

Following point 5 at the November 1976 low, the correction was completed. From here, the normal expectation was a major new bull leg, an upwave which should have corresponded with the speculative third phase of the bull market. But at X (Dow 1004) the price movement fizzled. The Dow simply "died." This *extraordinary failure* under Elliott went a long way towards turning me cautious at the time. I didn't know why the Dow failed at X. Maybe the market was appraising President Carter, maybe it was looking at the dollar and the deficit situation, I don't know. But I do know that something "changed," and the Dow produced an amazing Elliott failure on the upside, then turned down.

Since that failure in December 1976, the Dow has moved down in a major Elliott correction or an Elliott bear market. I show the Dow as having completed two major downward legs and one corrective rallying leg. The completed legs are marked in Roman numerals. Leg I carried down to a May 31, 1977 low. Leg II then rallied the Dow to a July peak. Leg III, then slammed the Dow down to the recent October 25 low of 801.54.

The big question, of course, is this: "Have we completed a 1-2-3 Elliott correction? Or is the most recent rally part of upward corrective leg IV, the preamble to downward leg V which will finish off this phase of the pattern?"

As this is written, there is really no way of my telling whether the advance that began on November 2 is going to develop into (1) a more extended (upward) corrective leg IV, or (2) whether the November 2-11 rally completed a substandard upward leg IV, or (3) whether the market will come down and trace out a double bottom, preparatory to a much more extensive upward leg IV. All that remains to be seen, and there is no sense guessing about it at this stage of the game.

**November 30, 1977**

*FIBONACCI*: By the time you read this, it is possible that Industrials will have bettered the 845.89 point, and, in that case, this study will be meaningless. Nevertheless, I thought the following was interesting in the light of my Fibonacci studies.

In the last Letter [November 9, 1977], I showed how, according to my Elliott count, major declining wave III terminated for the Dow at 801.54 on October 25, 1977. Since then, the Dow has been in (upward) corrective wave IV. I show part (or conceivably all) of wave IV on this chart from *The Wall Street Journal*. From the start of wave IV at 801.54 on October 25 to point C on November 11 is exactly 13 days. Now the Dow peak at C is 845.89.

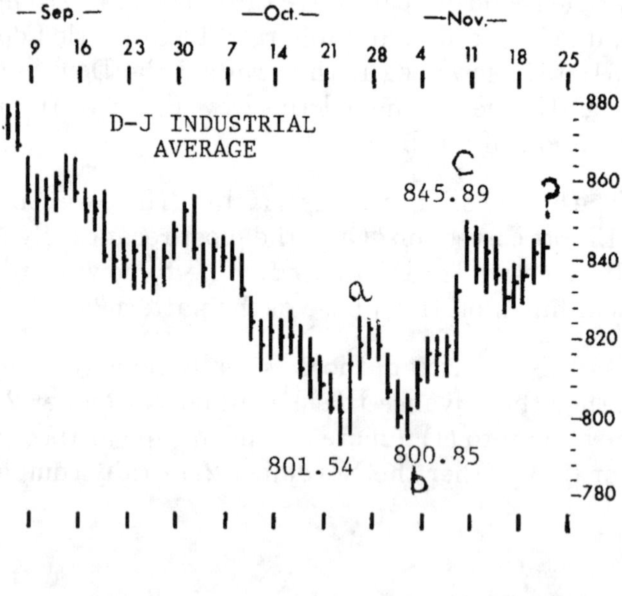

If you add up each number of 845.89 you get 34. Finally, the Dow rise from 800.85 to the peak at C of 845.89 represents a correction of exactly 21% of the entire 1976-77 drop in the Dow (from 1014.79 to 800.85).

Thus, we have three Fibonacci numbers which come up in connection with the recent October-November rally, the three numbers being 13, 21, and 34. That tells me that the 845.89 peak at C was quite important. It suggests (if the market turns down with the Dow having failed to better 845.89) that we may have seen the end of a rather short correction. If so (and I obviously can't tell at this writing), we could have a rather large leg V down. Abbreviated upward corrections often lead to extensive declines.

**January 18, 1978**

I want to update my Elliott interpretation of the market, a subject which I last discussed [on November 9, 1977]. As older subscribers know, Elliott and Fibonacci are "hobbies" of mine, but they are hobbies which occasionally help me tremendously with my market analyses. I also find (believe it or not) that a fairly large number of my readers are Elliott students.

At any rate, [the November 9 Letter] noted that "since the failure in December 1976, the Dow has moved down in what is either a major Elliott correction or an Elliott bear market. I made that statement because of the extraordinary "failure" following point 5 (November 1976) in the complicated triangle correction pattern as seen on the chart.

The Dow turned up from its November 1976 low in what "should have been the beginning of a final, major wave V." This is the wave that we expected would end the bull market which began in late-1974. But in January 1977, a most extraordinary failure occurred. The failure took place when the Dow was unable to better the upper trendline of the triangle. At the point of that dramatic failure, the Dow began a new bear market.

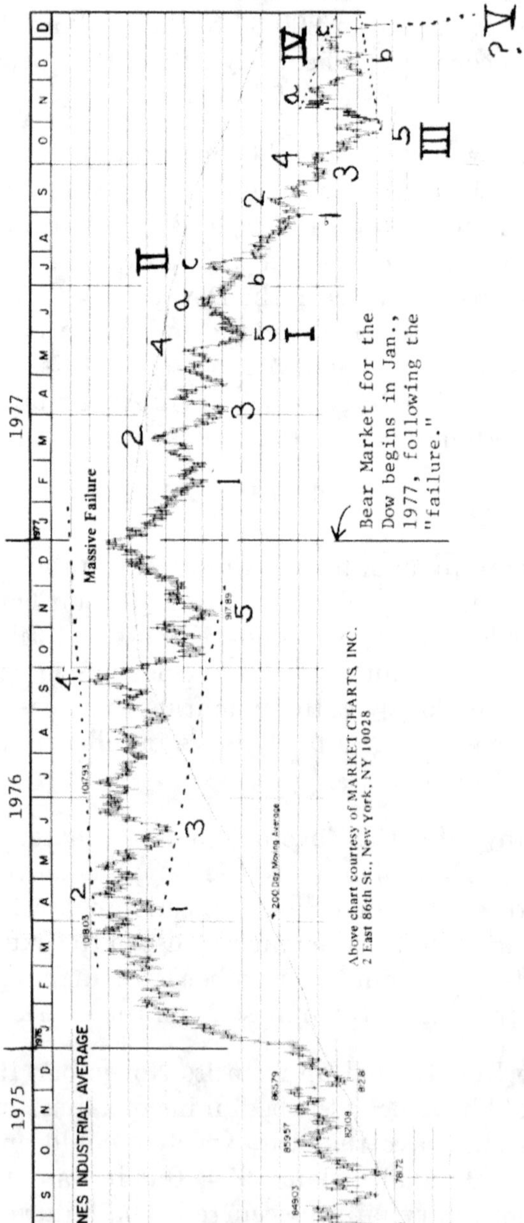
DOW-JONES INDUSTRIAL AVERAGE
1975
1976
1977
Massive Failure
Bear Market for the Dow begins in Jan., 1977, following the "failure."
Above chart courtesy of MARKET CHARTS, INC.
2 East 86th St., New York, NY 10028

Elliott bear markets take the form of large A-B-C downward patterns (A and C are down-waves while B is a rising or corrective wave). The A and C waves may be divided into a number of smaller waves, and I believe we have completed most of downwave A now, with only final leg V of wave A ahead. After leg V (and wave A) is completed, we should get a big upward correction which will probably take us up during the second half of 1978. Then declining wave C should develop during 1979, thereby completing the bear market.

The chart shows leg I (divided into five smaller movements) ending in late May 1977. We then had a very weak "flat" correction which took the Dow to a July peak, and this a-b-c pattern ended at II. Next the Dow declined another series of five minor legs down to the late October low of 801.54 (III on chart).

The movement from the November low into December (the final little a-b-c on the chart) was another extraordinarily weak correction with a "failure" at point "c" (I would have expected c to be above the 845.89 point at point a, but it became obvious that the correction at IV was turning into a weak triangle instead of a stronger upward zigzag).

*Conclusion*: I would now expect a final wave V to take the Dow down to new lows in a five-movement decline. It should be remembered that the last downwave or the 5 wave in a cycle is frequently the most intense. Thus, the coming leg 5 declining pattern for the Dow (which should wind up wave A) should be a nasty one, indeed.

**February 17, 1978**

I include my weekly chart of two segments of the bond market, the representative Treasury 7½'s of 1988 and the broad DJ 20 Bond Average. Both items are saying the same thing, namely, that the bond markets have been (and still are) weak.

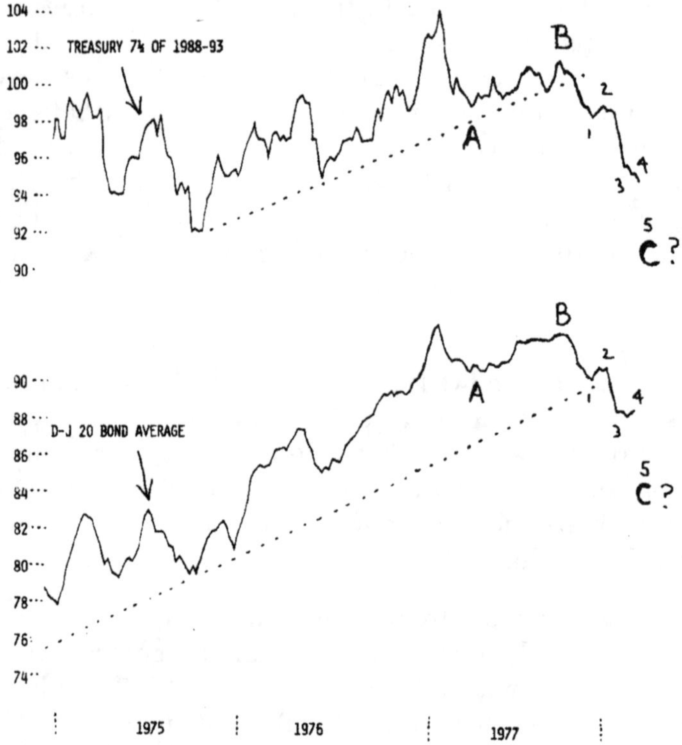


I count this as an Elliott bear market move for bonds, with an A-B-C decline in progress. A (down) and B (up) are completed, and the C (down) leg is in process. C should be divided into five smaller legs, and if I am correct, we are about to see the final leg 5 (down) to complete this bear market (or at least this phase of the bear market). Subscribers can see why I've been saying "Out of bonds and into T-bills" for so many months. And the worst (for bonds) could still lie ahead.

**March 1, 1978**

I have been doing a great deal of thinking regarding (1) the massive debt picture in this country, (2) the action of the market, (3) the very long term picture, and (4) all of this in terms of the Elliott Wave Principle. Mr. George E. Barber is an investment advisor who does extensive work with Elliott and moving averages, and his view of the market and Elliott is different from most that I have seen. I've studied Barber's work at length, and I believe his interpretation could be absolutely valid.[11]

One particular facet of this analysis interested me, and that is the conclusion that a great bull market ended in 1966. This has always been my contention; it was also the opinion of the late, great E. George Schaefer (whom I corresponded with during the 1960s and 1970s). Barber believes that the entire rise from 1932 to 1966 was simply final leg V of a massive grand Supercycle. Barber also believes in an approximate 54-year cycle, which implies that the final bottom of the bear market which began in 1966 will occur around 1986 (or 54 years from 1932, the bottom of the great 1929-32 bear market).

I have included this chart which shows Barber's concept of the Dow from 1932 to the 1966 bull market top, and then the bear market to the present. But it is the picture which lies ahead that I believe (if this interpretation is correct) will be of vital interest to subscribers. The bull market from 1932 took the Dow up in five Elliott waves (A,B,C,D,E) to the ***1966 top*** of 995.15 on the Dow. From there a great bear market began. The bear market will assume the form of three major legs down. The three legs will cover around 20 years in time (1966 to 1986) and they will take equities to lows perhaps not seen since the 1940s or 1930s.

The first bear market downleg took the form of an a-b-c-d-e wave down to the 1974 low of 577.60 on the Dow. This ended at ONE on the chart. The recovery wave (which

---

[11] This horrid study, which Frost and I independently protested vehemently at the time as a travesty of "Elliott," was published in *Dow Theory Letters* on the exact day of an hourly low that to this day has not been broken.

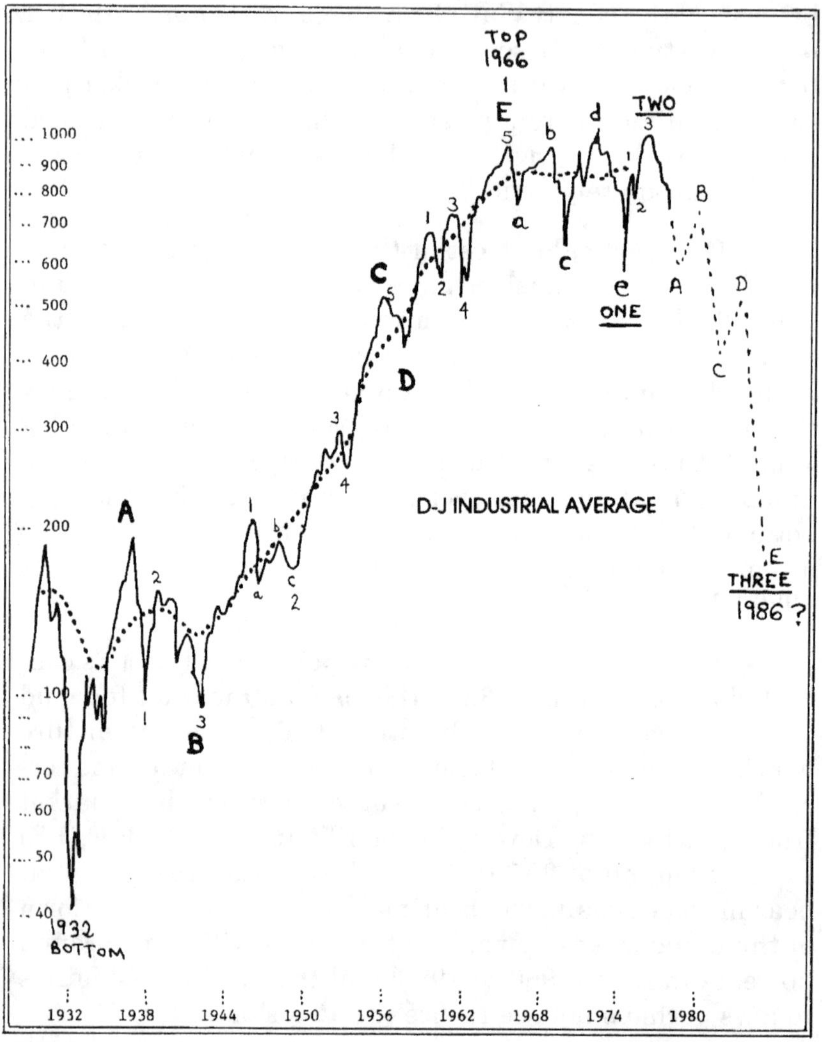


we refer to as the bull market of 1974-76) ended for the Dow on September 21, 1976 at 1014.79. This wave is labeled TWO on the chart. Currently, we are well into downleg A, the first leg of an A-B-C-D-E series of legs down, all of which comprise final major wave THREE as shown on the chart.

A number of further observations should be made here. (1) The dotted line on the chart is an 80-month moving average which is centered (it is charted between the 40th and 41st month). This provides a very long term picture of the Average Dow price, and as you can see this moving average is in the process of "rolling over" and heading down. The bearish implications of such a move are clear enough.

(2) Even though this Elliott view of the picture ahead is ominously bearish, note that there will be advances (leg B and leg D), and these advances could be powerful enough to be labeled mini-bull markets. Thus, even though a major supercycle bear market is now in effect, it will be punctuated by two mini-bull markets, each of which could be highly profitable.

(3) The question immediately arises, when does the current downleg A end, and when does leg B (which could be a very profitable rise) start? The only intelligent comment I can offer here is that current downleg A will end when this market stirs up enough FEAR to produce a major oversold condition. That could occur during this spring or summer, but as I have said so many times before, it is far easier to *identify* such areas than it is to predict them.

(4) Although the Elliott scenario presented here is a most discouraging one for the long-term, it fits into my presentation in the last Letter regarding "survival." It also fits into the section which deals with the necessity for investments which are very liquid (marketable) and the extreme need for proper timing over the period ahead.

(5) Finally, this Elliott scenario fits into my overall picture of a tremendous *liquidation of debt* in the period ahead. And that is what I think the whole bear market is going to be about — the liquidation of the unbelievable mountain of debt (in all sectors of the economy) that has been building up since 1932 — but much more importantly since World War II.

Speaking of liquidation, the latest (January) statistics show what could be a straw in the wind. January saw the first drop in NYSE margin debt from the $9.7 billion record high, a drop to $9.6 billion. During bear markets, it is normal for the margin debt to be steadily liquidated. It therefore would not surprise me to see margin debt drop to 15% to 25% of its record high before this bear market breathes its last. Despite the drop in margin debt, however, I note that the number of margin accounts actually increased by 5000 in January.

*LATE THOUGHTS*: By now, most of my readers should be familiar with the Fibonacci series of 1, 2, 3, 5, 8, 13, 21, 34, etc. In the series each lower number is 61.8% of the following higher number. This is the extraordinary 61.8% Fibonacci ratio.

Applying this to the present, note that the Industrial rise of 1974 to 1976 (577.60 to 1014.79) was 427 points. Now 61.8% of that rise is 270 points, and if we subtract 270 from 1014.79 we get 744. In other words, a 61.8% correction of the 1974-76 Dow bull market would take the Dow down to 744.[12]

The intraday low for the Dow on this entire decline was reached last week on February 23 at 742.98. This low was within a hair of the Fibonacci target of 744, and it occurred to me that the 743-45 level could set off a Dow rally. If so, the rally would not have an adequate base in that the market was NOT oversold at any time during 1978. My conclusion is that if the market rallies substantially from here, it will soon reach an overbought condition. Such a situation could easily set the stage for a broad new slide.

**April 14, 1978**

The market, even though it is overbought, is going to do what it has to do to fulfill its "pattern destiny." The

---

[12] Prechter's report on this target had just been published.

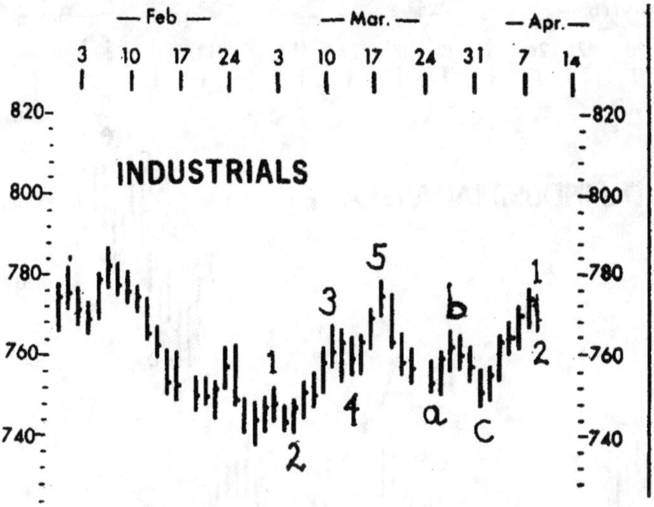


chart from *The Wall Street Journal* shows the daily Dow action from the March lows. I believe we are seeing an Elliott (upward) correction, a typical 5-3-5 pattern. I count five little legs up on the chart, a perfect little a-b-c down, and then the start of what should be the final part of this upward correction. At 5 (1 and 3 are probably completed), the Dow should be exhausted. I doubt whether the Dow can get back much above 780-800 since the initial upward corrective wave (1 through 5) was so unimpressive. It's taking a tremendous amount of volume to move this market higher. We'll stand aside.

**May 5, 1978**

Speaking of Elliott, I now have what I believe is a completed Elliott "count" for the Dow on this bear market rally. In [the April 14, 1978] Letter, I included a daily Dow chart and wrote as follows: "The market is going to do what it has to do to fulfill its 'pattern destiny'... I believe we are seeing an Elliott upward correction, a typical 5-3-5 pattern...."

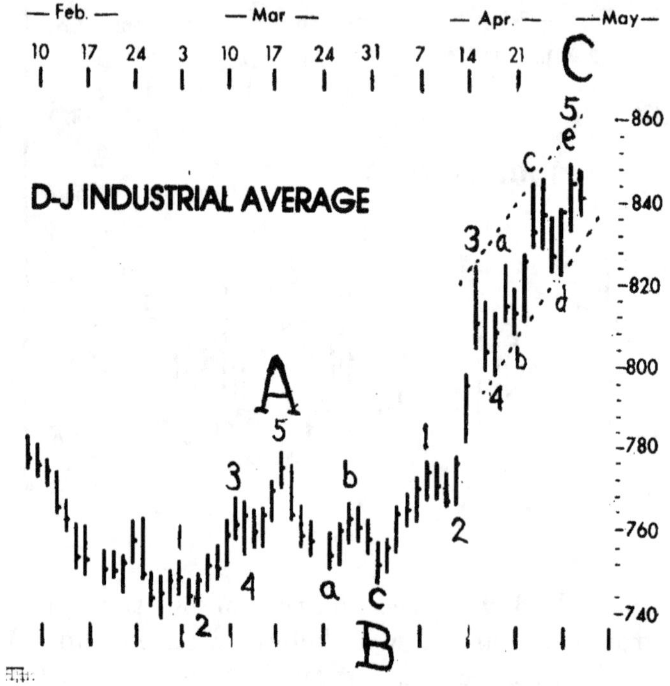


Now refer to the Dow chart. The first wave took the Dow up (in five little legs) to large A at 773.82 (March 20) Next we saw a little three-leg decline (a-b-c) to large B on April 3.

The leg to large C was a powerhouse. We saw an advance to point 1, then a little dip to point 2. A break-away "gap" exploded to point 3. Next we saw a two-day decline to point 4. And most recently, we have seen wave 5 develop in a perfect channel as it subdivided into an a-b-c-d-e.

At e (May 1), the large wave C should be just about completed. Unless the Dow can "extend" again, this time above the upper channel line (above 860-870), I would think the bear rally has run into exhaustion. The buyers should be about "used up." If so, then I would expect a move down towards or below 800, then another (but feebler) rally.

**January 17, 1979**

I have not reviewed my Fibonacci work for almost a year, and this seems like a good time to go into it again.

Veteran readers know that the Fibonacci series is an integral part of the Elliott wave studies.

I don't have time to go into the hundreds of ramifications of the Fibonacci series, but suffice it to say that the series has helped me immensely in my stock market work.

The following observations based on Fibonacci time sequences are listed. Those who wish to place them in the "coincidental" category are free to do so.

3 years from the 1976 top to the year 1979.

5 years from the 1974 bottom to 1979.

13 years from the 1966 top to 1979.

21 months from October 1977 (where most secondary stocks hit bottom) to July *1979.*

34 months from the September 21, 1976 Dow top to July *1979.*

55 months from the December 1974 Dow bottom to July *1979.*

Thus, the six time sequences listed above point to the importance of the year 1979 and more specifically to JULY 1979.

Combining the two studies, here is what we have.

(1) We know that February 1979 will be the 52nd month since the last historic bottom which occurred in October 1974. No market since 1949 has gone more than 52 months without producing a major bottom. But it looks as if this one will.

(2) May 1979 is interesting because May would be the 55th month since the October 1974 bottom — and *55* is a Fibonacci number (By the way, Richard Russell will also turn *55* years of age on July 22, 1979).

(3) July 1979 shapes up (from a Fibonacci standpoint) as a crucial month for the stock market. We could see a major bottom for the market in that month.[13]

*BONDS*: I show here my daily chart of the Treasury 8's of 1996. This bond has now come down from a 1977 peak price of 108 to the current price of just over 90. This

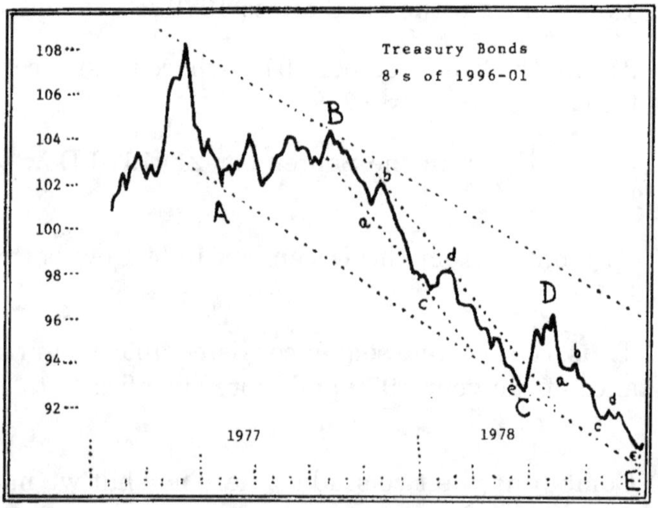


[13] Although nothing appeared to happen that month, *The Elliott Wave Theorist* identified that time as the end of a long period of contraction in the extent of the market's swings. From there, they expanded again.

represents an incredible drop of 16.6% on this highest-grade of all available debt paper. After all, this bond has behind it the full faith and taxing power of the U.S. Government. If it doesn't pay its 8% coupon, the U.S. Treasury is "broke."

The bond has declined in the classic Elliott five waves down, an A-B-C-D-E pattern as shown. The B leg is clearly subdivided into five smaller legs. The E leg is also subdivided into five smaller legs. At point E, the bond has resisted making contact with the lower trendline of the channel, and this is a *positive* point. I am now thinking that the Treasury bonds have probably entered a buying range. I base this (1) on my technical studies, (2) on contrary opinion, (3) on the fact that in the current area of 9% yields, the Treasuries offer what I consider "great value." At the current yield, the Treasuries (with almost no risk) offer average yields 53% above the Average yield on the DJ Industrial Average!

Consequently, I believe that subscribers should now watch the 8's of 1996 carefully (quotes are in the daily paper). At 91 bid, the 8's will have bettered their first minor declining trendline and also a minor preceding peak. At 91 bid, I recommend taking 1/3 the money that you are holding in T-bills and buying 8's of 1996. I believe the odds on profits in these bonds now *far outweighs the risk of loss.*

A number of years ago (I don't remember just when),[14] Bob Prechter of Merrill Lynch's research department got in touch with me and expressed interest in the Elliott Wave Principle as I occasionally expounded it. I had further correspondence with this brilliant young man over the years. About two years ago, A.J. Frost (probably the leading expert on Elliott) suggested that he and I write a new and much-needed book on Elliott. I thought about this and decided that the project (in view of my commitment to my own subscribers) was just too much for me.

---

[14] It was March 31, 1976.

It was a lucky decision. Frost decided to do the book with Prechter, and the results, I am sure, are far beyond anything Frost could have done with me. This is a definitive, excellent book on Elliott, and I recommend it to all who have an interest in the Wave Principle. *Elliott Wave Principle, Key to Stock Market Profits* is published by New Classics Library.

## July 5, 1979

I have been pondering the Wall Street situation long and hard, wondering how I should best approach it for my subscribers. For I believe that we are at a juncture in the market that is as IMPORTANT as it is confusing.

The most bullish case [for Wall Street] is the one that is made by many leading students of the Elliott Wave Principle (both Bob Prechter and A.J. Frost espouse the picture that I will now describe). The same case is graphically put forth in this chart. The chart shows a massive Supercycle which began at the 1932 low of 41 on the Dow. The first bull wave took the Dow to the 1937 peak of 194. The correction to point 2 returned the Dow to a 1942 low of 92. The third bull wave extended to the 1966 high of 995. And the very complicated corrective wave 4 smashed the Dow down to the 1974 low of 577.

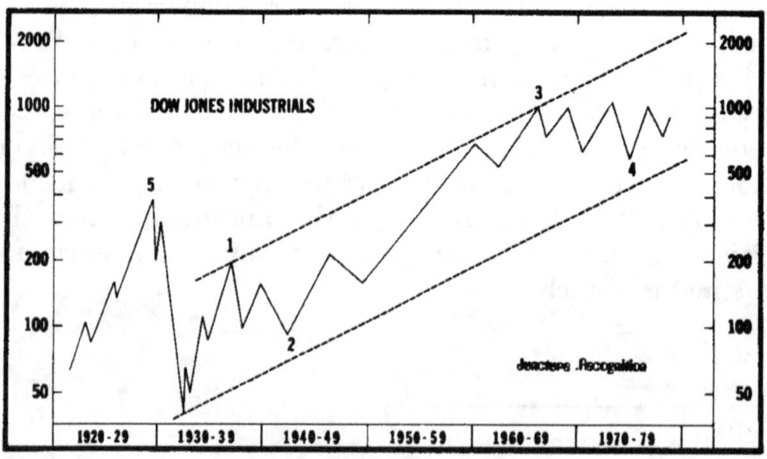

According to this view, we are now moving up in the final bull wave 5, even though the Dow is still only 265 points above its 1974 low. Both Prechter and Frost expect the fifth wave to carry very much higher. Prechter estimates 2860 on the Dow by 1983 (strangely, Value Line espouses this bullish view of the market but from the standpoint of fundamental analysis). What could occur to make this fantastically bullish case come true? First, we know that the Dow is "cheap" by historical standards. I think the second chart tells the story. In brief, the Dow is now in the "bargain zone" from the historical standpoint of price/earnings ratios, return on dividends and from the standpoint that it is currently selling below book value for only the fourth time since the 1930s.

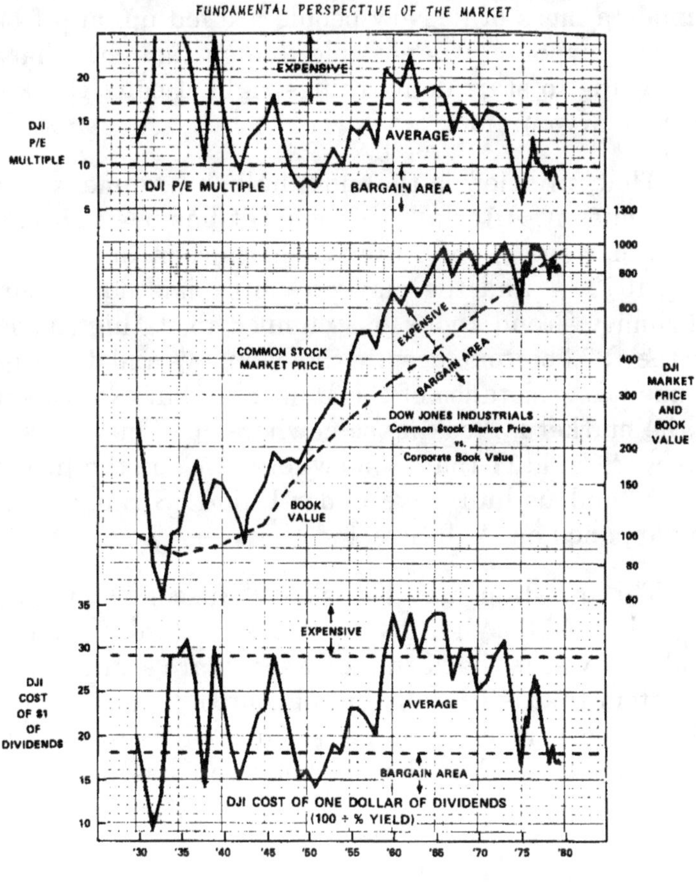

What could be the impetus to drive the Dow and the rest of the market into orbit, as projected by Elliott theorists? Inflation immediately comes to mind. After all, housing has careened into the wild blue yonder, collectibles have exploded in price, gold and the other precious metals have made major moves, commodities in general are now pushing higher. So what is left but common stocks? At some point (and possibly soon) the institutions and the public are going to realize that the only values left on the investment landscape are stocks — and then the rush could begin.

From a contrary standpoint, one could also say that for years and years the U.S. has done everything wrong. From Vietnam to inflation, from gaping deficits to pathetic Social Security mismanagement, you name it and the U.S. has made a mess of it. Now people are fed up, and from a contrary viewpoint it is possible (happy thought) that the U.S. is going to start doing things right. I can't think of a more contrary opinion!

That, in brief, is the most bullish argument. And I don't dismiss it. After all, this market has been absorbing wave after wave of the rottenest news seen in years here during 1979 — and the market simply has not caved in. My Primary Trend Index has climbed to its highest level since the 1974 bottom, despite the bad news and despite the monumental resistance of the Dow. Shouldn't we conclude that the market is "looking somewhere else" but not at the bad news? Couldn't that "somewhere else" be the fifth and final tremendous bull wave under Elliott? Stranger things have happened on Wall Street.

The question may be asked, "Russell, how do you personally see it? What do you actually think?" And here my only answer is that I think we today are seeing a pause in a system that is literally out of control. I sense that the market is now trying to make its mind up as to the whole situation. I sense that the market itself has not decided whether the bullish argument (the inflation hedge argument) can hold up, and thus the market is not yet ready to take off a la Elliott.

**August 29, 1979**

I have been writing for well over a year the importance (in the Fibonacci series) of not only the year 1979 but specifically of JULY 1979. I noted [in the Letter of January 17, 1979] that no less than six time intervals in the Fibonacci series underscored July 1979 as a key month in stock market history. I include an excerpt from that Letter below:

> "Six [Fibonacci] time sequences listed point to the importance of the year 1979 and more specifically to JULY 1979."

Yet, July 1979 came and went, and I was unable to uncover the "secret" of what had happened. In [the July 5, 1979] Letter I published an Elliott chart showing the four Supercycle wave movements since 1932. These movements form the first four waves of what should be a great, five-wave Supercycle bull market. The chart shows that we are now in the early stages of major wave 5. If so, if this is the *fifth wave* of a giant bull market that began in 1932, then we are dealing with a phenomenon larger than any living person has had any experience with.

For the fifth wave of a bull market is the final, speculative wave, and the fifth wave of a giant bull market (such as the one pictured in July 5, 1979) could be so powerful, so overwhelming, that it could wash away any counterforce in the same way that a tidal wave would sweep over a child's sand castle. And that may explain why so many time-honored market studies (many of them currently bearish) are not working at this time.

**January 30, 1980**

Another long-term study that I am watching intently now is the Elliott Wave Principle. My friend, Bob Prechter, is one of the true experts in this area (along with A.J. Frost), and I have borrowed the chart from Bob's most recent report. The chart traces the Dow from the end of 1936 to the present. The four major waves are identified, and if this interpretation is correct, we should now be moving into final wave 5.

One item worth noting is that despite a year of almost unending calamities, the Dow during 1979 never violated the lower trendline of the channel. Bob also notes that the Dow is now at the bottom of the channel which means that it is priced at bear market bottom value as was the case in 1932, 1942, 1949 and 1974.

The top of this channel is roughly in the 2860 area for the Dow. And that is where Prechter expects the Dow to go during the fifth wave of the great bull market that began in 1932 (the fifth wave is usually the most speculative wave and is accompanied by the highest volume). Prechter expects the fifth wave to end around 1984.

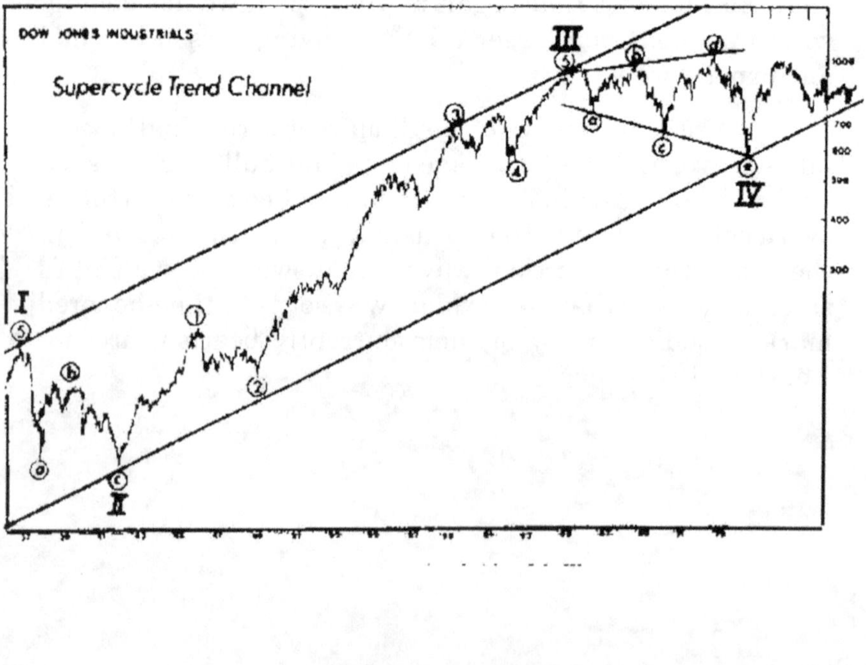

**April 9, 1980**

The most interesting and probably the most important phenomenon of 1980 so far has been the action of the DJ Industrial Average during the week of March 24. At this time, the Dow broke below the massive trendline which connects the 1942 and 1974 low. This action can be seen on the chart. Note parallel trendlines A and B. This great upward channel (formed by these two trendlines) has contained all the Dow action since 1942. But when the Dow broke below 800 two weeks ago, the picture changed.

My friend Bob Prechter (editor of *The Elliott Theorist*) is of the opinion that the break implies that the corrective wave 4 of a giant bull market has not yet been completed. As Bob sees it now, the completion of corrective wave 4 could take the Dow below the 1974 low of 577 and down to 520.[15]

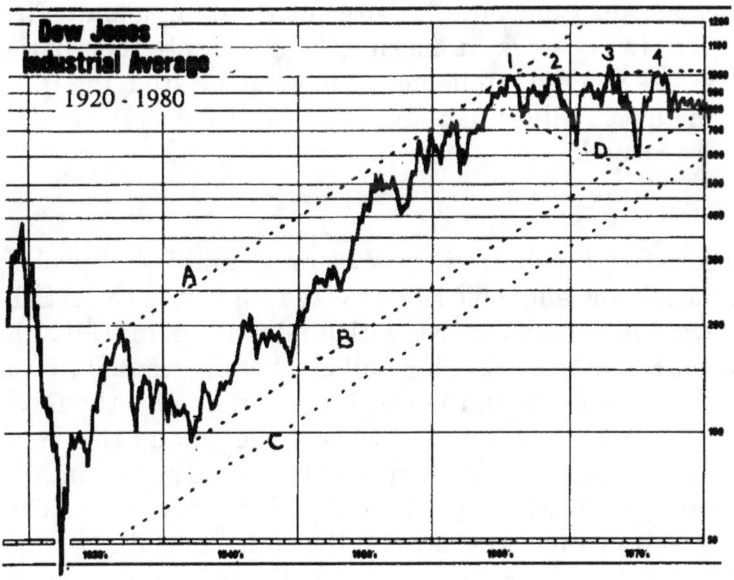


[15] It was true that wave IV was "not yet completed," as it ended in 1982. But its second "three" took the form of a contracting triangle, keeping prices higher than they would have been by any other pattern.

Bob could well be right. He's an excellent market student, and I always study his Elliott interpretations with the greatest interest. But the reason I include Prechter's Elliott observations here is that it helps to erase any preconceived notions I may have as to where this decline "must" stop. As far as I am concerned, the final termination could come at Dow 750, 700, 600 or even (as Bob suggests) 520. The fact is that no man on the face of the earth knows where or when THE bottom will come.

The recent March 27 lows were 759.98 for the DJ Industrials, 233.69 for the Transports, 96.04 for Utilities. At those lows the market looked short-term exhausted. It was a straight-line decline with not so much as a three-day rally from the February 13 peak.

**May 21, 1980**

*ELLIOTT*: I always keep one eye on Elliott, regardless of what market I am puzzling over or thinking about. Elliott doesn't always work; it doesn't always supply the answers. But it has worked often enough to keep me studying it. In a few instances Elliott has saved my life as far as the markets are concerned.

I talk to Bob Prechter every week or so, and Bob is probably the most knowledgeable Elliott Wave student in the U.S. Bob believes (and I tend to agree with him) that a giant Elliott bull market began in 1932. This bull market progressed through waves 1, 2 and 3 with the third wave ending for the Dow in 1966. From there corrective wave 4 began, and that fourth wave is still in force. The fourth wave should end in an A-B-C pattern. The A wave terminated in February, 1978. The B wave (subdividing as shown on the chart) ended in January 1980. We should now be in the final C wave, and the C wave should subdivide into five smaller waves.[16]

---

[16] It did, and they were already over!

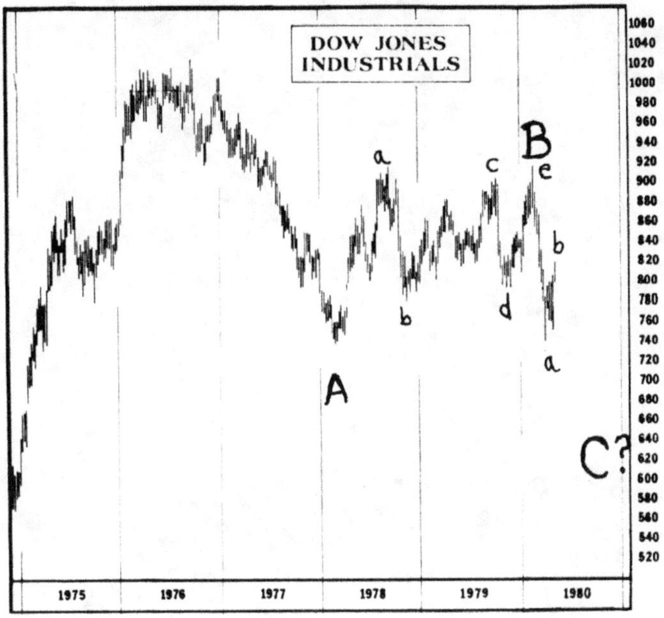


So far, this analysis makes sense on the chart, but unfortunately, if the final C leg is to be completed, the Dow has some more downside paths to travel. The termination of the current C wave should take the Dow well below the current levels, if this interpretation of Elliott is correct.

The good news: following giant corrective wave 4, there should be a superbull wave 5. This is the wave which will ultimately (if it occurs) take stocks into the stratosphere. What will happen to bring about the fifth wave? Easy: Russia falls apart economically, the U.S. again assumes world leadership with the help of a strong President, moral rebirth, an explosion in productivity and a dollar officially convertible into gold at $2000 an ounce. Russia dumps Cuba as an expensive failed experiment. An absurdly cheap oil-shale process is discovered and the biggest surprise of all — Saudi Arabia becomes the 51st State in the Union.[17]

---

[17] Six out of nine of these whimsical suggestions came true in the 1980s (seven if you include cheap oil).

# *RUSSELL ON GOLD*

**May 2, 1973**

I want to present a gold stock in terms of Elliott, and I have selected *American S. African Investment Trust* (a gold share holding Co.). The chart shows the bull market in ASA which took the stock from 9 in 1961 to 82 in 1968. During 1968-70, ASA underwent an A-B-C correction which took it back to 26. I have labeled the action since then (the action which began in early 1970) as "Bull Market" on the chart.

The first major leg of the *new bull market* (A on chart) took ASA to the *1971 peak* of 54. A typical 1-2-3 correction followed, taking the stock back to 32 and thereby completing

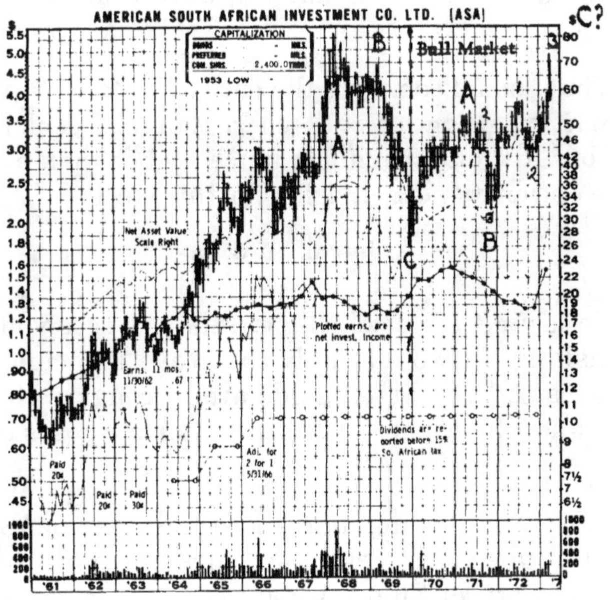

major corrective leg B. Major leg C commenced from the 1971 low. The first subwave of wave C (marked 1 on chart) ended at the 1972 peak of 57. Then came a drop to the late 1972 low of 41, and this is marked 2 on chart. *Most recently*, we have the rise to the 1973 peak above 75, and this I have marked 3 on the chart.

Now the question, why couldn't one claim that the move from the 1970 low to the current high constitutes a five-major wave bull market which is now about completed? I reject this interpretation on two counts: (1) corrective leg 4 dropped far below the peak of leg 1, and this should not occur in an Elliott pattern. (2) The first leg (A) should be the shortest leg. Thus, current leg C should be much longer than leg A, and I am of the opinion that the current major leg C will develop as a five-subwave rise with ASA now perhaps nearing completion of its third subwave. We should then have a correction (subwave 4), then a final very speculative subwave 5 up. Following that, a major correction should arrive, a correction which will constitute major leg D. Last, we should again witness a major upwave E made up of five subwaves.

That should complete the entire bull market in ASA. At this writing, no one can tell where that final peak for ASA will be, but it should be much, much higher than anything even the optimists now envision for this stock.

### July 6, 1973

Following the last Elliott study, I received many letters asking if I would apply the Wave Principle to the gold shares. All the listed golds are in roughly the same pattern, and I have chosen ASA Ltd. for purposes of wave study.

The accompanying chart shows the action of ASA from mid-1971 to date, on a weekly basis and drawn to arithmetic scale. As I interpret Elliott, we are now in a major primary

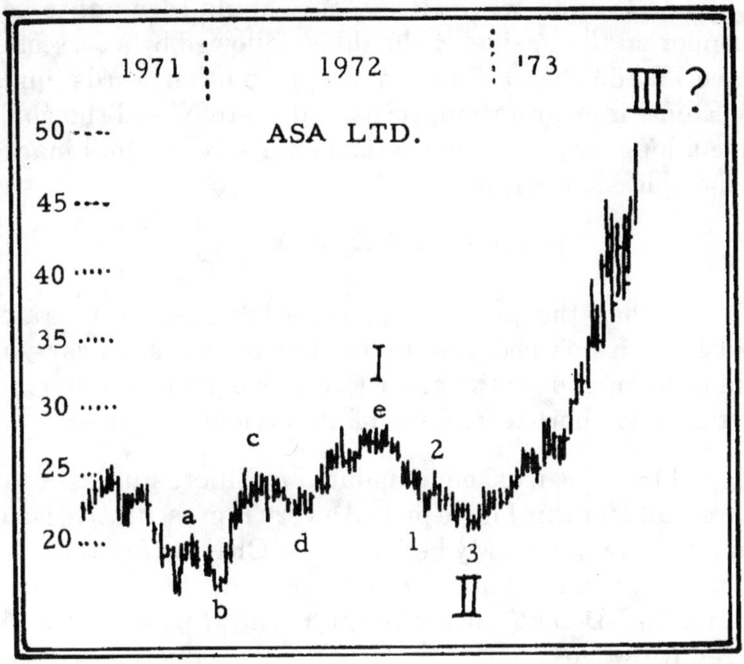


bull market in gold shares. The bull market began for most South African gold shares in 1971, and this is where I am placing the start of the bull market in ASA.

The first major upward wave of what should be a five wave bull market three waves up, two corrective waves down) began in late 1971, as shown on the chart. Wave 1 carried to mid-1972 and took the form of five typical smaller waves (marked a-b-c-d-e). Next, we had the classic three-leg corrective wave, which shows on the chart as II.

From late 1972, we went into major wave III, and this should assume the form of a five-leg rise. Wave III (so far) is very unusual because so far there is little evidence of correction, and at least two corrections should appear before leg III is finally completed (the first important decline in ASA could constitute the first correction of wave III).

As I see it, wave III in ASA should turn out to be a whopper on the upside. It should be followed by a correction (wave IV and then a final leg V up). In other words, under my Elliott interpretation, ASA (and therefore all the golds) have a long way to go on the upside before the bull market in the gold shares is over.

### August 17, 1973

Under the pressure of record high interest rates, gold bullion has been hit by (1) the high cost of carrying gold bullion, and (2) the attractiveness of debt instruments, particularly short-term debt, of 10% [yield] and over.

I have been asked to update my Elliott studies of gold shares, and for this I have picked a very representative issue, Campbell Red Lake. My belief is that CRK (as are the other golds) is in a major bull market, which should take the form of an A-B-C-D-E pattern with the B and D waves being the corrective waves.

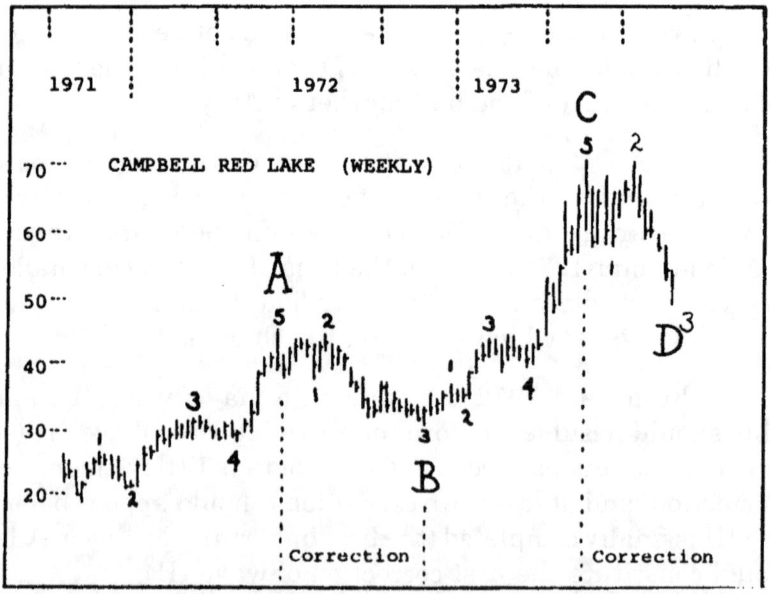

As seen on the chart, wave A ended in mid-1972, with corrective wave B terminating in late 1972. The booming move of 1972-73 assumed the form of a five-wave rise, the five waves constituting major upwave C. Currently, we are deep in corrective wave D, and this wave should terminate with (1) a discounting of the peak in interest rates (in other words, it will try to jump the gun on the interest rate peak), (2) a realization that inflation is continuing and that any cessation of record interest rates will simply intensify the continuing inflation, and (3) a business slowdown and a discounting of general easing of controls prior to new attempts to "re-flate" world economies (already Europe and Japan are experiencing some acute contractions in various areas of business). As an added note, as Phase IV starts (amid record interest rates), big companies are lining up to petition for increased prices. Thus, the *purchasing power of currencies* continues to erode.

Note on the chart that the current corrective wave D has now traced out a 1-2-3 downward zigzag, and this suggests that we could be nearing the end of this major correction in the golds. The high churning action of gold shares on August 14 suggested to me that some accumulation of gold shares was taking place, and on August 15 the gold shares began to turn firm for the first time in weeks.

According to my Elliott studies, the next movement in golds should be consistent with an E wave in Campbell. This should be the major upward leg, and it should take the form of a 1-2-3-4-5 series of rising [waves]. The fifth or final Elliott wave is often long, exponential and highly speculative. If this is what comes to pass, we should see a massive move up in gold shares and a great deal of turmoil in the world monetary picture.

## November 21, 1973

I show here my ratio-scale gold-silver chart. Note that at $90, gold bullion is still well above its long-term rising trendline. In Elliott terms, I place gold at the termination of its second correction (at large numeral 4), following a 1-2-3 correction (correction numbers in circles). The next move should be the final wave 4 to 5, and this should be a "really big show," as Ed Sullivan used to put it.

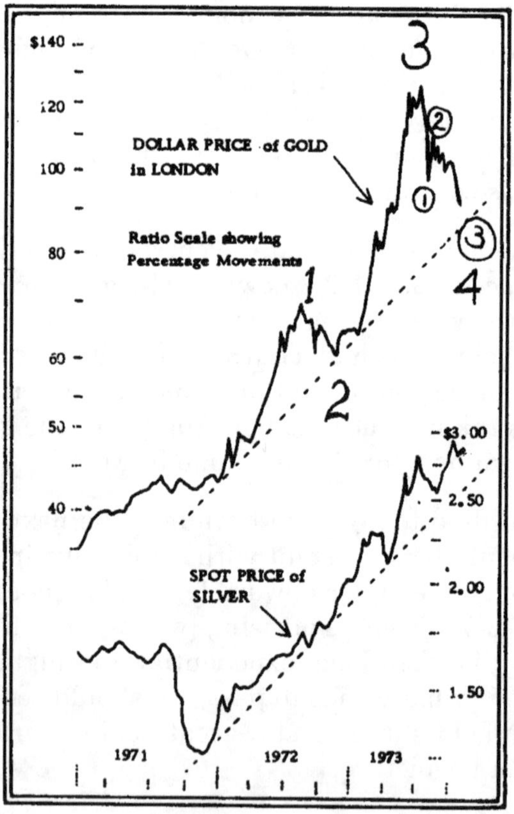

**December 21, 1973**

Now for the other side of the coin. I have also pictured here a semilogarithmic (ratio scale) monthly chart of Campbell Red Lake Mines, the leading Canadian gold producer. Here is the way I analyze the movements. A huge correction occurred in golds during 1968-70, taking Campbell (CRK) down from 47 to 14.5. The correction assumed the form of a typical 1-2-3 Elliott decline, as shown on the chart. From there, the current bull market in golds began.

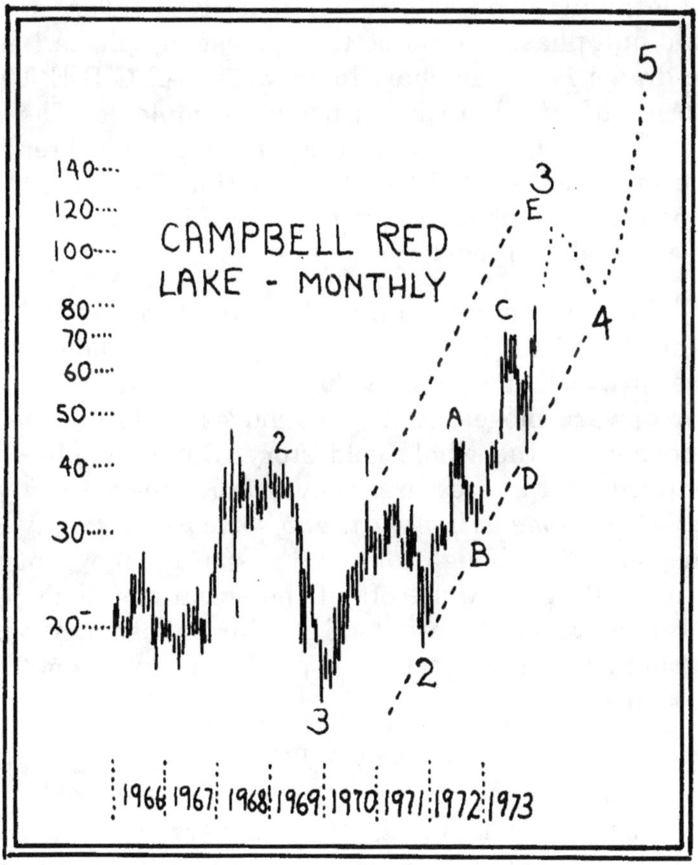

The first upward wave in CRK's bull market is labeled 1 on the chart; it carried from the 1969 low of 14.5 to the 1971 high of 35. This marked the first phase of the gold bull market, the phase in which informed investors took their initial positions. Following the 1971 peak, we witnessed the first bull market correction, which is labeled wave 2 (ending at the late 1971 low of 18.5).

The *second psychological phase* of the bull market in golds started from the 1971 lows. From here, gold shares began moving up in response to subtle but gradually bettering news on the gold front. Yet it was still the investors, not the public, who were buying the golds. The current second bull phase should be the longest "up phase," and I have drawn it on the chart to show an A-B-C-D-E Elliott pattern with the D to E leg not yet completed. The D-E leg could "extend," meaning that this leg could break up again into another A-B-C-D-E leg within the E leg. Then we should have the *second major* correction as shown, the correction labeled leg 4.

Finally, we will go into the third phase of the gold bull market. And this is what I want to talk about — the phase in which the penny gold stocks should make their major upward moves. And those moves could just be the eye-openers of the whole gold story. But remember, the low-priced gold shares are risky affairs, they are *highly speculative. Some will make it and some won't.* Penny gold shares should be bought only with "spare money," money you are willing to "write off" if the situations don't work out. But there will be profits if my third phase analysis of the gold picture is correct, huge profits of perhaps 500% to 2000% in some issues.

**January 4, 1974**

The gold shares ended 1973 in very strong fashion, despite the fact that they have been consistently ignored, talked down and dismissed by the investment fraternity. I show here a chart (ratio scale) of Homestake, a stock whose action can only be described as sensational during 1973. I have broken HM's price movements down into Elliott terms, and this could aid us in determining the potential 1974 action for the gold shares in general.

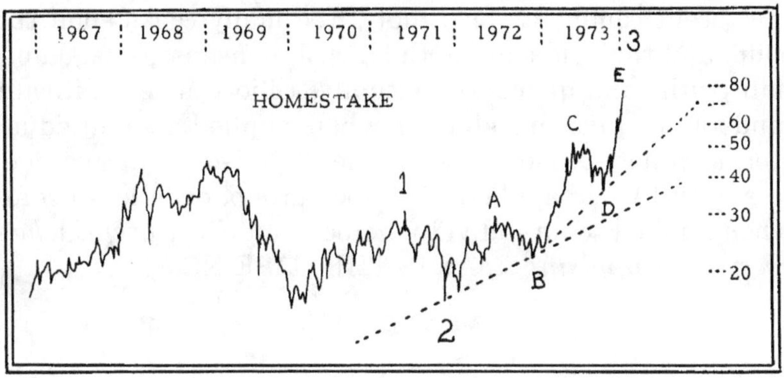


The big primary bull market in gold shares can be seen in terms of HM. The first upward wave (marked 1 on chart) began in early 1970 and carried late into that year. The first correction (wave 2) took HM to a low of 15.5 in late 1971. Then came major upward wave 3, a wave which should be considerably larger than wave 1 (which it already is). As I analyze it, HM is now into wave 3, a wave which I have broken down into a typical five-subwave A-B-C-D-E pattern. We are currently in the E wave, and unless E "extends" (meaning breaks down into five more upwaves), we could be nearing a correction in HM and the golds in general.

How big a correction I cannot tell, but usually if the first correction (in this case wave 2) is a severe one, the second correction (which will be wave 4) will be a shallow one. As seen on the chart, the 2 correction was a whopper. For this reason, I believe the next gold correction, when it arrives, will not be too bad.

**February 15, 1974**

Suddenly, everyone is an expert on gold price movements. Suddenly, all the advisors are specialists in Elliott Waves and five-leg movements and extensions and corrections. From all quarters come the soothsayer's warnings that the gold stocks are about to fall apart. I'm almost sorry I started the recent comments on Elliott. Too many cooks spoil the soup, and the gold soup is thick with nonsense, misquotes, half-truths and quackery. Actually, Elliott is very difficult (and often quite unreliable) when applied to individual stocks. Elliott is most useful when applied to an average, less useful when applied to a stock group, even less useful when applied to an individual stock, and *least useful when everyone is applying it,* AS IS THE CASE NOW!

**March 8, 1974**

I include a weekly ratio chart of Campbell Red Lake. I have been watching Campbell (CRK) closely, because it has been correcting longer than the other NYSE gold shares, and it may be telling us something. Note that CRK has now traced out the Elliott A-B-C downward zigzag correction. This could be calling the end of the gold correction all around. Note also that in January CRK actually touched the rising upper trendline. This is a sign of strength and suggests a milder rather than a severe correction. When the golds turn up, I expect the upward reversal to be violent.

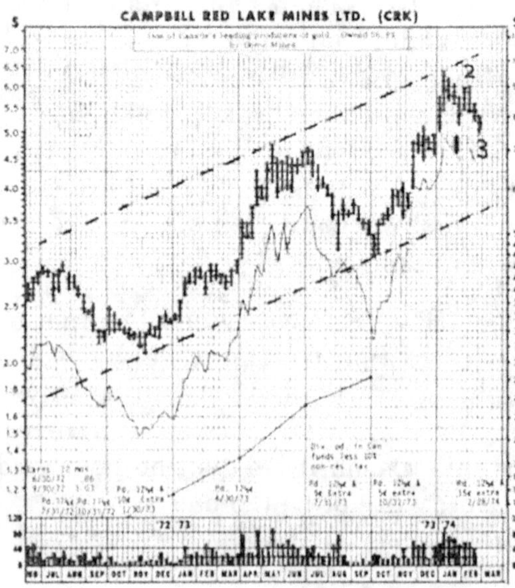

**May 22, 1974**

I have stated in the past that the normal Elliott wave correction is an A- B-C affair, with an A wave down, a B wave up and a final C wave down. The mild form of Elliott correction is termed a "flat," and here the termination of the B wave may approach or even better the point at which the A wave began. In the flat, the termination of the C wave is often not too far below the bottom of the A wave. That is what we may be seeing in the listed gold shares, charts of which I have included.

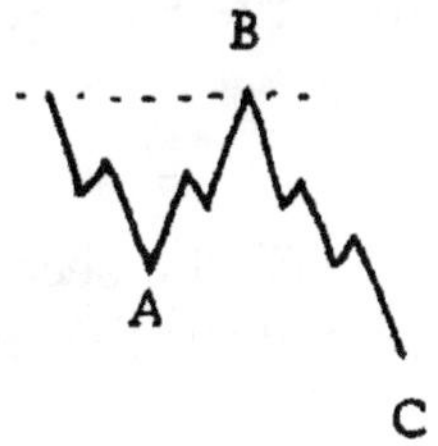


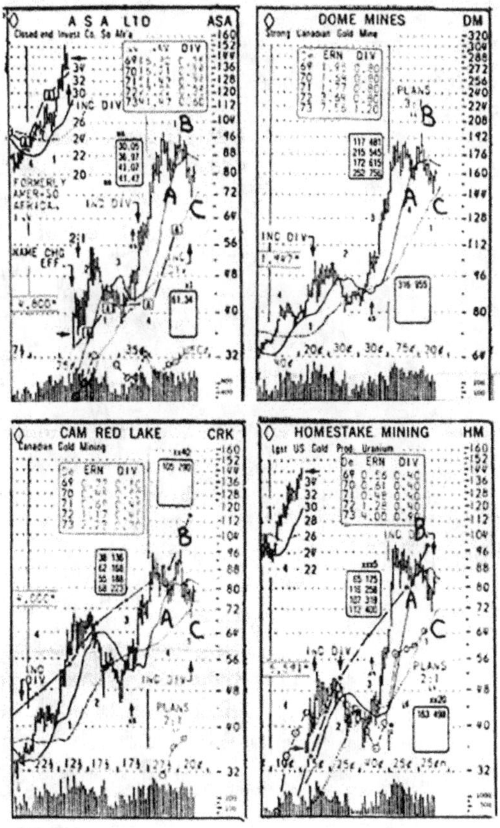

I have labeled the corrections with an A, B and C on the charts. Homestake is not clearly in a flat correction, looking more like the zigzag which is a more severe corrective formation. However, most of the golds are now "drying up" on the downside, which could mean that the golds have seen their lows.

**June 12, 1974**

The second psychological phase of the gold move assumed the form of an Elliott five-wave rise. These five waves

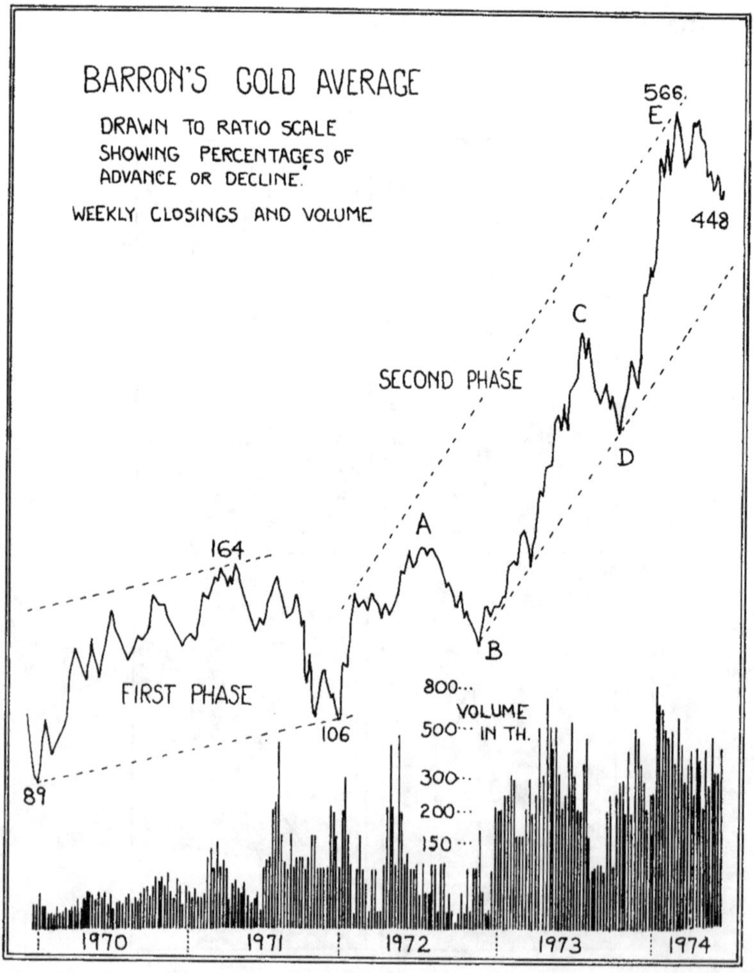

(A through E) gave way to the correction which has been in force in Barron's Gold Average since early 1974. I have stated that I felt that each subsequent correction in the gold bull market would tend to be *milder* than the preceding. Note the intensity and violence of the correction which ended the first phase (164 to 106). That was a correction of 35%. So far, the correction from the 1974 high to the May low (566 to 448) amounts to only 20%.

**July 2, 1975**

I just received a letter from *Mr. A.J. Frost* of Canada, in my mind the greatest living interpreter of the Elliott Wave Principle. Mr. Frost did a great deal of outstanding work with Hamilton Bolton, founder of the famous *Bank Credit Analyst*. Between them, they revived interest in Elliott in the 1960s, and that interest is greater today than ever. I would unhesitatingly say that if it had not been for Bolton's and Frost's efforts, Elliott would be unheard of today.

In Frost's latest letter to me, he outlined his thoughts regarding the gold picture. I consider it a privilege to be able to present those opinions to my readers at this time.

Almost all Bolton's and Frost's Elliott work was done on logarithmic-scaled charts, as they felt that log (ratio-scaled) graphs best showed the various thrusts of the price movement. Thus a rise of 2 to 4 shows as exactly the same vertical distance as say a rise from 45 to 90 on ratio scale.

I am including this tracing of the chart which Frost sent me. Frost writes: "The enclosed weekly gold chart (London morning and afternoon fix prices) shows a strong Elliott pattern. I have marked on it my Elliott reading. It is important to note that the B wave of the correction travelled into new high ground, indicating strength. This type of consolidation tends to generate a strong upward thrust. I would say that when the price of bullion breaks out of the pattern contained by its upper trendline (X on chart), the market price of bullion will quickly advance and exceed in amplitude the rise from the 1972 low to the March high of 1974, based on Elliott rules."[1]

Note that Frost places the first cycle peak for the gold bull market at point V (just under 180). He obviously believes that gold at point V completed the *first* major bull cycle of what will be a *supercycle* in gold.

Most readers (gold fans included) will probably be surprised at Frost's interpretation of the gold bull market having started in 1972 and ending in 1974 — rather than ending at the 1975 all-time high. However, those who read my [letter of May 30, 1975] are familiar with the Elliott A-B-C "flat correction," in which the B leg often betters the preceding bull market high (as was the case with the Dow in 1973).

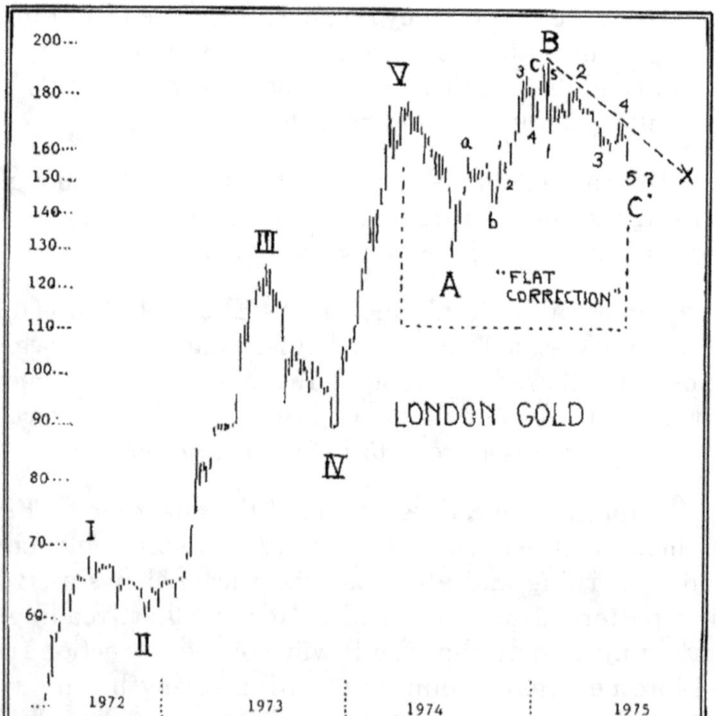


[1] This is a correct analysis in every respect except that wave C had much further to go.

Thus, according to the chart, the bear market correction for gold began at point V in 1974 and has already progressed through the A, B and a large part of the final major C wave. As you can see, the major A-B-C correction has assumed the form of a 3-3-5 (these are the breakdowns of the larger waves) correction. Currently, we are completing smaller leg 5 of major downward wave C. This should be the final leg down before the new major bull market in gold begins.

How far could leg 5 travel? The 1974 breakout point was 160, and this implies that 160 should be an important support level. But it may be that before the next primary bull market in gold, the market is going to have to "flush out" all the weak hands, and really turn all but the very strongest interest bearish on the future of gold. To do this, gold could break the 160 support level and perhaps drop down to test the 150 level, perhaps even temporarily provide a "panic breaking" of 150.

However, I believe we are getting closer to an important juncture in the gold story. Nobody can tell you how to make the "perfect play" in gold. Some like to average down; others like to buy on a upside breakout. I like to take a token position, "get my feet wet," then add to my position as the market gives consecutive technical "OKs." That is the reason I suggest token positions of up to 15% of assets split between Krugerrands and Homestake.

I want to watch the 160-161 level on gold carefully now. If gold touches those levels, it should bring out selling. If not, then I suspect the technical test is over, and we will shortly start up. In that case, a breaking of trendline X on the chart, which is now at the 170 level, should signal the beginning of the next gold bull market. If and when that happens, I will give my thoughts on why, how, and what to do.

**February 18, 1976**

I have labeled the Gold chart according to my interpretation of the Elliott Wave Principle. Most primary bear markets assume the form of a three-wave downmove, an A wave down, an upward correction to B and a final, usually crushing wave to the bottom of the bear market at C. These three major waves can often be subdivided into a 5-3-5 pattern, and I have shown this on the chart.

I show major wave A breaking down into five subwaves. Then I show a very weak correction to B, weak because point c did not advance above point a. Next I show the smashing collapse to the recent lows at C, and it is interesting to note that this collapse has taken (so far) the form of five subwaves. The current problem is that we do not know whether the final subwave 5 is completed.

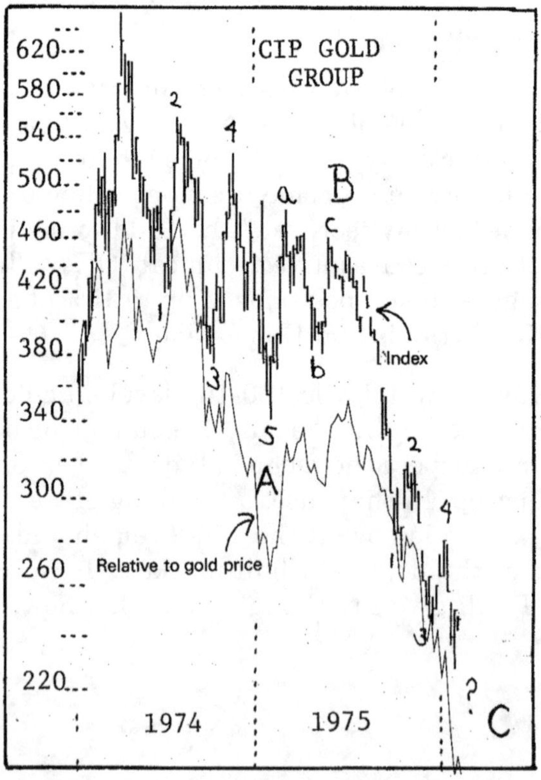

At any rate, it does appear to me that the bear market in gold shares could be nearing an end, at least based on Elliott. This does not mean that we should all rush in to load up on gold shares. Bear markets do not end in a day, to immediately give way to roaring bull market advances. However, based on this chart, I do not see the harm in assuming very careful positions in Homestake, as suggested in recent reports. For those willing to assume the political risks of investing in S. African shares, I would also recommend careful pilot positions in Amgold (ADRs).

**February 27, 1976**

I am of the opinion that the bear market in gold bullion and shares *has ended*. This does not guarantee an immediate gold boom, but it makes it a lot easier to purchase gold items. Veteran readers are familiar with my interpretations of the Fibonacci series (3, 5, 8, 13, 21, 55, 89, etc.) Each two numbers add up to the third. Each number is a ratio of 61.8% of its next higher number). From the late December 1974 bullion peak of about *200* (intraday) to the late January 1976 low of *123* (intraday) was *55* weeks. The number 55 is in the Fibonacci series. When 123 is divided by 200 we get approximately 61.8. This is the Fibonacci ratio. The twin figures seem almost beyond coincidence, and it fits in with my study of gold.

**January 5, 1977**

Gold bullion has now moved into a most interesting and critical pattern, as far as followers of the Elliott Wave Principle are concerned. As shown on the chart, gold bullion reversed to the upside (during the third quarter of 1976) when it pushed above the two-year descending trendline. The upthrust from the August 1976 low of 103.50 has assumed (so far) the pattern of a 1-2-3 wave form with a London high (afternoon fix) of *138.85* recorded on November 15, 1976. This high occurred at the termination of the second upwave at the point marked 3 on the chart.

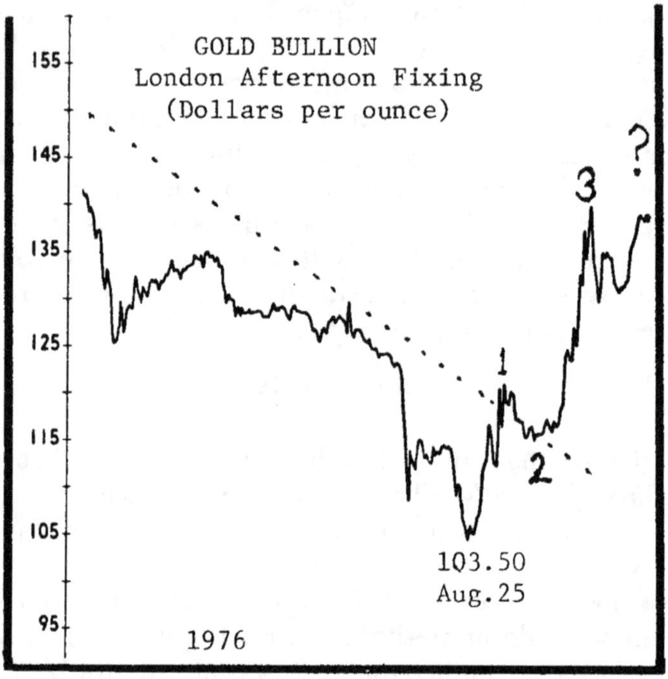


Following point 3, gold backed off, then pushed up again, but it has not yet bettered the 138.85 peak of November 15. Under Elliott interpretation, it will now be critical to observe whether gold rallies above 138.85 and records a new high which we will call peak 5 — or whether gold breaks down from here without showing any ability or inclination to better the 138.85 level at point 3.

Here is the reason why the forthcoming price action for gold is so critical. If gold hits a new high at a theoretical point 5, then we have a bullish 1-2-3-4-5 pattern, a pattern characteristic of the beginning of a bull market in gold. Remember, Elliott bull markets materialize in five-leg patterns while Elliott bear market corrections occur in three-leg patterns. If gold now breaks down, it will leave a typical 1-2-3 pattern which will very strongly suggest that all the upside action since the 103.50 August low was simply a completed 1-2-3 upward correction in a continuing bear market in gold.

*Conclusion*: If gold moves out above 138.85, I would say that we are definitely at the beginning of a new and very probably long-term bull market in gold. Following theoretical point 5 we would have a correction and a perfect spot to purchase some Kruggerrands. HOWEVER, if 138.85 (point 3 on the chart) can not be bettered, I would say that the 1974-76 gold bear market is continuing, and in due time, the price of bullion will break down below the 103.50 low of 1976!

Of course, this whole concept brings up the idea of "technical insurance" on gold at this point. The insurance plan would be as follows: sell gold here while it is just below point 3 or 138.85. Then buy it back if it hits 140. A price of 140 (just over the 138.85 high) would signal an Elliott bull market in gold, and it would indicate that gold was going into its leg 5 of the first major rise in the new bull market. If you sell gold here and it can't better 138.85, it could well go to new lows under 100. In that case, your sales would be well advised.

### January 24, 1977
### (Letter to *Barron's*)

In the January 10 issue of *Barron's*, this "*Barron's* panelist" made the statement (voiced some weeks ago) that "I think we saw the low on (gold) bullion last August at 103.50." I added that "I think we're in a long-term bull market in gold." Events since then have made me want to hedge, if not retract, those statements.

My concerns are technical in nature, based partly on my interpretation of the Elliott Wave Principle, and partly on my own experience. Normally, a bull market structure will trace a 1-2-3-4-5 rise with the 1, 3, 5 legs being rallies and the 2 and 4 legs being corrections. On the other hand, a bear market rally (against the main bear trend) will generally take the form of a 1-2-3 rise with the 1 and 3 legs being rallies and the 2 leg being a downward movement.

Gold bullion advanced in a characteristic 1-2-3 rise from its 103.50 August 1976 low. The peak of the 3 leg occurred on November 15, 1976, at 138.85. But then, instead of rising to a new peak (peak 5) above 138.85, gold began to sag. Now this is most critical. The stubborn refusal by gold to better 138.85 will (in my opinion) cast increasing doubt on the bullishness of the gold picture.

In fact, a failure to form a new peak 5 (above November's peak 3) will suggest that we have seen nothing more than a bear market rally in gold. If this is the case, it will only be a matter of time before the primary bear trend in gold takes hold and the 103.5 low of 1976 is attacked again.

From another standpoint, what the price movement does at halfway levels is important from a technical standpoint. The 1974-76 bear market in gold took the metal from 195 (1974) to 103 (1976). A halfway recovery would have advanced gold to 149. So far, gold has failed to reach the 149 level on any rise. That failure has negative implications.

The rally from last year's August low of 103 to the November high of 138.85 produced a halfway level of 121. If, on any forthcoming decline, the 121 level is broken, it will be extremely bearish for gold. Should gold break 121, I would put the odds at two-to-one that the bear market in gold is continuing.

Since weakness in gold these days is really an inverse function of strength in the dollar, it makes this writer wonder about the widespread opinions regarding "a weak dollar," "more and more inflation" and "continued strength in the leading European currencies." In short, there could be some extraordinary surprises ahead if the bear market in gold remains in force.

**August 10, 1977**

All right, now let's turn to the monthly chart of *Homestake*. I have marked the 1972-74 bull market in Homestake with a 1, 2, 3, 4, 5 and that action completed a perfect five-wave bull market under the Elliott Wave Principle. An extraordinary upside "blow-off" occurred in late 1974, a blow-off caused by white-hot speculative frenzy in gold shares. I marked the blow-off peak with an X on the chart. I consider the rise to X a "false rally."[2]

The aftermath of this frenzy to point X was the abnormal panic crash to point Y. During this crash, HM lost over half its market value! The stock then moved back to the

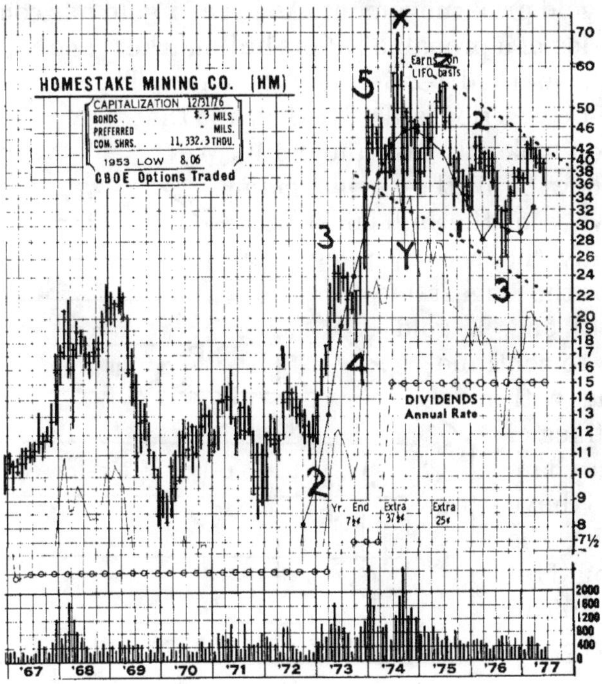


---

[2] Actually, counting from late 1971 (possibly the orthodox low) gives the 9-wave count of an impulse with extension right into the high.

55 area (Z), and at this point, with *volume dropping drastically,* it was clear to me that the bull market was over for the golds. I was recommending (in early 1975) that subscribers move completely out of gold and gold shares. The upside momentum had clearly been shattered.

From point Z a classic 1-2-3 Elliott bear market occurred. At point 3, just above a price of 25, the bear market ended for HM. I have drawn the bear market in the form of a giant descending channel. The question now is, what next for HM?

**November 9, 1977**

I want to close the gold section with a chart on the current gold price movement. As I see it, gold has completed the first leg of a probable Elliott bull market. The first leg is marked 1-2-3-4-5 on the chart. The mild a-b-c correction is also labeled, and that correction took gold just under 140. We should now be in the *second* major rising wave of the bull market. Classically, the second [up]leg should be the longest (most extended) one. If gold is going to continue following within the confines of the rising channel (as I have drawn it), the metal could hit around 200 in early 1978.

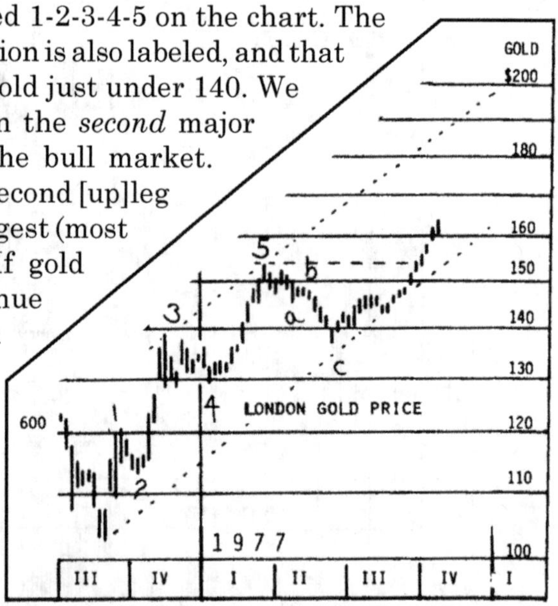

**March 1, 1978**

As long as I have discussed the [stock] market in terms of Elliott, I may as well go the whole hog and update gold in terms of my Elliott studies. As older readers know, Elliott views all bull markets as unfolding in a series of five rising waves (three upwaves and two intervening downward waves). Elliott bear markets take the form of two downwaves with an intervening rising wave. Of course, this is a very simple explanation, since each of the waves divides and subdivides.

At any rate, I include a long term arithmetic chart of Gold (1972 to present) showing the A-B-C-D-E bull market which took gold from $35 to a peak of 180 in early 1974. From here, we witnessed a corrective bear market (1-2-3 on chart) but we had a higher "unorthodox top" of 197.50 at point 2. Such tops are fairly rare, but they can materialize under the influence of heated speculation, a phenomenon which certainly appeared during 1974.

By August 1976, the bear market had slashed the price of gold to 103.50. From that level, a new bull market in gold was born. I have constructed a second gold chart to

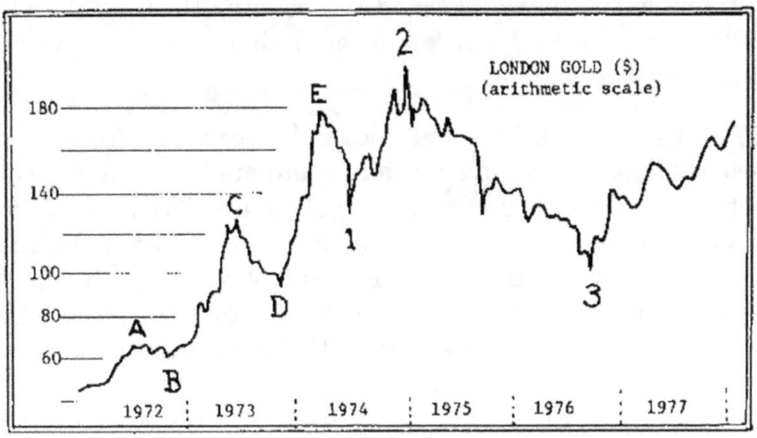

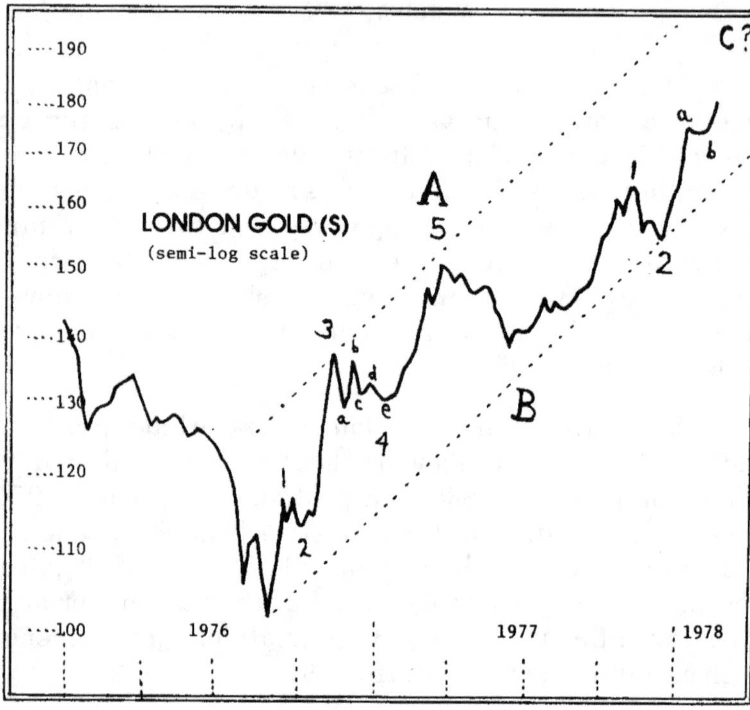


semilogarithmic (ratio) scale, and this scale is absolutely necessary if we are to use the device known as channeling. I have drawn a rising trendline connecting the 1976 and 1977 bottoms, with a parallel trendline passing through the late 1976 high. The bull market in gold should develop within this channel.

I see this bull market taking the form of an A-B-C-D-E series of waves. We have already completed wave A and corrective wave B, as you can see on the chart. We should now be in rising wave C, a wave which should break down into five subwaves. We are currently in subwave 3, which follows the correction marked 2 on the chart. Leg A increased the price of gold approximately 48%. If the current rising wave C was merely to match wave A, gold could rise to the 205 area. My guess is that the current wave C should be greater than wave A in terms of percentages, but of course, that's only my guess. Following the current wave C, we should have another correction and then final rising wave E. This should be the most speculative movement since 1974, but this final rising wave might not appear until 1982 or even later, so at present I'm centered on analyzing wave C.

Incidentally, this morning I heard that Switzerland was reducing bank interest to foreigners to 1% while barring foreigners from buying Swiss stocks. Thus, the Swiss are cutting off entrance of new dollars, and this should mean more dollars siphoning into gold.

Thought for the week: We're at the point now where if the U.S. Government doesn't inflate fast enough, it's deflationary!

## May 5, 1978

On my weekly arithmetic chart of gold, I have labeled the rallies and declines in Elliott Wave terms.[3] Thus, I believe we are in a large A-B-C-D-E Elliott bull market in gold. Wave one (subdivided into five smaller legs) carried to March 1977. The correction to point B ended in June 1977. A new wave to C subdivided into five smaller legs.

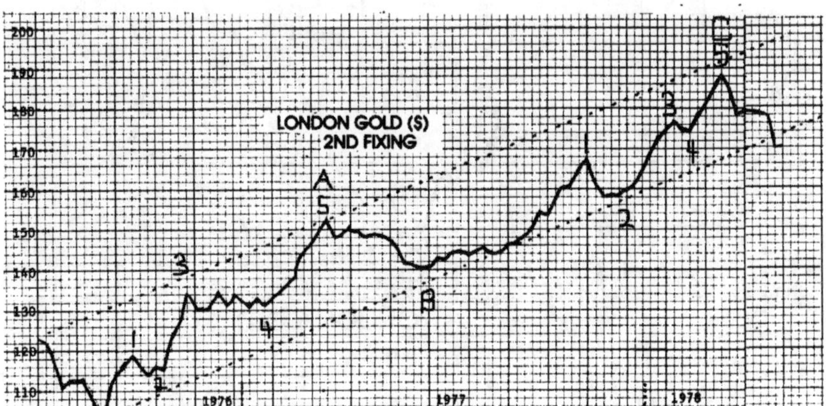


[3] Labels were inadvertently omitted from the original chart. We have added them here according to Russell's commentary.

Since the end of leg C at 190, gold has corrected down to the 167-168 area. In doing so, gold broke just below the lower channel line. This is all right, and it served to turn about three out of every four gold followers bearish. In my opinion, gold is now basing. The 168 area could hold, or gold might even slide to even stronger support at 161-164.

**June 28, 1978**

I have filled in my own Elliott count for gold. The bull market in gold should run in five waves in an A-B-C-D-E pattern with waves A, C and E being rising bull waves and B and D being corrective waves.

We have already completed rising wave A, a wave which divided into five smaller legs. The correction to point B is now completed. Currently we have completed 1, 2, 3 and 4 of major rising wave C, and we are on wave 5 of larger wave

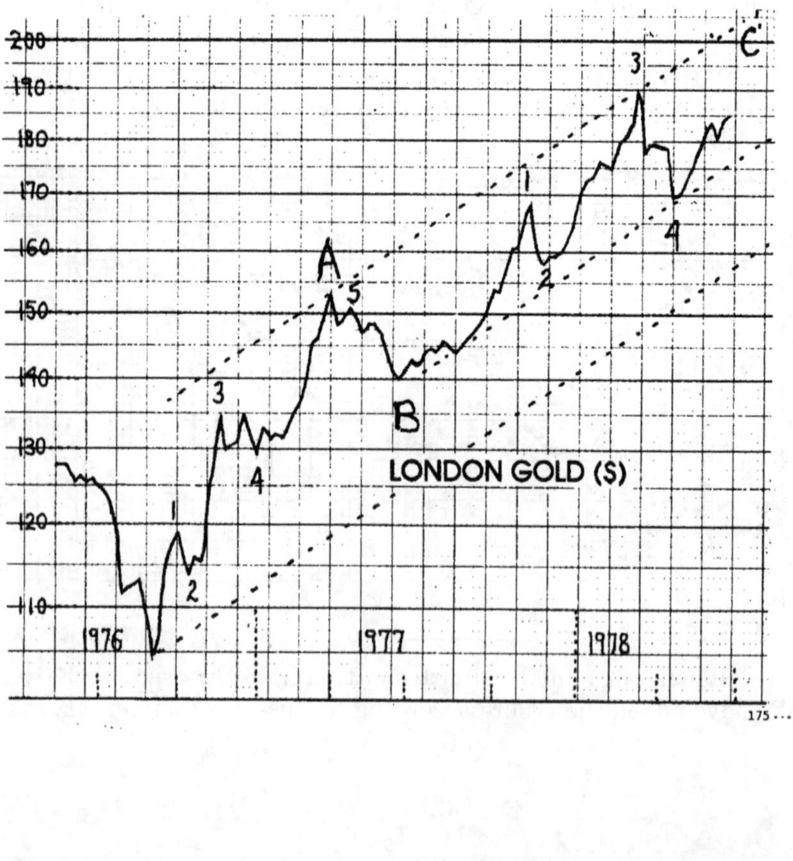

C. The 5-leg is usually the most violent and most speculative, and I find it most interesting that current leg 5 is the one that will grow out of a breakout from the huge base.

I have not written this before, nor have I seen it said anywhere else. But gold is now poised to push out of its head-and-shoulder base and complete leg 5 or major upward wave C. If all this comes to pass, gold could mount an upward move that could be as spectacular as it would be frightening. On this basis, gold (quiet as it appears now) could be like the oncoming train. Either get on it or get out of its way.[4]

**July 26, 1978**

My weekly ratio chart of gold shows gold in terms of percentage of rise or fall. Since 1976, gold has risen on a path that has held it well above the lower trendline. Then in early 1977, gold held above a higher (but not steeper) trendline. All of this was, of course, bullish. This chart

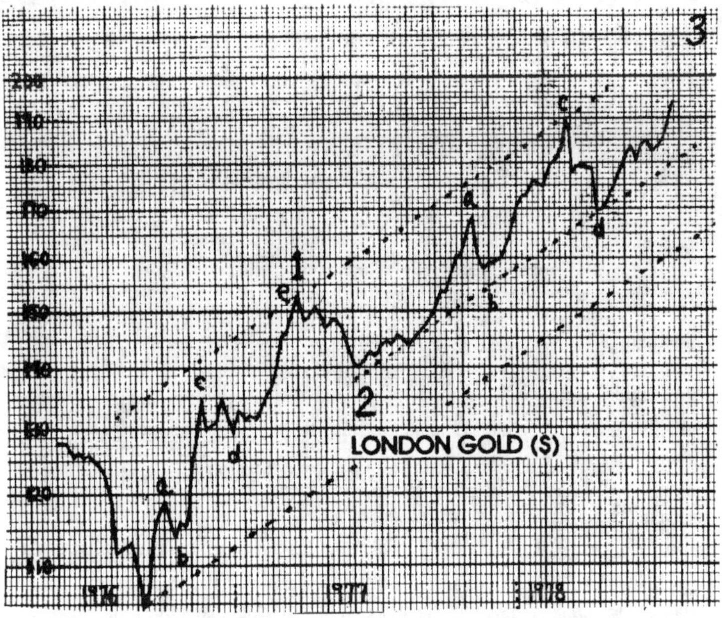


[4] Gold more than quadrupled from here.

also shows my Elliott Wave count. Wave 1 contained five waves and ended in late 1976. Wave 2 corrected wave 1, taking gold from 153 back to 140. By my Elliott count, gold is now in wave 3, and this wave should divide into smaller a-b-c-d-e waves. The a through d waves are now completed and gold is currently in wave e. The e wave should wind up major wave 3. It should also be the strongest and most speculative subwave in larger wave 3. Following a wave 4, correction gold should embark on bullish wave 5. That wave should be something to see.

**October 4, 1978**

Gold has been rising within the two trendlines which make up the *channel* on the chart. I have numbered the movements in Elliott terms according to my interpretation. We completed a 1-2-3-4-5 rise during 1976-77. An a-b-c correction took gold down to 140 in early 1977. The latest rise is also a 1-2-3-4-5 advance, and by my reckoning, gold is still in leg 5. So far, this has been a very subdued fifth leg, even

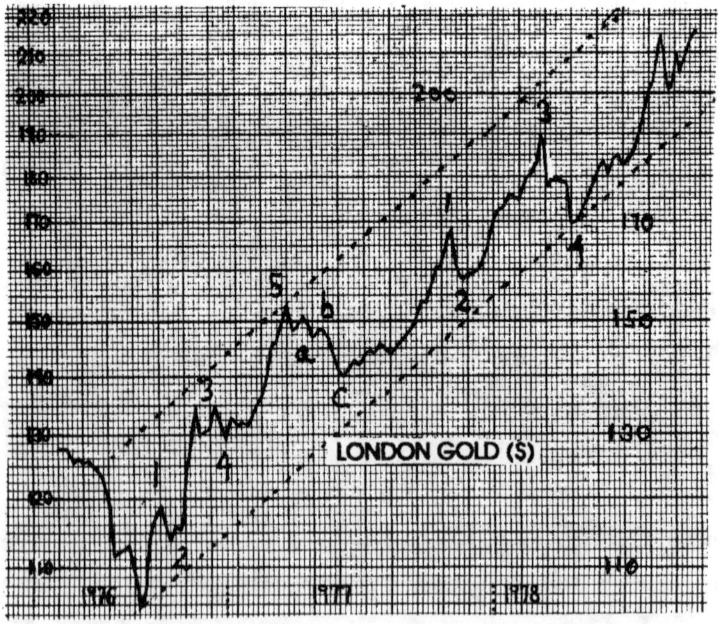

though it has carried from 169 to 219. My guess is that the fifth leg is extending and that it will become emotional and speculative before it's over. The top of the upper channel line intersects the price at about 250, and it wouldn't surprise me to see that figure touched or surpassed before the next six months are out. Somewhere along the line in this fifth leg, gold should start to "bubble and boil." But it will do so on its own good time.

### October 18, 1978

In the last Letter, I updated (in Elliott Wave terms) my chart of gold. I think that the technical considerations regarding gold are now telling us a great deal about the coming scenario for the U.S. economy and the markets. This is how I see events unfolding.

As I explained in the last report, gold is now in its second major advancing wave from the 1976 bottom. The first rising wave took the form of a classic 1-2-3-4-5, and these subwaves are numbered on the chart. The first wave ended at 152.20 on March 25, 1977. We then had a normal a-b-c correction, which carried down to 138.40 on June 14, 1977. From here, the second major wave began its upward climb. As you see on the chart, subwaves 1 through 4 have been completed. We are now in subwave 5. The fifth wave of any rising wave structure is usually the speculative wave, and that is why in the last Letter I stated that I thought the current rise in gold was close to becoming emotional and speculative.

Note that gold has been climbing higher within the channel formation as shown on the chart. The top of the channel at this time comes in at about 250 for gold, but with each passing week, the channel top moves higher. If gold becomes speculative and emotional, I would expect it to push up to or even above the top of the channel (around the 250 area).

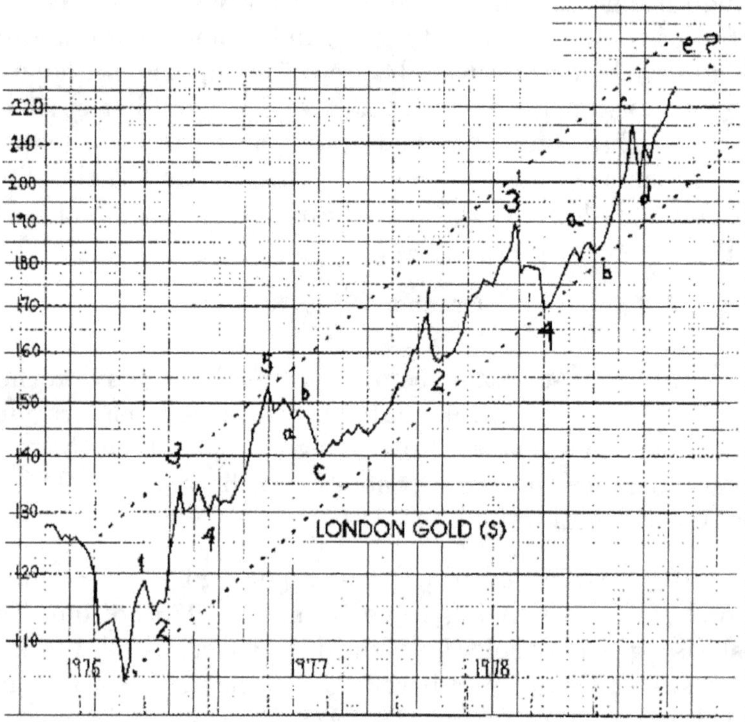


**November 22, 1978**

I have applied technical analysis to the trade-weighted dollar, and the results are rather interesting. So far, what I believe we have is a giant A-B-C bear pattern in the dollar. The A leg carried down to 1975. The B leg rallied the dollar to mid-1977. And the C leg smashed to a low in November 1978.

What interests me in particular is that the C leg has assumed the form of five sub-legs (numbered 1-2-3-4-5 on the chart). The C leg has the *look of a major completed leg* to me. This is the reason why I believe we could have a stronger dollar and a more extended dollar advance than most skeptics on the dollar now think possible. I believe that the dollar is now in an important advancing leg. Whether this leg will carry above point B I do not know. Obviously if it does, the

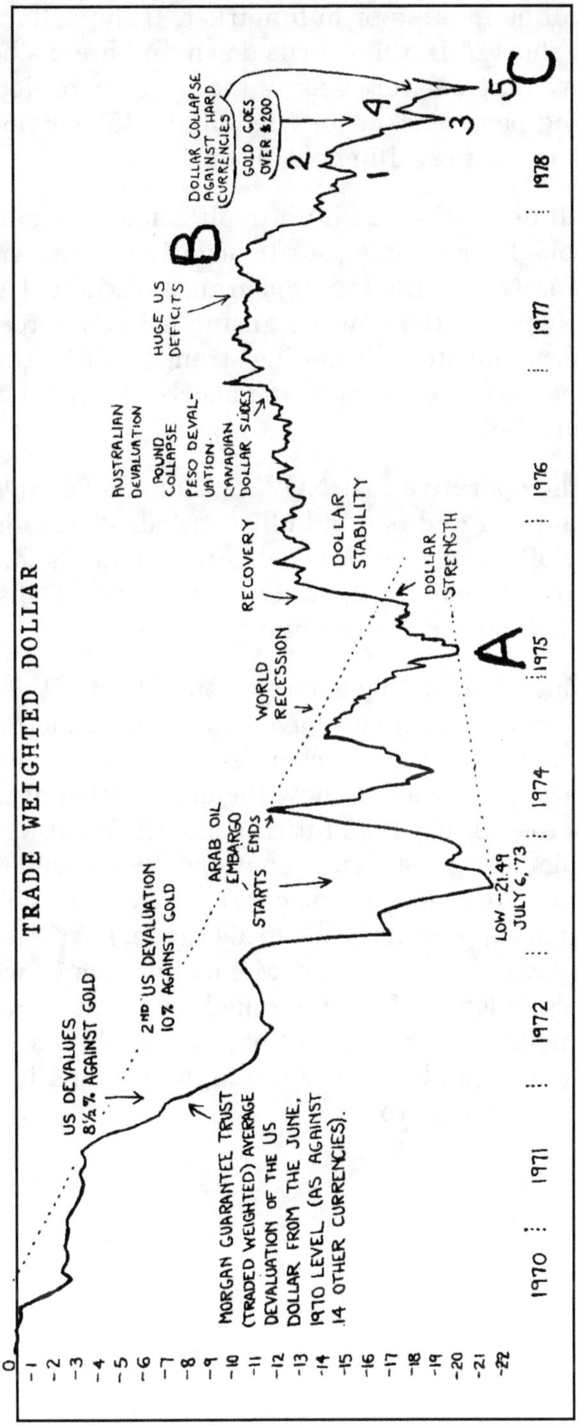
TRADE WEIGHTED DOLLAR
US DEVALUES 8½% AGAINST GOLD
2ND US DEVALUATION 10% AGAINST GOLD
MORGAN GUARANTEE TRUST (TRADED WEIGHTED) AVERAGE DEVALUATION OF THE US DOLLAR FROM THE JUNE, 1970 LEVEL (AS AGAINST 14 OTHER CURRENCIES).
ARAB OIL EMBARGO STARTS ENDS
LOW – 21.49 JULY 6, '73
WORLD RECESSION
A
RECOVERY
DOLLAR STABILITY
DOLLAR STRENGTH
AUSTRALIAN DEVALUATION
POUND COLLAPSE
PESO DEVALUATION
CANADIAN DOLLAR SLIDES
HUGE US DEFICITS
B
DOLLAR COLLAPSE AGAINST HARD CURRENCIES
GOLD GOES OVER $200
1 2 3 4 5
C
0 -1 -2 -3 -4 -5 -6 -7 -8 -9 -10 -11 -12 -13 -14 -15 -16 -17 -18 -19 -20 -21 -22
1970 1971 1972 1974 1975 1976 1977 1978

dollar will be in a major bull market. If the dollar halts its advance short of B, then turns down and breaks below C, I would say that we were seeing the next major decline in a continuing bear market for the dollar. But for now, dollar strength is the prevailing condition.

All of this has definite implications for gold. One of the reasons I turned cautious to negative on gold in the last Letter was the completed appearance of the C leg on this chart. As long as the new advancing leg is in force, I doubt that gold can muster any lasting strength. But if the current advancing leg is abbreviated, if it aborts, then gold will sense it and turn bullish.

The operative fact NOW is that the dollar has completed its C leg and is in a bullish trend. That tells us that holding dollars is now preferable to holding gold. A small amount of gold coins will still be a valid form of "insurance," but any holdings of gold should be *minimal.*

Many readers have never seen a chart of the currency futures, but here again we have a fascinating picture of sudden dollar strength and a completed "top out" move in one of the hard currencies. I show the daily action of the Swiss franc via the March, 1979 future contract. What we see here is a completed 1-2-3-4-5 rising pattern, then a wild downside panic plunge (the dots on the chart are "limit down" moves), then a bit of support in the .63 to .64 range. Last week Swissy plunged down the limit again. Meanwhile, the 10-week moving average (dotted line) has rolled over and turned down, completing the violent top-out pattern for Swissy. The odds on Swissy moving back over the high any time in the near future are slim to zero.

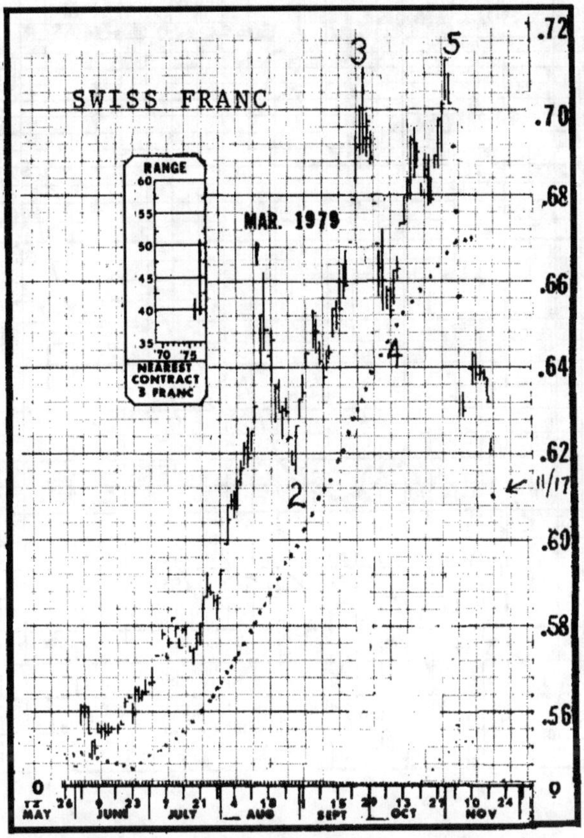


I want to turn now to the ratio (semilog) chart of gold. The chart shows gold climbing up a two-year rising channel. As long as gold held within this channel, it was clear that the metal was holding to a steady rate of growth. What I was afraid might happen did occur last week. On November 15, gold dropped below the bottom trendline of the channel. This tells me that the odds favor a severe, rather than a mild correction in gold.

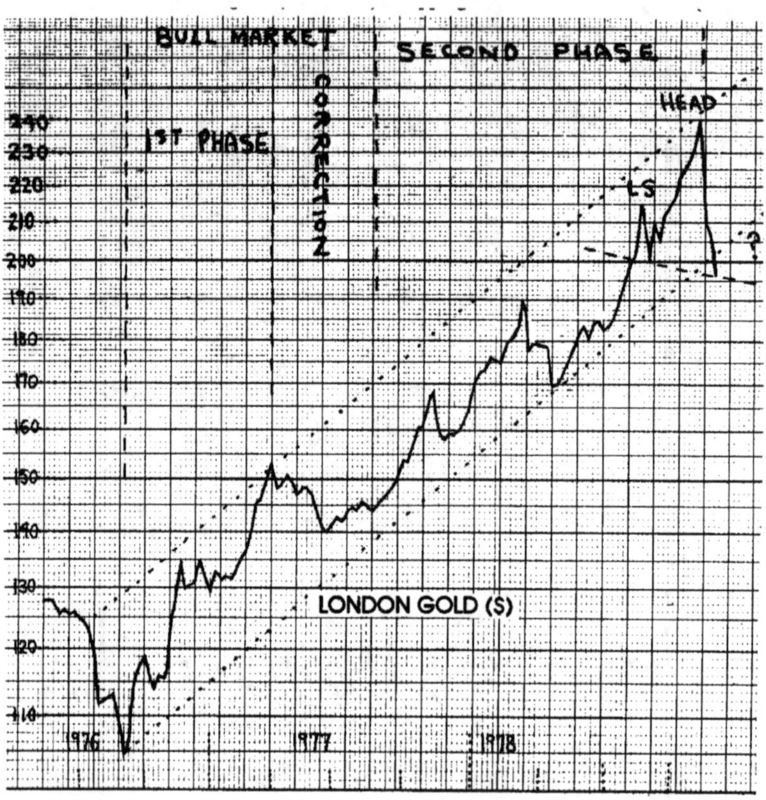


I have labeled the phases of the bull market in gold (so far). When gold hit 243 and then aborted (because of the record high in the discount rate), the second phase of the gold bull market ended. Second phase corrections tend to be severe and costly. It is during the second phase correction that I would expect gold to move from weaker to stronger hands. When gold finally bottoms out, following this correction, it should be in rock-strong hands, and it should then be ready for its third phase or final rise, but such a move could be months away, and we have to deal now with the corrective situation.

I said that I expected gold to trace out an A-B-C correction. So far, I would say that gold is in its first or A-leg down. It is a negative that the first leg ruptured the two year rising trendline. The next rally in gold should be the B-leg. Unfortunately, I don't think the B leg will take gold very far into the channel again (if indeed it can rise within the rising channel at all). Following the B leg from wherever the B leg starts, we should get the final C leg down. I would guess, from what I see now, that the C leg could carry gold down to the 150 to 170 level.

My daily chart of gold and the gold stock average (GSA) shows gold finally confirming the GSA by breaking below its (gold's) August low of 197.50. However, note that gold has now taken the form of an a-b-c-d-e pattern down

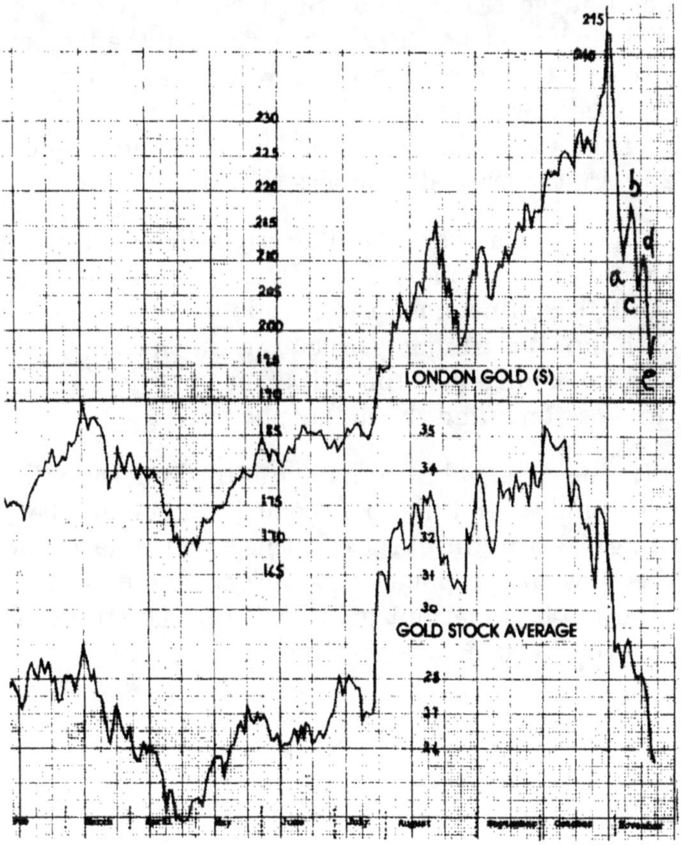

and this could end the first leg down. Therefore, gold should be ready to rally, and the strength of the rally back will tell us something important about the gold picture. If you have not lightened up on gold so far, any rally from here should give you the opportunity. I would cut down to a peak position of 15% of assets in gold.

**January 17, 1979**

I believe that we've now seen the end of the B-leg (upward corrective leg) of the A-B-C pattern which should be a major corrective pattern for gold. If I'm right, then we should now be in the C leg or the final down-leg of the correction. Certainly everyone had a chance to lighten up on this B leg (as I suggested they do). Since the upward B leg was extended via news (the OPEC price rise and the Iran mess), gold prices obtained on the B leg were even better than I had expected they would be. So from here on, we should be watching the unwinding of the C leg to the downside. 212, then 202 are the critical numbers to watch

Don't get me wrong, I still firmly believe that only gold is real money and all paper is an IOU against gold (if paper is not an IOU against gold, then, as John Exter says, it's an IOU-nothing). But timing is crucial in the markets, and the markets are saying that the dollar, at least for a while, is going to be strong (and the dollar pays interest).

In due time, gold will have its third phase (bull market) boom, and when that boom comes, it's going to be quite something else. But the purpose of this second phase reaction in gold is to wear everyone out, knock them out, scare them out – and in so doing, put gold back in rock-strong hands again. Once that is done – watch out!

**March 14, 1979**

Poised on "the edge" is my weekly chart of the Morgan Guaranty "trade-weighted dollar." This is the dollar measured against 14 other currencies (the currencies weighted for volume of trade). Following the crushing downward smash (a smash that was divided into five distinct waves down), the trade-weighted dollar has now formed a base and a potential "head-and-shoulders" bottom. If this chart can break out into the minus 16 area, the dollar will be showing remarkable strength, and in that case I would expect a 50% retracement of the entire 1977-78 collapse.

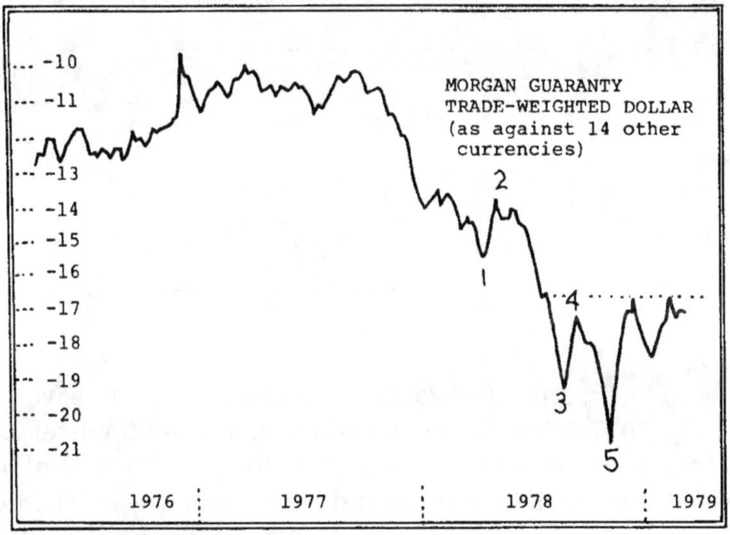


**April 25, 1979**

[Here] I show my ratio chart of gold starting from the 103 low of August 1976. I have all along pictured the move in gold in terms of the Elliott Wave thesis, and I believe this analysis is still valid (although it has been misinterpreted and mangled by many analysts).

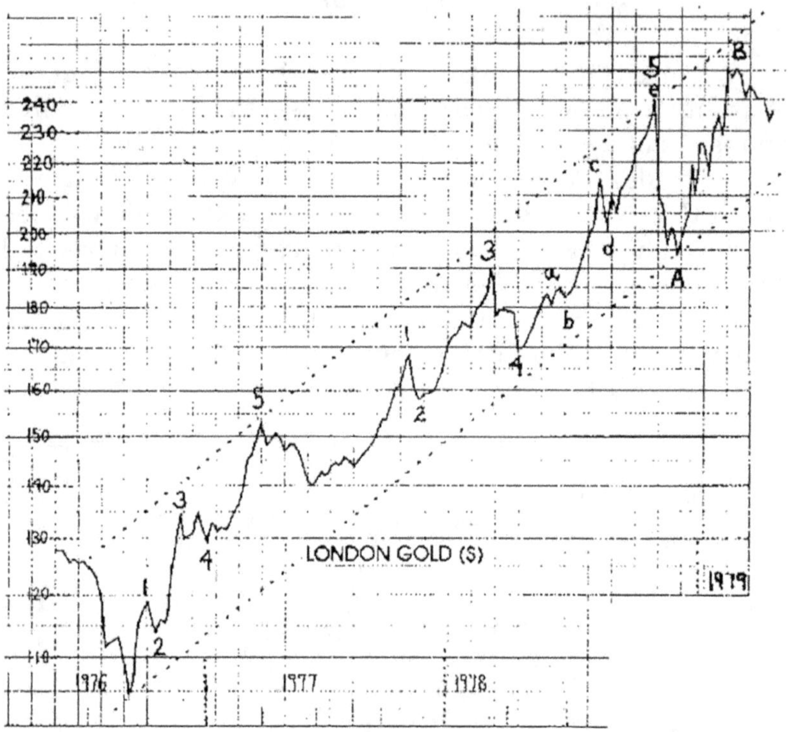


The first phase of gold took the metal to just above 150 in early 1977. This phase traced out a 1-2-3-4-5 pattern. A mild correction took gold back to the 140 area. The next phase took gold to 243 in late 1978, and here again we saw the bull move follow at a 1-2-3-4-5 rising pattern. The fifth wave of this pattern extended, and I show this with an a-b-c-d-e on the chart. Extensions are never the end of a move, but they are often followed by good corrections.

Gold broke to 193 in November 1978 (A on chart). Then with the help of all kinds and varieties of political crises, gold rose (actually above the previous high) to point B on the chart — to 253. From there gold turned down again, and that's where we find gold now having backed off to the 236-239 area, and still in a corrective phase.

## June 6, 1979

This gold chart shows the monthly action of gold on semilog (ratio) scale. This is gold in Elliott terms, as seen by A.J. Frost (co-author of the new Elliott book). The huge rise to the 1974 high of 193 is seen as major wave I for gold. Then we see corrective wave II down to the 103 low of late 1976. Frost sees the advance to the late 1978 peak of 243 as the orthodox top of subwave I. Then came the panic to 193, and this was seen as wave A of an A-B-C correction. The new high of last week is part of wave B of a flat-type correction (in flats the B leg often rises above the orthodox high). A C leg down to 200 to 220 should complete the move.

I've asked myself whether the flat correction is the correct diagnosis of the action since last year's 243 high, and frankly I don't know. It surprised me that the current

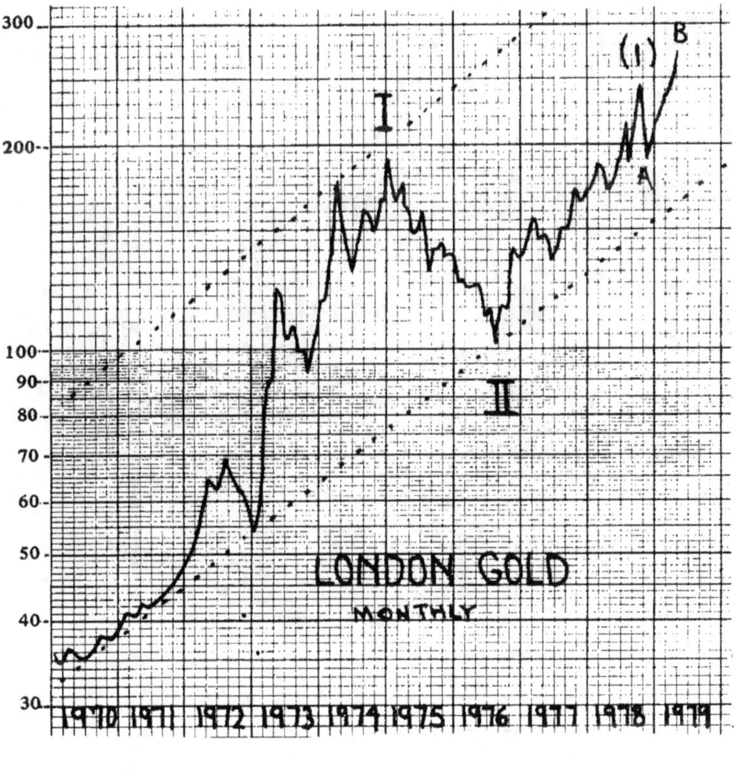

B leg went as far as it did above the old 243 high. However, the laggard action of ASA and Campbell Red Lake could be saying that the "flat correction" is the correct view of this gold move. I just can't tell at this time. If the flat correction view is the right one, I would expect gold to start correcting at any time.[5]

**December 3, 1980**

I must admit that the near-term or daily chart looks better than the long-term chart, but the story is still being

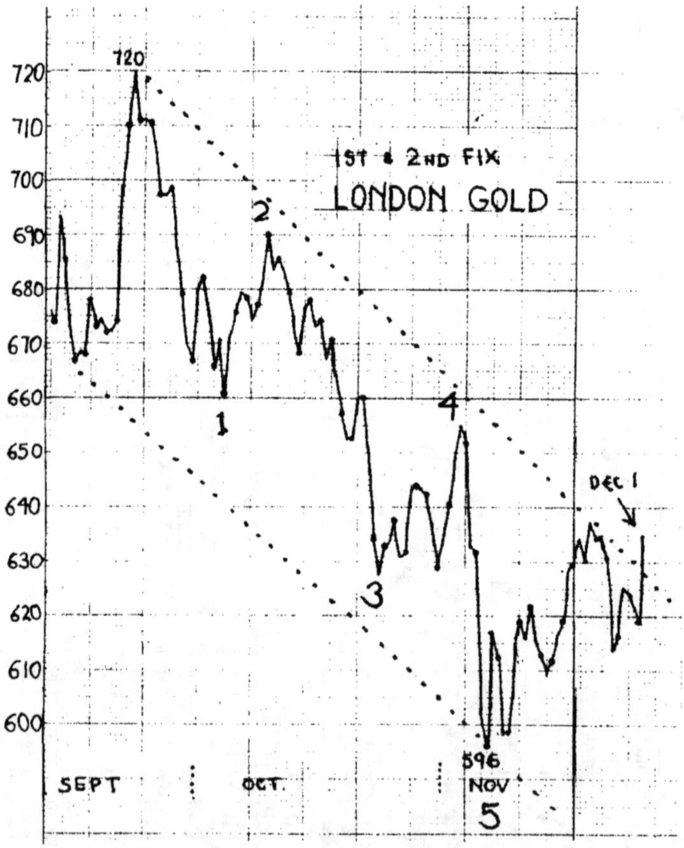


[5] It was not a flat correction, as gold kept on going up.

told. On the daily chart note that gold has corrected down from its September high of 720, and the correction has taken the form of five waves down — all within a descending channel. Now five waves down usually completes a movement,[6] so it was not surprising to see gold correct upward following the termination of the fifth wave at a price of 596 in early November.

[6] It also signals the new direction of the larger trend, which in this case is down.

# A.J. FROST'S ELLIOTT WAVE FORECASTS

## 1978 - 1991

*After his departure from the money management business in 1963, Frost continued to keep an hourly chart and analyze the market according to the Elliott Wave Principle through 1991. His forecasts were captured in numerous newspaper articles and a 1989 special report published by Elliott Wave International. The following section includes most of these published accounts and a few letters to Prechter, which together give readers the full Elliott Wave rationale behind Frost's forecasts.*

## *LETTER TO SLOAN WILSON*

**April 1, 1978**

Wave IV of the big Supercycle from 1932 has been long and frustrating, but the long-term message of the big picture has been constant. It simply says that wave V will carry the DJIA to the level where it will touch the upper parallel or boundary line in the 1982-84 period at approximately 2700 DJIA.

In trying to pinpoint the demise of wave IV, most Elliotters bet on the 1974 low as the terminal point of a fourth-wave triangle. However, I am not so sure that this is the correct interpretation, as subsequent action does not confirm the beginning of a new bull market in December 1974. In fact, the move up from that point to September 21, 1976 (1014.79 DJIA) looks like a three-wave affair and the move down from September 1976 to March 1, 1978 another three. If this is the correct reading, wave IV is a seven-wave sequence, or double three, lasting from February 1965 to March 1, 1978, a period of 13 years plus a few days.

In Elliott's terms, fifth waves often match first waves if the middle wave extends. On this basis, the move up from March 1 (740 DJIA at 11 a.m.) should eventually match the wave I from July 1932 to early 1937, lasting approximately 55 months and reaching a level 4 to 4½ times its base. So if waves V and I are to match in time and amplitude, we can expect a rip-roaring bull market over the next few years. And why shouldn't we? Everything that can be discounted seems to be reflected in stock prices, with bargains galore all around us, even in Canada.

2700 DJIA looks high, but with today's rotting dollar, the Dow at 2700 on a weighted basis would likely only approximate the 1966 high of 1000 DJIA. So in real time, 1966 at 1000 = 1983 at 2700 or thereabouts.

I shudder for the future, but the next few years may not be too bad.

### VICTORIA TIMES, SATURDAY, OCTOBER 27, 1979

## Wall Street crash not till '83: analyst

Al Forrest

Fears of a stock market crash are about four years premature, says A.J. Frost, a market analyst.

Frost said his studies indicate a major crash is coming but not until late 1982 or early 1983.

In fact, the present market should recover strongly and hit all-time highs before it collapses.

Frost, author of *The Elliott Wave Principle*, a book on technical factors in the Dow Jones index, made the comments Thursday night in a speech at the Union Club to the Vancouver Island branch of the Fellows of the Canadian Securities Institute.

The FCSI was established by the Investment Dealers Association to provide advanced education in securities.

Frost said his studies of long-term market trends indicates the Dow Jones will soar to 2,000 points, possibly up to 2,600 "before the market falls out of bed."

The index has been over the 1,000 mark but closed Thursday at around 800.

Frost said he began his studies in 1962, during President Kennedy's Cuban missile crisis, when the Dow Jones showed severe up and down movement.

He noted an Elliott Wave pattern, an idea developed in the late 1930s but not promoted by stock analysts.

He began a painstaking hour-by-hour study of the up-down fluctuations of the Dow Jones Index and put the patterns into a book with the help of co-author Robert Prechter of New York, a market counsellor.

Frost was educated in Ontario where he became a legal accountant. He has now retired to Victoria.

He said he continues to chart the Dow Jones every day.

The recent actions of the transportation index have been the most promising, he said.

They show the typical five moves upward, three moves down, that precede an upward swing in the market.

And across the board there is a growing confidence in the market that will soon be reflected in higher stock prices, he said.

He urged salesmen to stress fundamentals (company earnings, dividends) when studying an individual stock but to use technical factors when considering the swing of the index.

Any well-based stock that is moving up in a parallel trend with the index should be a solid buy, he said.

Frost said the Dow Jones index is a reflection of people's emotions, more than a statement about the economy. And while the economy may be difficult to chart, emotional reactions are fairly predictable to anyone who has studied them for a period of time.

As a result, the Dow Jones index seems to move according to some natural law, he said.

A sudden emotional outburst may push the index higher or lower than expected in any given week but on a longer term the predetermined trend will continue unimpeded because severe fluctuations are countered by the opposite move, pulling the market into equilibrium, just as in nature.

## *LETTER TO PRECHTER*

**May 5, 1980**

I have a feeling that the market is not going to drop below the April 21 low of 755.38. If it does, then an update will be required.

## *LETTER TO PRECHTER*

**July 1980**

In broad general terms, I feel it is safe to say that if the long consolidation from 1965 did not end in 1974, it has now ended or is ending. My analysis suggests that last October when the market dropped by over 100 Dow points, then climbed in a three-wave sequence to 910 DJIA on February 10, 1980 only to fall by over 150 points to March 27, 1980 can be identified as an ABC flat of a completed Primary wave from March 1, 1978. This means we are now entering the third Primary wave of the last Cycle move up from 1932, which could be exponential in character. The proof of the pudding will be in its eating. In my opinion, good stocks are literally going to be eaten up in an orgy of buying. Tony Reid, writing in the *Financial Post* on April 12, 1980 said,

"Stocks on an earnings basis are today the cheapest in more than a century." Coming off an ABC flat from October 1979 to March or April 1980, the investor can anticipate a very strong upward thrust, under Elliott's rules.

Market action this year is reminiscent of the 1962 collapse ending in a selling climax on June 26, 1962 at 523 DJIA, followed by a rising wedge containing a series of Elliott patterns and ending in a five-wave decline to the Cuban crisis low of 554 DJIA. At that point, the market never looked back. The collapse of the DJIA from February 10 to March 27 of this year followed by a similar rise and a five-wave sequence down from 796 DJIA on April 11th to a low of 755.38 DJIA at 3 p.m. on April 21 suggests that the March 27 low of 739 DJIA was an unorthodox low and 755.38 the orthodox low. Again, we don't expect the market to look back as we have now seen the lows for many years to come. At least, *them's my sentiments.*

## *LETTER TO PRECHTER*

**August 18, 1980**

We seem to be headed for the bull market of the century and the crash of the ages.

The Sunday Sun, June 26, 1983

# Elliott's Wave Sinks Gold

**Tony Reid**

In the interests of presenting different opinions, this week I had the pleasure to interview an old friend, A.J. Frost, aged 75, who is now retired and living in Victoria, B.C.

We met in Vancouver in 1959 when we both worked at my father's investment management company. Our working relationship continued at Bolton Tremblay in Montreal, in the early 1960s, where Frost worked with A. Hamilton Bolton, then the leading authority on the Elliott Wave Principle.

What is the Elliott Wave Principle?

*Frost*: Briefly, the Elliott Wave Principle is a cyclical theory of change based on an underlying principle of order. Order is implicit in the stock market, because the market is people. Scientists claim that there is order in the universe which generates a great web of interrelated processes, all of which expand and contract in harmonious relationship to each other.

*Sun*: That's very interesting — but what does the Wave Principle tell you right now?

*Frost*: The Elliott Wave Principle (EWP) tells me we are still in the first leg up in a strong primary bull market dating from August 13, 1982 when the index was 776.92. I expect this first phase will continue until March or April, 1984 with a short term Oct. 1983 massacre bringing the market down about 100 points.

My view on the stock market generally does not apply to gold. Gold, in my opinion, is the least attractive investment vehicle and has the greatest downside risk. I fully expect gold bullion will be trading below $200 U.S. an ounce in late 1986. This is based on my interpretation that gold is about to enter wave C of an A, B, C, correction.

*Sun*: That, of course, is the exact opposite of my viewpoint on gold. I believe the price of the metal — currently at $419 U.S. — is just about ready to start on its next major move upwards, towards a 1986 high above the $2000 U.S. mark.

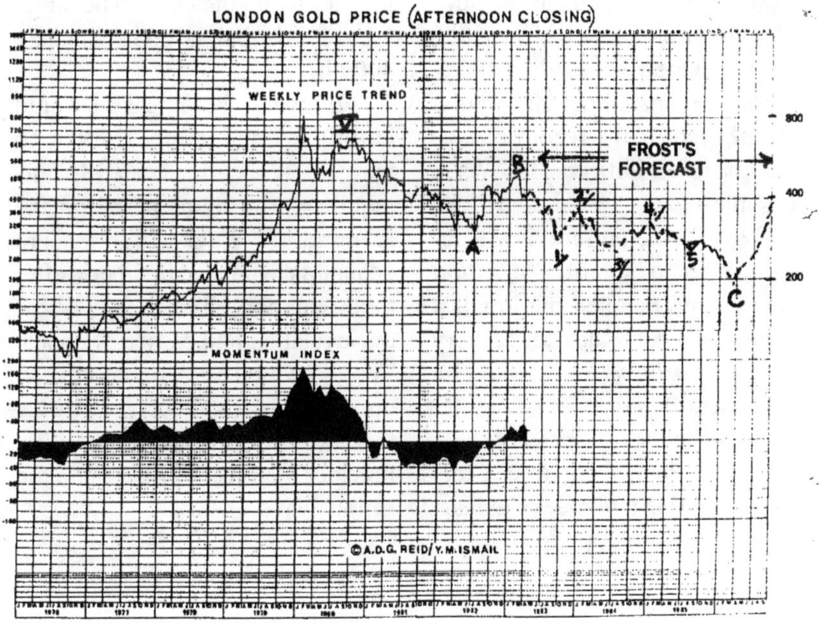


**REID'S CHART** shows past price movements of an ounce of gold — including that point in 1980 where an ounce of the shiny stuff soared over the $800 U.S.-mark. Follow the dotted line and you see Reid's friend, A.J. Frost, is predicting dire things for the flashy metal, including a $200 U.S. low by late 1986.

**$2000, or $200 by 1986?**

Why do you feel that gold is going down?

*Frost*: Gold has not completed its cycle that began in the late 1960s and terminated in Sept. '80 at $710 U.S. The absolute high of $850 U.S. set in Jan. '80 was an irregular or unorthodox top in Elliott terms. I expect the current price to drop precipitously over the next few months, breaking the $300 U.S. level before year end.

*Sun*: I guess then, you would see the same thing happening to all precious metals?

*Frost*: Yes, and to their related assets such as gold stocks etc. I would like to add that in the long run, possibly 10 years from now, gold bullion will be over $3000 U.S. an ounce.

*Sun*: OK, that's enough for gold. Tell me what is the record of correctness for Elliott and his Wave Principle?

*Frost*: At the present time Robert Prechter, editor of *The Elliott Wave Theorist*, called the low last August and continues to be very accurate. *Business Week*, May 30, 1983 states Prechter is a dissenter to be watched.

At that time, most forecasters were predicting a retrace of at least one-third of the 57% advance in the DJIA from last August. As you well know, Tony, the market has ignored such predictions, confounding many pros who use various market approaches. On October 20, 1982, Prechter said the market would hit 1200 by April, 1983. In my opinion Prechter has an enviable record of market predictions.

*Sun*: On this basis, where do you think the stock market is going and over what period of time will your prediction be based?

*Frost*: Based on Elliott Theory, I would project a target of 3600 on the DJIA by 1987. For the TSE 300 (Toronto Stock Exchange composite index), I would anticipate a move up paralleling the DJIA. The target I have in mind is approximately 4000 in 1987.

Following these peaks I would anticipate a decline similar to that which occurred in 1929. This parallels projections based on the Kondratieff Wave (the Russian economist who died in Siberia after the revolution). That is, a 54-year cycle relating to the price of goods. The "K" wave is an economic cycle, not a stock market cycle, however the "K" wave seems to parallel Prechter's projections based on the Elliott Wave Theory.

The Sunday Sun, September 22, 1985

Tony Reid

# He sees boom, then depression

*Technical analysis is somewhat like sex; timing is everything.*

— Jack Frost

The 78-year old exponent of the Elliott Wave theory last week addressed the Canadian Society of Technical Analysts, an association formed late last year and already with 88 members.

Ron Meisels, a technical analyst with Nesbitt Thomson, welcomed Frost as the first honorary member of the fledgling society, which was formed to promote technical analysis as a decision-making investment tool.

With stock markets crashing down early last week, Frost made a bullish forecast. The market, he said, will see a spike down to a selling climax in a "correction" phase, and climb from that point.

Frost also dwelled on yesterday's technical analysis experts, including Ralph Elliott, originator of the wave theory who made his name in the early 1930s by successfully calling the bottom of the 1929-32 bear market – within two hours.[1] He later went on to develop his theory, which has been resurrected by modern market watchers.

Another pioneer was Hamilton Bolton, a Montrealer who in the Fifties wrote on Elliott's theories. Bolton founded the firm of Bolton, Tremblay and originated the *Bank Credit Analyst*, still considered the bible of the banking industry.

In 1978 Frost and Robert Prechter published the first edition of *Elliott Wave Principle*, outlining all previous works on the subject, and interpreting the effect on future markets.

Prechter later became the darling of Wall Street, after winning the prestigious U.S. trading championship. He is now one of the most widely-followed U.S. market forecasters.

Frost says "the spirit of man is technical, but the mind of man is fundamental." He also believes there's an order in the universe and in man's mind, "so it follows there is order in the stock market.

"There is a tendency for the market to move in increments of its square root."

---

[1] Reid is probably referring to 1935, when Elliott first demonstrated the utility of the Wave Principle by calling a low in the market via telegram to Charles J. Collins.

For example, the 1932 market low in New York of 41 rose to 194 in 1937, which is a gain of 4.7 times. Applying Elliott's theory, then the low of 777 in 1982 should peak at 3676 some time in 1987.

Frost feels we're in for a fantastic bull market over the next few years, and says the Dow index will double to 2600 next year, then fall back to 1800 and peak at that 3600 figure.

In Toronto, he feels the TSE index will mirror the Dow, and rise to well over 4000 by 1987.

Frost says that following the markets' explosive top in 1987 a crash is due, and will be brought about because of parallel conditions in the banking system to those of 1929. The combined external debts of Argentina, Brazil and Mexico, he reminds, could wipe out the 50 largest U.S. banks – and Frost says default is likely.

That will lead to an exodus of foreign money from U.S. banks; high real inflation; a bank collapse and depression dealing a serious blow to the American financial system.

Last year I interviewed Frost, when he called for a strong market in Canada and the U.S.; a strong American dollar; and weak gold and oil prices. In particular, he forecast a drop in gold prices from $419 U.S. to below $300.

He was right on all counts, and now says gold will fall more to between $105 and $175 in 1987 and oil will sell for $16 U.S./barrel next year.

So there you have it: Avoid oil and gold; plunge into the stock market for the next 12 months; wait for it to fall 30% and buy again to get the last surge in 1987.

The Sunday Sun, June 29, 1986

## Stock market will peak, then crash says leading Elliott Wave philosopher

**Tony Reid**

It was unseasonably cool when Jack Frost arrived in town last week to address the Canadian Society of Technical Analysts.

Frost, 78, spoke to the group last September when he was made its first honorary member. He has had a varied career. He is both a lawyer and chartered accountant and has held executive positions in a trust company and in investment counseling as well as serving on the National Capital Commission, the Tax Appeal Board and the Boy Scouts of Canada.

But he is best-known as Canada's foremost expert on the Elliott Wave Theory. In 1978, he co-authored a book on the theory with Robert Prechter. *Elliott Wave*

*Principle* is now in its fifth edition. Prechter, the leading advocate of the theory, is considered to be one of the top stock market forecasters in the U.S.

Elliott's theory is based on a number of waves and cycles and it made his reputation in the early '30s when he successfully called the bottom of the 1929-32 bear market within two hours.[1]

It was in the early '60s, in association with A. Hamilton Bolton, founder of Bolton Tremblay and Co. and an exponent of Elliott, that Frost intensified his studies of the theory.

Elliott's work is really more of a philosophy than a theory. And in many ways, Frost is the philosopher's philosopher as he likes to interpose quotes from ancient Chinese, Indian and other writers.

In applying the principle to the stock and security markets, Frost describes it as the cycle in security price movements. And he has been right more often than wrong.

Last September, he correctly forecast strong markets in Canada and the U.S., a strong U.S. dollar, weak oil prices and the decline of gold from $419 U.S. to $300.

He foretold the TSE rising to 4000 by 1987 and that the Dow Jones Industrial Index would double to 2600 this year, fall back to 1800, then peak at 3600 in 1987.

Further, he recommended avoiding gold and oil and said oil would drop to $16 U.S. a barrel.

His stock-market forecast is dead on so far, and he really did call the tune last September. In fact, the market has risen virtually straight up since. As we all know, oil prices collapsed at the turn of the year, plunging from the $27 U.S. level in September to a low of about $10 U.S. in April.

As for gold, it was about $335 U.S. in September, has been as low as $315 U.S. in December, as high as $385 U.S. in January and is currently about $345 U.S., so Frost is still a long way from his projected price of between $105- 175 U.S. in 1987. In this category, as a gold bug, I hope he's wrong.

What does Frost say now? He thinks bond prices have peaked and interest rates (long-term) are going to start rising. Frost also believes the stock market is "the best show in town" and that prices will continue to rise toward his earlier projected target in 1987.

He doesn't think this will be the case however, believing instead that the Dow Jones will move up 50% to 2800, then react to 2600 before completing its fifth wave, which will carry it to a peak of between 3400 and 3600 in 1987. But then, he says, "it will fall and fall hard, in a crash worse than 1929-1932."

He believes the U.S. system is already strung out and has no more elasticity left for the next crisis — therefore the collapse. He continues to cite the third world debt situation as the event that will bring down the banking system.

As for oil, he sees the price falling to between $8 and $10 U.S. a barrel. He bases that prediction on his former professor at Queen's, Frank Knox, who said: "Based on a free market, the price of a commodity as determined over the short term will come down to the cost of the marginal producer."

With those thoughts, Frost wound up with one more quote:

"Nature alternates dynamically. When it completes what it is doing, then it starts all over again. All that is springs from such alternation."

Sunday Sun, March 1987

## Here's a market update for Elliott Wave fans

**Tony Reid**

Last June I did an update on Jack Frost, Canada's 79-year-old expert on the Elliott Wave theory. Frost co-authored a book on the theory with Robert Prechter, the hottest market forecaster in the U.S.

In our last interview, Frost forecast that the TSE 300 would rise to 4000 in 1987 and the Dow would move up 50% to 2800, then react to 2600 before completing its fifth wave to a peak of between 3400 and 3600 in 1987. Following that there would be a "crash" worse than 1929.

Currently the TSE 300 is 3820 and the Dow is 2371, so Frost is well on target.

*This week I received a letter from Frost dated March 10:*

For the last 12 months the Dow has been flexing its muscles. The phenomenon can be seen in the impulse waves which are moving up strongly and in the Dow's corrective patterns. The result has been a clear parabolic curve from November, 1986. When this curve is shattered it could be game over for stock prices.

Currently we are in the last phase of a Supercycle trend up from 1932. This last phase started in August 1982 and has not been completed. In the next few months the market should rack up one of its best gains in history. The question is: How far will this market go before it turns turtle or, like Humpty Dumpty, breaks to pieces?

Cycle Wave 1 from 1932 to 1937 advanced 4.7 times from its low over a period of five years. If we apply this formula to the low of 1982, the DJIA could reach 3686.

The only problem I see with this interpretation is that the low of 1932 could have been a throwover of the lower trend line. If this is true, the July 8, 1932 low may be an unorthodox low, which leads me to suspect that the market may not reach a much higher level than 3686 by the fall of 1988.

Another count which has validity under the Wave Principle is to apply the rule that a fifth wave is often related by a Fibonacci Ratio to the net advance from the beginning of Wave 1 to the top of Wave 3. If we apply this principle, it appears to me that the Dow is not likely to extend beyond 3415 by early September, 1987. At this point the dow could fail to reach its upper parallel line from 1932.

Under the rule of alternation, the Dow could fall at this point, as it started out in 1932 with a likely throw-over in the opposite direction.

According to my count, the market entered Cycle Wave 5 on Aug. 11, 1982 at DJIA 744. We now are in Primary Wave 5 of Cycle 5. Primary 5 has so far subdivided into four Intermediate waves, placing the market in the 5th of the 5th of the 5th from 1932.

Primary Wave 4 started, in my view, on March 21, 1986 and ended Sept. 29, 1986. Within Primary 5, Intermediate 3 started Jan. 2, 1987. From Jan. 2, I anticipate a third-wave intermediate extension and possibly an extension within an extension. If this should develop, the final Intermediate up wave could be very short, indeed. My guess is only 160 points, which could terminate the long-term move from 1932.

If the reader is in doubt about my wave count, especially Primary 4, I suggest he try counting backwards from Aug. 4, 1986 or Sept. 29, 1986. On this basis, it could well be noted that there are a series of contracting flats back to March 21. Counting backwards is not part of EWP, but it sometimes clarifies the count.

*For those of you who don't understand or care what Elliott and Frost are saying, essentially the message reads: "Hang onto your hats! We now have embarked on the final and most dynamic phase of the bull market that began way back on July 8, 1932 when the Dow bottomed out at 41.22. With that same index now at 2362.64, the market could be expected to explode as high as 3600 by 1988 or, as Frost says, sharply higher by this fall. And then it's all over.*

Sunday Sun, June 28, 1987

## For technical analysts, it was a wave of a week

**Tony Reid**

Last week was a doubleheader for the Elliott Wave theorists in Toronto as the theory's leading exponents addressed two sessions of the Toronto Society of Technical Analysts.

Before a packed, standing-room only crowd, Bob Prechter, from Gainesville, Ga., said the Dow Jones Industrial Average, currently at 2444, would peak at 3686 in 1988 to show a 50% gain.

That would cap the stock market boom that began on Aug. 12, 1982, when the index was 766.92.

Next day, at lunch, before another packed audience, A. Jack Frost, the dean of the Canadian Followers of the Elliott Wave Theory, also spoke on his forecast for the stock market.

He agreed with Prechter on the Dow Jones Average but thought that the market could peak in 1987 at roughly the same level.

On gold, however, Frost was not bearish at all.

In fact, on the long-term outlook, he was quite bullish

Frost and Prechter wrote the book *Elliott Wave Principle*, published in November 1978 outlining the theories of R.N. Elliott, who was popular throughout the 1920s and '30s, and was more recently followed by A. Hamilton Bolton, the founder of Bolton Tremblay and the original author of *The Bank Credit Analyst*.

The lunch was more than just Frost's annual speech to the technical analysts.

It was, in fact, a time for the Canadian Society of Technical Analysts to honor Frost.

Many special guests came to honor Frost.

Following Frost's speech, CSTA past president Ron Meisels presented Frost with a silver bull as a memento of the respect the group holds for him.

He will be 80 next January and has been involved in the financial community for almost 60 years.

## *LETTER TO PRECHTER*

**August 23, 1987**

Two of your girls asked me about my projected end of the current bull market. I decided to put my views in print and enclose herewith how I see the market's future. A reverse mirror image is a technique Hamilton Bolton often used in trying to determine the turn-around in a bull market. As the chart indicates, this will be rather a short rise — say three or four months at the most.

ELLIOTT IN PROGRESS

Supercycle(V) began July 8, 1932
Cycle Wave V began Aug.12,1982
Primary Wave ⑤ began Sept.29, 1986?
Int Wave (3) began May20,1987
Minor Wave 3 began July23,1987
Minute Wave .5 should begin within a day or two, taking the market up,up,up.

See chart #2

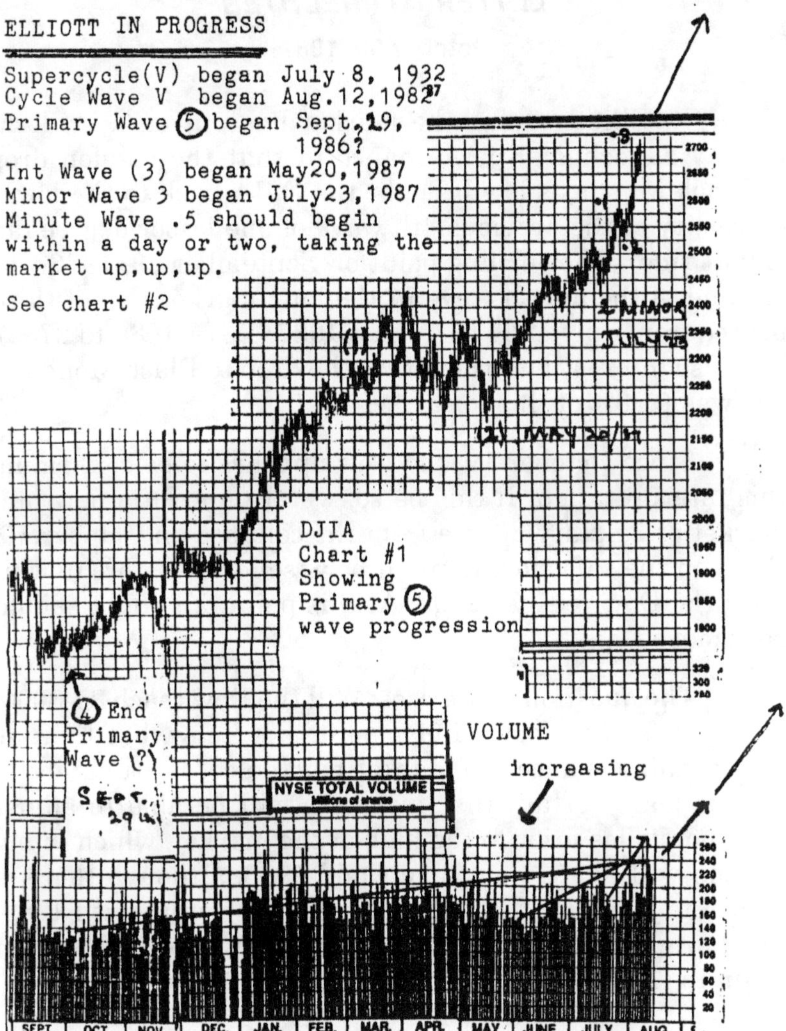


The Final wave structure up could fail to touch the long term upper parallel line, giving the 5-wave up a truncated appearance. The subsequent decline could trigger one of the worst depressions in history and a shift in world trade domination. A.J. F. Aug.15,1987

## *LETTER TO PRECHTER*

**October 30, 1987**

In Elliott terms, the market has put on a brilliant display of technical performance in that the sudden drop to Black Monday's low brought the DJIA back to the lower extremity of the previous 4th wave of one lesser degree (an Elliott rule). The turning point on September 29, 1986 was the end of the fourth wave in the long market rise of third degree from July 1984 to August 1987 (DJIA 1086 to 2732). It is also interesting to note that the drop to Black Monday's low was 61.8% of this long rise.

Since October 19, the Dow appears to be confirming this interpretation. If this be so, we are now in a new bull market of Primary degree from the collapse on October 19. To be on the safe side, it might be wise for investors to wait until the Dow reaches 2500. At this point, all doubt should be removed.

The question now arises: Will the Dow reach 34-3600, or will it fail? Unfortunately, we do not know, but there is a reasonable chance the market may do so. Fortunately, it now appears certain that investors will be able to adjust their portfolios prior to the high of the market, which in my opinion will likely occur about mid-1988, although there is reason to think that the market might continue until 1989. In other words, I do not feel Black Monday's low will be seen again in the cycle upwave from 1982.

Sunday Sun, November 8, 1987

Shocking Forecasts (As Usual) from Jack Frost

# Rising rates and $1,000 gold?

**Tony Reid**

In the past few weeks I had a number of calls expressing appreciation from my June 28 column on Jack Frost. In that column, A. Jack Frost, whom I consider to be the dean of the Canadian exponents of the Elliott Wave Principle, called for a peak in the Dow Jones Industrial Average (DJIA) in the fall of 1987.

Frost and Bob Prechter, from Gainesville, GA., wrote the book *Elliott Wave Principle,* published in November 1978.

It outlined the theories of R.N. Elliott, who was popular throughout the 1920s and '30s, and was more recently followed by A. Hamilton Bolton, the founder of Bolton Tremblay and the original author of *The Bank Credit Analyst.*

This week when I passed on the congratulatory messages to Frost, who will be 80 years old in January, I thought it would be interesting to update his current view subsequent to the great crash of 1987.

In fact, he already had sent me a clipping of a recent interview in the Victoria papers. In that article, Frost indicated that he sold the last of his stock market holdings on Oct. 3, thus avoiding the massive losses suffered by most investors in the last few weeks.

When I asked Jack Frost what his current views were he gave me the following comments:

"With the DJIA at 1945, in 'Elliott' terms I think the market has put on a display of technical performance in that the sudden drop to that Black Monday low (1738) brought the DJIA back to the lower extremity of the previous fourth wave of one lesser degree."

At that point I said, what does that mean in English?

He responded "It means that the turning point of Sept. 29, 1986 was in reality the end of a fourth wave of a long bull market from July 1984 to August 1987 when the index rose from 1086 to 2722.

"In other words, the drop to the 'Black Monday' low was a normal correction (Reid's comment: 'That's normal?) of 61.8% of the previous gain. If that analysis is correct then we are simply in a new market from 'Black Monday.'

"However, to be on the safe side we have to wait a few weeks to be sure that the market doesn't break the previous low of 1738. If it does then we have a five-wave structure which will be very similar to 1929 — and it's game over then."

I then asked what the chances were for this event to occur.

Frost replied: "I don't think that the 1738 point is going to be broken, which means simply that we are now in a new bull market of primary degree."

At this point I almost swallowed the telephone and suffering writer's cramp as I listened in shocked disbelief at Frost's next words:

"If this is the case, the DJIA could easily reach 3400-3600, which is Bob Prechter's prediction."

Frost added: "On my analysis, the real damage to portfolios is somewhere in the distant future."

So, if you believe my friend Jack Frost, you can now step down from that window ledge and relax.

## *LETTER TO PRECHTER*

**November 9, 1987**

The U.S. economy is on the horns of a dilemma, but not the stock market. For instance, Paul Volcker in 1981 was told to protect the dollar by keeping interest rates high, and recently at the Venice Summit, seven Western nations agreed to protect the dollar. Now the policy is to forget the dollar, to assist the farmer and boost other exports to foreign countries. Keep interest rates up. Keep interest rates down. U.S. economic policies are as clear as mud. The tragedy of it all is that the U.S. dollar appears to be losing its status as a world reserve currency.

The question now arises: where are we in the stock market cycle? Although Black Monday is the topic of the day, it does not give the answer to this question. The devastating collapse on October 19 has generated a feeling of insecurity and is no doubt a forerunner of things to come, but it is not the root cause of our plight. Market shocks are not generated by Black Mondays or any other antecedent.

To determine where we are, it is important to review the principles of Elliott Theory. The Dow has put on an extraordinary performance of technical accuracy. If the long market rise from July 1984 to August 1987 (DJIA 1086 to 2732) is a Primary ③ in the bull market from 1982, it leaves little doubt that we are now in a new bull market of Primary degree from Black Monday's low for the following reasons.

1. The Dow came down to a low on Black Monday in an ABC structure with the last leg subdividing in a clear cut 5. This low appears to be the previous low of one lesser degree which occurred on September 29, 1986 at 1740.

2. The drop represents approximately 61.8% (an Elliott ratio) of the third Primary rise from mid '84 to mid '87.

The chart showing the gyrations on Black Monday October 19, 1987 represents an analysis on a 15 minute interval basis. Neither the hourly charts or half-hourly charts reflect the true Elliott pattern shown very clearly in the *Newsweek* chart [labeled at right].

My Elliott count suggests that we are now in a Primary Bull Market of the fifth degree up from Black Monday's low and is not likely to last more than 13 months unless it extends as did Primary ③ mentioned above.

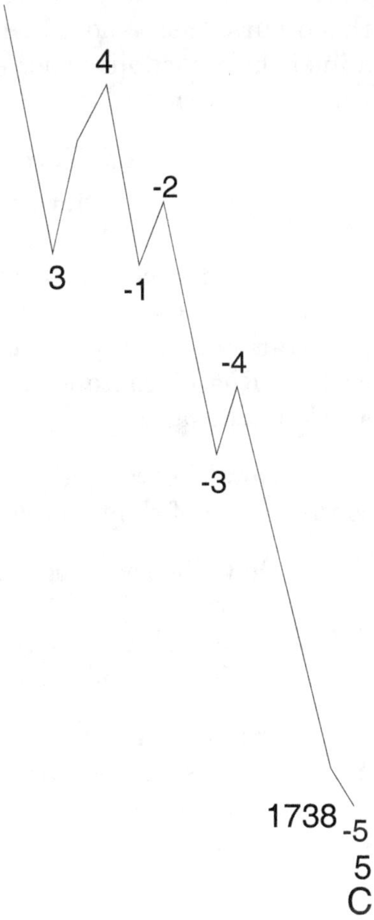

It is generally agreed that we are in the terminal stage of a bull market from 1982. Several possibilities appear. The market could move into new high ground of the current cycle, or it could form a double top. If it moves into new high ground, it is quite possible that a high of 34-3600 could be reached. It is also possible that the market could form a double top around 27-2800. Once the market gets past 2500, euphoria could permeate the equity markets and a new era philosophy develop. On the other hand, if Black Monday's low is broken in a five-wave sequence down, it could well be that my count above is wrong and we are in for a long sustained bear market, mass liquidation on a world-wide basis and a lower standard of living. However, if this occurs, there should be one last chance for investors to adjust their portfolios as the market moves up in a Primary wave ② correction.

## *LETTER TO PRECHTER*

**November 28, 1987**

In the eleven days preceding Black Monday, the DJIA declined over 903 points with the Industrials and Transports penetrating their September lows. As a result of this action, Richard Russell contends that we are now in a Primary Bear Market. I disagree.

Dow Theory is essentially a trend theory based on the confirmation of the two main Dow averages (up or down).

Dow Theory recognizes three types of trends.

1. Primary Trend
2. Secondary reactions
3. Minor trends or ripples

Primary trends are the all-engulfing trends of the market and secondary trends are the main components. It is my submission that if the move up from 1982 is an all-engulfing trend, it is not realistic to say that the drop from the market's high to its September low constitutes a secondary reaction in terms of Dow Theory. In my view, the Dow must penetrate Black Monday's lows to constitute a Dow Theory signal.

Under Dow Theory, authentic signals can only be given in the third phase of a bull market. In my opinion, the current move down is playing itself out. Until this move is completed, we cannot say for certain when the final wave will have started.

To gain perspective on where we are in the stock market cycle, I suggest we cast back to 1962. Mr. Blough wanted to raise the price of steel six dollars per ton. Jack Kennedy blew a fuse and compelled the steel companies to roll back the price of steel. It was a real fight and may well have generated the precipitous fall to 532 DJIA. Subsequently, the Dow rose in an A-B-C structure, then declined in a five-wave sequence to the Cuban crisis low of 544.

At the time, Bolton was in Greece and didn't catch the low but indicated to me that he would have done so had he not been out of the country. I suggest that the market is unfolding in a pattern similar to 1962 and that both under Dow Theory and the Elliott Wave Principle the final up wave lies ahead and will either end in a double top or come close to 36-3700.

## *LETTER TO PRECHTER*

**December 21, 1987**

Just one more kick at the can.

Two dates and their lows cause me concern.

| | | |
|---|---|---|
| September 29, 1986 | 1738.75 | 2pm |
| October 19, 1987 | 1738.74 | close |

If September 29 terminated a fourth wave correction, then in my opinion, Black Monday's low touched a previous low of one lesser degree to the exact round figure. However, if we extend the low figures by two decimal points, then Black Monday's low came within 1/100 of 1%, which I feel has to have some Elliott significance.

Following through on my view that the A-B-C correction from the April high of 2420 to December 4 low of 1966 is a 1962 configuration in disguise, then we can still expect a new bull market rising off that correction and we could still reach a final terminal point around 3600.

Unfortunately, Black Monday's action was so alarming that it appeared to change the whole picture, hence I feel we are still at the crossroads. The picture will become clearer as time goes on and your alternate count may prove to be correct.

### January 8, 1988

*Frost sent the following chart to Prechter, labeled through year-end 1987, including the comment, "a 1962 scenario, not 1929." His 1962 analogy was complete, as wave 5 had failed to register a new low. Primary wave ⑤ was underway.*

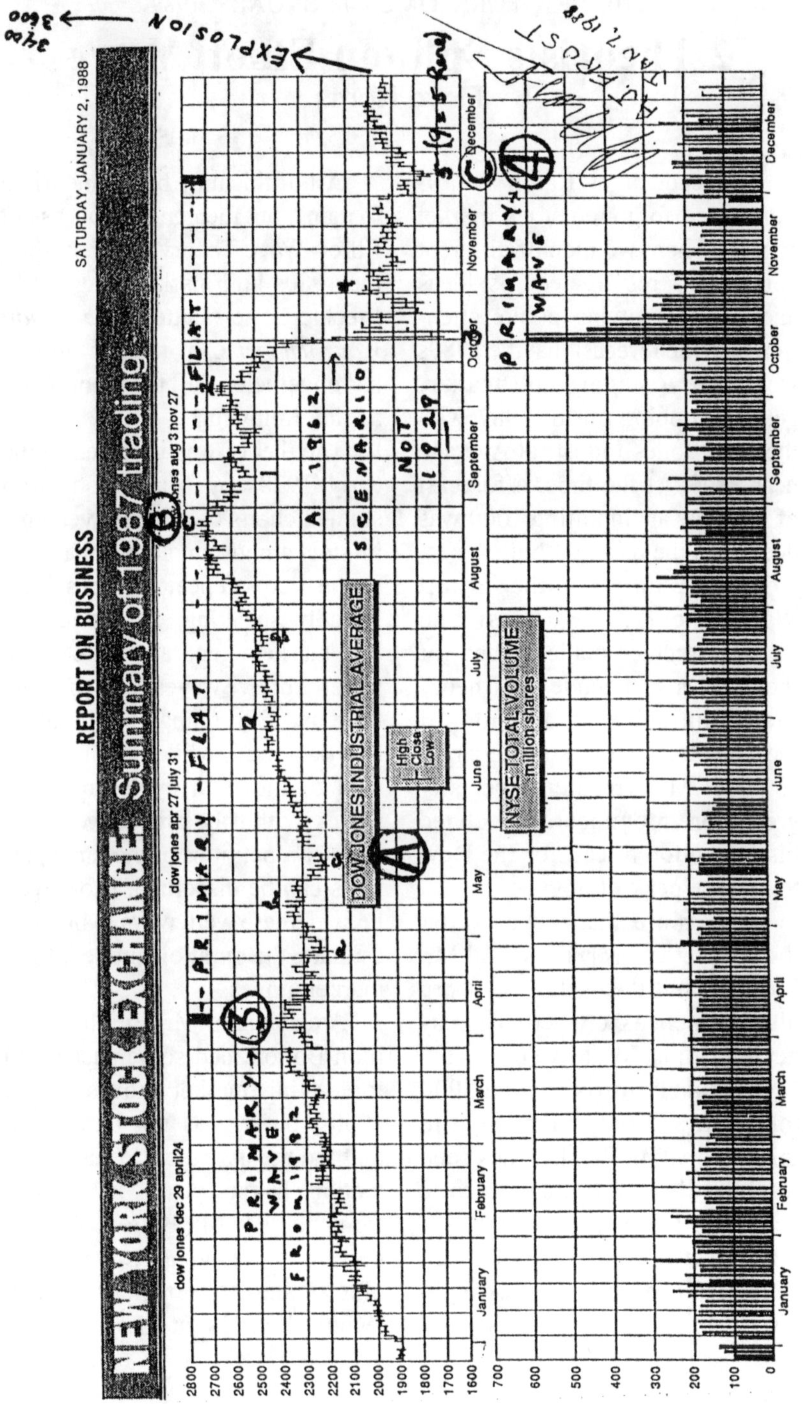
REPORT ON BUSINESS
SATURDAY, JANUARY 2, 1988
NEW YORK STOCK EXCHANGE Summary of 1987 trading
dow jones dec 29 april24
dow jones apr 27 july 31
dow jones aug 3 nov 27
DOW JONES INDUSTRIAL AVERAGE
High
Close
Low
NYSE TOTAL VOLUME
million shares
January
February
March
April
May
June
July
August
September
October
November
December
PRIMARY WAVE FROM 1982
PRIMARY FLAT
A 1962 SCENARIO
NOT 1929
EXPLOSION
PRIMARY WAVE

THE NEW YORK TIMES, FEBRUARY, 1989

# 2 Theorists Split on Elliott Wave

**Floyd Norris**

A decade ago, Ralph N. Elliott was a forgotten stock market analyst. Then two men of different generations resurrected his ideas and gained growing public attention with the forecast that the 1980s would see a surging bull market, perhaps topping out in 1987 with the Dow Jones Industrial Average near 2800. At the time, a forecast of the Dow again hitting 1000 was deemed to be daringly bullish.

By popularizing the Elliott Wave Theory, A.J. Frost and Robert Prechter made names for themselves and made the theory the technical phenomenon of the decade. As the stock market zoomed, Mr. Prechter especially grew more prominent. He refined his prediction to call for the Dow to reach a peak of 3600.

Now, more than a year after the 1987 crash, Mr. Frost and Mr. Prechter find themselves in sharp disagreement as to where the market is heading. Mr. Frost thinks the Dow is likely to rise above 3000 this year, and only then begin to fall sharply. Mr. Prechter has been resolutely bearish. He concedes he may have to change his stance if the market continues to rise much further, but so far he is sticking to his guns.

All of this may be arcane trivia to many, but the general success of Elliott Wave Theory in forecasting the 1980s bull market, and of Mr. Prechter's newsletter, *The Elliott Wave Theorist*, in market timing, has nonetheless left the theory with a wide following.

The theory was invented in the early 1930s by Mr. Elliott, who studied charts of price movements in stocks and concluded that certain patterns repeated themselves. Broadly speaking, he found that bull markets generally proceed in patterns of five waves, with the first, third and fifth rising and the other two declining, while bear markets tend to move in cycles of three waves. Within the large movements, smaller repetitions of the same patterns can be discerned. Moreover, he said, there were ways to broadly estimate the duration and length of market moves.

A disciple of Mr. Elliott, Hamilton Bolton, had some success in forecasting market moves in the 1950s, but it was not until 1978 that the theory began to regain attention. In that year, Mr. Frost, a former aide to Mr. Bolton who had become a Canadian Government official and Mr. Prechter, then a technical analyst at Merrill Lynch

& Company, published a book with the forecast of a roaring bull market in the 1980s.

Mr. Frost is now retired and living in Victoria, British Columbia, where he keeps a close eye on the market. By his count of Elliott Wave cycles, the fourth wave ended in December 1987, and the fifth, and final, wave is still in progress.

"In my view, the technical side indicates a strong move up for the next six months," Mr. Frost said in a telephone interview. "I think this market will go above 3000, and possibly peak around 3250. But when it breaks, it will keep declining until 1993 or 1994."

Mr. Prechter said the third wave of the five peaked in September 1986, when the Dow hit 1922. He said the pullback following that peak and the move to a new high of 2722 in August 1987 constituted the fourth and fifth waves. The October 1987 crash convinced him that the five-wave structure had ended.

For followers of Elliott Wave theory, the disagreement is a bit disconcerting, but both men concede the other could be right and say they are likely to reach agreement soon. A fallback to 1700 on the Dow would persuade Mr. Frost to change his view, while Mr. Prechter said that a move up to much above 2400 would cause him to reconsider his wave count. "That's my alternate wave count," he said of Mr. Frost's view, "but I give it very little probability." He called the January rally "very unimpressive," with little movement by secondary stocks.

Mr. Prechter noted that the two men had disagreed before, including a period in 1980 when Mr. Frost had correctly concluded the market had bottomed in April while Mr. Prechter disagreed. "It was June or July before I realized he was correct," Mr. Prechter said.

In any case, the two men are in agreement that the 1980s bull market, whether it is over or has one last gasp, will be followed by a depression and plunging prices as a major and prolonged bear market begins. "Once the market turns, it won't be just Black Monday, but Black Tuesday and Wednesday and Thursday and Friday," said Mr. Frost, who saw the rising tide of debt as one of the problems that would cause a financial collapse.

"Bob and I aren't really that far apart," Mr. Frost said, "because over the longer term we expect a very large decline. Once the five-wave structure completes itself, we've had it."

Mr. Prechter's views: "I hope that A.J. is right. His interpretation would mean that we have another year or so to prepare for the bear market that we've both been forecasting for 10 years."

The Sunday Sun, July 23, 1989

## THAT TIME OF YEAR FOR FROST TO RETURN

**Tony Reid**

It's that time of year again — Jack Frost has returned to Ontario.

Happily, it's not that Jack Frost, the harbinger of winter, but the other Frost, my favorite expert interpreter of the Elliott Wave Principle.

I've known and worked with the Victoria-based Frost for more than 30 years, featuring him in a number of columns over the years.

To remind you, Jack Frost and Bob Prechter wrote the book *Elliott Wave Principle*, which was originally published in 1978. It's been through a number of printings and is the current bible of Elliott followers.

R.N. Elliott was a popular market technician in the 1920s who believed that markets moved in a series of waves. His work was documented by A. Hamilton Bolton, founder of Bolton Tremblay.

Frost studied with Bolton in the late 1950s and has been a popular Elliott exponent ever since.

In June 1987, I quoted a speech that Frost made before the Toronto Society of Technical Analysts in which he predicted the market would peak in 1987 above the then 2444 level of the Dow Jones Industrial Index (DJII). He also said the market would crash later that year.

We all know that the DJII peaked at 2722.42 on Aug. 25, 1987 and then plunged to a low of 1738.74 on Oct. 19, 1987.

So what does Frost think now? As he approaches his 82nd birthday, he says: "Watch out, all hell is going to break loose!

"I think the market is unfolding as expected and I feel it will peak out some time in 1990 at 3250 although I wouldn't rule out Bob Prechter's original projection of 3400 to 3600."

Frost says we're presently in a strong bull market.

"When it peaks next year it will create not just a Black Monday but a whole series of Black Days.

"Short interest rates have been declining recently (7.9% in U.S. in the short term) but should start to rise in early 1990 by 200 to 300 basis points. With long-term yields remaining stable, this will create a negative interest rate curve which will be the signal to get out of the market. It will be the harbinger of the next stock market collapse and a severe economic depression."

What are the odds of this happening, I asked.

"Eighty percent! I expect a severe depression and one of the worst economic collapses in economic history.

"The real estate market in both Canada and the U.S. is very much overpriced and will tumble in the order of between 50% to 60% by the mid-90s. Canada is in a much worse position than the U.S. due to our higher per capita debt load.

"In light of this decline, both the U.S. and Canadian dollars will decline sharply in world markets with the result that the Federal Reserve and the Bank of Canada will beef up the money supply to cure the ills of the economy.

"That will be to no avail because markets tend to follow their own set of laws and nothing can stop it this time.

"The purchasing power of the dollar has declined to 5¢ or 6¢ since 1908, when I was born, and today's dollar will lose the same value between now and the year 2000," Frost said.

"That's the reason I feel investors should orient the major portion of their assets to gold and gold-related assets."

I asked Frost for some hard numbers to go with his forecast.

"The DJII, currently at 2575, will rise above 3000 to 3250 by early 1990," he said.

"Then it will drop to 1700, which will be the first stopping point of any importance. Gold, currently at US$371, has bottomed out and will rise to US$1,000 in the next two to four years.

"My favorite stock purchase is Placer-Dome ($17.50), a major gold producer."

So there you have it—Frost updated.

And it seems to me this time he resembles more the herald of colder times than his normal warm wind from the West.

## *THE OUTLOOK FOR STOCKS, GOLD AND THE ECONOMY*

**September 1989**

**Published with "A Philosophy of Markets" (see page 377)**

The world today is changing rapidly. Corporate business is becoming a worldwide enterprise. Plants are moved from one nation to another and funds are transferred among world markets with ease. About 600 large corporations are buying in their own stock and fewer and fewer good stocks are available for investment. The drop in the U.S. dollar since 1985 has increased the cost of imports and lowered the cost of exports, making the U.S. a good country to buy from, but a poor country to sell to. Industrial production is on a binge, with the Industrial Index at 84% of capacity, near an all time record. It's an enviable position for a great nation, but can it last?

Currently, the action of world financial markets and economic fundamentals is being interpreted by leading economists as indicating the likelihood of merely a "soft landing" for the economy (i.e., a slowdown, but no recession) to be followed by continuously expanding business conditions and more prosperity for everyone. In my view, this is not supported by developing trends and should be viewed as so much wishful thinking.

Man is an emotional creature and subject to alternating periods of optimism and pessimism. When man is optimistic, the future looks bright. He anticipates better times and takes risks. If he is in business, he anticipates sales to expand and profits to increase. As an investor, he anticipates higher stock prices. Everything has a rosy hue. During such periods, the economy and the financial markets expand, and inflation often results. However, we all know emotions can turn on a dime. When this happens, a period of deflation suddenly asserts itself, leading to depression, falling prices and often, panic conditions.

As our 1978 book explained, we are not unaware of bad times ahead, based on the Elliott Wave Principle. The fundamental conditions appear to support our conclusions. Nations around the world are in a financial dither. We borrow and spend, expecting everything to go up and up. So far, that is exactly what is happening. The thrifts are in deep trouble, as are the U.S. and Canadian banks, and will be more so if foreign debts are not paid. If Argentina, Mexico and Brazil defaulted tomorrow, it would wipe out the capital of the fifty largest banks in the U.S. and cripple our Canadian banks, with one or two exceptions. We are no doubt living in an economy that cannot be sustained for long. Real estate is over-priced and over-mortgaged. Interest payments in the U.S. are over 30% of cash flow, and continue to grow. It has been estimated that the debt of large corporations worldwide has grown to over one trillion dollars in the last ten years. The Fed has the difficult task of keeping interest rates high enough to attract new capital and low enough to hold the line on costs.

The basic principles of change are constant, but how is that going to help us? In this way: to be forewarned is to be forearmed. The economy is often its own best indicator. Not since 1930, based on economic signs, has the outlook been so ominous. The current pumping up of inventory assets is a harbinger of things to come and will be the cause of another great depression. It happened in the 1930s and it will happen again. As I read the future based on developing trends, the economy is headed for a serious meltdown triggered by a stock market collapse. Such an event or the start of it could occur late this year or in early 1990.

As deflationary forces take over, they will wreck the world's financial system, not just major banks of the United States. Roosevelt said in the last depression, "We have nothing to fear but fear itself." Fear is already at work. Banks are finding it more and more difficult to make creditworthy loans to creditworthy customers. Loan write-offs are bound to increase, and real estate values are too high to support the current rate of lending on this particular asset. As unemployment takes hold, homeowners will not be able to meet their obligations. Houses in foreclosure could then be a drag on the market in most cities in the United States.

As business and spending contract, unemployment will rise and most prices will tumble. Debts incurred at high rates of interest will become an intolerable burden. This situation will threaten bank deposits and defaults will become commonplace. Panic conditions could prevail. Government deficits will expand at an increasing rate and government will become increasingly meddlesome and restrictive.

When will it all end? It will end when the world economy hits rock bottom and there is nowhere to go but up. Then the cycle of pessimism will roll over and the bright new light will shine at the end of the tunnel.

You, the reader, may not agree with my forecast. If so, you are probably in good company. Sixty years ago my economics professor, after a discussion, exclaimed, "Frost, you speak with all the assurance of stolid ignorance." On the final examination, he gave me a brilliant "pass" of 51%, the last in the class.

In our 1978 book, we indicated that the Dow had hit a Supercycle closing low of 41.22 in 1932 and had completed four waves of Cycle degree from there. We indicated that the market would ultimately see a fifth upwave of Cycle dimension (a major bull market), in turn composed of five Primary waves. The market unfolded as expected, starting with the 1982 low of 776.92, which finally completed the market's sideways fourth Cycle wave, which began in 1966.

After reaching Bob Prechter's long cited upside target for 1987 of 2700+, the market traced out a small bearish pattern. Bob issued a sell signal at Dow 2640. After the 900 point decline which followed, he concluded that the best course of action was to remain in Treasury bills, since the odds of reaching his original 1982 target of 3600 for the final high, in his opinion, had diminished to the point that continued stock market investment could not be justified. T-bill rates were high and rising, providing a safe place to park capital, while providing a good return.

Since October 19, 1987, the market's form has allowed for more than one acceptable Elliott Wave interpretation at Primary degree. Bob has been detailing the two best interpretations in *The Elliott Wave Theorist*. The first, which Bob has preferred, is that the orthodox high of Cycle wave V in the DJIA occurred in 1987, and that any rallies (slight new highs notwithstanding) will be part of a corrective pattern.

The second count is that the 1987 drop was Primary wave ④, and that Primary wave ⑤ to substantial new highs is in progress. Since I have been partial to the wave count which would call for substantial new highs, Bob has asked me to spell out my reasoning in detail.

On October 24, 1987, five days after the "crash," Bill Millar, *Times-Colonist* business writer of Victoria B.C., interviewed me. At that time I said, "It is too soon to tell if we are really in a new bear market, but we should know in a couple of months." My doubts vanished, however, within a few days, as I came to the realization that the drop had brought the Dow to within 1% of the previous fourth wave low of *1738.75*, made on September 29, 1986 at 2 p.m. The actual hourly low at noon on October 20, 1987 was *1726.46*. This remarkable performance confirmed the value of the Elliott Wave Principle and supports the more bullish count.

One current question of interpretation with respect to wave structure is: when did the first wave begin? Many analysts have seized on the period between December 1974 when the Dow stood at 577.60, and September 1976 when the Dow stood at 1014.39, as the first impulse wave. On this interpretation, one is forced to conclude that the third and final phase of the bull market terminated in August 1987.

I believe this view, although widely held, is incorrect. As the great Horace would probably have said, "It should be written in sand and running water." The mistake from an Elliott Wave perspective is so obvious that one almost blushes to mention it; the period from December 1974 to September 1976 is a three-wave structure and thus corrective in nature. Have it any way you like, but in my opinion, 1982 was the beginning of the current Cycle degree bull market.

Figure 1 shows the market's path from 1982 at the end of Cycle wave IV to the current date. The Cycle wave breakdown is as follows:

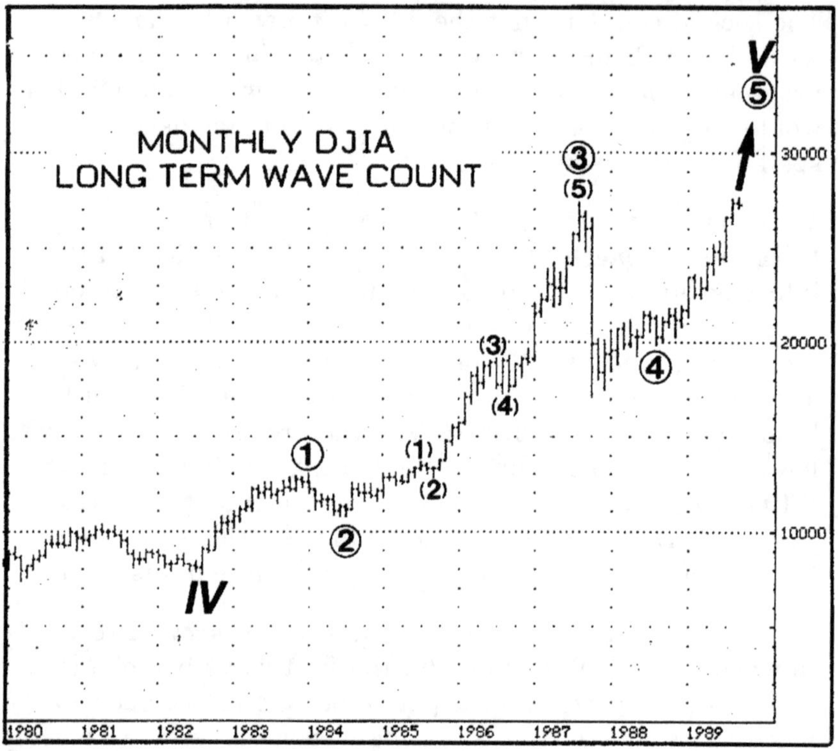


*Figure 1*

| Date | Wave | DJIA |
|---|---|---|
| Aug. 82 to Jan. 84 | ① | 777 to 1286 |
| Jan. 84 to July 84 | ② | 1286 to 1086 |
| July 84 to Aug. 87 | ③ | 1086 to 2704 |
| Aug. 87 to Aug. 88 | ④ | 2704 to 1984 |
| Aug. 88 to ? | ⑤ | 1984 to ? |

2722 was the actual closing high, but not the orthodox high. In other words, the Dow generated a false picture in the minor trend at this point. DJIA 2704 appears to be an important level, for these reasons:

1) 2704 is the top of Primary wave ③, from which point the market dropped and then advanced in a three-wave structure to DJIA 2722.

2) 2704 is contained within an exponential curve drawn below Primary ③, whereas 2722 is outside the line.

3) Primary wave ③ from 1086 to 2704 DJIA has an amplitude of 1618 Dow points, a number which reflects (though perhaps coincidentally) the Fibonacci ratio, 1.618.

4) 2704 equals 52 squared.

The Fibonacci ratio, which governs the Wave Principle, has square root aspects. If the market happens to top at 3249, it will be equivalent to $57^2$, reflecting a move from 2704 of 5 in terms of square root. If the market tops at 3600 ($60^2$), it will have moved in the square root increment of 8 from the top at 2704. Further (and this is most crucial), if wave ③ and wave ⑤ are the same length, that is, 1618 Dow points, we can project wave ⑤ to peak at 3602 DJIA, as 1984 DJIA, the orthodox low of Primary ④ in August 1988, plus 1618, equals 3602.

I favor my projected high of 3249 to that of 3602, because 5 represents a move in the direction of the main trend whereas 8 represents a completed cycle (5+3). Still, I do not rule out the latter possibility. It should be noted that Primary wave ③ was exponential in character and that wave ⑤ appears to be developing exponential characteristics as well. Thus, Bob Prechter's forecast of 3600 for the final high made back in 1982 is still a real live possibility under the aegis of the Wave Principle.

Numbers in the Fibonacci sequence applied to duration suggest that a top is ominously close. In particular, August 12, 1982 plus a Fibonacci 89 months = January 12, 1990. This fits the alternate year for a top given in Bob's "Forecast Update," which was added to our book *Elliott Wave Principle* in 1983. As he pointed out then, 1990 is a Fibonacci 8 years from the 1982 low.

Looking to the future, it would appear that the Dow is enjoying its final run-up in the long term bull market that began in 1932 and the Cycle degree bull market which started in 1982. The days ahead could be among the most exciting or devastating in world market history, depending on where you sit. Those on the wrong side of the fence will be engulfed with problems. Following the peak, it will take about four years for investors to be wrung out psychologically.

If you follow banking figures and the Elliott Wave Principle, you should be right about the Primary trend 80% to 90% of the time. Nevertheless, the October 19, 1987 sudden drop of over 500 Dow points clearly indicated that at times the DJIA can be extremely volatile. For this reason, the prudent investor should not wait until the last minute for a market top or play the short side. Futures and options are not for the investor, either. Be prudent, and the knowledge provided by Elliott will serve you well.

### *GOLD*

No better example of unorthodox market action can be found than in the way gold bullion reacted to President Carter's embargo of Iranian assets in 1980. The market didn't like what Carter did and moved well above the basic trendline, reaching an unorthodox high of $850 per ounce. A three-wave sequence took gold down to $474, and then a five-wave sequence brought it to its orthodox high of $720.50 in September. This terminated a five-wave sequence from $35 per ounce.

From the orthodox high, we get the following ABC corrective pattern, as shown in Figure 2:

Wave A: $720.50 to $296.50 in 1982;
Wave B: $296.50 to $511.50 in 1983;
Wave C: $511.50 to $284.25 in 1985.

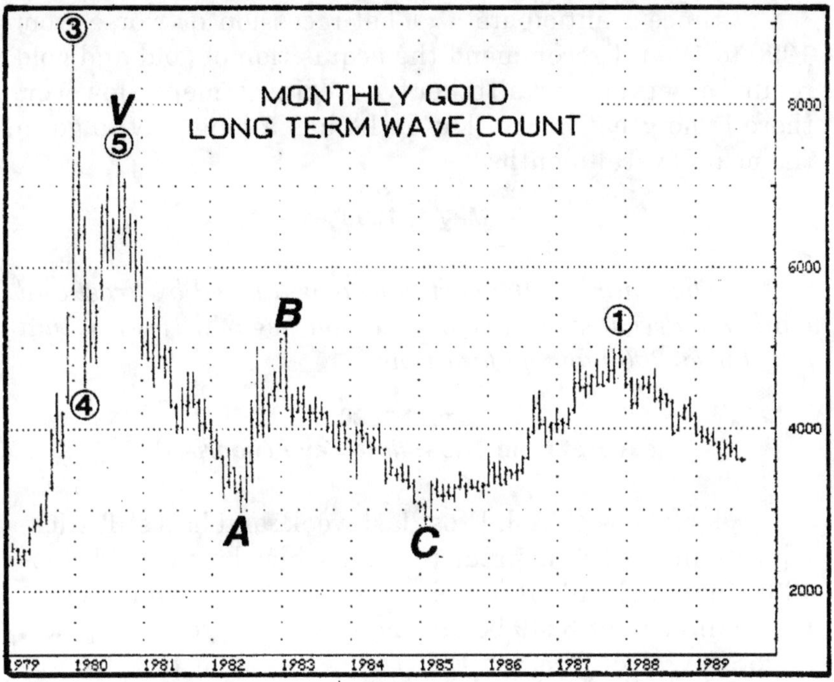


*Figure 2*

Applying the 1.618 ratio, we might reasonably expect the next high in the vicinity of $1050 to $1100 per ounce, although an extension could provide a much higher figure, as gold bullion has now entered its third wave up from $35 per ounce.

How does this count tie in with fundamentals? Gold is ultimate money and has not lost its value as such. It is also a commodity, but the currency feature is more important. When investors lose confidence in their beloved governments, usually gold takes on a special identity all its own. It is hoarded and retained at all costs. Paper assets decline in value and gold bullion grows in value as governments flood the market with paper to pay off debt and stimulate economic growth.

Since I anticipate a global recession or worse from 1990 to 1994, I recommend the acquisition of gold and gold related assets against all other types of investment. However, there is no great hurry. The DJIA has a long way to go in the next several months.

**May 1, 1990**

*The chart on the next page was labeled by Frost and mailed to Prechter right before the Dow began a 15% rise that put it over 3000 for the first time.*

**August 1990**
**(excerpt from *The Elliott Wave Theorist*)**

I spoke with A.J. Frost last week, and he's still sticking with his two main predictions, to which he has held since 1987, that gold will ultimately soar to $1000/oz. and that the Dow will peak at 3249 before the next collapse takes place. As for the latter forecast, the Dow is less than 10% away, a great call already as far as I'm concerned.

**September 1990**
**(excerpt from *The Elliott Wave Theorist*)**

When the Dow broke 2500, A.J. Frost told FNN viewers that a new bear market had begun and that 3249 was no longer in the cards. Although the market fell short of his target, A.J. has long advised his listeners to exit above Dow 3000.

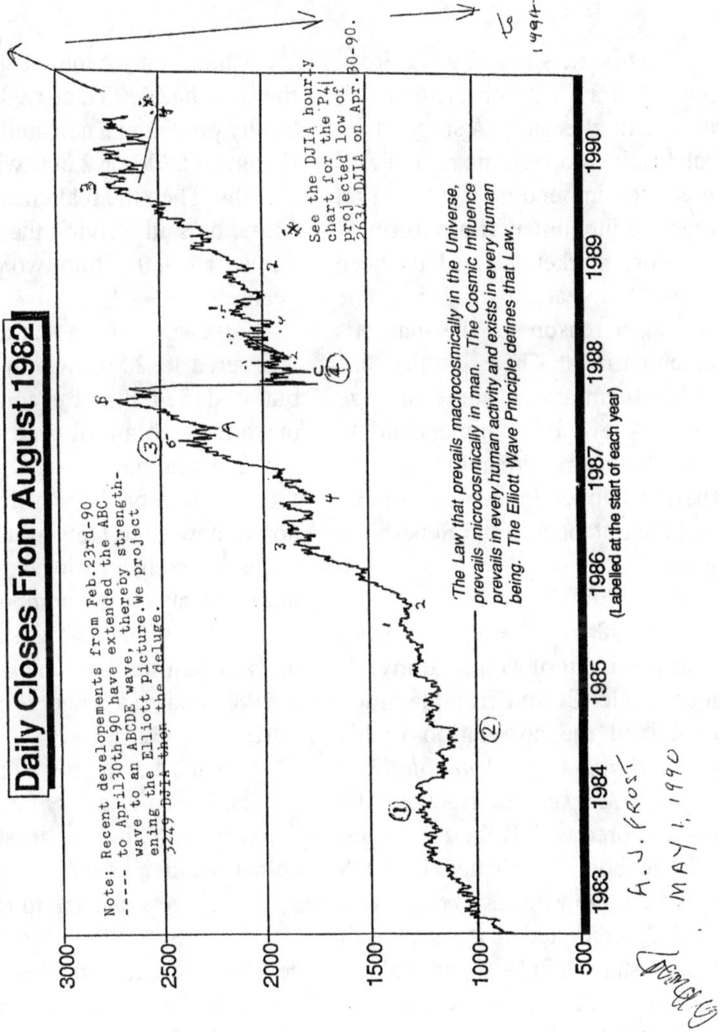
Daily Closes From August 1982
Note; Recent developements from Feb.23rd-90
----- to April30th-90 have extended the ABC
wave to an ABCDE wave, thereby strength-
ening the Elliott picture. We project
3249 DJIA then the deluge.
See the DJIA hourly
chart for the 'P4'
projected low of
2634 DJIA on Apr. 30-90.
'The Law that prevails macrocosmically in the Universe, prevails microcosmically in man. The Cosmic Influence prevails in every human activity and exists in every human being. The Elliott Wave Principle defines that Law.
3000
2500
2000
1500
1000
500
1983
1984
1985
1986
1987
1988
1989
1990
(Labelled at the start of each year)
A. J. FROST
MAY 1, 1990

**The Vancouver Sun, December 20, 1991**

## BULLS, BEARS...AND BUNNIES?

David Baines

This is the story of Jack Frost. No, it's not a Christmas story. It's a stock market story. A story which relates the propagation rate of rabbits to an impending stock market crash of monumental proportions.

Stock market players have been trying for years to discern some rhyme or reason for the market's machinations. Their inquiry has taken them down some strange roads. A few, for example, claim to have found a correlation between the Dow Jones Industrial Average and the outcome of the Superbowl game.

But rabbits?

Frost, 84, of Victoria, a former vice-president of Montreal investment dealer Bolton Tremblay Inc., explained the correlation in his book, *Elliott Wave Principle: Key to Stock Market Profits*, which he co- authored with Robert Prechter.

The book, published in 1978 when the Dow Jones average was at 777, predicted a massive bull market starting in 1982 and peaking in 1987 at 2,860, followed by the worst crash in history.

In fact, the bull market peaked in August 1987 at 2,722 — almost dead on target — and the ensuing crash in October 1987 was indeed the worst in history.

A month after the crash, when the Dow had settled at 1,900, Frost boldly predicted a new bull market rising to 2,700 or 2,800 within 13 months. Then the real crash would come, he said, driving the Dow to a low of 1,000 within two or three years.

Frost was right in that the Dow recovered to 2,800 within a year, but it defied him by continuing upward — to an all-time high of 3,082 last month.

Despite a plethora of bad economic news, the Dow still resides at the relatively lofty level of 2,914, but Frost says this is temporary.

"It's just one last gasp in an upward bull market which started in 1982, and on a longer term basis started in 1932.

"The market might go up, but if it does, it won't be very far. I think the Dow will drop at least 1,000 points within a year."

Which gets us back to rabbits.

The Elliott Wave theory was developed by Los Angeles accountant R.N. Elliott in the aftermath of the 1929 crash, and is based on a numerical progression called the Fibonacci sequence, named after the Italian mathematician, Leonardo Fibonacci.

The sequence is derived from the question, "How many pairs of rabbits placed in an enclosed area can be produced in a single year from one pair of rabbits if each pair gives birth to a new pair each month starting with the second month?"

The answer is 1,1,2,3,5,8,13,21 and so on.

Frost and Prechter note in their book that these numbers have many interesting relationships. For example, the sum of any two preceding numbers equals the next higher number. Also, the ratio of any two consecutive numbers is approximately 0.618, which is known as the Golden Ratio or the Golden Mean.

This ratio forms the basis of the logarithmic spiral, which occurs in many natural forms such as snail shells and galaxies.

The Golden Mean also forms the basis for the Golden Rectangle, which is reflected in many forms of art, such as the shape of playing cards and the Parthenon.

The ratio is also apparent in musical relationships. A piano keyboard, for example, has eight white keys and five black, 13 in all.

Frost, who plotted the Dow Jones average on an hourly basis for 20 years, says the stock market has the same mathematical basis. It rises and falls in waves, five up and three down, each wave relating to the previous one by a similar ratio.

There are also waves within waves. Hourly movements are microcosms of daily movements. and daily movements are microcosms of monthly, and so on.

It gets more complicated from there, which explains why Elliott Wavers can look at the same chart and come up with different interpretations.

Frost says there is no question we are in the fifth and final wave of a bull market. However, the wave has extended into an even bigger wave, which explains why the Dow is still at a relatively high level.

But make no mistake, he says, the cycle of optimism currently reflected in the Dow Jones average will soon crumble into a cycle of pessimism.

"Look what's happening to General Motors. Look what's happening to employment. I think our economy is in the worst shape since 1932, when the Dow hit 42."

# *A.J. FROST — REFLECTIONS*

## *1961 – 1990*

## A PHILOSOPHY OF MARKETS[1]

### September 1989

In 1975, Professor Fritjof Capra authored a book entitled *The Tao of Physics*, in which he explored the parallels between modern physics and Eastern mysticism. Dr. Capra's findings are based on the most recent research in physics, the revelations from which he compares to the age-old traditions of Taoism, Hinduism and Buddhism. Capra's studies support the supposition that there is an underlying principle of order in the universe generating a great web of interrelated processes, all of which expand and contract in harmonious relationship to each other. This cosmic order reflects a never-changing principle in an ever-changing world. The laws of physics and Eastern mysticism speak to us of the orderly Oneness of the universe. Research with respect to the stock market supports the proposition that the parallels which exist between the laws of physics and Eastern mysticism can also be found in stock market behavior.

In the 6th century B.C., Lao-Tzu, a Chinese philosopher, wrote one of the world's greatest classics, the *Tao Te Ching*. He believed that Order is one and indivisible and implicit in both man and the universe. Lao-Tzu said that Order is macrocosmically in the universe and microcosmically in man, a concept which has been at the heart of Chinese thinking

---

[1] This is the heart of A.J. Frost's final work, published by Elliott Wave International. It encompasses a lifetime of thought and brings him full circle from his early interest in religion to his success in the markets and back to speculation on the great mysteries of life. This exposition is followed by chronologically arranged excerpts from his private correspondence, speeches and other writings.

for thousands of years. Thus, man is an individualization of the eternal order, and although all the laws of the universe are personal to him, they are otherwise impersonal. Tao (God, the Absolute, etc.) can be regarded as either personal or impersonal, but the main point is that Law, or Order, prevails everywhere and is in and forms part of everything. In this connection, it is interesting to note that the word "universe," a combination of "uni" and "versum," implies a single unity, one world. If this is so, then all parts must form one integrated whole, subject to *one* set of laws. This Cosmic Influence prevails in every human activity and is in every human being. Human thought has the same cosmic beat as the heavens.

To the Occidental mind, these concepts may sound strange, as they *seem* to conflict with our ideas of free will. We do not normally think in terms of an overriding principle of order influencing us in everything we do or think. However, for those of us brought up firmly in the Christian or Jewish tradition, it should be noted that the Old Testament contains many references to this law. Further, the words of the Lord's Prayer imply that God's will prevails on earth as it does in Heaven. All the great religions of the world teach that we are free to assume our own attitudes, subject to the laws of life. We reap what we sow, and we are only what we attain spiritually. The law within is umbilically linked to the Law without. In the scheme of things, man must take full responsibility for himself. He is "free," but not above the Law.

Taoism teaches that there are two inseparable forces arising out of nature called Yang and Yin. These forces are sometimes referred to as "opposites," but they only appear to be in opposition. Actually, they complement and complete each other and are constantly rising and falling in harmony. The complementary nature of Yang-Yin duality is the ordering principle of unity behind all created things.

The *Tao Te Ching* (as translated by Professor Archie J. Bahm) contains two statements touching on the Yang-Yin principle which may be of particular interest to stock market analysts.

> 1. "Ultimate reality involves initiation of growth, initiation of growth involves the completion of growth, and completion of growth involves returning to that whence it came." (Ch. 25)
>
> 2. "Nature alternates dynamically. When it completes what it is doing, then it starts all over again. All that is springs from such alternation." (Ch. 40)

In a non-technical account published by the National Research Council of Canada with respect to the work of the Dominion Astrophysical Laboratory, Victoria, B.C., the following statement appears:

> The work of astronomers has gradually shown that the laws which govern matter and form here on earth hold sway in the remotest spaces we can scan. Ancient man, even medieval man, thought of the skies as the literal abodes of gods and angels. The modern vision of a vast, perhaps endless, universe controlled by a few simple laws of nature is scarcely less marvelous.

This account also states that there are millions of solar systems in our Milky Way, with the whole rotating about its centre every 220 million years. It is no less startling to hear that our galaxy will, about 50 billion years from now, become so dense that it will cease to expand and start falling in on itself and then, during the next 50 billion years, will reverse its progress so that in 100 billion years (more or less), it will be back where it is today. Beyond this point, one might theorize that our galaxy would become a black hole in space, at which point the galaxy cycle would be completed, only to begin again. This phenomenon of expansion and contraction is also evident in stock market behavior and apparently is governed by the "few simple laws" which control matter and form here on earth. These same laws impact everything about us.

It was no less an authority than William Peter Hamilton who stated in *The Stock Market Barometer* that "Order is Heaven's first law." Hamilton Bolton, the founder of the *Bank Credit Analyst*, added, "The stock market is part of life and subject to the Cosmic Influence."

R.N. Elliott, however, was the first analyst to state how the law of the market operates and to spell out its mathematical base. He discovered that all completed cycles have essentially the same design characteristics. When one is over, another begins, based on the root principle of polarity. There is little or no cause-and-effect relationship between cycles. Their relatedness is acausal and can be explained only by reference to a common basic pattern of behavior.

Study of the wave patterns and characteristics of the stock market over an extended period of time gives the analyst an ever-increasing sensitivity to the laws of the market and a feeling for what is likely to happen. As technical analysis, under the basic tenets of the Wave Principle, is more an art than a science, the "feel" that one acquires can be most important. However, one must never ignore what he sees in technical data; otherwise, the whole approach becomes subjective and worthless. There is an intuitive element in the rational, but there is also a rational element in the intuitive.

Back in January 1981, we had a demonstration of what can happen in markets. Joseph Granville, a well known investment analyst, advised his clients to "sell everything." This announcement was followed by a wave of selling, which brought the market down from a close of 1004.69 DJIA on January 6th to a close of 965.70 two days later, a sudden precipitous drop which was generally attributed to Granville's "sell" recommendation. If this drop developed as a direct result of the advice Granville gave to his clients, then one must conclude that there *was* a causal connection between those sell orders and the decline. However, the basic tenets of the Wave Principle reveal that an apparent cause and effect such as this is merely that, apparent. As usual, the market itself gives us the answer. On December 11, 1980, the DJIA registered a low of 899.12. In the 16 trading days which followed, the market rose 105 points, closing at 1004.69, a very strong advance for such a short period. This move up was, in Elliott's terms, a five wave sequence of Intermediate degree, the last Minor of which subdivided into five waves of Minute degree. Granville's recommendation accurately *caught* the turning point of the end of that intermediate wave, namely the fifth of the fifth, at which time the market was due for a decline to the travel area of the fourth wave of one lesser degree, in the vicinity of 960-970 DJIA. The two day decline brought the market to 965.70, the middle of that area. If Granville's sell signal had any effect at all, it served only to speed up the decline. *It did not affect the technical wave pattern of behavior.*

Occasional news-related coincidences are pointed out by many to be proof of an external cause of market behavior, but the number of seemingly important events which are followed by no or apparently contradictory market action far outweigh them. Subsequent signals by Mr. Granville, for instance, were followed by nary a ripple in prices, proving the point.

The art of applying the Elliott Wave Principle can be characterized as applied Taoism. Taoism starts with an understanding of the way things really are as opposed to the way they merely appear. One must then use that knowledge constructively. For instance, music in the Taoistic sense is an interpretation of the Tao in life conceived and expressed through musical symbols. The art of technical analysis is another approach to a part of life conceived and interpreted through stock symbols and the ticker tape. If the proper study of man involves man's behavior and creations, then the stock market as an emanation of man can be regarded as an integral part of such a study. Every facet of life carries out its structured function under the aegis of the whole.

If this is so, it is useful to explain market behavior in new terms, using old Taoist concepts. Such an explanation might run as follows:

The market rises and falls, only to rise again and fall again in a higher or lower degree. Bull markets come under Yang, the positive force in nature, and bear markets come under the returning or negative force, designated as Yin. The two forces alternate indefinitely, resulting in a series of compensated oscillations tending at all times to be in balance with each other. After the positive force becomes dominant, the negative force overtakes the positive and completes the cycle. Then, *of themselves*, the two forces enter a new phase and a new cycle appears, generating patterns of movement similar to those that have gone before. Stock market action is always a reflection of the Yang-Yin principle of movement, or the core polarity of opposites. As the stock market holds to this basic design, it parallels nature. Once a pattern is completed, a similar pattern starts all over again, repeating the five up, three down scenario.

Although it may sound somewhat ridiculous to suggest that the study of the stock market can enculturate man, the stock market does provide us with a practical philosophy which can be helpful when applied to other fields, such as economics. As one studies the stock market, one develops a growing sensitivity to the law hidden behind the mask of prices and other surface phenomena. The forces of nature which sculpt *form* and enliven *being* shape the universe in every detail. This philosophy is an ancient wisdom developed over thousands of years, and has been lost and rediscovered over and over again. To see its practical applications leads to wise investing and better living.

Thus, there is no point in grumbling at the stock market. It is more realistic to try to understand it and accept it for what it is. The only way the investor can be nearly assured of making money is to study the technical position of the market and keep in step with the primary trends. There is nothing wrong with making money, and there is a lot wrong with losing it.

The Elliott Wave Principle is the key to stock market profits when properly understood and applied. The principles behind stock market behavior are indestructible, immutable, and understandable. In application, the rules and guidelines are subtle, and few can read them at first blush. The stock market can "turn on a dime" and catch unaware investors with more money than experience. The rationale of the stock market seldom reflects the sort of behavior we are accustomed to in our every day experiences of life. Why? Because the market "feels" what cannot be observed. For this reason, it is often said that the market discounts the unknown. It is continually alerting us to those things which are not readily foreseeable. As the unknown is always greater than the known, the market is a leading indicator of what is in progress in both the economy and the stock market. Cycles of optimism and pessimism, which affect supply-demand relationships, are generally reflected by market action, which in turn foreshadows the economy. Thus, the proper study of the stock market is the stock market itself, an informative study which can alert us about what to expect in the economy. Economists do not know what makes the economy tick, but the analyst who understands market action in Elliott terms does. Under the basic concepts of Elliott, the market is the message. Unveiling the messages of the stock market is an exciting and rewarding experience.

The stock market is a reflection, or possibly an abstraction, of man's intuitive awareness. It is felt rather than observed. It is *not* a by-product of reason. Investors who worry themselves sick about the stock market are not likely to make much money. It is better to take a detached, playful attitude, but at the same time to study it intensely. In this way, it will not cut you down. Always wait for the moment when it tells you something you can capitalize on. Invest with patience, be decisive, and cut your losses if an error is indicated. Once you understand its basic patterns, the market will warn you of impending changes in the direction of stock prices. Under the guidelines of the Wave Principle, these patterns seldom fail to foreshadow the directions of the movements of the market.

## *SPEECH TO COMMERCE CLUB OF QUEEN'S UNIVERSITY, KINGSTON ONTARIO*

**November 9, 1961**

The stock market is a tricky place, especially for the amateur. People with more money than experience frequently lose heavily when they dabble in stocks. The reason is that the small investor usually acts from an emotional bias and with little knowledge of trends. The little fellow reacts to the only thing he can react to, namely, rumors and press headlines. The professional, with more knowledge and reserve, will use the little man's mistakes for his own gain. My advice is to *take* advice before investing in the stock market, or study the theory of market action intently before exposing yourself to undue risk. Even then, it may be that advice should be sought before making investments.

Christopher Morley once said: "Dancing is a wonderful training for girls. It is the first way they learn to guess what a man is going to do before he does it." When you learn to guess what the stock market is going to do, you will also get clues as to what is likely to happen in the economy as a whole. I can think of no more rewarding pastime than trying to figure out the future course of stock market trends. Commerce students with a background of economics, statistics, corporate finance and accounting should be well equipped to study seriously the theory of market action. It will lead you into all sorts of interesting fields of study and knowledge.

It was in the spasmodic booms and sharp credit panics of the late 19th century that Charles H. Dow, the founder of *The Wall Street Journal* and one of the foremost financial observers of the era, made a notable contribution to the theory of stock market investment. Dow's editorials in the Journal appeared frequently up until the time of his death in 1902, and are quite remarkable in their analysis of stock market trends. The basic tenets of Dow Theory have been added to since his death by William Peter Hamilton, who succeeded Charles Dow as editor of *The Wall Street Journal* and by Mr. Robert Rhea, who for years was a leading exponent of the Dow Theory.

Under the inflexible credit conditions which existed before 1914, the Dow Theory worked well. Today, it appears to be out of step with the times, and many analysts do not accept it. However, Charles H. Dow was the granddaddy of all stock market analysts, and the theory is still the best known of all stock market theories.

Dow discovered that the stock market as a whole had a *trend*, and that most stocks moved in unison despite the constant fluctuations of individual stocks. To measure this trend in the stock market, two sets of averages were developed by Mr. Dow in 1896 and have been published ever since by Dow, Jones & Co. One average was composed of railroad stocks, and the other was made up of industrial stocks. These averages were used by Mr. Dow to develop his trend theory ideas, which later grew into what is now known as Dow Theory. The rail and industrial averages are the main tools of Dow Theory. The only other tool is volume. The Dow Theory is a 100% technical approach to the market, as it only considers factors internal to the market. It may be worthwhile reviewing the main features of the Theory as it has been developed. The following tenets are a summary:

1. The movements of the averages break down into three trends of different magnitude: a) Primary movement or trend; b) Secondary movement or trend; c) Minor movements, or daily fluctuations.

The primary trend is the broad main movement of the market. Such a movement may be classified as either a bull market or a bear market and lasts a comparatively long time. The primary trend is the "all-engulfing" tide.

Secondary movements are advances or declines which interrupt the main or primary trend. They usually last three weeks to three months and retrace 1/3 to 2/3 of the preceding movement.

Daily, or minor, movements are of no significance except where a *line* is being formed. A line is a price structure lasting two or three weeks during which time prices fluctuate within a 5% range. Lines are not considered of importance unless they occur in both averages at the same time, with volume steadily decreasing.

2. *Averages Discount Everything.* A fundamental proposition of Dow Theory is that averages are an index of what everyone knows about business prospects. The averages "see all and know all" except acts of God, and even acts of God are supposedly evaluated almost immediately. The discounting function of the averages is explained on the ground that the market taps every important source of information as soon as it is known. The averages therefore reflect matters of financial significance before the information becomes public knowledge. All Dow purists are insistent on this point. It sounds superficial, but it is part of the theory. It means, of course, when the averages "speak," one doesn't have to look further to ascertain the future trend of the averages.

3. *Confirmation.* The confirmation principle states that movements of the industrial average and railroad average must be considered as part and parcel of the same underlying trend and that any reversal signal by one average cannot be regarded as genuine until confirmed by the other average. A reversal signal by one average unconfirmed by the other has no "forecasting" value. It is sometimes spoken of as half a signal, but to the Dow theorist it is meaningless.

4. *Trend Determination.* In primary bull markets, as long as the Averages keep breaking into new high ground by

penetrating previous highs and keep holding above preceding lows, the primary trend is bullish. In a primary bear market, the opposite is the case.

5. *The Three Phases.* A primary bull market comprises three phases:

a) Following depressed market conditions, the market rebounds to known values. This is the first phase.

b) The second is usually the longest phase, as the market rises in response to improving business conditions. This is the steady mark-up phase.

c) The third phase is the blow-off period when speculation tends to raise the price of stocks to comparatively high levels. As Rhea said, "stocks are advanced on hopes and expectations."

6. *Signals.* Under Dow Theory, signals are always late. The averages never reveal that a bull (bear) market is over until the highs are past. At some point in the third phase of a bull market, reversals (secondary trends) will occur in both averages which will not be fully retraced. One or both averages will fail to reach new highs, *on diminishing volume.* This is a danger signal, but not conclusive, that a change of trend under Dow Theory is imminent. The actual signal occurs when both averages penetrate the lowest point of the preceding secondary reaction. This is a full-fledged bear signal and is usually accompanied by volume on the downside. A bull signal is the opposite. Authentic signals can only occur in the third phase of a bull or a bear market, according to modern Dow Theorists. Third phase theory is now held to be the key to whether or not a signal is genuine. However, Dow Theory doesn't give the analyst any clues on this point, and present day exponents do not agree.

The Dow Theory has a mixed record of successes and failures.

In 1929, it was put to a real test and came through commendably. Dow Theory devotees have been talking about it ever since. On September 3, both the rail and industrial averages reached their peaks and then declined. On October 25, William Peter Hamilton published his famous editorial, "A Turn in the Tide," in *The Wall Street Journal* and said the bull market was over. At the time, the Rail Average had declined 12% and the Industrial 22% from their highs. The signal, however, wasn't too late to rescue devotees from the collapse which followed. It should not be forgotten, however, that in 1926, Hamilton announced a bear signal which proved to be false.

The record since 1929 has been very spotty, with no notable successes except for 1937, when the theory gave a clear-cut signal shortly after the market reached its peak. In 1946, the theory failed badly as it confirmed a bull market a day or two before the peak and registered a bear signal after the market had sustained a 45% loss for the year. In May 1948, the Averages signaled a bull market after 80% of the rise had already taken place. However, 1948 was not a turning point.

Following the low point in June 1949, the theory worked fairly well. In August, the Industrials penetrated their previous high and the Rails confirmed in early December.

In the years 1953, 1957 and 1960, Dow Theory worked badly, giving bear signals only to have the averages follow an opposite course.

In the past few years, the record has not been very creditable, having been marked with rather conspicuous failures. Many followers have been whipsawed.

By the very nature of the theory, all signals are late. It is only after a trend has been established in the opposite direction that a signal can be given. If the signal isn't too late and isn't *false*, it is better than nothing. It is better to be taken out of a bear market after a 25% decline than to ride the entire downward movement. However, you can't count on the Theory at any time unless you know where you are in the stock market cycle. This is something the Theory cannot tell you.

Dow Theory exponents seem to be the most equivocal of analysts. The theory has no forecasting value beyond confirming a trend already established. The follower may have to wait for years for a clear-cut signal and *then* can't be sure of it. Confirmation is often slow and reflects only surface indications. The theory doesn't deal with underlying forces or anything of a fundamental or economic nature. It is important to know the theory, but don't be deceived by it. Use it in conjunction with other market tools if you like, but don't let it burden you.

[2]The Dow Theory is a valid approach to stock market analysis, but like the Elliott Wave Principle, it is often misinterpreted. These two approaches are first cousins. This anatomy of the market first observed by Dow was further analyzed by the late R.N. Elliott, who observed that there was a rhythmic regularity to the market. He discerned that the stock market tended to unfold according to basic patterns and that Dow's three primary trends, with secondary reactions in between, could be subdivided and re-subdivided into waves of smaller degree, and that each complete primary wave was a part of a yet larger wave formation. Elliott concluded that waves were not simply of the order of primary, secondary and minor but of a much wider spectrum.

Hence you can go up and down the ladder until you reach waves of such minute degree or such large degree that neither has any practical significance. If you don't pursue the Theory too far, it can be very helpful in understanding

---

[2] This paragraph is added from Frost's 1989 monograph, *A Philosophy of Markets*.

something of the theory of market action. It may be that the Elliott Wave Principle should be considered more as a philosophy than a precise tool for forecasting trends, but when the legs (waves) are clear, it is rather surprising how accurate a tool the Elliott Wave Principle can be.

[2]Hamilton Bolton said that if the principle behind "Elliott" had been discovered first, Dow Theory would never have been heard of.

### *LETTER TO J.W. BERRY*

**December 14, 1964**

My friends sometimes tell me I am a bit of a maverick, but then I feel this may be the way to success in the battle of investment survival.

### *LETTER TO REGINALD STEERS*

**February 5, 1965**

To misquote Shakespeare:

"The stock market like an angry ape,

Plays such fantastic tricks before high heaven

As make the brokers weep."

We are most ignorant of what we are most assured, especially when it comes to the stock market. The angry ape is a sentimental being as well as an economic creature. I would love to place salt behind the ape's ears, but I have never quite succeeded.

One can never worship a chart with impunity, but that doesn't nullify the value of charts. Most analysts keep myriads of charts. I am not exactly a chartist, but I do find a few of considerable value.

Charts are not a substitute for judgment. Accurate foresight is impossible because in the economy, exactly the same thing doesn't happen twice. Charts, by the very nature of economics, have definite limitations and can never be regarded as the sole basis for forecasting the stock market. We need them, however, to formulate our judgments and to get perspective on the market. Personally, I feel there is a conjunction between observational economic data and mathematics. The Elliott Wave Principle seems to fit market behavior and in my view is not without practical application in the study of the phenomena of movement. As you know, I keep an hourly chart for the express purpose of trying to read Elliott. I find that very frequently I read it incorrectly, but I find it helpful and, in retrospect, can see my errors which I use as guidance for the future.

## *SPEECH TO KIWANIS CLUB OF OTTAWA*

**March 19, 1965**

The stock market fascinates me. It is one of the great institutions of the capitalistic system. If we did not have a stock market, free enterprise would soon invent one. Every free country in the western world has an exchange. The NYSE is the world's largest, accounting for more than 85% of the dollar value of all stocks traded over U.S. markets. 18 million people own 9 billion shares registered in New York. The New York Exchange, because of its size, is the greatest manifestation of mass psychology in the financial world. All other markets are little more than pocket editions of New York.

The first point I would like to make is that the stock market does not always act on strictly rational principles. New investors, with more money than experience, have a hard time understanding the rationale of the market. They expect it to respond to the sort of logic they have been accustomed to in their everyday business experiences. The market, however, has a logic all its own. You can only appreciate the market if you accept and are in sympathy with the way it operates. Hundreds of thousands, possibly millions, of investors dream of making a lot of money on the market. As in dreams, investors' hopes expand and fade with terrific velocity. If 1% of U.S. shareholders decide suddenly they want to swap their securities for cash, 90 million shares would be thrown on the market and the NYSE would have to close its doors. The volume could not be handled in less than one week. A 1% scramble for cash would also create a panic, as buyers would withdraw their bids. A bidless market is a panic market.

As I have said, the market has a dream function because of its peculiar psychology, but behind the dream lies the reality of business. The market has two faces — the economic and the emotional. I am not suggesting that the market is a disorderly thing, although disorder can and does develop on occasion. For the most part, market action has meaning. It is governed by the laws of psychology and economics. All market transactions produce their effects. Each individual transaction is a short-lived affair, but in a minute way, it is worked into the fabric of the market structure. Each successive advance or decline grows out of what has gone before and so enters the chain of causes which makes the market what it is at any given time. For this reason, the market has form and lends itself to analysis and study.

"The race is not always to the swift or the battle to the strong," but in the stock market, that is the way to bet.

The stocks to buy are those which are fundamentally sound and are backed up by strong technical positions. To accomplish this, a great deal of work must be done in the broad fields of fundamental analysis and technical analysis. The fundamentalist studies data external to the market and the technical analyst studies data internal to the market. Remember, there are always those two faces to the market — the technical or psychological, and the fundamental. The fundamentalist is interested in all external factors which have a bearing on business conditions or which may provide clues as to future prospects. The technical analyst is interested in the prevailing psychology of investors as a key to changes in investment sentiment and ensuing shifts in the supply-demand relationship of stocks which affect prices.

At times, sentiment seems to completely dominate the market. Take, for instance, the period immediately following World War II. Everyone seemed to think at that time that a postwar depression was inevitable. The market declined from a high of 212 on the Dow Jones Industrial Average in April 1946 to a low of 161 in June 1949. During this period, earnings rose substantially. In fact, earnings on the 30 Dow stocks more than doubled. Later on in the stock market cycle (1955-61), earnings stabilized at around $32 on the Dow and stock prices trebled. To give you another example of sentiment, two weeks ago a leading journal in Canada published an article which contained implications with respect to a certain stock. The article contained nothing new, but the headline was so worded that investors became nervous and the stock dropped 20% in value. Back in the spring of 1962, you may recall, the DJIA dropped 200 points in a first-class technical debacle. The market was due for a technical correction, but what helped prices to turn turtle was when President Kennedy lectured Mr. Blough, president of U.S. Steel Corp., over a proposed increase in the price of steel. There was no sound fundamental or economic reason for the sharp decline in stock prices and no reason for the decline has since been uncovered. The drop can only be explained in technical or psychological terms. The business outlook in the spring of 1962 was excellent and banking trends were strong.

## *LETTER TO PRECHTER*

**1977**

On a long-term basis, the pattern of the market is usually quite clear. On a short-term basis, the pattern too can be clear enough if the market is moving impulsively.

However, on a short-term basis during corrective periods, the market is reacting, and the pattern is often profuse and unclear. In retrospect, it is usually quite easy to read, but in prospect, the task of reading (or in more technical language, "counting" the waves), becomes more difficult. When the market becomes sluggish and unclear, the best policy is usually to wait until the air clears. Nit-picking is generally a waste of time.

## *LETTER TO PRECHTER*

**March 28, 1977**

Bolton was never entirely convinced that his 21-year triangle theory (from 1928 to 1949) was correct, and on a number of occasions hedged by saying it would do until a better interpretation came along. Shortly before he died, he was my house guest at Manotick and we spent some delightful hours discussing Elliott.

The question as to when the current supercycle began came up, and Bolton said, "I am probably wrong about 1949." Bolton adopted this theory originally because, as he said, the 1928 to 1932 concept was too much of a [time] "mouse" to be a Supercycle. I agreed and fell into a trap. In my search for an explanation, I took 1942 as the most likely year. Elliott first said 1932 but changed his interpretation to 1942. Collins said 1932 and never changed his mind.

Consider the five fingers on your hand — the thumb is the strongest, the middle finger the longest and the fifth is thin and looks the weakest. In a representative five-wave sequence, wave 1 often has the steepest slope, wave 3 is usually the longest and wave 5 the weakest and subject to failure. I don't know if this analogy is a sound one, but it seems to fit. However, I fully expect the current fifth wave from 1974 to reach the 2400-2800 DJIA area before it folds. Say 2400 DJIA as a minimum target and 2700 as a probable turning point.

In my view, the current supercycle is a fifth wave within the Grand Supercycle which started in 1789 or earlier. When it terminates, say five to seven years from now at 2700 DJIA, which is not an unreasonable target, it will likely mark the beginning of decades of corrective markets coinciding with drastic changes in our economy and life styles. This could be a period when technical analysis will come to the fore and outrank fundamental considerations. Elliott often works extremely well in corrective markets with their clear-cut rallies.

The irregularity of today's markets brings up a most important point — what did Elliott mean by "length"? He said in *Nature's Law* that third waves are often the longest but never the shortest of the impulse waves. Was he referring to time or amplitude? Bolton said "amplitude," and I would think in most cases this might be so. On the rule of alternation and the fact that the wave up from December 1974 appeared to be longer than the developing move from October 1975, I assumed that a new series of five waves from October 1975 was likely to develop within wave 1 from December 1974. Now I am not so sure. By silence, Elliott kept his options open. Let us assume that "length" includes duration and that the September 22, 1976 high of 1020 DJIA was a terminal point.

## *LETTER TO PRECHTER*

**May 26, 1977**

With respect to your comment: "What the devil is the A and B base Elliott describes at the end of *Nature's Law*, page 61?" I would say that Elliott, himself, probably could not answer that question satisfactorily in terms of his own theory. If you analyse wave 5 of Elliott's "Special Index" on page 61 you can get a nine-wave sequence, which is all one really needs to know if the wave is to be analysed as an impulsive up move. The count Elliott used suggests a three-wave breakdown of the first minor of 5. He offsets this by throwing in a minor a, b later. An "A and B base" suggests that the first wave of any five can subdivide as a three. While any five can be counted as a three, a three cannot be counted as a five — otherwise the system breaks down.

## *LETTER TO RICHARD RUSSELL*

**November 15, 1977**

Joe [Collins] is a delightful fellow and most remarkable for his 92 years. He knew William Peter Hamilton and Bob Rhea. Rhea and Collins had a working arrangement to write each other's letters should one become ill. Collins rather startled me with the remark that he has always felt that Rhea knew more about the market than he was prepared to divulge, which ties in with Bob Prechter's observation that Rhea came very close to discovering the same principle that now bears Elliott's name. I find this rather fascinating.

As you can appreciate, working in a judge's chambers and courtroom does not supply me with the resources I need to write a book. However, I have completed it and have rewritten much of the earlier chapters. Prechter, who is very interested in the work, is coming up here shortly and I hope and expect he will work with me as coauthor to complete a worthwhile book. Collins agrees and will write an introduction. He has invited Prechter and me to be his house guests in Florida once the book is completed.

At turning points, the Elliott Wave Principle delivers. In a sense, Elliott promises you the world, but this is not the correct view to take on Elliott. I view it simply as a most reliable indicator in determining the primary trend of the market.

## *NOTES TO* ELLIOTT WAVE PRINCIPLE
### 1978

On occasion, subminor waves tend to get a bit tangled. When this happens, the analyst must wait for the larger pattern to emerge. Meanwhile, it often helps to characterize waves according to their personality. If the analyst recognizes the character of a single wave, he can often correctly interpret the complexities of the larger pattern.

* * *

Irregularities tend to disappear as wave formations increase in size.

* * *

Life is ruled by law and not by accident.

* * *

Action and reaction is part of life's mystery. Why are men impelled to do things? Man likes to think he is above the forces of nature which control his destiny, but is this true? Because we may assume our own attitudes, we often conclude that we are not part of any controlled phenomena. However, our assumptions in this respect may not be correct. Shakespeare said our destinies are "shaped" by a divinity which *is*.

It is an open question whether or not man is a puppet on a string. In the short term he is not, but over the longer period he may be. One thing, however, can be said with some certainty: there is a relationship between his behavior and that which triggers recurring events in the physical world. The universe per se is an unfathomable unity in which each man plays a part. Parallelism is neither a cause nor an effect, but a sign of unity. Man must be considered as part of those forces which are manifest everywhere and everywhere *un*manifest. As the *Desiderata* suggests, we are all part of the universe, which is unfolding as is should. The Elliott Wave Principle supports this viewpoint.

* * *

Nature has no straight lines.

* * *

The market is a reflection of the tides of erratum. The tides of erratum parallel the ordered growth of natural phenomena, mathematically speaking.

* * *

A trader tries to scalp the market on a short-term basis. The market, however, is often the scalper and the trader the scalpee.

## LETTER TO PRECHTER

### January 19, 1978

As you know, one of my objects is to advance the Elliott theme. Truth stands so tall in a garden, the galaxies, mathematics and so many other facets of life that it is somewhat of a revelation to find it in such mundane parts of life as the stock market. For this reason, advancing the Elliott Principle may have some greater significance than we can appreciate at this time. Besides, it is a great way to make money and a fascinating study.

## *NOTE TO PRECHTER*

**April 29, 1978**

> New York (AP) — ...Basically, the analysts' surprise was over the fact that the market performed as well as it did despite economic developments that weeks ago would have been blamed as the latest reasons for steady losses.

Bolton always said it is not the news but the construction placed on the news by the market that confirms the trend.

## *LETTER TO PRECHTER*

**September 1978**

Elizabeth I (1533-1603), "The Virgin Queen," came to the throne of England during this Supercycle period. Although the country was weak and in despair following a devastating war with France, Elizabeth's England became the most dominant and prosperous nation in the world. She defied all the powers of Europe and expanded her empire to four corners of the earth. It was a great epoch in world history, the likes of which may not be seen again until the occurrence of the next Millennium Cycle's third wave, say, a thousand years from now.

It makes one think. What is a thousand years?

## *LETTER TO PRECHTER*

**September 6, 1978**

After I wrote the sentence, "The ever-changing stock market follows a never-changing principle found in Nature," I asked a Frenchwoman what it was that Voltaire said. She gave me this quote:

"Plus ça change, plus c'est la meme chose." (The more things change, the more they remain the same.)

## *LETTER TO KENNETH THOMSON*

**January 12, 1980**

20 million investors expecting the stock market to respond to the sort of logic they are accustomed to in their every day experiences of life and unaware or unsympathetic to its real rationale make it a fascinating study.

## *LETTER TO PRECHTER*

**March 22, 1980**

I must say I get sick and tired with analysts who say Elliott is too subjective for them, as I feel they do not use the word in its real sense but rather as a pretext to excuse themselves for their own prejudices and preconceived notions. Having said this, however, one must recognize the fact that there is some subjectivity in Elliott based on the wonderful reason that its depth and universality reflects both the beauty and mathematical excellence of the mean proportion.

## *DRAFT FOR PREFACE TO THE SECOND EDITION OF* ELLIOTT WAVE PRINCIPLE

**May 5, 1980**

Since completing the first edition in 1978, the authors feel more than ever that it is possible to read into stock market behavior a philosophic significance under the basic tenets of the Elliott Wave Principle. Bear markets alternate with bull markets as the rhythms of the market wax and wane, reflecting cycles of optimism and pessimism. The question arises: which came first? Periods of optimism and pessimism or bull and bear markets? The odds suggest from a philosophic viewpoint that neither may be the case, but they arise and fall together. If this is the case, the Wave Principle becomes more significant, as it would seem to indicate that the basic forces which control the universe may also be in effective control of our emotions, which in turn manifest themselves in the behavior of stock prices. True or otherwise, the important point is that the Elliott Wave Principle gives an invaluable perspective as to where we are in the stock market cycle and is measurable.

## *SPEECH TO THE SOCIETY FOR THE INVESTIGATION OF RECURRING EVENTS*

**July 1980**

The Elliott Wave Principle is a theory known to most investors in name only. It is little understood and frequently misinterpreted but nevertheless has stood the test of time.

There are three main reasons why I personally follow Elliott:

1. It makes the market enjoyable. Since 1962, I have kept an hourly chart of the DJIA and have studied every hourly boggle and twist. I never cease to be amazed at how accurately Elliott fits market behavior and the events in the world around us as they unfold. It is an interesting and intellectual exercise. It is particularly enjoyable in fast-moving markets.

2. Elliott keeps one outside the market without getting whipsawed by minor changes in trend. (Moving averages tend to whipsaw one to death at tops and bottoms.) This is one reason why so many analysts go wrong.

3. It is relatively easy to catch turning points and to prepare oneself for changes in direction of the market in advance of major turns.

Elliott is a truly remarkable tool in the hands of the intelligent investor, provided he treats the Principle objectively. He must believe what he sees. Elliott himself had such a highly disciplined mind that he was able to develop a set of principles covering all market action known to him up to the mid-1940s. After he discovered the basic principles of market action, he made a further discovery, namely that market movements align themselves with a *form* contained in the Fibonacci sequence of numbers or the law of the logarithmic spiral.

Because a spiral is three-dimensional and charts are two dimensional plotted on paper, we have to deal with two forms, but they are similar in concept. They are:

1. The Elliott in stock market form, and

2. The logarithmic form.

The Elliott form is basic. Every analyst, if he wants to understand the Wave Principle, must keep this form in mind. He must appreciate how the market expands and contracts without changing its basic design.

If the analyst wants to delve a bit into the esoteric, he must familiarize himself with the second form that is the log spiral.

Both conform to the same basic mathematics.

The one form is necessary to understand Elliott, but the other helps to enjoy Elliott. It is not necessary to be familiar with both forms, but it helps. Both expressions have the same basic beat.

Many analysts have a bias against the Elliott Wave Principle. They rebel at the very thought that there is a universal law which asserts itself in our everyday affairs. Yet this appears to be one of the central facts of life, and the essence of stock market behavior. The evidence is overwhelming, in my opinion. However, to satisfy, if we can, those rebellious

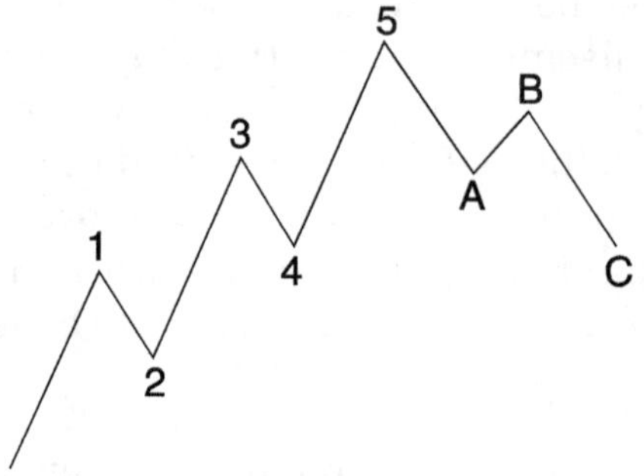


Elliott Form

Logarithmic Form

souls who feel the Wave Principle is nonsense, let us delve into other fields: religion, astronomy, physics, Chinese philosophy and falconry.

**1. RELIGION**

Many of us, probably most of us, have been brought up in the Christian tradition and are not unfamiliar with the Lord's Prayer. Many times we have repeated — "Thy will be done on earth as it is in Heaven."

Think about it. What do the words imply? In positive terms, I would say the only inference to be drawn is that God's will prevails on earth as it does in heaven. The same law or laws that exist here prevail everywhere. What is implicit in heaven is implicit on earth. That which is manifest everywhere, is everywhere unmanifest. According to Paul Bruntun, thoughts have the same beat as breath. In other words, that which is microcosmically in oneself is macro-cosmically in the universe, or the other way around if you prefer.

The Old Testament is literally loaded with references to God as law. Take a few phrases from the 19th Psalm:

"The law of the Lord is perfect."

"The statutes of the Lord are right."

"The testimony of the Lord is pure."

"The judgments (effects) of the Lord are true and perfect all together."

The heavens declare the glory of God and the firmament his handiwork. The very word "lord" means law, or laws and "in the keeping of them there is great reward," again a quote from the same psalm.

If you should think religion is out of place in this context, let's talk about astronomy — not astrology, astronomy. There is no trace of hocus pocus here — all is order.

## 2. ASTRONOMY

The National Research Council of Canada publishes a brief nontechnical account of the Dominion Astrophysical Observatory at Victoria, B.C. and its work and some aspects related to astronomy. I shall read two quotes:

> The work of astronomers has gradually shown that the laws which govern matter and motion here on earth hold sway in the most remote spaces we can scan.
>
> The modern vision of a vast universe controlled by a few simple laws of nature is scarcely less marvellous than the ancient view that the skies were the literal abodes of the gods.

Believe it or not, modern astronomy confirms the Lord's Prayer with respect to universal law and so does Elliott, in the sense that the same law or laws which govern *motion* govern *emotion* en masse.

Our galaxy, the Milky Way, contains about 100 billion stars, and there are many millions of galaxies on a per capita basis for each person alive today. There are literally millions of planets or earths within the range of our modern telescopes. Our home galaxy is a logarithmic spiral, following the same law as the New York stock market. One round trip of the Milky Way takes about 220 million years and is controlled by a few simple laws of nature which no man can explain. The very same laws that govern matter also govern motion.

So don't get too discouraged about stock market behavior. All market analysis is a footnote to a few simple laws of nature. No wonder economists have such a tough time in making their economic forecasts. At least the financial analyst has a toe-hold on the design of movement and emotion. As analysts, we are not specialists in what happened yesterday. That field belongs to the economists since they aren't much good at forecasting.

### 3. PHYSICS

Recently Dr. Fritjof Capra, a research physicist, wrote a book titled *The Tao of Physics,* exploring the parallels between modern physics and Eastern mysticism. He claims in this book that the models of modern physics lead to a view of the world which is in harmony with Eastern mysticism. Dr. Capra says that the unity of all things in nature is a revelation of physics, and for this reason, it can be asserted that the stock market, as part of nature, beats time with the laws of the universe. Please (for heaven's sake) don't write off the Elliott Wave Principle before you even understand it.

## 4. CHINESE PHILOSOPHY

We have talked about religion, astronomy and physics. Now let us move back into antiquity to the 6th century B.C., to the time of Lao Tzu, who wrote one of the world's greatest classics, the *Tao Te Ching*, or the *Power of the Way*.

According to Lao Tzu, man has his roots in the bosom of the cosmos (Tao). The old sage lived in the serene knowledge that man could enjoy cosmic security forever and that this phenomenon could be discovered within oneself and as well in the visible world.

In Lao Tzu's philosophy, polarity is symbolized by yang and yin, the two poles of cosmic force. These forces are always in balance, and one cannot exist without the other. The yang is positive and dominant, the yin is negative and yielding — as in the sexes. The two principles come together in harmonious relationship as two aspects of a single unity. The yang-yin opposites are always in harmony; one does not win over the other. "Being and non-being grow out of one another." The principle, therefore, is an implicit unity of all things founded in nature. It is called the Tao.

To reduce this philosophy to stock market parlance, we find that:

1. Action (bull markets) is followed by reaction (bear markets).

2. Movements, both up and down, reflect a form similar to the form known as the logarithmic spiral of nature.

3. This form has a mathematical base.

4. Completed cycles reflect a harmonious relationship in time and amplitude but are independent of both fixed periodicity and fixed amplitude.

In other words, the forces of the universe (yang and yin, if you like) repeat themselves in our affairs because of man's emotional or spiritual nature.

In Chinese philosophy, all manifest things return to their source.

### 5. FALCONRY

Mr. Louis Rukeyser of *Wall Street Week* humorously refers to market technicians as "elves," presumably playful little creatures who do more harm than good. I wish he would stop it. This constant reference to technical analysts as elves has in my opinion set our profession back 25 years, as it places the technician in an inferior place to that of the fundamentalist in the eyes of many investors. He does it with a smile. Giving us the gracious taunt is invidious. *When* to invest is 10 times more important than *what to buy*. Any half-baked analyst can pick a few "solid" stocks for investment purposes, and that is about all we hear about on *Wall Street Week*. The real problem is not *what* but *when*. I would suggest to Mr. Rukeyser that technicians are *falcons*, not *elves*. A falcon first frightens his prey by soaring in ever widening circles and then spirals down in quickly narrowing circles, throwing its victim into complete confusion. It hits its prey at speeds of over 100 miles per hour. A falcon, like a stock market technician, employs the law of the logarithmic spiral — no mean tool. And no mean bird — the falcon for its weight is the strongest thing alive. Technicians, if they would flex their muscles more, could be an equally strong bird.

## *UNPUBLISHED ESSAY*

### July 1980

Hamilton Bolton always viewed the stock market as part of life and subject to the laws of nature. As the Wave Principle is implicit in market action at all levels, its clocklike mechanism finds continuous expression in the form of trends within trends, conforming to the basic rule of five up and three down. Because of the empirical nature of these rules, the stock market can be measured, analysed and projected once the nature of the rules is understood.

As a general proposition, the workings of the Wave Principle can best be seen in the DJIA, and no other average is required to interpret market action in Elliott's terms. However, if the picture is blurred (no average is perfect), other averages or indices can be helpful. Unfortunately for the interpreter, we have come through a long period when the Dow isn't too clear as to pattern, and this is why we are currently looking at charts of other indices to give us some dependable clues. You should always remember Elliott is only a tool in the kit of the technician. All technical analysis is but a footnote to Elliott. Hence its great importance.

However, let's not fool around too much with the esoteric nature of Elliott. It is more important to ask practical questions: Where are we in the stock market cycle and how long can we buy stocks with impunity?

## *LETTER TO SLOAN WILSON*

**November 25, 1980**

In my view, Elliott is the root principle of polarity inherent in motion and form, a reflection of which can be seen in the behavior of bull and bear markets. Although Elliott discovered the principle in stock market action, the same principle has been at the heart of Chinese philosophy since the 6th century B.C. when Lao Tzu wrote his famous classic, the *Tao Te Ching*. The principle can be seen in the sum of related things, but is not the sum. It is the cosmic power of universal harmony which arises of itself. It is the sovereign laws of the universe manifest everywhere and everywhere unmanifest which continually assert themselves in our every day affairs from the price of frozen pork bellies to the DJIA. In this connection, it is interesting to note that a pamphlet prepared by the National Research Council of Canada and issued here by the Dominion Astrophysical Observatory states, "The few simple laws which govern matter and form here on earth holds sway in the remotest spaces we can scan." The stock market is no exception. It has form, and no one would suggest that it does not have motion. The hourly figures show this conclusively. Since October 15th, 70 hourly registrations (DJIA) have displayed a continuous progression of pattern and form without a single irregular beat. How can anyone say that stock prices are a random walk? True, a million monkeys pecking at the key board of a million typewriters ad infinitum would ultimately produce a novel, but in the stock market the process is continuous. Hour by hour — forms, forms, forms — all meaningfully interrelated. As these forms are constant in design but continuously changing in amplitude and duration, the stock market becomes intelligible to the analyst and hence predictable.

Bob Prechter visited us here in Victoria two weeks ago. I discussed with him the possibility of Elliott being a composite of all cycles, the 41-month, 18-year etc. We do not see it as such, despite the fact that many cycles reflect the Wave Principle. Bob views the Golden Spiral of Elliott as fully representing the form of natural growth and all growth as an extension of the past. My friend Alan Drengson, professor of philosophy at Victoria University, has referred to the Elliott Wave Principle as applied Taoism. Their views in my opinion are not incompatible.

## *LETTER TO DAVID WILLIAMS*

**December 17, 1980**

As I see it, the forces of nature which initiate upturns and downturns at all levels of the stock market cycle have a common root in polarity but nevertheless lend themselves to interpretation despite the fact that they defy explanation. These forces are always felt but practically never observed. Elliott stands for the proposition that the forces that make the market have a constant mathematical base and are umbilically linked with the rhythm of the universe. I would submit that the evidence of this is overwhelming and rules out any causal relationship between fixed cycles and price movement over the longer period. For this reason, I look askance at such theories as Kondratieff and Benner dreamed up.

The Benner-Fibonacci chart in our book was my own creation, blending their concepts as best I could for the greater part of this century. I first projected the Benner cycles forward. They did not seem to fit, but some of the concepts did. As one might expect, the fixed cycles got out of whack. For this same reason, I do not think the chart we published will hold for very long. I fully expect it to fade, but I am reasonably satisfied that it will at least reflect the next high in 1983 and the next low in 1987.

## *LETTER TO PRECHTER*

**July 8, 1981**

I often wonder why the stock market is ruin and loss for so many investors. Gain is seldom realized until one stops looking for it. If one has the patience to wait for the right moment, gains will take care of themselves. All that seems to be required is perspective, and that is where Elliott comes in. Hammy Bolton used to say, "Elliott gives perspective." I feel you have it. So from now on, I must pay more attention to you and less to my own analysis, although I have done extremely well over the last 37 years (a 15% annual compounded gain after taxes).

There is something very strange about market action which defies explanation. A bear market usually complements a bull market in time and amplitude. Each is dependent on the other and cannot exist without the other. Cycles follow an invisible law of nature which we call Elliott. When values move in one direction and cut a pattern, they recede and form a complementary pattern and, like the waves of the ocean, return to a state of rest. The packet nature[3] of stock market behavior communicates in its own way what is likely to follow. A force seems to pass through one series of cycles to the next, following one of nature's laws. It is intransitory and swallows the law of cause and effect in its stride. It is mysterious and exciting. Be a turtle; drag your tail in the mud. Go the easy way, and snap when things fit.

## *LETTER TO PRECHTER*

### 1982

The Kingdom of Heaven refers to a state of mind, a higher level of being, the state of enlightenment, bodhi, vidya. Truth makes for freedom. When Jesus says: "Repent," He refers to a change of consciousness. The Greek word translated as repentance is meta-noia. It is a change of consciousness, an inner evolution, a higher level of understanding. The heart of man can comprehend the higher reality. It is not penitence or regret but a complete change of mind and heart, a revolution is our outlook, the displacement of ignorance, avidya by knowledge, vidya. It is a new way of thinking, feeling and acting. It is a rebirth. "Unless a man is born anew, he cannot see the Kingdom of God," said Jesus to Nicodemus. Rebirth belongs not to the natural man, but the secret, internal, the spiritual man. It is another step in evolution. "Repent and be turned." It is a whirling round of our consciousness. "Except ye turn and become as little children." There is the child in us that is responsive to the magic and mystery of the world. We

---

[3] By "packet nature," Frost is referring to a term from Fritjof Capra's *The Tao of Physics*. A packet wave is a sequence of waves that starts from a point of rest. It first expands and then contracts, eventually returning to rest at the level at which the entire sequence began.

are generally lost in the world of objects and the things of sense. The mystery of life is destroyed by life and remains only a memory, dimly felt at moments recalling for a fleeting instant something that we knew once and possessed. We must recover this lost possession, recapture freshness and spontaneity. Man must change himself. The writer to the Ephesians says: "Awake thou that sleepest and arise from the dead." Christian teaching in its origin before it became organised and externalised was awakening from sleep through the light shed by the inner wisdom. Jesus, like the Buddha, was one who had awakened and taught others the way of awakening. The Kingdom of Heaven is not something in the future. It is at hand. It is within us. When we attain this state, we are freed from law. "The Sabbath is made for man and not man for the Sabbath."

Both religion and science affirm the unity of nature. The central assumption of science is the intuition of religion that nature is intelligible. When we study the processes of nature we are impressed by their order and harmony and are led to a belief in the divine reality. St. Thomas put it, "By considering what God has made we can — first of all — catch a glimpse of the divine wisdom which has in some measure impressed a certain likeness to itself upon them." We should see in the order and constancy, the beauty and pattern of nature, the divine wisdom and not in the exceptional and the bizarre. To suggest that the whole course of history is bound up with some unique event which happened at one time and in one place in a universe which has had nearly 6,000 million years of existence may strain the scientific conscience of even ordinary people. Heaven mingles with earth from the very start.

God is all-embracing infinity and is found in even the smallest thing.

## *"PROSPECTS FOR 1982"*

## THE SIDNEY REVIEW

### January 20, 1982

The Elliott Wave Principle is an approach to the stock market developed by R.N. Elliott from 1932 to 1947. He discerned that the stock market tended to unfold according to a basic rhythm or pattern, which he called the law of the market. Under Elliott's theory, broad patterns of market behaviour, including time and amplitude relationships, reflect the process of expansion and contraction in nature.

Q: Could you give us an example of the practical importance of the Elliott Wave Principle of market behavior?

A: Yes. In February of 1980 my coauthor, Robert Prechter, said gold would trade as low as $388 per ounce. At that time London gold was well above $650 per ounce. He was the only market analyst I am aware of who predicted that gold was in a severe bear market and that the bear market would last until mid-1981.

Prechter later refined his prediction and said the low would occur in August, 1981. On August 4, gold traded at $385.50 in London and the nearest futures contract on COMEX had a low of exactly $388.

Q: You have a story I know you love to tell. It bears repeating. Do you mind?

A: No, certainly not. A little chicken sitting comfortably in the henhouse without a care in the world was startled by the appearance of a man and ran away. When it came back, the man was gone but there was some corn lying on the ground. Having a degree of scientific curiosity, the chicken began to watch, and it soon noticed that when the man appeared, the corn appeared.

It did not want to commit itself to any theory in a hurry and watched the sequence 999 times. There were no exceptions to the rule that the appearance of the man meant food, so it swallowed its skepticism and decided there must be a necessary connection between the man and the corn.

In the language of causality, this meant that whenever the man appeared, the corn must appear. On the basis of this conclusion, the chicken went out to meet the man on his 1,000th appearance to thank him for his kindness and had its neck wrung.

The moral of this story is that for the most part, events have no discoverable cause and effect relationship. The Elliott Wave Principle implies the interconnectedness between events and stock market movements, but no causal connection.

For instance, a decline in interest rates does not mean that the price of gold in London is going up on the ground that it makes gold a more attractive buy. Events may be conjoined, but event A does not cause event B. The sequence of events may follow one another time and time again but not necessarily the next time around.

That is why the wise investor diversifies, rather than place all his funds in one basket. Overdiversification is unwise. It does help to cover up one's mistakes, but it is not the way to survive in the stock market.

Q: Do you see President Reagan's program working?

A: I see Reagan's program working and bringing the U.S. out of its recession early in 1982. However, I must say I feel he is going to be right for the wrong reasons, at least for the most part.

I fully expect the late 1980s will be the most difficult period for all of us since the dirty 1930s.

## *LETTER TO CHARLES J. COLLINS*

**November 1, 1982**

As I see it, the DJIA "houses" the emotional forces of nature which we call Elliott, not the other way around. The Dow may well reflect those underlying forces better than any other average, but it is far from perfect. At one point, R.N. Elliott endeavoured to construct a new average which would better reflect the law of the stock market. When the Dow does not do the job as I see it, my natural inclination is to turn to the Toronto Stock Exchange industrial average, the New York Composite, or some other average which I think reflects the underlying market forces more realistically. In my view, there is nothing sacred about any average. Using this conglomerate approach, I feel that the third primary wave up from 1974 failed and that from June 1982, the stock market entered the fifth of the fifth from 1932.

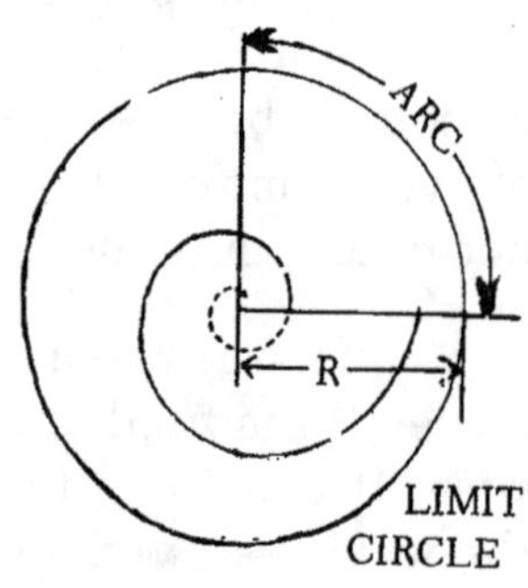


In Walter White's appendix to *Elliott Wave Principle*, he raises a very intriguing point by drawing a limit circle around the logarithmic spiral. Walter claims that the ancients often drew a circle in this manner to indicate that when the forces of nature generating the spiral exhausted themselves, the spiral would momentarily become a circle and fall in on itself and then return to the center from which it came. At this point, that is when the forces return to the center, they would recompose themselves and then start up all over again. Carl Sagan in his TV series, *Cosmos*, said much the same thing. He indicated, for instance, that about 50 billion years from now, the Milky Way would likely become a ring circle to other galaxy formations in the heavens, at which point, the forces of nature which are equal and opposite would reverse themselves so that in another 50 billion years, our galaxy would be back to the point where we are today, only moving in the opposite direction. In other words, the galaxy would unwind, and a few billion years beyond that point, the galaxy would become a black hole, trapping space and light curves only to recompose itself and start up all over again. This process of expansion and contraction is reflected in the treble clef symbol, only the circle in this symbol is drawn above the spiral before returning to its center to start up all over again.

## *LETTER TO PRECHTER*

**March 25, 1983**

Elliott is more of an art than a science, prevalent everywhere, or should we say manifest everywhere and everywhere unmanifest? I love the Principle, but at times it drives me "up the wall." As I get older, I tend to give up on limitations and try to assess the underlying forces of stock market behavior which Elliott represents. In the long run, the theoretical tends to be the most practical in most fields of inquiry. Hence, Elliott is our most practical approach and for the most part, technical analysis can properly be regarded as a footnote to Elliott, in much the same way as western philosophy is a footnote to Plato.[4]

## *LETTER TO PRECHTER*

**February 10, 1984**

The question is often asked: Is technical analysis an art or a science? Since the underlying *order* of market action has a mathematical base, catching important turns is more of a science than an art, but projecting future movements and tops, with the options open to the market, the opposite would appear to be the case.

In sum, the Elliott Wave Principle and ancient Chinese philosophy deal with concepts of change. The *I Ching*

---

[4] And Aristotle.

(*Book of Changes*) was a manual 40 centuries ago. Today it is regarded as the first and most ancient of Chinese classical works. Its authorship extended over 800 years! Later works, namely the *Chuang-Tzu* and Lao-Tzu's *Tao Te Ching,* written in the 4th and 6th centuries B.C., respectively, also deal with the basic philosophy of changes in *man* and *nature.* The same basic thinking runs through all these works: that which is is the was of what shall be.

## LETTER TO WARREN HAVENS

**October 13, 1984**

There are over 80 translations of the *Tao Te Ching.* In one of the early German translations, God was referred to as a ratio. There is lots more, but let's leave it at that.

## TAPED CONVERSATION WITH PRECHTER

**mid-1980s**

I feel that all things essential to the soul's welfare, i.e., man's well-being in a spiritual sense, can be found in the 110 verses of the Sermon on the Mount, which reflect the ideas of Buddha and Lao-Tzu, and three or four of the parables, including the Prodigal Son, the Good Samaritan, and the parable of the Wise and Foolish Virgins. Christians later added all sorts of creeds and rites, which ruined the basic message and made it "a religion of belief." The Kingdom of Heaven is not a place, but an expanded state of awareness. It's in the here and now.

## LETTER TO PETER KENDALL

**May 23, 1987**

The Wave Principle appears to be a reflection of the fourth dimension.

## *LETTER TO GURNEY WATSON*

**December 12, 1987**

In my opinion, there is an underlying tendency for the stock market to reflect a law or set of laws which are absolute in their character. This leaves some room for fundamental considerations which seem to affect the amplitude of market swings but have very little impact with respect to timing.

Bolton remarked to me several times that any investor who accepted the leadership of the Elliott Wave Principle should be right 80% of the time with respect to the general trend of the market. Many times, he was asked to publish his views on Elliott more frequently than once a year. I think it is quite remarkable that Bob Prechter has undertaken to write about Elliott so frequently and with such amazing accuracy. He is doing what Bolton said was virtually impossible. This could be Prechter's one error, but, then again, he has done such a wonderful job that I feel he must be complimented for it. I say this despite the fact that Bob and I do not always agree.

## *LETTER TO DAVID SUZUKI*

**March 18, 1988**

I am a fan of yours in that I agree with you that all men have a built-in genetic link with nature, but my reasons are not based on science, as I have no knowledge of biology or any other science. I am, however, a student of the cultures of the world and stock market behavior in depth. I co-authored *Elliott Wave Principle* with Robert R. Prechter, Jr., who for the last three years has been regarded as the darling of Wall Street.

In this book, we explore the proposition that there is a mathematical link between the mind of man and nature.

To state the proposition in different words, man is part of Nature and subject to the cosmic influence.

This concept is a very old one. Lao Tzu in his *Tao Te Ching* contended that (1) that which is microcosmically in the universe is microcosmically in man; and (2) that the mind of man is an entity with the soul as its centre and thereby assumes that man's body does not possess a soul, but the soul of man possesses his body (reincarnation and karma).

Although we do not know what precisely makes the mind of man, the universe and the stock market *tick*, we do know that it has a mathematical base. As nature has many forms but only one form which moves to zero and infinity with no change in mathematical relationship, we must assume that this form is closer to ultimate reality than anything we are aware of.

When I was at Queen's University, back in 1927, my Professor of Mathematics asked me three questions:

1. "What is zero x 16?" I said zero.
2. "What is infinity x 16?" I said infinity.
3. "What is infinity x zero?" I said I didn't know. He said, "It is 16 or any given quantity."

He then demonstrated that zero x infinity = 16 or any given quantity. If I were to answer that question today, I would say that the product of zero times infinity gives rise to consciousness. If this be true, we live in an unending sea of consciousness and the "genes" of consciousness are impersonal in the everywhere but individualized and personalized in man, making us all different despite the fact that all men have a common heritage (Sons of God, never God).

Prior to the days of Constantine, when Christianity became a religion of belief over a period of 20 years, St. Augustine said, "Christianity had existed from time immemorial, but the advent of Jesus gave it a new name." When

Augustine was elevated, he was obliged to recant the statement as Bishop of Hippo.

The Dead Sea Scrolls and the discovery of the 52 Gnostic texts discovered at Nag Hammadi in upper Egypt have compelled us to reconsider our historical views with respect to the origins of Christianity. These texts reveal that TRUTH is LAW and arises from within, and further, that there is no third person between ourselves and ultimate reality. In this sense, I am not a modern Christian as I am quite convinced that God does not smile or frown upon us but we may have frowns or we may have smiles provided we seek it and find it. In my philosophy, science and religion are compatible. If we keep the law, we will be kept by it. Life is progressive and renews itself and no man can be separated from these basic fundamentals. To progress, we must live love and love life and not under any circumstances let any "bastard" get us down.

## THE OBSERVER

***(church newspaper)***

**June 10, 1990**

I would like to congratulate Ruth C. Studd on her Front Page editorial which appeared in *The Observer* dated May 1990. If she had been at Queen's a few years earlier, she might have influenced me to continue in my chosen career to become an ordained minister of the United Church.

I was raised a Methodist but in the Quaker tradition, as my forefathers were Pennsylvania Dutch. At an early age, I unequivocally accepted the teachings of Jesus in all their simplistic grandeur. I was never a great fan of St. Paul as his teachings seemed to conflict in substance with what Jesus taught. Jesus said The Kingdom of Heaven is within (Luke 17:21) He also said that what defiles a man comes from within. Paul, on the other hand, often spoke of Heaven as a place as opposed to a state of consciousness or being. These differences are not too difficult for a layman to understand once it is recognized that Mind is an entity per se.

Thousands of years before the time of Jesus, the Upanishads of India taught that beginnings and ends are dreams and that our souls will exist through all eternity. Later, Lao Tsu wrote in the *Tao Te Ching* that that which is manifest everywhere is everywhere unmanifest.

To me, the aim, object and purpose of our earthly lives is to seek enlightenment through the power of the inner spirit. We are only what we attain spiritually. It is all within.

*The Elliott Wave Theorist*, May 28, 1999

## A.J. FROST — IN MEMORIAM

*A.J. Frost by Joan Frost Oman 1998*

Alfred John (Jack) Frost died at 9:00 a.m. on Tuesday, May 4, 1999. He was 91 years old. He is survived by his daughter Joan Oman and his granddaughter Margaret Oman.

Frost led a varied and productive life. Originally a student of theology, Frost became a CFA and obtained a law degree. He worked for Canada's Board of Review, the Canada Trust Corporation, Mutual Funds Management Corporation, the financial firm of Bolton-Tremblay and Guaranty Trust Company of Canada. In the late 1960s, he served on the National Capital Commission under Prime Minister Lester Pearson. He finished his career as a judge for eight years with the Federal Tax Court of Canada. Frost's awards and appointments were legion. He served on two university councils, was elected a Fellow in the Institute of Chartered Accountants, served as president of the Association of Canadian Better Business Bureaus, earned titles as an Honorable Life Member of the Ottawa Historical Society and an Honorary Life Member of the Victorian Order of Nurses, served as trustee for the Boy Scouts of Canada, became an Honorable Vice President of the organization's National Council and was awarded the silver acorn for distinguished service. In 1993, he received the Commemorative Medal for the 125th Anniversary of the Canadian Confederation for years of distinguished service in business, government and academia.

Perhaps his most lasting contribution is his work in the field of the Wave Principle via his association with A. Hamilton Bolton, his writings for *The Bank Credit Analyst* and his collaboration with Robert Prechter on the book *El-*

*liott Wave Principle — Key to Market Behavior*, which is now in its ninth edition and has been translated into ten languages. An engaging speaker, Frost offered popular weekly stock market commentary on CNBC in the early 1990s and frequently addressed professional organizations such as the Market Technicians Association and the Canadian Society of Technical Analysts, which elected Jack as its first honorary member. His analytical legacy is preserved in the book, *The Elliott Wave Writings of A.J. Frost and Richard Russell.*

Frost's funeral was held at Turner and Porter Funeral Home in Toronto on May 8, after which his body was interred at Capital Memorial Gardens cemetery. In memory of Jack, the Canadian Society of Technical Analysts (CSTA) has just instituted the annual A.J. Frost Memorial Award for Outstanding Contribution to the Development of Technical Analysis. The first presentation* will be at this year's International Federation of Technical Analysts (IFTA) conference in Toronto and will be presented annually thereafter at the CSTA conference. The award will be for outstanding lifetime achievements in order to reflect "AJ's outstanding and diverse career." The family welcomes donations in his name to the Boy Scouts of Canada Trust, Box 5151, Stn. LCD-Merivale, Ottawa, Ontario, Canada, K2C 3G7 (phone 613-224-5131; fax -3571).

If you would like to read a full biography of A.J. Frost along with numerous photos, you are welcome to read "A.J. Frost: A Life Remembered" at http://www.elliottwave.com/frost.

I was fortunate to have been Jack's friend for nearly 22 years. All who knew him will miss his engaging personality and sparkling genius.

—Robert R. Prechter, Jr., Gainesville, GA, May 1999

---

* IFTA invited Prechter to address its conference that year. In a surprise announcement, the CSTA presented the first annual A.J. Frost Memorial Award to Robert Prechter. Joan and Magi Oman were in attendance.